The Politics of Backwardness in Hungary

THE POLITICS OF BACKWARDNESS IN HUNGARY

1825-1945

Andrew C. Janos

PRINCETON UNIVERSITY PRESS
PRINCETON, NEW JERSEY

TO THE MEMORY OF MY PARENTS

Contents

List of Tables

List of Tables

List of Maps and Diagrams

Preface

POLITICAL CHANGE: EVOLUTION OF A PARADIGM

Although the study of political change is as old as the study of politics itself and goes back to the various cyclical and evolutionary theories of antiquity, a systematic inquiry into the social and economic roots of the phenomenon began only in the early nineteenth century. It was then that, under the impact of the great scientific and technological revolutions of the age, the disciplines of political sociology and political economy emerged, together with a three-tiered paradigm that, until very recently, has served as the cornerstone for all theories of political change. According to this paradigm, economic, social, and political changes are interrelated: as the economy of a particular unit changes, so will the social structure, and when the social structure changes, pressures will arise for the transformation of dominant ideologies and institutions so as to keep the social order in a state of equilibrium.

Within this classical paradigm, however, we can discern a number of different theoretical orientations, each with a distinct conceptual focus and point of departure. The first of these is Saint-Simonian and Comtean in origin, but is most fully developed in the writings of Herbert Spencer. This mode of theorizing focuses on the categories of technological innovation and industrialism and holds that as levels of technological sophistication in production increase, so will the differentiation of the social structure. This, in turn, produces new orders of social complexity, which then require adaptations in the organization of political authority and controls. In this theory, carried forward by a number of contemporary economists and sociologists,[1] the principal task of the analyst is to identify critical thresholds in the advancement of technology. Once this is done, the "progress" or "development" of a social unit may be plotted as passing from one stage to another, either toward a final stage of "modern," "industrial," or "mass consumption" society, or else be seen to proceed with a

---

[1] See, for instance, Marion Levy, Jr., *Modernization and the Structure of Societies* (Princeton: Princeton University Press, 1966), or Gabriel A. Almond and G. Bingham Powell, *Comparative Politics: A Developmental Approach* (Boston: Little, Brown and Co., 1966).

cheerful open-endedness toward higher and higher developmental stages.

If one of these theoretical orientations could, at its inception, be described as a French intellectual's attempt to come to grips with the industrial revolution of England, another may be seen as a German and Central European response to the commercial revolution that began to engulf these societies in the second half of the nineteenth century. Associated with the names of Max Weber, Ferdinand Tönnies, and later with Karl Mannheim and Karl Polányi, these theories focus our attention not on industrialism and technology, but on the market mechanism. As the market becomes the predominant instrument for the allocation of scarce resources, so this theory goes (most explicitly perhaps in the formulations of Karl Polányi[2]), the value orientations of society will undergo transformations in conformity with patterns typical in market relationships. In this process of "rationalization," or "demystification" (*Entzauberung*), the personal warmth, particularism, and ascriptive orientations of the traditional *Gemeinschaft* will pass and be replaced by the impersonal, secularized, and performance-oriented norms of the modern *Gesellschaft*. As part of this overall change political relations, too, will undergo transformation, for as the fundamental orientations of society become rationalized, this process will undermine the legitimacy of traditional, divinely ordained authority, and replace it with the authority of the charismatic leader, or else with the legal authority of the modern state. Out of this generalized concept of social change, then, arise a number of popular hypotheses concerning the "politicization," "mobilization," or "fundamental democratization"[3] of the body politic, processes whereby large numbers of people, by having gained "new insights"[4] into the social mechanism, become available for sustained and systematic political participation.

Marxian theory, the most comprehensive of all the intellectual constructs bequeathed upon us by the nineteenth century, may be described as a most ingenious synthesis between the above two intellectual trends, even though in strict chronological terms the genesis of the theory is located between the earlier French and the later German

---

[2] Karl Polányi, *The Great Transformation* (Boston: Beacon Press, 1957).

[3] For a classic formulation, see Karl Mannheim, *Man and Society in an Age of Reconstruction* (New York: Harcourt, Brace and World, 1958); also, Karl Deutsch, "Social Mobilization and Political Development," *American Political Science Review*, 55 (1961), 493-502, and Daniel Lerner, *The Passing of Traditional Society* (Glencoe: The Free Press, 1958).

[4] Mannheim, *Man and Society*, p. 45.

schools of political sociology. On the one hand, Marx was fascinated with the industrial revolution of England, so much so that he made technological innovation—or, in his own words, changes in the "means of production"—the "demiurge," or principal motor force, of all important change in human history. Much as in the earlier Comtean and Spencerian schemes, in Marx's universe society passes from one stage to another when the technology of production undergoes some critical transformation. While feudalism was the product of the hand loom, Marx explained in one of his oft quoted lines, capitalism was the product of the technology of the power loom. But if the technology of production occupies such a key place in the scheme, it does not occupy the entire stage of modern history, for Marx also assigned considerable weight to the methods of appropriation and allocation, among them the methods of entrepreneurship in the context of a market economy. True, Marx's attitude toward the market was somewhat ambivalent in that he was inclined to see it as guided as much by political forces as by the laws of supply and demand. But still, he had enough appreciation of the importance of commerce and economic risk-taking to devote more attention in *Das Kapital*[5] to the entrepreneur than to the technical innovator when writing about the makers of the modern world. There can be no doubt that for Marx capitalism meant far more than industrial technology and the advent of the machine age.

It was from this synthesis of the commercial and industrial revolutions that Marx's two-stage theory of social and economic modernization emerged. In the first stage, a group of bold, risk-taking entrepreneurs accumulate sufficient wealth and power to challenge the warrior aristocracy and to replace the antiquated feudal political structure with their own rationalized and demystified bourgeois state. This victory sets the stage for further developments, specifically for great capital concentrations, and for the rise of the industrial economy. It is in the context of this economy that the bourgeoisie achieves its greatest glories and fulfills its mission in history. But it is also in this context that it begins to decline, for industrialism and capitalism produce a growing political awareness among the working classes, and mobilize them for a final onslaught against class rule and capitalism.[6]

[5] Karl Marx, *Capital*, trans. S. Moore and E. Aveling (New York: International Publishers, 1975), 1, Pt. VIII, 713ff. See also, Marx, "The German Ideology," Pt. I in Robert C. Tucker, ed., *The Marx-Engels Reader* (New York: Norton, 1972), 140-146.

[6] For Marx's own theory of social mobilization, i.e., his references to the growing social consciousness of the masses in the course of the industrial revolution, see "The Communist Manifesto," in Tucker, *Marx-Engels Reader*, pp. 342-343.

Preface

One by one and together, these three bodies of social thought—the Comtean-Spencerian, Weberian, and the Marxian—had an enormous intellectual impact, and rightly so, because they identified critical elements in the social process and reduced the infinitely complex historical experience of the occidental world to a few manageable categories. If nothing else, they created three outlines for social and political history that no student of the Occident could henceforth ignore. It was this achievement that has won these theories their popularity among both historians and sociologists. But it was also this achievement that has raised some of the most vexing questions concerning their universal validity. For once the theories were taken outside the narrow confines of the Occident, they could not account for many of the social and political phenomena encountered. This was already evident to Marx himself, as he pondered the phenomena of oriental despotism and the Asiatic mode of production in relation to his own categories. The same dilemma tormented his Russian disciples, among them Lenin, who tried to resolve the intellectual problem by resorting to an essentially face-saving formula that retained the concept of historical stages, but allowed for skipping, or "telescoping" them under conditions of backwardness and late development.

The conflict between theory and reality was even more sharply posed in the years following World War II, when American and other western scholars began to carry their intellectual baggage to the study of what they called in succession the "backward," "underdeveloped," "developing," "emerging," and "late developing" societies of the non-western world. Here the gaps could not be easily papered over with semantic devices, but called for significant revisions in the classical paradigm. To be sure, even today there remains a staunch group of strict evolutionists convinced that the experience of our industrial civilization will be replicated by the late developing countries, and that the latter will faithfully follow the path of the former, progressing from stage to stage, either by the successful transfer of technologies,[7] or by the diffusion of a rationalized value system, fulfilling Weber's vision of the *Entzauberung der Welt*.[8] The large majority of modern scholars, however, set out on different intellectual paths and, instead of searching for stages and uniformities in history, began to mark out

[7] One of the best known of these is Walt W. Rostow, *The Stages of Economic Growth* (Cambridge, England: The University Press, 1962).

[8] Apart from Lerner, *The Passing of Traditional Society*, see Alex Inkeles, "Making Men Modern," *American Journal of Sociology*, 75 (1969), 138-150, and Alex Inkeles and David Smith, *Becoming Modern* (Cambridge: Harvard University Press, 1974).

xvi

critical differences between western history and the dynamics of change in the contemporary Third World.

This class of revisionist scholars falls into two general categories. In the first one we find theorists who postulate the ultimate convergence of social and political patterns but, at the same time, point to the prospect of different paths to modernity and development. Most frequently, they focus attention on the process of transition from tradition to modernity, attempting to identify sources of stress that explain differences between "early" and "late" development. Among this category of scholars, some point to economic strains produced by the rapid mobilization of savings for development[9]; others attribute the pains of transition to cultural strain produced by the confrontation between the ideas and institutions of the West and those of the non-western world.[10] In the second category of revisionists, then, we find those who believe that the "crisis" of non-western societies may be more than a transitional phenomenon. Instead of searching for the different "roads" to modernity, their quest is directed toward identifying different political outcomes in the modernization process. Among the latter, Samuel P. Huntington relieved the theory of development from the strains of teleology and historical determinism by pointing out that there was nothing inevitable about the diffusion of technologies or rationality,[11] and that while some societies may successfully industrialize and consequently develop stable institutions, others will merely experience economic stagnation and political decay.

[9] The theory was first advanced in Isaac Deutscher, *Stalin* (New York: Random House, 1960); also David A. Apter, "System, Process, and the Politics of Development," in Bert Hoselitz and Wilbert Moore, eds., *Industrialization and Society* (The Hague: Mouton, 1963), still further elaborated in Apter, *The Politics of Modernization* (Chicago: Chicago University Press, 1965).

[10] Works in this category are numerous and they tend to emphasize stress produced by adaptation to western culture or institutions. Some of the most important of these are Lerner, *The Passing of Traditional Society*, Lucian W. Pye, "The Nature of Transitional Politics," and Jason L. Finkle and Richard W. Gable, *Political Development and Social Change*, 2d ed. (New York: Wiley, 1971), pp. 538-549, David A. Apter, *Ghana in Transition* (New York: Athenaeum, 1963); and many of the essays in Harvey G. Kebschall, ed., *Politics in Transitional Societies* (New York: Meredith, 1968). The concept and term of "transitional society" is also used by Fred Riggs in his *Administration in Developing Countries* (Boston: Houghton and Mifflin, 1964), without impairing the validity of his conclusions concerning the nature of bureaucracy in the societies of the non-western world.

[11] The thesis was first advanced by Samuel P. Huntington in his "Political Development and Decay," *World Politics*, 17 (1965), 386-411, and further elaborated in his *Political Order in Changing Societies* (New Haven: Yale University Press, 1968).

Preface

Other scholars, most prominently perhaps Barrington Moore and Reinhard Bendix, point to potential contrasts in the character of modern industrial states, and link contrasts between democracy and autocracy either to the cultural makeup of the preceding traditional society[12] or to the configuration of the social classes that lead the struggle for industrialism and modernity.[13]

Impressive as the contribution of these scholars was to the general body of literature in social science, in recent years their findings have been challenged by a number of writers who set out not to modify modernization theory but to replace it with a new paradigm of political economy. Most strikingly in view of the accumulated heritage of political sociology, this new school of thought has focused inquiry not on discrete processes to explain particular outcomes—such as the industrialization of France or India to explain the nature of French or Indian politics—but on relationships of interdependence within a larger global socioeconomic system possessing its own logic, division of labor, and operational principles. This new mode of thinking about society does not ignore discrete processes of industrialization, commercialization, mobilization, rationalization, and so on. But it assumes that such processes acquire different meanings over time and space, depending on whether they occur in one period or another, or whether they take place in the center (core) or on the periphery and semi-periphery of the larger world system.[14] The social, economic, and political implications of a factory built in eighteenth-century Manchester were different from those of a factory built in nineteenth-century Moscow or in twentieth-century Bombay. An assumption to the contrary ignores the validity of this fundamental precept and introduces an element of artificial simplicity into social comparisons to the detriment of their explanatory power.

Because most of the progenitors of this new paradigm are radicals in the Marxist intellectual tradition, they described the modern world system as an arena of scarcity and inequality in which the economies of the periphery are dependent on the center, which exploits them by transferring their surplus resources from one geographical sector to another. Different theorists offer different explanations about the ways in which this is accomplished, thus producing certain variations

[12] Reinhard Bendix, *Nation-Building and Citizenship* (New York: Wiley, 1964).

[13] Barrington Moore, *Social Origins of Dictatorship and Democracy* (Boston: Beacon Press, 1966).

[14] This terminology first appeared in the mid- and late-1960s, but became popularized by Immanuel Wallerstein, *The Modern World System* (New York: Academic Press, 1974).

on the general theme. According to some, exploitation is a political act, accomplished by a variety of coercive or quasicoercive means, ranging from outright plunder to the setting of prices and to the maintenance of subservient "client classes" in the countries of the periphery.[15]According to others, exploitation is an economic phenomenon. These writers regard the market itself as the culprit, describing it as an instrument for stimulating artificial needs and hence a dependence on the commodities of the advanced nations that is to be satisfied either by cheap raw material exports or by a kind of "dependent development" that in the long run serves only the interests of the core economies.[16] Or, as yet another version has it, economic exchanges between labor and capital intensive economies are inherently unequal because they result in different rates of return and hence in the transfer of value from the peripheral to the core nations. In this version of the theory, dependence and exploitation result from the mere inclusion of the backward producer in the world economy.[17]

The present study owes unquestionable debt to this new school of thought for redirecting scholarly interests from a narrow concern with developmental stages to the broader global sources of scarcity, inequality, and political consciousness. But if so, the study also takes issue with some of the premises on which these neo-Marxist theories rest. First and foremost, while it would be a folly to deny the obvious fact that perhaps all too frequently in history powerful nations have used force to expropriate the resources of others, some important questions still remain concerning how critical such forcible transfers were in creating the present structure of global inequalities. Second, while it is easy to accept the proposition that the market functions as the most important distributive mechanism in the modern world, it is less easy to concur with a view of the market in which the supply of labor is unlimited, in which demands are subject to the volition of

[15] See, for instance, Susanne Bodenheimer, "Dependency and Imperialism," in K. T. Fann and Donald C. Hodges, eds., *Readings in U.S. Imperialism* (Boston: Porter and Sargent, 1971), pp. 155-181; André Gunder-Frank, "Economic Dependence, Class Structure and Underdevelopment Policy," in James D. Cockroft, André Gunder-Frank, and Dale J. Johnson, *Dependence and Underdevelopment* (New York: Doubleday, 1972), pp. 19-46.

[16] Among others, Fernando H. Cardoso and Enzo Faletto, *Dependency and Development in Latin America* (Berkeley: University of California Press, 1979); also Theotonio Dos Santos, "The Structure of Dependence," in Fann and Hodges, *Readings in U.S. Imperialism*, pp. 225-237.

[17] See, especially, Arghiri Emmanuel, *Unequal Exchange: A Study of the Imperialism of Trade* (New York: Monthly Review Press, 1972); also, Wallerstein, *The Modern World System*.

the stronger party, and in which value is principally accounted for by the amount rather than by the productivity of labor. Third, while one can take no exception to the proposition that political action is most frequently motivated by deprivations and scarcities, one should also remember, as Marx did in his own time,[18] that these categories are relative and that they acquire meanings only through juxtaposition to the wealth and gratification of others. This is to say that immiseration, poverty, and the resultant frustrations may not only be the result of plunder and expropriation but also of failure to keep pace with the progress of others. That such progress invariably involves a zero-sum relationship in which someone's gain is always someone else's loss, that such qualities as inventiveness have little or no bearing on the relationship, are propositions that go against the grain of elementary human experience.

Whatever its immediate, or ultimate, sources, the problem of international inequality, like all other asymmetric relationships, raises a question of legitimacy. The term itself, as all social scientists will know, refers to beliefs in the higher moral qualities of an order, be it national, subnational or supranational. Whether such beliefs represent a form of false consciousness, or whether they answer to some deeper human need, is for Marxist and Weberian sociologists to argue. In either case, however, we must realize that the legitimacy of an order is not a fixed condition. On the contrary, as one of the foremost students of the phenomenon has observed,[19] legitimacy implies fluidity and a perennial quest for proof. It is a quality that imposes on any incumbent elite the daily task of demonstrating its own merit, of fulfilling promises, of squaring ideological formulations with ever-changing realities. Thus the legitimacy of an order, whether national or international, is not only the function of changes in the socio-economic structure but also of particular human decisions, not only of great, epochal trends but also of fortuitous events. Elites, as a succession of social thinkers from Macchiavelli to Pareto and Mosca reminds us, will not only fall because their virtue crumbles under the weight of necessity, but also because of the element of *fortuna*, that is, because they make a wrong decision at the wrong time. This formulation, to be sure, is at variance with the generally aprioristic thrust of contemporary sociology. Yet such fortuitous events as wars, assas-

[18] In his own words, "let a palace arise beside the little house, and it shrinks from a little house to a hut." See, Marx, "Wage-Labour and Capital," in David McLellan, ed., *Karl Marx: Selected Writings* (Oxford: Oxford University Press, 1977), p. 259.

[19] Reinhard Bendix, *Work and Authority in Industry*, 2d ed. (Berkeley: University of California Press, 1974), especially pp. xxv-xxvii.

sinations, revolutions, and discoveries will frequently provide critical thresholds for political change, and it is precisely on account of these that human history cannot be reduced to a more or less predictable and predetermined developmental scheme.

THE HISTORICAL STUDY

The principal purpose of this study is to test the validity of these propositions, and to elaborate them further by examining the political history of Hungary from the beginning of the nineteenth to the middle of the twentieth century. For these purposes the country and the period seem to be eminently well suited. To begin with, during the period under consideration Hungary was a backward country located on the periphery of the world system and laboring under the same material and psychological handicaps as are today's "emerging" nations in the so-called Third World. This circumstance should permit us to look for analogies and, more ambitiously, to develop a generalized concept of peripheral politics. Further, the body of materials at hand is lodged in the past and spreads over a period of more than a century. During this period the world system itself underwent significant transformations. This should enable us to go beyond the search for analogies, and to identify differences in the behavior of peripheral societies within various chronological frameworks. Finally, the case of Hungary offers a unique opportunity to study the phenomenon of backwardness in a country that possessed a distinctly occidental religious and institutional heritage. This should not only make it possible to discover historical analogies but also to test various hypotheses concerning the role of culture in a changing society.

Culture is a complex concept, and the hypotheses in question refer to a number of different formulations that will have to be examined here briefly even at the risk of encumbering the flow of discussion. To start with the definition itself, for the purposes of this volume culture will refer to patterns of behavior shaped by the injunctions (or sanctions) of religious belief and/or collective memories. In the most general sense, then, cultural hypotheses address the nexus between such beliefs and traditions on the one hand, and social, economic, and political outcomes on the other. While this will permit us to seek out an infinite number of connections, in most recent years social scientists have been particularly interested in the nexus between occidental culture and specific outcomes in economic and political development. Even here, however, we have to distinguish among three separate scholarly orientations. The first emphasizes the motivational

Preface

factor and treats certain elements of western culture—the asceticism and achievement orientation of religion and the universalism of the medieval institutional order—as the most important forces behind economic growth and the rise of a viable civic polity. The second formulation is less ambitious in that it treats culture as a necessary rather than sufficient condition of economic and political development,[20] while the third avoids the pitfalls of causality by emphasizing the continuity of cultural patterns and by assuming that these continuities will account for significant variations among the institutions of different societies.[21]

If one of the objectives of this study is to test and develop general hypotheses, another is to reexamine the political history of modern Hungary. This last objective stemmed from a degree of dissatisfaction with the ways in which conventional historiography, both nationalist and Marxist, has treated the general subject. To put it succinctly, the many studies that are available on politics and political change tend to fall into one of two categories: they are either phenomenological in orientation, emphasizing the unique and the idiosyncratic elements of history, or else they examine their subject within categories that have been borrowed directly, and sometimes quite uncritically, from the occidental experience. Specifically, there has been an unfortunate tendency throughout the past decades to place an undue emphasis on the processes of industrialization and commercialization at the expense of other processes, such as the bureaucratization of political life. As a corollary, political history has generally been written in terms of the conflicts of economic classes—landowners, entrepreneurs, workers, and peasants. This point of view ignores one of the most outstanding features of Hungarian history, the periodic rise and decline of political classes living by and off the institutions of the state.

Even more striking perhaps is the failure of conventional historiography to come to grips with the implications of backwardness for the dynamics of political and social change. Historians of the past were probably too weighted down with national pride to be able to build their analysis around the concept, while the Marxist historians of the postwar period remained the captives of a conceptual framework that viewed social change as an essentially uniform and unidirectional process in which the advanced country is supposed to show its less developed counterpart the mirror image of its own future. All

[20] This distinction, and the literature pertaining to it, is elucidated in Robert N. Bellah, "Reflections on the Protestant Ethic Analogy in Asia," in S. N. Eisenstadt, ed., *The Protestant Ethic and Modernization* (New York: Basic Books, 1968), pp. 243-252.

[21] See Bendix, *Nation-Building and Citizenship*, pp. 1-32.

this should not be taken to mean that the state of backwardness has been consistently overlooked or strenuously denied. Indeed, studies dealing with the economic aspects of the problem are numerous and perceptive. But while the existence of the problem has been acknowledged, little attempt has been made so far to address its psychological or international dimensions, or to integrate it within the overall experience of social, economic, and political change.

As a historical study of politics the present volume follows a chronological outline. After a general survey of the accumulated historical experience, it begins at a time when Hungary entered the rising global socio-economic system, and ends with the advent of communism in 1945. This last event, to be sure, did not end Hungary's backwardness vis-à-vis the Occident. But the year signals Hungary's entry into a larger and more tightly organized regional unit—the Soviet Bloc—whose policies were often formulated outside the boundaries of the country. Moreover, 1945 also signals the rise of a bi-polar international system with new rules of the game that present a different analytic problem for the student of political change.

As an analytic enterprise devoted to the exploration of historical patterns and relationships, the study has tried to avoid lengthy narrative and the detailed description of particular historical events. For this reason, the volume will mainly appeal to two categories of readers: to those who are already familiar with Hungarian history, and to those whose chief concern is not with Hungary, but with the history of other countries and with the more general problem of interpreting political change. A number of readers, no doubt, will fall between these two categories in that they will have some interest in Hungarian history, but will lack familiarity with its particulars. For them it may be useful to consult first a standard work on the subject, or else to study the chronology of major historical events appended to these pages.

NOTE TO THE READER

In any work covering a period of more than one hundred years, the problem arises concerning the consistent use of proper names, titles, measures, and the like. In our case, this problem is further compounded by the fact that during the period of history discussed here, a number of important legal, territorial, and economic changes took place, together with a conscious effort at the standardization of administration and systems of measurement.

To begin with, even the designation of the territorial unit presents certain problems for, prior to 1848, the term "Hungary" was used in

Preface

reference to two territorial units. One was Hungary proper, the other the larger Kingdom of Hungary (or, officially, the lands of the Holy Crown of St. Stephen) which included also the Voivodship (later Principality, and still later, Grand Duchy) of Transylvania, the associated kingdom of Croatia-Slavonia, and a Military Frontier District detached from these territories in the eighteenth century and administered separately under the authority of the Ministry of War in Vienna. After 1867, all these parts were united, except for Croatia-Slavonia, which retained its constitutional autonomy. These complex divisions would be of little consequence to the modern reader, except that they impinge on the collection of statistics. Certain data were collected for Hungary, but not for Transylvania; other data are available for the kingdom at large, but not for its constituent units. These differences will be duly noted in the tables and in the accompanying references.

A further complication arises out of the fact that for almost four centuries the Hungarian Kingdom was associated with a larger political unit, an empire ruled by the Habsburg dynasty. The legal and political ramifications of this relationship will be described elsewhere. Here it should be sufficient to remind the reader that the emperor of Austria—before 1804 the Holy Roman emperor—and the king of Hungary were one and the same person. In the text both titles have been used in reference to the wearer of the crown, depending on the capacity in which he acted. If he clearly acted in his capacity as the Hungarian sovereign (e.g., by opening the Diet or by appointing a prime minister) the use of the royal title appeared to be more appropriate, whereas in any other context he was referred to as an emperor.

A question that had to be faced while preparing the volume was how to render Hungarian first names. After some hesitation this was resolved in favor of translation or, in the case of lesser personalities, in favor of initials, with the exception of the footnotes and bibliographical references in which, for obvious reasons, the original forms had to be preserved. Similarly, and to avoid unnecessary confusion, Hungarian titles and the names of institutions were translated, often liberally, by adopting their British equivalents, rather than translating them literally. Thus I use the generally accepted term of county to designate the principal unit of local self-government, prime minister (instead of minister president) in reference to the head of the cabinet, and lord lieutenant (instead of chief bailiff) with respect to the head of the local administration. Likewise, the names of geographical regions were translated, since the original Magyar versions convey little meaning to the English-speaking reader. Thus, I use the "Plain," or

"Plainland" instead of *Alföld*, "Highlands" instead of *Felvidék*, and so on.

On the other hand, the names of cities are rendered in their Magyar original, except in a few cases where the German version was more current at that time, or was better known in foreign countries, as in the case of Pressburg (Pozsony), Kronstadt (Brassó), Hermannstadt (Szeben), and a few others. The use of the present Slovak or Rumanian names of these cities (Bratislava, Braşov, Sibiu, etc.) in a historical context seemed to be anachronistic.

Some dispute among prospective readers may arise concerning the use of the two adjectives, "Magyar" and "Hungarian." In the Magyar language only the former is known, while in English customary usage favors the latter, a derivative of the Latin "Hungaricus." In the Middle Ages, each term was used in reference to both the inhabitants of the kingdom and the people who spoke the Magyar idiom. This habit at times generated much argument, and before 1918 was often cited as evidence for Magyar intransigence. Since the usage goes back to the earliest days of the country's history when national sentiment was unknown in the modern sense, this argument makes little sense. At the same time, for our purposes a distinction may be useful. Thus, throughout the book the term "Hungarian" will be used to denote association with the legal entity, whereas "Magyar" will be used to designate ethnic solidarity and affiliation by language. However, this distinction cannot always be made crystal clear, for too often these two meanings overlapped in the minds of particular speakers and writers, especially after 1920 when the political unit was reduced essentially to the Magyar-speaking population.

A few words may also be said here about Hungarian money and measures. The traditional Austro-Hungarian currency was known in Hungary as the *forint* (Florin, abbrev. Fl.), with its value constantly changing between the Napoleonic wars and the end of the century. In 1894, the Florin was stabilized and exchanged for the Krone (in Hungarian, *korona*), at a rate of two to one in the approximate value of U.S. $.20. After the dissolution of the dual Monarchy, the Hungarian government retained the now heavily inflated Krone until 1926, when it was exchanged for a new monetary unit, the Pengő, originally at the value of the old Krone.

The measures used in old Hungary, as in the other countries of pre-modern Europe, were varied and inconsistent, and wherever necessary, footnotes refer to their metric or Anglo-American equivalents. One of the most important of these, the Hungarian, or Pressburg bushel (*mérő*, *Metzen*) equals 1.74 American bushels, while the old

Preface

quintal (*mázsa, Zentner*) translates into 123.58 English pounds. The traditional measure of land, the Hungarian acre (*hold*) almost equaled its Anglo-American counterpart (1:1004), while the traditional Hungarian mile converts to 4.97 English statute miles. In 1854 most of these measures were abolished and the metric system introduced, except for the measurement of land, where the Austrian, or cadastral acre, equaling 1.41 English acres, was introduced. For the second half of the nineteenth century and thereafter, all statistics will be given in these changed measures.

ACKNOWLEDGMENTS

The subject, purposes, and design of the volume thus having been stated, there remains only the pleasant task of expressing my gratitude to those who by their aid or example helped to accomplish this project. In the first place, these acknowledgments are due to social scientists whose own work provided inspiration and theoretical underpinnings for the project, whether or not my conclusions ultimately converge with theirs. Of these scholars, Fred Riggs provided me and the entire discipline with insights into the phenomenon of bureaucratic politics, so significant within the context of a backward society. Richard V. Burks' penetrating study of East European nationality introduced me to the important problem of ethnic marginality; Alexander Gerschenkron's essays raised a number of incisive questions concerning the nature and dynamics of change under conditions of economic backwardness; Reinhard Bendix's volumes sensitized me to the role of culture in politics, and to many related subjects; Karl deSchweinitz's book on industrialization and democracy called my attention to the implications of the international demonstration effect; finally, the work of Immanuel Wallerstein introduced me to the basic categories of analysis of the modern world system.

While archival research was not feasible in conjunction with the study of history covering a period of more than a century, throughout all phases of the work an effort was made to develop the argument from such primary sources as the Proceedings (*Napló*) of the Hungarian Parliament, items from the contemporary press, collections of published documents, and the speeches, diaries, or other writings of participants. But a work of this kind and scope could quite obviously not have been written without reliance on secondary materials. For this reason, acknowledgments are also due to a number of historians who either provided a starting point for research, or else a shortcut to the conclusions offered by the study. Among the great writers of the past one should mention the name of Henry Marczali whose magnificent study of Hungary in the eighteenth century proved to be a treasure trove of information on the economics of the period, and of Gyula Szekfű, whose numerous works, among them his five-volume history of Hungary (written in collaboration with Bálint Hóman), served as an invaluable reference work. Among more recently published works one should mention the comprehensive, two-volume history of Hungary written by a collective of writers under the general editorship of Erik Molnár, Zoltán Horváth's study of Hungarian intellectual life in the early 1900s, Iván Berend's and György Ránki's numerous essays on various aspects of modern economic history, Tibor Süle's competent essay on the radical intelligentsia and the socialist movement, Peter Sipos' monograph on Béla Imrédy, Sándor Kónya's biography of Gömbös, and Miklós Lackó's volume on Hungarian national socialism, the last three works based almost entirely on hitherto unknown materials buried in Hungarian archives. Among works published in the English language, one ought to mention George Bárány's biography of Stephen Széchenyi, Rudolf Tőkés' volume on Béla Kun and the Hungarian Soviet republic, William McCagg's seminal studies of the Hungarian Jewish nobility, intelligentsia, and political figures, and finally A. C. Macartney's still unsurpassed two-volume history of Hungary (1929-1945). Full references to these works will be found in the footnotes and in the accompanying bibliography.

In a more direct and personal manner I am indebted to a number of institutions and persons who, over the years, provided me with moral and material assistance. Of these, the Center for Slavic and East European Studies and the Institute of International Studies, both at the University of California at Berkeley, have supported the study with funds for research and clerical assistance. Their financial assistance enabled me to hire a number of competent research aides, of whom Magda Czigány and Stanyan Vukovich deserve special mention. In addition, the International Research and Exchange Board awarded me a fellowship which made it possible to spend a number of fruitful months to study, for the sake of analogy and contrast, social patterns in Rumania and other East European countries. I am indebted to my colleagues Reinhard Bendix, Richard V. Burks, A. James Gregor, William Griffith, Chalmers Johnson, Peter Kenez, Giuseppe di Palma, and Rudolf Tőkés for reading the manuscript at various stages of its development. Competent editorial assistance was provided by Sanford G. Thatcher and Marsha Shankman. The tedious task of indexing was largely accomplished by Kathe Thelen. The University of Cali-

Preface

fornia Press has kindly granted permission to use portions of my essay, "The Decline of Oligarchy," from the volume *Revolution in Perspective: Essays on the Hungarian Soviet Republic* (Berkeley and Los Angeles: University of California Press, 1971), edited by myself and William B. Slottman. Acknowledgments are also due to Joseph Grosz and Alice J. Boggs (for the estate of W. Arthur Boggs) for permission to reproduce a translation of the poem "Poet of the Steppe" by Endre Ady.

In addition to the above I wish to express thanks to my wife and to a number of personal friends for their moral support, patience, and good-humored needling about my repeated dodgings of self-established deadlines. However, they, like all other persons and institutions mentioned above, merely gave me the benefit of their advice and their doubts, and should in no way be held responsible for any of the shortcomings of the finished product.

Hungarian Spelling and Pronunciation

Hungarian spelling is phonetic and its pronunciation consistent in that each sound has a letter, or combination of letters, corresponding to it. Several of these letters, all of them vowels, include diacritical marks, which English-language works sometimes omit for technical reasons. Such omission, however, is somewhat irritating to the eye trained to read Hungarian texts, for in the Magyar language, just as in German or French, the marks are used to indicate significant differences. In the case of á, é, ö, and ü, these differences are qualitative; in the case of í, ó, ő, ú, ű, the difference is quantitative, that is, the diacritical marks are used to indicate merely a change in the length of a particular sound.

While the accurate rendering of these vowels, as well as of some of the consonants, is difficult short of using phonetic signs, the following list of equivalents, or near equivalents, may serve as a rough guide to both reading and pronunciation.

a	is like	*au*	in	fl*au*nt
á	"	a	"	German V*a*ter
e	"	e	"	d*e*bilitate
é	"	a	"	l*a*ke
i (archaic y)	"	ee	"	s*ee*
o, u, ö, ü	"	same	"	German
c (archaic cz)	"	ts	"	*ts*ar
g	"	g	"	*g*arden
j	"	y	"	*Y*ork
s	"	sh	"	*sh*irt
cs (archaic ch)	"	ch	"	*ch*alk
gy	"	soft d	"	British *d*uty
ny	"	soft n	"	British *n*ew
sz	"	s	"	English
ty	"	soft t	"	*t*une
zs	"	j	"	French *j*our

Chronological Survey of Relevant Events

896   The Magyar tribes enter the Carpathian basin.

896-971   Semi-nomadic, kinship society. Magyar expeditions of plunder to western and southern Europe.

972-1000   Chieftain Geyza of the clan of Árpád. Settlement of the Magyar tribes. Christian missionaries invited to the country.

1000-1038 Geyza's son Stephen (István) first king of Hungary.

1000-1222 Patrimonial kingdom and institutions under kings from the dynasty of Árpád.

1222   King Andrew II issues the Aurea Bulla charter in which he recognizes the hereditary rights of barons and the privileges of royal servitors and freemen.

1222-1514 Gradual development of legal, political, and economic institutions of feudalism.

1301   Extinction of the Árpád dynasty. The monarchy becomes elective.

1351   The second Aurea Bulla confirms hereditary property rights and privileges of the nobility.

1458-1490 King Mathias Corvinus. Attempts to strengthen royal authority at the expense of the nobility.

1490-1514 Feudal reaction. It provokes the peasant uprising of 1514.

1514-1517 Commissioned by the estates, Stephen Werbőczy issues a collection of noble rights and privileges in the *Tripartitum Corpus Juris*. King and nobility are described as equal partners in a Corporation of the Holy Crown. All freemen—magnates and "common" nobility—said to have equal rights. At the same time, the rights of serfs, including their earlier freedom of movement from one estate to another, are severely curtailed.

1526   Battle of Mohács. The Hungarian feudal army annihilated by the Turks. Death of King Louis II on the battlefield.

1526-1540 The country and the feudal estates divided between Ferdinand I of the House of Habsburg and John I of Zapolya, the latter under Ottoman patronage. The beginnings of the Protestant reformation in the country.

Chronological Survey

1540   Tripartite division of the kingdom among Habsburgs, Ottoman Turks, and the principality of Transylvania.

1547   The National Assembly abolishes restrictions on the peasants' freedom of movement. Growing differentiation of the peasantry between serf tenants and cottagers (*zsellérs*) settled on the lords' domain (*allod*).

1566   The Diet of Transylvania declares the equality of the Catholic and Protestant denominations.

1572-1606 Incipient royal absolutism under King-Emperor Rudolf of Habsburg.

1605-1608 Religious and civil strife. Protestant rights recognized in royal (Habsburg) Hungary. Public Law ɪ/1608 transforms the National Assembly of freemen into a bicameral Diet.

1670-1687 Protestant rights under attack. New wave of royal absolutism. The Diet of Pressburg recognizes the hereditary succession of kings from the House of Habsburg.

1683-1699 Turks expelled from the Carpathian Basin by the joint forces of Catholic coalition. Transylvania under Habsburg sovereignty.

1703-1711 War of independence against Habsburg domination, led by Prince Franciscus Rákóczi. Ends with the victory of Habsburgs, who nevertheless restore the constitution of Hungary, and recognize the special status of the kingdom within their realm.

1722   The Diet passes the Pragmatic Sanction Act, extending the rights of succession to the female line of the ruling house, and declaring Hungary "inseparable" from the other countries of the Habsburg realm.

1711-1780 Decline of foreign trade and industry. Regression into subsistence farming. Massive immigration and colonization to replace population lost during the Turkish wars.

1767   Royal decree (*Decretum Urbarium*) regulates the feudal obligations of the peasantry.

1784-1787 First Hungarian census.

1793-1814 Napoleonic wars. Commodity production in agriculture stimulated by the rising price of grain.

1814-1825 Economic depression, and political attack on feudal parliamentarism. Emperor-King Francis I refuses to convoke the Diet.

1825-1848 The "Age of Reforms," or *Vormärz*. Impoverishment of the lesser, or "common," nobility, and the rise of liberal ideas among them.

1830   Count Stephen Széchenyi publishes his *Hitel* (Credit) propagating measures for the modernization of Hungarian agriculture and legal institutions.

1833   Louis Kossuth enters public life as the editor of *Parliamentary Reports*. In subsequent years he is tried and imprisoned for sedition (1837-1841), becomes the editor of the liberal *Pesti Hirlap* (1841-1844), and the leader of the radical wing of the liberal opposition at the Diet (1847). In this capacity he acts as the chief advocate of political reform to modernize the institutions of the national state.

1836   Urbarial Law permits the cash commutation of the feudal obligations of serf tenants.

1841   The first Jewish Emancipation Act. Jews free to settle and buy property in cities, with the exception of seven economically depressed mining communities.

1848   *March 15.* Revolution in Buda and Pest. *March 19-30.* Diet abolishes feudal institutions, modernizes parliament, and sets up Hungarian cabinet with ministries of finance and defense independent of their counterparts in Vienna. *June-September.* Rebellion against the Hungarian ministry among Serbs, Croats, Rumanians, and Slovaks. *September.* War breaks out between the Hungarian and the imperial governments.

1849   *April 14.* Hungarian Declaration of Independence, and dethronement of the House of Habsburg. Louis Kossuth "governing president" (regent) of Hungary. *June 15.* Imperial Russia enters the war and sends expeditionary army to Hungary. *August 13.* The surrender of the Hungarian armies.

1849-1867 Hungarian constitution suspended. Autocratic rule of Francis Joseph I.

1855-1873 Cereal prices booming.

1860-1861 Various attempts to restore constitutionalism while maintaining the centralized administrative structure of a unitary empire.

1867   The *Ausgleich*, or Compromise, between emperor and Hungary restores constitutional monarchy. Francis Joseph king of Hungary, the Austrian Empire transformed into Austro-Hungarian Monarchy. Julius Andrássy prime minister of Hungary.

1868   Second Jewish Emancipation Act. Also, Nationalities Act providing for a limited use of non-Magyar languages in

education and administration. Both Hungarian nationalists and the representatives of the minorities reject the
provisions of the act.

1875   Formation of the Liberal party. In opposition, the National
Independence (1848) and Conservative parties.

1875-1890 Premiership of Coloman Tisza. Institutionalization of electoral corruption. Rise of the Liberal political machine.
Repression of national minorities.

1878-1896 Commodity crisis and the final ruin of the gentry, the
lesser landowning nobility.

1881-1887 Fiscal reforms, and various acts of parliament to establish
a system of subsidies for new industries.

1890-1906 The industrial revolution "takes off" in Hungary.

1892-1895 Anti-clerical debate and legislation in parliament. Representation of Jewish religious communities in the House
of Lords.

1901-1905 Parliamentary crisis aggravated by the dissatisfaction of
various classes of agrarian producers. Perennial filibuster
of defense appropriations.

1903-1905 Count Stephen Tisza premier.

1904   Tisza attempts to break the filibuster by parliamentary
maneuver.

1905   Electoral defeat and collapse of the Tisza machine.

1906-1910 Hungary governed by an ineffectual coalition of the National Independence (1848), Catholic People's, and conservative Constitution parties under the premiership of
Alexander Wekerle.

1910   Stephen Tisza forms the neo-liberal National Party of
Work, and restores machine politics.

1910-1912 Tisza speaker of the House of Representatives. Forceful
repression of the opposition filibuster.

1912-1917 Second premiership of Stephen Tisza.

1914-1918 Hungary in World War I.

1916-1918 Karl I (IV) succeeds Francis Joseph as emperor of Austria
and king of Hungary.

1918   *October 31.* Revolution in Budapest. Stephen Tisza assassinated. Count Michael Károlyi premier. *November 16.*
Hungary proclaimed an independent republic. Rumanian, Serbian, and Czechoslovak troops enter the territory
of the country.

1919   *January 11.* Michael Károlyi president of the republic.
March 21. Democratic republic falls under foreign and

domestic pressures. Proclamation of the Hungarian Soviet Republic. *Summer.* War against Rumania and Czechoslovakia. Red terror. *August 1.* Fall of the Soviet Republic. *August 3-November 16.* The Rumanian occupation of Budapest.

1919-1921 White terror and governments of "Christian" political orientation.

1920 *January.* Election of a new, unicameral National Assembly. *March 1.* Admiral Nicholas Horthy regent of Hungary. *June 4.* Peace treaty signed in Trianon palace, independent Hungary reduced to about 29 percent of the territory and 37.5 percent of the population of the prewar kingdom. *August-September.* Counterrevolutionary legislation: religious quotas for university admissions, restoration of corporal punishment, and a moderate land reform law.

1921 *April and October.* Two attempts by King Karl IV to reclaim the throne of Hungary.

1921-1931 Premiership and "liberal-conservative" government of Count Stephen Bethlen. Formation of the Unitary party. Restoration of the old political machine. Neo-liberal, mercantilist economic policies, protection of urban enterprise and the Jewish religious minority.

1929-1934 Economic depression.

1931 Bethlen resigns. Count Julius Károlyi premier.

1932-1936 Right radical government under Prime Minister Julius Gömbös. Abortive design for a one-party corporatist state.

1936-1938 "Grand coalition" of the radical and the conservative Right under Coloman Darányi. The first "Jewish law" establishes quotas of 20 percent in business and professions.

1938-1939 Right radical government of Béla Imrédy. Another attempt at establishing a one-party, mobilization regime. Second Jewish law drafted, establishing quotas of 12 and 6 percent for business and the professions respectively. Pursuant to the first Vienna Award, Hungary recovers part of Slovakia and Ruthenia.

1939-1941 Count Paul Teleki's government attempts to steer a middle course between the conservative and the radical Right in domestic policy, between a pro-German and pro-British orientation in foreign affairs. Under terms of second Vienna Award Hungary recovers northern Transylvania from Rumania.

1941   *April.* Hungary enters war against Yugoslavia and recovers part of territory lost in 1918. Premier Teleki commits suicide in protest. *June 26.* Hungary enters the war against the Soviet Union. *December.* Hungary in war with western allies.

1941-1942 Ladislas Bárdossy premier. Right radical, pro-German policy orientation.

1942-1944 Nicholas Kállay premier. Conservative, pro-western orientation of national policy.

1944   *March 19.* Horthy detained in Klessheim. Eleven German divisions occupy Hungary. Döme Sztójay premier. Arrest of conservatives, socialists, and democrats. *March 30.* Anti-Jewish decrees. *May.* Deportation of the Jewish population of the countryside and provincial cities. *June 30.* Bethlen's secret memorandum urges resistance, armistice, and the end of deportations. *August 29.* Sztójay dismissed, General Géza Lakatos premier. *October 15.* Abortive attempt to surrender the Hungarian army. Regent Horthy arrested. *October 16.* Francis Szálasi premier and "leader of the nation." Proclamation of national socialist Arrow Cross regime.

1945   *April 4.* Retreat of the last German troops, and of the national socialist government from the territory of Hungary. The Soviet army occupies the country.

The Politics of Backwardness in Hungary

I.

Historical Background

STATE AND PEOPLE

The Hungarian State in History

The Danubian Basin, which for the most part of this volume serves as the locus of the narrative, is a relatively closed geographical unit in the middle of the European continent. The arc of the Carpathians that surrounds the Basin on three sides arises at the Danube near Vienna and runs unbroken to the east, south, and then to the west until it rejoins the river at the Iron Gates, embracing a territory of approximately 128,000 square miles.

Inside the mountainous arc the landscape is variegated, which makes it possible to differentiate among regions in purely topographical terms. In the center of the area the countryside is flat and open, its monotony broken only by a few rivers of which the Tisza (Theiss) is the most important. Located north of the Plainland is what Hungarians called the Highlands, corresponding to the territory of contemporary Slovakia and the Carpatho-Ukraine. Transylvania is a high plateau, east of the Plain, while in the west the rolling hills of Transdanubia stretch from the Danube to the foothills of the Austrian Alps. In the south, crossing the river Drava, we enter the historical province of Croatia-Slavonia. Here the terrain changes slowly from plains to gentle hills, and then to the more rugged mountains of the Adriatic coast, an area attached to the larger unit less by geography than by political ties.

The Hungarians, or Magyars, who lent their name to these parts for the better half of the second millennium came here relatively late, toward the end of the ninth century. A warrior people of semi-nomadic cattle herders, they found it easy to destroy the weak and poorly integrated societies of the local population, but they found it hard to adapt to a sedentary way of life and to organize their own state. Indeed, for decades they persisted in their earlier habits, and instead of tilling the land they organized expeditions of plunder that brought havoc to the neighboring countries. These forays came to an end only when the German princes mustered their forces and, after wiping out

Historical Background

some of the Magyar marauding parties, prepared to wage a war of extermination against the obstreperous intruders. It was mainly under this threat that the Chieftain Geyza, head of the largest clan from the line of Árpád, made a decision to settle the roving tribes and, using the loyalty and superior numbers of his kinsmen, forced the rest of Magyardom to accept the creed and institutions of occidental Christianity. The task begun by Geyza was accomplished by his son Vajk who, under the name of Stephen (István), accepted a royal crown from Pope Sylvester II in the year 1000, and became the first, subsequently canonized, king of the country. In the intervening years recalcitrant tribal chiefs and their clansmen were put to the sword and their lands were confiscated and donated as fiefs to foreign knights or to more pliable tribesmen.

The center of the original Magyar encampment was on the Plainland between the rivers Tisza and Danube whence the conquerors fanned out in every direction. Transdanubia and the Highlands were occupied by the Magyars in the tenth century, while Transylvania was added to their domain in the eleventh, though the latter province, with its dense forests and sparse population, continued to enjoy a measure of institutional autonomy under governors, or voivods, appointed by the Hungarian kings. In the twelfth century, the kings of Hungary acquired the crown of Croatia-Slavonia and turned the lands between the Drava and the Adriatic into an "associate kingdom" without subverting the integrity of local laws and institutions. Over the centuries, other provinces and fiefs were temporarily attached to the kingdom by conquest or dynastic arrangements, but Transylvania, Croatia-Slavonia, and Hungary proper continued to form the core of the medieval realm under the "holy crown of St. Stephen."

The principal ambition of the first kings of Hungary from the native dynasty of Árpád (1000-1301) was to consolidate this realm and to defend it from both imperial encroachments and the incursions of such steppe nomads as the Cumans, Pechenegs, and Tartars. But their successors, elected from various royal houses of Europe, set their sights higher and made repeated attempts to gain much wider influence on the Continent. Thus in the fourteenth century Kings Charles Robert and Louis of the royal house of Anjou took advantage of the favorable balance of power following the decline of Byzantium, and made Hungary the center of a far-reaching dynastic union from which they ruled their Italian, Polish, and Balkan possessions. In the fifteenth century, Sigismund of Luxembourg moved from the Hungarian royal throne to the German imperial throne, though in the process he was arrested and held for ransom by unappreciative local

4

magnates. A few decades later Matthias Corvinus, son of the voivod of Translyvania, attempted to follow in Sigismund's footsteps. As king of Hungary he waged numerous wars in Bohemia, Poland, and Austria, and, in his quest for the imperial throne he moved his residence to Vienna where he died in 1490 before he could attain his lifelong objective.

These fleeting moments of dynastic glory were soon followed by political decay and disintegration. After the death of Corvinus a long pent-up feudal reaction set in to check the incipient trend toward royal absolutism. The feudal reaction quickly dismantled the appurtenances of a centralized dynastic state, among them Corvinus' standing army. This development took place at a singularly inauspicious time, for it coincided with the rise of Ottoman power on the Balkan peninsula, and with the preparations for a Turkish assault on the Danubian kingdom. When the assault came in 1526, the raw and undisciplined feudal levies were no match for the vast and superbly trained Ottoman army and suffered a debilitating defeat at their hands in the historic battle of Mohács. Since King Louis II himself fell on the battlefield, the consequences of the defeat were compounded by wrangling among the estates over succession, which eventually resulted in the tripartite division of the country. The western and northern parts of the country passed under the scepter of the Austrian branch of the House of Habsburg. The Plainland, including the former royal residence of Buda, became incorporated into the Ottoman empire, while Transylvania emerged as a principality which, under its native and elected princes, maintained its precarious independence by paying tribute to the Sublime Porte and by playing off one great power against another. The changing fortunes of war kept the boundaries of these three political entities in constant flux and brought devastation upon property and people caught between the stalemated Habsburg and Islamic armies (see map, p. 7).

This precarious state of affairs was aggravated by religious conflict between the adherents of Catholicism and Protestantism. The new faith had been introduced into the country in the 1520s and took root first in some of the German trading and mining centers of northern Hungary. But it truly began to flourish a few decades later among the Transylvanian nobility and among the population of the territories under Turkish domination, whence it spread to Habsburg Hungary so fast that by the first decade of the seventeenth century only a handful of noble families and their retainers remained constant to the Catholic faith. In the interim, Protestantism also won a number of significant political victories. In 1566 the Diet of Transylvania de-

Historical Background

clared the equality of all faiths, while in 1606 the estates of Hungary gained royal consent to the freedom of worship. These spectacular advances were subsequently reversed by a combination of force, persuasion, and judicious concessions on the part of the Crown that removed many of the root causes of religious and political protest. But even after the successes of the counter-reformation led by the able Cardinal Pázmány, almost a fourth of the country's total population (and an even larger percentage of the nobility, bourgeoisie, and free peasantry) remained adherents of one or another of the Protestant denominations, Lutheranism in the cities, Calvinism in Transylvania and the Plainland, and Unitarianism in some of the remote Magyar villages of the eastern Carpathians (Table 1).

The division of the country, aggravated by intermittent religious warfare in which Transylvania fought on the side of the Protestant coalition of Europe against the House of Habsburg, lasted until the end of the seventeenth century when the armies of a Catholic alliance expelled the Turks from the Carpathian Basin and reunited the country under Habsburg authority. This victory of the Christian armies, however, was greeted with less than uniform enthusiasm by the population of the country, for the prolonged war of liberation (1683-1699) caused enormous losses throughout the country, and was accompanied by the prosecution of Protestants and by depredations of the foreign soldiery. In protest, a peasant rebellion broke out in 1703, and the peasants were soon joined by other elements of Hungarian society. Under the leadership of Franciscus Rákóczi, the descendant

TABLE 1
RELIGION IN THE KINGDOM OF HUNGARY, 1839
(thousands)

Religion	Hungary		Entire Kingdom	
Catholic	5,030	51.8%	6,130	47.4%
Greek Catholic (Uniate)	856	8.8	1,322	10.2
Evangelical (Lutheran)	783	8.1	1,006	7.8
Reformed (Calvinist)	1,614	16.6	1,846	14.5
Unitarian	9	.1	47	.4
Greek Orthodox	1,169	12.1	2,283	17.8
Jewish	240	2.5	244	1.9
Total	9,701	100.0%	12,878	100.0%

SOURCE: Elek Fényes, *Magyarország statistikája*, I, 33-34 and Table 52B.

6

Aachen

GERMAN ROMAN

•Prague

POLAND

EMPIRE

Vienna   •Pozsóny

•Buda   •Debrecen
         •Kolozsvár
Zagreb   TRANSYLVANIA
               •Szeben

OTTOMAN

EMPIRE

HUNGARY in EUROPE
1450 - 1550

━ ━ ━ Boundary of Hungary
.... Boundaries of Ottoman territory and
           Transylvania, 1540

0   500 KM

of Transylvania princes and the wealthiest landowner of the country, the forces of the peasant *jacquerie* and the noble *fronde* were welded into an effective nationwide alliance whose initial success persuaded the estates in 1707 to declare the royal rights of the House of Habsburg null and void.

The war of independence dragged on for eight years, but was eventually put down by a seemingly inexhaustible flow of troops from the imperial holdings of the ruling house. Nevertheless, the scale of the rebellion convinced the imperial side that Hungary could not be governed effectively without the consent of her nobility. The Peace Treaty of Szatmár (1711) and the subsequent Act of Pragmatic Sanction (1722) represented compromises—neither the first nor the last ones—between the Hungarian nobility and the Habsburg dynasty. On the one hand, these documents confirmed the hereditary rights of the dynasty to the Hungarian throne, and made the kingdom an "indivisible and inseparable" part of the larger imperial domain. On the other hand, they guaranteed Hungary's constitutional autonomy and identity within a customs frontier between herself and the other provinces of the realm. The head of the House of Habsburg was to rule the country not as an emperor but as the king of Hungary, governing with the aid of an indigenous officialdom within the traditional limits of royal authority (see map, p. 9).

Demographic Change and Ethnic Divisions

When the nomadic Magyars entered the Carpathian Basin at the end of the ninth century they found a number of peoples left behind by earlier waves of cross-continental migration. In the process of conquest and settlement those peoples who lived on the plains in the center of the country were assimilated into Magyardom. But those who lived in relatively compact settlements on the mountainous periphery of the Basin—among them the ancestors of today's Slovaks, Ruthenians, Croats, and Rumanians—escaped assimilation and succeeded in maintaining their cultural and linguistic identity. In subsequent centuries the complexity of this ethnic picture was compounded by the arrival of new groups of immigrants. Among them were several nomadic peoples—the Pechenegs, Jazygs, and Cumans—who were quickly absorbed by the surrounding Magyar population, as well as substantial numbers of German (Saxon) colonists, who managed to preserve their language and customs in the cities of Transylvania and northern Hungary.

In the absence of regular conscriptions, the numbers and ethnic stratification of this medieval population must remain a matter of

8

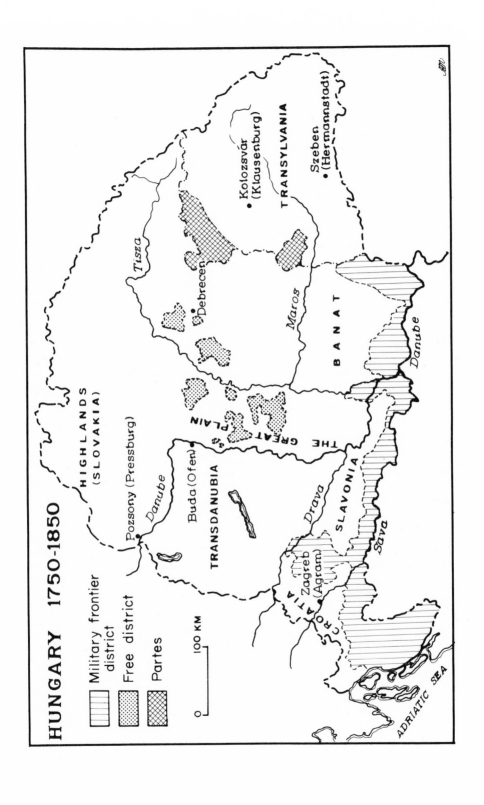

HUNGARY 1750-1850

Military frontier district

Free district

Partes

0   100 KM

HIGHLANDS (SLOVAKIA)

Tisza

TRANSYLVANIA

Kolozsvár (Klausenburg)

Szeben (Hermannstadt)

Debrecen

Maros

BANAT

Danube

THE GREAT PLAIN

Pozsony (Pressburg)

Danube

Buda (Ofen)

TRANSDANUBIA

SLAVONIA

Drava

Sava

Zagreb (Agram)

CROATIA

ADRIATIC SEA

conjecture. According to Hungarian historians, at the end of the fifteenth century the population of the country was five million, of which
as much as eighty percent is said to have been Magyar.[1] This estimate
may well be slanted by nationalist bias. In any case, in the next two
centuries the demographic structure of the country underwent profound transformation. As a result of protracted warfare, the population of large parts of the country was greatly reduced, with the
Magyar-inhabited Plainland bearing the brunt of the losses. Thus the
census of 1720 found only 2,582,000 inhabitants in the kingdom, of
whom 44.1 percent were subsequently estimated to have been Magyar
in language and custom.[2] Thereafter, the population losses of the
previous centuries prompted a new and systematic policy of colonization that brought close to one million settlers from southern Germany to Transdanubia and the Voivodina (Bánát), adding to the already existing German community of Saxons another community of
"Swabians" in southern Hungary. Other immigrants, responding to
labor shortages in Hungary, came to escape oppressive conditions in
neighboring countries. Among the latter were hundreds of thousands
of Serbians and Rumanians, who crossed the borders of the Ottoman
Empire and settled in the regions adjacent to them. As a result of this
influx, the population of the country increased dramatically from
2,582,000 in 1720 to 8,003,000 in 1787, but the proportion of Magyars
declined to 39.1 percent according to one estimate, and to 29.0 according to another.[3] From this point on, however, the Magyar element
began to increase once again due to a process of natural, and as yet
unplanned, assimilation, so that in 1839 the statistician Fényes could
report that 37.4 percent of the population of the entire kingdom, and
42.2 percent of the population of the country without Croatia-Slavonia, were ethnic Magyars. Meanwhile the population of the country,
including Croatia-Slavonia, had grown to 12,878,000. This population
was ethnically divided in the manner indicated on Table 2.

In the Middle Ages, the ethnic division of the population was the
source of few frictions. Indeed, the first king of the realm, Stephen,
issued a series of "Admonitions" in which he emphasized the importance of ethnic diversity, presumably because it enabled him to deal
more effectively with the primordial tribal instincts of his Magyar
subjects. And if the latter-day nationalists were deeply embarrassed
by this "error" of the great king, his immediate successors acted upon

[1] See Hungarian Ministry of Foreign Affairs, "The Development of the Population
Since the Cessation of Turkish Rule," *Hungarian Peace Negotiations* (Budapest: Horánszky,
1922), I, 43-46.
[2] Ibid.   [3] Ibid.

TABLE 2
NATIONALITIES IN THE KINGDOM OF HUNGARY, 1839
(thousands)

Nationality	Hungary		Entire Kingdom	
Magyar	4,335	44.7%	4,812	37.4%
Slovak	1,679	17.3	1,687	13.1
German	1,020	10.5	1,273	9.9
Rumanian	1,070	11.0	2,202	17.1
Croat	148	1.5	886	6.8
Serb	391	4.0	828	6.5
Other South Slav	339	3.4	469	3.6
Ruthenian	442	4.7	442	3.4
Others	277	2.9	279	2.2
Total	9,701	100.0%	12,878	100.0%

SOURCE: Fényes, *Magyarország statistikája*, I, Table 52B.

it by transforming the tribal state of the Magyars into a supranational commonwealth whose official language (up until 1841) was Latin, and whose institutions were devoid of ethnic identity. Thus while the Magyars continued to be overrepresented among the warrior and administrative classes, the term *populus Hungaricus*, or *natio Hungarica*, referred to all the freemen of the country whose privileges were granted and enjoyed with no regard to ethnic origin.

Religion and Culture

All over the European continent, the settlement of nomadic peoples and the rise of organized societies in the post-migration period were closely linked to the spread of Christianity. The tenets of the faith provided much needed ideological cement to emerging social relationships, and contributed significantly to the consolidation of the political order by teaching obedience to established authority, and by condemning murder and plunder as a way of life. Thus when a heathen chief and his people embraced the faith, this was usually taken as a declaration of intent that they would abide by the rules of civilized international conduct, to be reciprocated by the gift of a crown from either Rome or Byzantium, the two great fountainheads of the creed in the Middle Ages.

When the chieftains of the heathen Magyars turned to Rome rather than Byzantium, their choice was dictated not so much by cultural and theological as by momentary political considerations. Wedged between the eastern and the western empires, and facing a papacy feuding with the German emperors, Hungary was in a relatively fa-

Historical Background

vorable bargaining position which she used to maximum advantage. Her rulers extracted from the Pope concessions that had been granted to few occidental monarchs. Thus in the course of negotiations that preceded his conversion, the future king of Hungary and his successors were given "apostolic rights" which included, among others, the right of veto over all ecclesiastic appointments, and the right of refusing to promulgate any of the papal bulls.

While the choice of Rome over Byzantium was thus the result of momentary expediency, and hence can be regarded as an accident of history, its consequences were far-reaching, for the emissaries of the Pope not only brought with them particular forms of liturgy and church organization, but a set of principles as well, which in the Dark Ages represented the single most important link with the legalism and universalism of antiquity. These principles tended to emphasize individual rather than collective responsibility before God, and a concept of salvation that hinged upon the fulfillment of specific obligations, with the Church acting as an intermediary. In Catholicism "God has established certain laws for man. By sinful conduct man violates these laws. Justice requires him to make amends to God. The Church supervises this relationship. . . . Just as [Roman] jurisprudence has drawn up scales of crime and punishment, so also the Church has drawn up scales of sins and necessary penances. The business of the Church's legal agents is to apply this scale to particular cases."[4]

Originally, this doctrine of legalism was constructed to regulate spiritual life and purely ecclesiastical functions. But in time, due to the vast spiritual and temporal influence of the Church, these teachings spilled over into many areas of private and public life and, whether by analogy or direct injunction, provided models and sanction for diverse forms of secular behavior. For one, they lent legitimacy to the idea that men should be judged according to their own deeds rather than those of their kinfolk, and encouraged the view that the relationship between superiors and subordinates—between king and vassal, lord and peasant—should rest on a system of well-defined and reciprocal obligations regulated by contract. For another, the position of the Church and its relationship to the secular state provided a model for the autonomy of other social and political entities, as well as for their immunity from arbitrary coercion by the Crown and its agents.

The universalism and legalism of Catholicism may be fully appreciated only in comparison with some of the tenets of Greek Orthodoxy.

[4] Ernest Benz, *The Eastern Orthodox Church* (Chicago: Aldine, 1963), p. 44.

12

Unlike the former, which grew directly out of a tradition of Roman law, the latter was shaped by Near Eastern philosophies and, under their influence, eschewed the philosophical foundations of western Christianity. If in Catholicism the ideas of retribution and divine justice seem to overshadow the themes of God's love and infinite forgiveness, the eschatology of the Orthodox creed rests on altogether different principles. "From the very beginning," writes the theologian Benz, "the Eastern Church secretly inclined toward the idea of universal salvation."[5] Thus in the third century, the church father Origen developed the doctrine according to which the Last Judgment would not set apart the saved and the damned, but only "assign men their place in a new age of the universe in which everyone will have a fresh chance to ascend to glory. At the end . . . the fallen angels, and even Satan himself, will turn back to the divine Logos."[6] As a corollary, the conditions of salvation are not laid down with any precision, but are subsumed under the diffuse obligation to love God, with the act of sinning seen not so much as a breach of rules, but as a "diminution of essence."[7] In sum, these canonic principles came down strongly on the side of community and affect, and inspired a far more diffuse set of social and political relationships than the tenets of occidental Christianity. The ruler is a stern father, not a supreme judge or legislator. He requires the love of his subjects, but also retains the prerogative to define and redefine their duties, and to expect total filial devotion from them rather than mere compliance with specific commands.

These differences between eastern and western Christianity were brought into an even sharper focus by the doctrinal innovations of the Reformation. If Catholicism provided a model for a state in which authority was divided and subject to restraints, Protestantism challenged a whole mode of life dominated by hierarchy and, through the examples of synodal-presbyterial forms of church government, presented a model for participation in the affairs of the state, thereby giving the faltering institutions of medieval parliamentarism a renewed raison d'être. Furthermore, while Catholicism carefully established the criteria for salvation through penance, the Reformation transformed the very concept of service to God, by teaching that the transcendental end of salvation may be attained by such empirical means as the pursuit of perfection in one's own occupation. Out of this notion of "calling" arose not only the celebrated work ethic, but also the emphasis on asceticism, which encouraged total devotion to

---

5 Ibid., p. 52.   6 Ibid.
7 Ibid., p. 51.

Historical Background

the task of salvation without the distractions of material, aesthetic, or physical indulgences.[8]

Inspired by these religious principles, the Protestants of Hungary developed the stubborn individualism and sense of manifest destiny that have reminded many an observer of some of the qualities of contemporary English, Scottish, and Dutch religious dissenters in their inhospitable overseas environments.[9] To be sure, neither religious doctrine nor circumstance made the inhabitants of Hungary into carbon copies of colonial Dutchmen or Scotsmen. But religious doctrine instilled in them a number of traits that Weber, Tawney, Troeltsch, and other students of Protestantism have linked to the rise of modern economies and societies. Thus, like the citizens of Calvin's own Geneva, those of the German cities of northern Hungary became subject to the rigor of ethical and legal codes that reflected a puritanical conception of virtue and vice. Most of these cities for instance, possessed strict codes of dress which, like that of the city of Kassa in 1708, not only banned "indecent, luxurious or extraordinary garb,"[10] but also specified the number of items that a man or woman could possess. Violators of these codes were fined or pilloried. Vagrancy and sloth were usually outlawed and punished by flagellation, while adultery and other sins of the flesh carried the penalty of death or torture on the rack. The virtues of hard work and accomplishment were celebrated in many ways, often in the form of inscriptions on the walls of proud patrician houses and Lutheran churches that survive to this very day. They were also embodied in the *Meisterstück*, a most elaborate piece of workmanship that secured its creator admission to the guild and to full-fledged membership in the community.

In the Calvinist countryside similar rigor prevailed, although it was less closely tied to explicit legal sanctions. The memoirs of the Calvinist Count Bethlen (1642-1716),[11] lord chancellor of Transylvania, and of the more humble George Rettegi (1718-1786)[12] are replete with

[8] For these elements of the doctrine see Weber, *The Protestant Ethic*; Ernst Troeltsch, *Protestantism and Progress* (Boston: Beacon, 1958), especially pp. 90-150. Also, T. H. Tawney's "Foreword" to the above work, and Eisenstadt, *The Protestant Ethic and Modernization*.

[9] The Austrian historian Joseph Redlich, quoted in Oscar Jászi, *The Dissolution of the Habsburg Monarchy*, 2d ed. (Chicago: University of Chicago Press, 1961), p. 303.

[10] Sándor Domanovszky, ed., *Magyar művelődéstörténet* [The cultural history of Hungary] (Budapest: Magyar Történelmi Társulat, 1939), IV, 328-329.

[11] *Bethlen Miklós önéletleírása* [The autobiography of Nicholas Bethlen] (Budapest: Szépirodalmi könyvkiadó, 1955), I, 116-135.

[12] György Rettegi, *Emlékezetre méltó dolgok* [Things worth remembering] (Bucharest: Kritérion, 1970), pp. 80-81.

praise for the importance of modesty, industry, and self-reliance, together with occasionally lurid stories of victory over the temptations of the flesh. The Calvinist squire George Bossányi, eulogized as the prototype of his class in the memoirs of his grandson, Francis Kazinczy, "lived in a thatched cottage . . . wore the same clothes in the winter and summer," and was content to eat a simple dish of lentils on his wedding day, "even though his barns were filled with corn, straw and hay."[13] Moreover, Bossányi no longer sought recognition simply by performing a single, spectacular act of valor in the manner of the knight-hero of the Middle Ages. Instead, he endeavored to prove himself by the meticulous performance of daily, often pedestrian, duties in the service of God and community. In his honorific position as grandjuror (*táblabíró*), he patiently listened to all applicants irrespective of their status, never ceased to show concern for the welfare of his clients, and when the boundaries of the county were surveyed, acted as a commissioner without accepting any fees.[14]

These anecdotal characterizations of Hungarian Protestants seem to be borne out by a more comprehensive view of the social scene. While reliable statistical information and aggregate data are unavailable from the seventeenth and eighteenth centuries, information dating from the early nineteenth century shows that Protestants as a group were more literate and educated than members of the Catholic and Greek Orthodox denominations.[15] Indeed, it was men trained at the Calvinist colleges of Debrecen, Enyed, and Patak who laid the foundations of modern language, literature, and science in the country. The spheres of production, mining and the more sophisticated arts and crafts, and even the cultivation of vineyards were the near monopoly of Lutheran Germans, while Calvinists were represented among the yeomanry and the squirearchy (though not among the owners of the large estates) far above their proportion in the general population. In politics, likewise, the Protestant minority played a con-

---

[13] Ferenc Kazinczy, *Pályám emlékezete* [Recollections of my career] (Budapest: Franklin, 1900), pp. 4-5.

[14] Ibid.

[15] In the first half of the nineteenth century the 5,236,000 Catholics of the larger Hungarian Kingdom possessed 66 "institutions of higher learning," i.e., Latin schools, three colleges, and one university. At the same time, 992,000 Lutherans had 21 Latin schools and one college, the 1,842,000 Calvinists 21 Latin schools and five colleges, the 1,705,000 Greek Orthodox altogether two institutions of higher learning. Literacy rates were estimated as 9.38 percent among the Lutherans, 7.4 percent among the Calvinists, 6.89 percent among Catholics, and 2.08 percent among the Greek Orthodox. See Elek Fényes, *Magyarország statistikája* [The statistics of Hungary] (Pest: Trattner, 1842), III, 60-99.

spicuous role at the diets and local assemblies, standing in the fore-
front of opposition against imperial overbearance and dynastic absolutism. They were, in the words of Oscar Jászi, the "real bearers of
constitutional independence in noble society."[16] The British historian
Harold W. V. Temperley agrees, and adds his opinion that "in no
land [had] Calvinism exercised a more important [political] effect than
in Hungary, and without it there can be no doubt that its constitution
would have perished" in the turbulent seventeenth and eighteenth
centuries.[17]

FEUDAL SOCIETY AND INSTITUTIONS

The Evolution of Privilege

Under the influence of these religious and cultural norms the structure and institutions of feudal society developed along lines familiar
from the historical experience of the Occident, and like the West
passed through two distinct stages. In the first stage the old communal
and tribal organization gave way to a patrimonial order in which land
was declared to be royal property and was administered by familial
retainers (*servientes regis*) from the clan of Árpád, or else reassigned
as non-hereditary fiefs to royal vassals whose obligations were specified by contract and confirmed by the sacred oath of fealty. In the
second period, roughly between the thirteenth and fifteenth centuries,
the fiefs became de facto hereditary,[18] and while the fiction of royal
ownership was retained (to bedevil credit relations in a later age),[19]
the highly personalized relationship between king and vassal gave way
to a more neutral, legal relationship between the Crown and a number
of corporate entities, or estates, whose rights and obligations were
regulated by successive royal charters and acts of parliament.

The most important of these estates, the nobility, came into being
when the familial retainers of the king, after a brief rebellion, were

---

[16] Jászi, *Dissolution*, p. 303.

[17] Harold W. V. Temperley, "Introductory Essay" to Henry Marczali, *Hungary in the
Eighteenth Century* (Cambridge: The University Press, 1910), p. xliii.

[18] Hereditary fiefs were established in 1351 when the Act of Aviticity (*ősiség*) of that
year abolished the royal right of repossession except for cases where a line became
extinct, or where the proprietor had been convicted for *lèse majesté*.

[19] Since landed property could not be sold under the law it could not be mortgaged
either. Hence all transactions involving land were technically long-term leases, which
led to innumerable and interminable lawsuits. This, in turn, was at least one of the
reasons why "the chief occupation of the gentry became legal science." See Jászi, *Dissolution*, p. 7.

16

granted the same rights and immunities as were already enjoyed by his tenants-in-chief and principal vassals. As formulated by the *Aurea Bulla* of 1222, and expanded by successive constitutional documents culminating in the Tripartite Code of 1514, these included, apart from the right to hereditary fiefs, seigneurial rights over serfs and an exemption from all direct taxation by either royal or ecclesiastic authorities. In criminal law, noblemen were immune from arrest (except when caught *in flagranti delicto* committing a capital crime) until convicted by due process that was to exclude all forms of torture or corporal punishment. Under civil law, their status was to be superior to that of commoners, in that the latter were not allowed to bring suits against noblemen in their own name, but were to be represented by their town, landlord, or county. In exchange for these impressive privileges, nobles were obliged to render military service upon the call of the king, and to contribute to the costs of warfare as long as the hostilities took place within the boundaries of the country.

While the Tripartite Code and other public documents going back to the *Aurea Bulla* emphasized the unity and indivisibility of the nobility, differences in wealth, power, and, less obviously, in legal prerogatives, continued to divide the privileged estate into two separate classes, the magnates, or aristocracy, and the common nobility. The former included a few score of grandees, the descendants of the erstwhile tenants-in-chief and principal vassals of the kings, who after the sixteenth century became recipients of the hereditary titles of baron, count, and duke. The families so graced owned vast estates which, in the Middle Ages, sprawled over hundreds of thousands of acres of arable land and encompassed hundreds of serf villages. In the seventeenth and eighteenth centuries some attempt was made to break up excessive concentrations of wealth and power. But even so, in 1778, the 108 aristocratic clans native to Hungary and Croatia-Slavonia[20] still exercised seigneurial rights over forty percent of all the enfiefed parishes of the country (Table 3), and the single largest fief, that of the ducal branch of the Esterházy family, still encompassed some 800 parishes with 800,000 acres of land attached to them. (The sixty-two aristocratic families of Transylvania were less prosperous. But even here, members of such illustrious clans as the Bethlen, Bánffy, and Teleki owned substantial estates and were, by virtue of their wealth, prestige, and easy access to public office, a ruling class in name as well as in fact.)[21]

[20] Marczali, *Hungary in the Eighteenth Century*, p. 123, n. 1.

[21] Bálint Hóman and Gyula Szekfű, *Magyar történet* [Hungarian history] (Budapest: Egyetemi Nyomda, 1936), v, 113.

Historical Background

TABLE 3
DISTRIBUTION OF FIEFS IN 27 COUNTIES,
1784-1787

Category of Owner	No. of Fiefs	% of Total
Total	6,581	100.00
Magnates	2,651	40.28
Church	817	12.41
Treasury (Crown)	423	6.42
Common Nobility		
Individual Holdings	1,497	22.77
Communal Holdings	1,140	17.32
Other[a]	53	.80

SOURCE: R. Danyl and Z. Dávid, eds., *Az első magyarországi népszámlálás, 1784-1787*.
[a] Parishes held in fief by royal free cities, foundations, and other legal entities endowed with noble rights.

In contrast to this small and exclusive group, the original members of the common nobility were descendants of onetime royal servitors whose number, quite substantial to begin with, continued to swell over the centuries, particularly during the Turkish wars when both Hungarian kings and the princes of Transylvania were eager to grant exemptions and immunities, sometimes to the inhabitants of entire villages, in order to secure a steady flow of fighting men into their armies. As a result of these practices, and some laxness in certifying titles after the Turkish wars, the number of common nobles reached 389,146 in 1787, and was estimated at 617,521 in 1839, representing some five percent of the population of the country.[22] About one-fifth of these[23] were a *possessionati* nobility whose members held in fief another forty percent of the peasant villages of the country, twenty-three percent as individual holdings, seventeen percent as communal holdings (*compossessoriats*) in which a group of noblemen exercised seigneurial rights collectively over a few households of serfs. It was this essentially middle-class element which in the nineteenth century began to refer to itself as the gentry, using the very English term, or else its Hungarianized form, the *dzsentri*. The remaining four-fifths of the common nobles were a "petty" (or peasant) element whose

[22] For 1787, see R. Danyl and Z. Dávid, eds., *Az első magyarországi népszámlálás, 1784-1787* [The first Hungarian official census, 1784-1787] (Budapest: Állami Nyomda, 1960), pp. 50-51; for 1839, Fényes, *Statistika*, I, 120.

[23] In 1809 the census of the nobility listed 3,112 *bene possessionati* noblemen whose income exceeded 3,000 Fls. per annum, together with 27,166 *possessionati* nobles whose income was between 500 and 3,000 Fls. See István Kiss, *Az utolsó nemesi felkelés* [The last feudal levy] (Budapest, 1909), p. 35.

18

members had no economic ties to feudalism in that they exercised no seigneurial rights; they sustained themselves as small freeholders, tenants, and employees of other nobles, or as petty public servants—constables, jailkeepers, custodians of public buildings—whose economic and cultural standards were not noticeably different from those of the serf peasantry. For this reason, once military exigencies diminished, several attempts were made to curtail their legal prerogatives: Public Law vi/1723 provided that the tenants of other nobles be subject to the payment of certain taxes, while Public Law xx of the same year stipulated that only noblemen of good standing should be eligible for elective public office. But such legislation notwithstanding, the petty nobility survived as an identifiable juridical entity whose members would serve as a reservoir from which the upper strata of society could replenish their ranks.

By historical accident, these differences in wealth, status, and privilege between the two major strata of the nobility were further accentuated by differences of religion and nationality. On the one hand, the aristocracy (with the exception of the Transylvanians) was throughout its history a polyglot entity[24] which maintained a record of stout adherence to the religious tenets of Catholicism. On the other hand, the common nobility never lost its original Magyar character,[25] and in time became closely associated with the Calvinist branch of Protestantism. From these ethno-religious differences, then, emerged different systems of political outlook and identity: while the aristocracy viewed itself as the paladin of Christian universalism in the service of a European dynasty, the common nobility liked to portray itself as the patriotic defender of parochial institutions and constitutional liberties. In possession of vast holdings, the aristocracy was an embodiment of hereditary privilege, a class whose status was secure and could be transferred from generation to generation. Conversely, the offspring of the economically marginal gentry could often survive as gentlemen only by engaging in economic activity, public service, or the practice of law. This made them the principal representatives of meritocratic principles in the midst of noble society.

As in all countries of Catholic Europe, the status and privileges of the nobility were fully shared by the clergy of the established church,

[24] According to one source only 34.3 percent of the aristocratic families were of Magyar ethnic origin. Ernő Lakatos, *A magyar politikai vezetőréteg* [The Hungarian political elite] (Budapest: Élet Nyomda, 1942), p. 19.

[25] According to Fényes (*Statistika*, i, 118), of the 544,472 noblemen and noblewomen of Hungary proper 464,806, or 85.37 percent, were Magyar in language and custom in the year 1839.

while the Church itself enjoyed powers of taxation and had jurisdiction over a vast array of religious and temporal matters, including the administration of family law and the adjudication of disputes between the established church and the "non-established" Protestant and Orthodox churches. In the Middle Ages, these legal prerogatives were bolstered by substantial landholdings, the virtual monopoly of the clergy over education, and its vigorous participation in defense and administration of the country which, despite the apostolic rights of the kings, made the Church a virtual state within the secular state.

In the sixteenth century, however, the political position of the Church was shaken by a number of concurrent developments. In the territories administered by the Turks the clergy was not only expropriated, but often expelled. In Transylvania, the Church was disestablished, and the Calvinist princes often looked askance at the activities of Catholic priests, suspecting them of pro-Habsburg sympathies. Throughout the kingdom, Protestantism shattered the cultural monopoly of the clergy. Some of this damage was repaired upon the reunification of the country under the Catholic dynasty by restoring ecclesiastic properties and prerogatives. But even so, the Church possessed only about twelve percent of all feudal fiefs, and only about one-half of all schools in the country, while its flock had been reduced to less than one-half of the population. These circumstances made the Church insecure and dependent on the dynastic state whose support the Church reciprocated by acting as the chief ideological defender of centralization and royal authoritarianism.

Next to nobility and clergy, the third estate of feudal society consisted of 498,000 townspeople (1787), inhabiting 70-odd privileged settlements across the kingdom.[26] Originally, the inhabitants of these cities were regarded as royal serfs, and their settlements as royal boroughs, exempted from the jurisdiction of the nobility in exchange for the performance of specific economic services to the Crown. In later centuries, royal insistence on servitude and dependence were gradually modified. The cities were granted a variety of new rights, among them the right of parliamentary representation and self-government, and to symbolize the change, the adjective "free" was added to the original designation of "royal borough."

As we have already noted, in both Hungary and Transylvania, the overwhelming majority of townspeople were Germans who came at

---

[26] Danyl and Dávid, *Az első magyarországi népszámlálás*, pp. 50-51; the settlements included forty-nine Hungarian "royal free cities" represented in parliament, sixteen cities of the Szepes region, and seven Saxon cities in Transylvania.

the call of the Hungarian kings from Lower Saxony in the thirteenth century. Since most of the cities banned Magyars, Rumanians, and Slovaks from residency by explicit provisions of their charters, their ethnic character had been well preserved through subsequent centuries. In Transylvania, as late as 1848, the words "Saxon" and urban resident were virtually synonymous. In Hungary proper, there were a few urban centers inhabited by Magyars, among them the Calvinist cities of Debrecen, Kecskemét, and Komárom, and a few cities, like Pécs, with mixed populations. But the most important urban centers, among them Buda, the residence of the kings, and Pozsony (Pressburg), the seat of the Hungarian Diet after 1526, were solid bastions of a bourgeoisie whose cultural roots reached outside the boundaries of the country.

In the hierarchy of pre-modern society the most exalted positions were occupied by the nobility and the clergy, followed by the burghers, whose cities and corporations were regarded as legal entities endowed with noble privilege. Below the burghers, but above the grey mass of the "common folk" (*misera plebs*), there was yet another category of people, neither noble nor commoner, whom many constitutional scholars described as "semi-privileged,"[27] for they were legal owners of freeholds and were exempted from the tutelage of feudal overlords without enjoying the personal freedoms and privileges of the nobility.

In the eighteenth and nineteenth centuries this semi-privileged stratum comprised no less than 13.5 percent of the general population, most of them livng in "free districts" established by the Crown at different times in history.[28] The first of these was as old as the Hungarian state itself and was occupied by the Transylvanian Szeklers, the descendants of a Magyar tribe who were never subjected to the authority of patrimonial officials, but were granted titles of ownership to their lands in exchange for defending the eastern marches of the realm. The second of these districts was founded in the thirteenth century when the Jazyg and Cuman (Jász-Kun) tribes were settled on the plains and exempted from servitude so that they could render military service. Four centuries later, Prince Bocskai of Transylvania created a third district when he settled the Hajdús—a group of freebooters of martial inclinations—on the wastelands surrounding the city of Debrecen in the hope of putting an end to their plundering

---

[27] In Fényes' words "neither peasants nor nobles but between the two." See *Statistika*, I, 119.

[28] 1.6 million including the inhabitants of the Military Frontier Districts. Ibid.

and of winning their support for his anti-imperial campaigns. The Habsburgs on the whole accepted these arrangements, and in the eighteenth century extended them to parts of reconquered Croatia and the Bánát by creating a number of Military Frontier Districts under the jurisdiction of the Austrian Ministry of War. Like the Szeklers, Cumans, and Hajdús before them, the Serbian, Croat, and Rumanian inhabitants of these districts were exempted from feudal obligations and granted communal titles to their lands, in return for their services as permanent frontier guards in the defense of the Empire.

The economic position of this free peasantry was not markedly different from that of the petty nobility, but their legal and social status was more ambivalent. For while the nobility was exempted from taxation in exchange for military service, and the burghers were exempted from service in exchange for taxation, the inhabitants of the free districts had to carry both burdens. This was an obvious instance of inequity and a perennial source of grievance which made the free districts hotbeds of rebellion against the feudal order. The Jazyg-Cuman district was the locus of the great peasant uprising of 1514 under the leadership of the Szekler officer George Dózsa. The Szekler lands themselves rebelled repeatedly against both princely and royal authority, while the *jacqueries* of Horia, Cloşca, and Pero Segedinać in the eighteenth century all originated in the Military Frontier Districts. The latter were also the centers of the anti-feudal and anti-Hungarian movements of 1848-1849, while the Jazyg, Hajdú, and Szekler districts provided the mainstay for Kossuth's anti-Austrian campaign. Indeed, over the centuries this spirit of rebelliousness hardened into a political culture that not only was anti-authoritarian but also denied the legitimacy of any form of governmental authority. It therefore provided a fertile ground for all opposition parties in the age of modern parliamentarism.

Political Institutions and Authority

The history of the medieval state and its constitution was, in the first place, the history of relationships between kings and privileged estates. As these relationships changed over time, so did constitutional theory and the various institutions designed to formulate and enforce public policy.

In the first centuries of the kingdom these relationships were, at least in principle, strictly hierarchical. The monarchy of the Árpáds was hereditary and legitimated by the principle of divine right which was reinforced by the periodic canonization of deceased rulers and members of their family. The crown, the symbol of royal authority, was regarded as the personal property of the kings. The state was a mere extension of the royal household, and its institutions, among them the annual gathering of freemen at the royal court, were mere appendages of the monarchy performing judicial and administrative, rather than legislative, functions.

Between the thirteenth and fifteenth centuries, however, the balance of power between king and estates gradually shifted toward the latter, and as it did, relationships within the body politic became not only more predictable, but also more infused with the principles of reciprocity and equality. In 1301 the monarchy became elective.[29] The proprietorship of the crown passed from king to the nation, and the theory of divine right was supplemented by a new doctrine that vested legislative powers in a public corporation in which the king and estates were equal partners, neither enjoying historical or legal precedence over the other. For while the "king created the estates" (by issuing letters of patent), "the estates created the king" (by the act of election or confirmation). In practice this meant that henceforth legislative business would be conducted by the parliament within which the estates exercised the power of the purse, while the king retained a right of unconditional veto over all the acts of the estates.

In Hungary proper, the powers of parliament were first exercised by genuine national assemblies to which all freemen were invited to participate in the deliberations and voting. These assemblies were usually convened at the camp of Rákos, near the royal residence of Buda (and just outside the fishing village of Pest), and were boisterous affairs. Thousands of armed men milled about, although from earliest times on the lesser nobles and freemen were separated from the magnates who deliberated and then submitted their decisions for the approval of the multitude. In 1608 this division became formalized when the landmark Parliament Act of that year transformed the National Assembly into a bicameral Diet consisting of a Magnates' Table and a Lower Table (officially the Table of the Estates and Corporations). The membership of the former included the great temporal and spiritual lords of the realm, while the latter consisted of an assortment of "delegates" (ablegati): two from the fifty-odd counties, a number of abbots and canons representing the lower orders of the clergy, a variable number of deputies from the royal free cities,[30] and

---

[29] The monarchy was elective de jure and de facto between 1301 and 1526. It remained de jure elective until 1687 at which time parliament granted the male issue of the House of Habsburg hereditary rights of succession. In 1722-1723 the same rights were extended to the female successors of Charles III.

[30] Irrespective of voting rights, many of the cities sent large delegations. Thus the

a few representatives of the free districts. Nominally, the king continued to be present at the deliberations. In reality, he was represented by the Palatine (Viceroy) presiding over the sessions of the Upper Table. Legislation involved innumerable exchanges of messages between the Diet and the Royal Chancellery.

The system of public administration likewise evolved gradually from the patrimonial institutions of the early monarchy. Under the first kings royal landholdings and the servitors residing on them were organized into counties (*megyék*) under the supervision of appointed officials: the lord lieutenant (*főispán*), his deputy (*alispán*), the high sheriff (*főszolgabíró*, or, literally, the chief judge of the servitors), and others whose titles are clearly indicative of the patrimonial and familial nature of the institution. At a later date, however, the royal servitors became part of the hereditary nobility, and the county evolved into an institution of self-government. The lord lieutenants continued to act as royal representatives and as nominal heads of the administration. But real administrative powers were transferred to the deputy lord lieutenant and the other officers of the county who, after 1504, were elected by an assembly, or *congregatio*, composed of all noblemen residing in the particular county. Meanwhile, as a curious, and unwittingly incongruous, reminder of the patrimonial past, the elected officials remained responsible not only for the performance of local administrative and judicial functions, but also for collecting royal revenues and for enforcing royal decrees. It was by virtue of this anomaly that, from the sixteenth century onward, the county became the single most important bastion of "ancient liberties" against the newly ascendant foreign monarchy. For while parliament could be manipulated, coerced, or simply bypassed by the kings, the local assemblies and their officers were in the position to seek redress by means of "passive resistance," i.e., by refusing to collect taxes or deliver their quota of conscripts to the royal authorities.

It was also in this period, roughly between the fourteenth and sixteenth centuries, that the cities emancipated themselves from royal tutelage and developed institutions of municipal self-government. In many ways, these institutions were similar to those of the counties. The conduct of local affairs was vested in a council elected by the ten or twelve percent of the residents who enjoyed "full citizen's rights."[31] In contrast to the county, however, the urban councils in most cases

---

forty-nine royal free cities of Hungary were represented by eighty delegates in 1808, seventy-seven in 1825, and seventy-five in 1832. See Fényes, *Statistika*, ii, 71.

[31] Hóman and Szekfű, *Magyar történet*, v, 242.

also included a *tribunus plebis*, elected by and from among the privileged, but charged with representing the interests of the non-voters. Yet another difference between self-government in town and country was that in the former the nominal head of the administration was not a lord lieutenant, but a mayor or magistrate who won his office by election. Under this arrangement the towns were in an even stronger position to outwit the sovereign than the counties. Yet they never rivalled the counties in the art of resisting arbitrary measures, for, as the historian Marczali points out, "it is not the institution but the spirit which it manifests that is most important, and, tried by such test, the towns must be deemed to have failed."[32]

Like the elective branch of government, the executive grew out of the patrimonial institutions of the first centuries of the kingdom. The banus of Croatia, the voivod of Transylvania, the palatine of Hungary and other dignitaries were originally familial retainers who became salaried officials charged with the performance of specific administrative functions only under the Habsburgs at the turn of the seventeenth century. It was at the same time that the executive branch was reorganized to reflect the realities of the personal union between Hungary and the "hereditary" provinces of the Habsburg realm. In the process of this reorganization, the Royal Chancellery was moved to Vienna to serve as a liaison between the parliaments and the Crown, while back in Hungary the business of the Crown was entrusted to a Council of the Lieutenancy, a kind of pre-modern ministry divided into Departments of the Interior, Finance, and Internal Security, or Justice. The departments were in charge of the supervision of the mines, the administration of royal courts, the postal service, customs, and the royal monopoly of the mining and sale of salt. However, in the shadow of a powerful parliament and county system, the powers of this bureaucracy remained as limited as the staff at the disposal of individual departments. As late as 1840 the Royal Chancellery had only 208 employees (including clerical personnel and menial workers), while the Council of the Lieutenancy had a staff of 267 supervising the work of 401 customs officers, 412 salt inspectors, 336 treasury agents, and 552 inspectors of the mines.[33]

In Transylvania and Croatia, the two provinces associated with the Hungarian kingdom, public institutions passed through the same stages of development and reflected the same constitutional principles, though in form they deviated somewhat from the Hungarian model. In both provinces the Hungarian county had its counterparts,

[32] Marczali, *Hungary*, p. 151.   [33] Fényes, *Statistika*, I, 120.

but in Transylvania these were supplemented by the self-governing "seats" (*sedes, székek,* or *Stühle*) of the Szekler and Saxon population whose popular assemblies functioned under the supervision of elected captains. In both provinces most legislation was handled by unicameral local assemblies, the Sabor in Croatia and the Diet in Transylvania. In Croatia the Sabor included the same elements as the Hungarian Diet: local magnates, clergymen, elected representatives of the nobility, and a few royal officials. In Transylvania the Diet consisted of the local magnates and the elected representatives of three "nations," the Magyar, Szekler, and Saxon. This terminology is deceptive, however, for the nations in effect refer to three feudal estates, Magyar standing for the nobility, Szekler for the free peasantry, and Saxon for the bourgeoisie. At different times these local legislatures maintained different institutional ties with the Hungarian Diet. From its establishment in 1437 until the year 1526 the Transylvanian Diet sent eight representatives (4 Magyars, 2 Saxons, and 2 Szeklers) to the Hungarian parliament. Thereafter the practice was discontinued although the Catholic bishop of the Transylvanian diocese and a number of magnates had seats in both parliamentary bodies by virtue of their landholdings in both parts of the kingdom.[34] In contrast, the Croatian Sabor had no liaison with the Hungarian Diet until 1642 at which time all Croatian magnates were invited to attend the deliberations of the Upper Table, while the Croatian counties began to send deputies to the Lower Table, thereby gradually diminishing the jurisdiction and overall importance of the provincial assembly.

Serfdom and Economic Feudalism

Under the feudal constitution just outlined, one of every five inhabitants of the country were privileged freemen with some access to the country's political institutions and with some share in the "liberties" as they evolved over the centuries. By the standards of the period this figure was unusually high, and, as Hungarian writers of a later age never tired of reiterating, it put Hungary well ahead of most countries of the continent. Nevertheless, this system still left four out of five subjects of the Hungarian king outside the feudal nation. While the constitution did not altogether ignore this multitude, it placed them under the tutelage of landlords in a system of land tenure that was and remained the chief economic pillar of the feudal order.

As all other institutions of feudal society, the system of land tenure

[34] Fényes, *Statistika,* II, 71.

passed through several developmental stages over the centuries. In its first, more rudimentary, stage large tracts of land were assigned to royal retainers who, in exchange for their services to the Crown, were allowed to expropriate part of the peasant's produce in the form of a tithe or other payments in kind. At a later date, the system became progressively more complex in that the fiefs became divided among the *demesne* (the lord's freehold, called in Hungary the *allod*), the commons, meaning the forests and pastures available for use by both lord and peasant, and the parcels, or sessions (*telek*), of the village community or the individual farmers. In this arrangement, the lord retained title to the entire estate, while the peasant became a serf tenant (*jobbágy*), responsible not only for the tithe and a whole array of ecclesiastic and royal taxes, but also for rendering the *corvée* (known in Hungary as the *robot*) or labor needed for the cultivation of the lord's manor.

Within this institutional arrangement the lot of the peasantry varied according to economic exigencies and the changing balance of power between landowners and the monarchy. In the fourteenth and late fifteenth centuries the constellation of these variables generally favored the peasant. Thus, while he continued to be excluded from the *pays légal*, his standing in society underwent slow but steady improvement. As part of this improvement, there was an increasing tendency to depersonalize the relationship between lord and peasant and to make it into a purely contractual association in which reciprocal obligations were summarized in carefully drafted copyhold agreements (known as *urbaria* from the Magyar word for the lord's rent). As a corollary, the law granted the peasant hereditary and inalienable rights of usufruct to his parcel, without infringing on his freedom of movement, provided that he fulfilled his contractual obligations. Finally, there was in the fifteenth century a growing trend toward village self-government centering around the office of the village judge (*judex villicus*) with jurisdiction over a wide range of civil and criminal matters. These trends culminated under the reign of Corvinus (1458-1490) whose government methodically protected the peasantry from lordly excess in an attempt to expand the tax base and to increase the revenues of the royal treasury.[35] These policies created an emotional bond between monarchy and peasantry and, despite the heavy taxes levied by his treasury, Corvinus would enter popular lore as the most just of Hungary's rulers.

---

[35] István Szabó, *Tanulmányok a magyar parasztság történetéből* [Studies from the history of the Hungarian peasantry] (Budapest: Athenaeum, 1948), pp. 12-14.

Historical Background

In the feudal reaction that took place after Corvinus' death there was a sweeping attempt made to reverse these trends and to increase the amount of *corvée* and the size of the lands belonging to the *allod*. Against these attempts the peasantry revolted in 1514, ravaging hundreds of manor houses across the Hungarian Plainland. The rebellion was repressed with great cruelty and the National Assembly that convened immediately after the uprising reduced the peasantry to "eternal bondage" declaring with engaging frankness that the lives of most rebels were spared only because "without them the estate of the lords [was] of not much value either."[36] Subsequently, in 1547, restrictions on the freedom of movement were abolished. But the prescribed amount of labor services continued to increase for the next century, and the autonomy of the peasant village was effectively subverted by extending the authority of the manor courts, or lord's benches (*úriszék*), over the village and by degrading the office of the village judge. Henceforth, the *judex villicus* was held responsible if the community defaulted on the tithe or labor services, so that in most instances reluctant candidates had to be pressed into service under the threat of severe penalties.[37] At the same time, the use of corporal punishment became widespread for default in dues and services. Its harshness was underscored by the haughty and contemptuous attitude of the privileged classes, who proceeded to subvert the social morale, self-esteem, and identity of the peasantry. It was in this period that the very word "peasant" (*paraszt*, derived from the Slavic *prost*) came to be a term of disparagement, conveying a sense of callous simplicity that made the word nearly unfit for use in polite society.

The peasant's condition, so debased in the sixteenth and seventeenth centuries, improved again in the eighteenth. This was partly because the massive wartime losses of life made the working serf a precious commodity, and partly because in the interim the monarchy reverted to its dual role of both taxing the peasantry and protecting it from the excesses of landlords. With these objectives in mind, the governments of Maria Theresa (1740-1780) and Joseph II (1780-1790) issued a number of patents and edicts designed to regulate relations between lord and peasant. The most important of these, the Urbarial Edict of 1767, restored the sixteenth-century quota of labor services: one day per week with, or two days without, a team of oxen for the tenant of a statutory parcel fixed between sixteen and forty-eight acres depending on the quality of land. The edict also attempted

---

[36] For the legislation of the National Assembly of 1514, ibid., pp. 67-71.

[37] For the history of the decline of village self-government, ibid., pp. 265-310.

to curtail the arbitrariness of the manor courts by banning landowners from juries hearing the cases of their own serfs, and by making appeal to royal courts mandatory in all capital cases. There is no doubt that landowners evaded some of these provisions, and that the entire system tolerated, if not encouraged, a measure of "patriarchal indulgence."[38] But it is also true that in the monarchy the peasant found a powerful protector, however distant. For this reason, the literary works of the time show not only evidence of noble haughtiness and depredations, but also of peasant audacity that the modern mind does not readily associate with the institution of feudal land tenure. In fiction, Michael Fazekas' Matt the Gooseherd "thrice walloped" his own lord in revenge for indignities suffered.[39] Closer to reality, George Rettegi's memoirs make casual references to landowners killed by their serfs, and speak of others involved in interminable litigation with villeins over the refusal of services. The author himself complains about having been cursed in the vilest possible language when insisting that his peasants fulfill their labor obligations.[40] In short, due to royal intervention, the particular constellation of economic forces, and the well-entrenched tradition of legalism, the Hungarian peasantry escaped the worst forms of social degradation that the agrarian classes of Russia, Rumania, or of the German lands east of the Elbe were subjected to after the sixteenth century. Nothing testifies more eloquently to the validity of this observation than the massive influx from the east and west of peasant colonists into the country.

The same economic and political forces that blunted the edge of the feudal reaction after Corvinus' death also slowed down the tendency toward expanding the *demesne*, and by the end of the eighteenth century stabilized the relationship between the lands of the manor and of the villein at fifty-eight to twenty-seven percent in Hungary, and at sixty to fifteen percent in Transylvania (leaving the remainder to pastures and forests used in common by lord and peasant).[41] But if economic and political circumstance checked the tendency toward excessive allodization, they did not stem the spread of a new type of

---

[38] Marczali, *Hungary*, p. 145.

[39] *Ludas Matyi. Egy eredeti magyar néprege* [Matt the Gooseherd. An original Hungarian folktale], written by Fazekas in 1804, and published in Nagyvárad anonymously in 1815.

[40] Rettegi, *Emlékezetre méltó dolgok*, pp. 38, 297, 305-307.

[41] See Pál Z. Pach, *Magyar gazdaságtörténet* [Economic history of Hungary] (Budapest: Tankönyvkiadó, 1963), i, 311, ii, 9; also Győző Ember, "A magyar parasztmozgalmak 1848-ban" [Hungarian peasant movements in 1848], in Aladár Mód, ed., *Forradalom és szabadságharc 1848-49-ben* [Revolution and war of independence in 1848-1849] (Budapest: Szikra, 1948), p. 144.

Historical Background

villeinage: *métayage*, cottage tenancy or, in Hungarian, *zsellérség*. This is to say that while the *demesne* had not conspicuously increased in size from the sixteenth century onward, Hungarian landowners made it their habit to settle peasants on the *allod* proper, rather than carving out parcels from their own estates under the legal statutes. This tendency continued throughout the eighteenth century, so much so that by 1787 the majority of peasants (952,482 families or 51.9 percent of the peasant households) were cottagers as opposed to 635,568 families of serf-tenants (34.1 percent of peasant households).[42] Under the Urbarial Edict the former enjoyed the same legal protection as the latter, and were subject to the same services as were the serf-tenants. However, their tenancy was non-hereditary, and hence they were subject to eviction on the whims of their masters. Having no legal title or claim to the lands they cultivated, these peasant families would acquire no proprietary rights under the Act of Emancipation of 1848 and, together with the remaining fourteen percent of the peasant population (who appear in the official census as "day laborers and farm servants"), would form the bulk of the agrarian proletariat of the nineteenth and twentieth centuries.

MATERIAL CONDITIONS

While from a cultural, religious, and institutional point of view medieval Hungary was an integral part of the occidental family of nations, in terms of material conditions, the sophistication and the productivity of the economy, it lagged behind the Atlantic and Mediterranean countries of the Continent. The origins of this lag were historical and go back to the late start of agricultural, commercial, and industrial pursuits in a society that continued to be ravaged by nomadic incursions for more than two centuries after the foundation of the state. As a result, in the twelfth century when Paris, London, and Bologna were already well-established trading and cultural centers, Hungary had as yet to possess a single settlement deserving the designation of a city. In this early period, even the royal residence was moved from place to place, so that the retainers of the king could consume the meager surplus of particular regions.

It was only after the last Tartar invasion in the second half of the thirteenth century that the Hungarian economy began to develop along European lines. This advance was due to the influx of skilled artisans, the discovery and export of precious metals,[43] and the stra-

---

[42] Danyl and Dávid, *Az első magyarországi népszámlálás*, pp. 50-51.

[43] In the fourteenth and fifteenth centuries the Carpathians produced one-quarter

tegic position of the country between the two great trading centers of the contemporary world, the Hansa and the Levant. For the next two or three centuries, the methods of farming were improved by switching from the old two-track, to the more up-to-date three-track, system; handicrafts and trade flourished in the urban centers populated by Germans, and the country became an exporter of gold, silver, cattle, and grain to Austria, Bohemia, Poland, and Venice.

Economic boom and development continued throughout the sixteenth century despite the dislocations caused by the Turkish wars, for while certain parts of the country suffered serious material damage, others thrived on the steady demand for comestibles generated by the presence of large garrisons in the country. But as the Turkish wars came to an end this demand dropped suddenly. At the same time, trade and manufacturing began to suffer the consequences of the shift of global trade routes from the Mediterranean and the Hansa to the Atlantic countries. To be sure, this shift of trade affected the economies of all southeast European countries. But in Hungary, its consequences were aggravated by restrictive imperial tariff policies to protect Austro-Bohemian handicraft industries,[44] and by the gradual exhaustion of gold and silver mines whose output had permitted the country to maintain a positive balance of trade for centuries. By the early eighteenth century Hungary effectively dropped out of the international economy, and while the countries of western Europe became the beneficiaries of expanding international commerce and technical innovation, the economy of Hungary not only stagnated, but declined in terms of both productivity and sophistication.

Whatever its ultimate causes, the decline of the economy was amply evident, most dramatically perhaps in the predominance of agriculture and the relative weakness of all branches of secondary production. The urban sector, normally the locus of trade and crafts, was

---

of all the silver used for coinage and about one-half of all the gold in Europe. Budapester Handels- und Gewerbekammer, ed., *Beiträge zur Geschichte der Preise ungarischer Landesprodukte im 19. Jahrhundert* (Budapest: Pesti Könyvnyomda, 1873), p. iii.

[44] The Tariff Act of 1756 imposed a duty of ten percent on all finished goods moving from Hungary to Austria, as opposed to a two percent duty on goods passing in the opposite direction. Meanwhile a duty of 33.3 percent was imposed on all finished goods imported from outside the empire. The discriminatory character of these measures became even more obvious when the imperial edict of 1775 exempted Austrian merchants from Hungarian transit duties when transporting goods to Transylvania, while Hungarian merchandise was prohibitively taxed in transit through Austrian provinces. See Ferenc Eckhart, *A bécsi udvar gazdaságpolitikája Magyarországon, 1780-1815* [The economic policies of the Viennese court in Hungary, 1780-1815], 2d ed. (Budapest: Akadémia, 1958), pp. 6-14.

small and steadily declining. Whereas at the end of the Turkish wars the population of the royal free cities may have been as high as 15 percent of the country's total population, by 1787 it had declined to as little as 5.75 percent,[45] and a substantial part—perhaps as much as 60 percent[46]—of even this minuscule population had gradually reverted to agricultural pursuits, cultivating lands adjacent to the cities and under the jurisdiction of the municipal administrations. Thus the conscription of 1787 found only 32,288 licensed artisans in the cities, among them 17,074 guild masters, 14,612 journeymen, and 6,102 apprentices,[47] while eighteen years later the census of 1805 listed 88,000 full-time artisans and craftsmen for the entire country, then inhabited by approximately nine million people.[48] The livelihood of the few artisans was protected by rigid production quotas and draconic punishments. Contemporary documents, among them numerous petitions to the Royal Chancellery, bewail the "impoverishment of many industrious and once prosperous artisans and merchants."[49] That this was not sheer rhetoric is proven by the fact that in the last decades of the century the Treasury collected no more taxes per capita in the privileged cities than among the cottagers and serf-tenants of the country.[50] Not surprisingly, in a society where privilege and economic prowess were closely related, the political rights of this impoverished bourgeoisie rapidly diminished. Thus, while in the seventeenth century the cities voted as an estate, by the end of the eighteenth century their representation was reduced to a single vote, as opposed to the fifty-five votes of the noble counties at the Lower Table.

The backwardness of the economy is evident also from the methods of farming used, which in the words of one historian, "were truly biblical in their primitive character."[51] At a time when England, France, and the Low Countries had already passed through critical stages of their agricultural revolutions, in Hungary most of the estates reverted to the old, medieval two-track system, in which half of the acreage was left fallow every year. The use of manure and other fertilizers was limited, harrows practically unknown, and the metal plow was rare. In areas where fodder was especially short and draft animals precious, men frequently took the place of beasts of burden. With such methods and instruments of farming, the cultivator was

---

[45] Danyl and Dávid, *Az első magyarországi népszámlálás*, pp. 50-51.

[46] Hóman and Szekfű, *Magyar történet*, v, 242-244.

[47] Marczali, *Hungary*, p. 29.

[48] Fényes, *Statistika*, I, 115; Hóman and Szekfű, *Magyar történet* v, 242.

[49] Eckhart, *A bécsi udvar*, p. 8. [50] Marczali, *Hungary*, p. 166.

[51] Ibid., p. 55.

lucky if he could quadruple the seed sown. Yet part of even this meager crop was wasted due to the crudeness of the methods of threshing and storage. Apart from these methods, the rudimentary character of agriculture is evident from the nature of the crops. "In the eastern half of the country," writes Marczali, "the main product was maize, which required little investment of capital."[52] In the rest of the country rye and millet were the chief products. Until about 1780, the production of wheat was relatively uncommon, so that white bread was regarded as a delicacy to be consumed only on festive occasions.

Given the self-sufficiency of the cities and the shift of international trade routes, the commercial sector of the economy was in an even more perilous condition. Trade between town and country was negligible, and the country's few imports reached the consumer through itinerant vendors or at regional fairs. The circulation of coin was limited, so much so that in 1783 a royal commission reported that certain rural areas of the country had no effective money economy, monetary transactions having been replaced by barter. In the very same year, a dozen or so counties requested the stationing of troops in the villages as a form of taxation in lieu of cash payments which the county administrations could not hope to collect from the peasantry.[53] In the absence of trade, there was very little incentive to maintain a regular transportation network. Indeed, the local administrations were happy to see the demise of this network so as to avoid harassment and intrusions by the royal authorities. Consequently, by the middle of the eighteenth century roads were either nonexistent or quickly rendered impassable by precipitation. "Between Pozsony and Nagy-Szeben [in Transylvania]," wrote an exasperated foreign traveler, "the roads are for the most part as nature and carriage wheels have made them. Below Pest, as far as Szeged, the road is entirely unmade. A mile this side of Szeged, the high road is entirely torn up—this part should be avoided by everybody. From Szeged to the frontier of Transylvania, the road is everywhere unmade."[54]

Notwithstanding the backwardness of technology and economic organization, the fertility of the land and the favorable ratio of land to population provided adequate nutrition for most, at least until the 1780s when demographic changes began to strain the economy. But even before that date, the pattern of life was simple. Peasants lived in adobe huts or hovels in which the whole family huddled around

[52] Ibid., p. 54.   [53] Ibid., p. 288.
[54] Murray Keith, *Memoirs*, quoted in Marczali, *Hungary*, p. 88.

33

an open hearth, while windows were plastered shut for the winter months to conserve heat.

The squirearchy's style of life was not particularly extravagant either. "In the 1780's," writes Marczali, "few noblemen lived in houses not made out of wood," and "glass windows were rarities even in the towns."[55] Inside the houses, glassware, eating utensils, silverware, and elaborate furniture were largely unknown. Noblemen and noble-women dressed in homespun "traditional" garb, in most cases wearing the same item year in, year out, often for an entire lifetime. Better items of clothing, made out of imported Moravian cloth, were so precious that they were inherited by sons and daughters. When nothing else could be conserved, the metal and horn buttons were cut off and passed on from one generation to another. Only half a century later these conditions seemed as woefully inadequate as they now seem to the modern observer. But to most contemporaries in late eighteenth-century Hungary they seemed to be natural and God given, and hence easy to bear, especially in an era of relative peace following centuries of warfare on the very soil of the country.

[55] Ibid., p. 69.

II.

The Impulse to Reform (1825-1848)

ECONOMY AND SOCIETY IN A CHANGING WORLD

Economic Development and Social Decay

These material conditions, and the effective isolation of Hungary from the European market, began to change rapidly toward the end of the eighteenth century, under the impact of forces at work within the core area of the rising global economic system. Between 1750 and 1850, European industrialization and urbanization grossly outstripped the rate of development in agriculture. This created a steadily rising demand for comestibles, and, in the absence of technologies for the transportation of large amounts of grain from overseas, generated pressure for the development of potential food-producing markets on the periphery of the Continent.

In the case of Hungary, its inclusion in the continental market was accelerated by the policies of the Austrian government under the reigns of Maria Theresa and Joseph II, and during the tenure of office of the economy-minded Chancellor Kaunitz, who was determined to transform the eastern half of the Habsburg realm into a granary for the industrial areas of lower Austria, Bohemia, and Moravia. As part of his design, in 1777-1779 the roads and the waterways of the country were surveyed. In the next decade new roads were built, parts of the Danube and Tisza were made navigable, and a number of smaller rivers were turned into canals to link some of the fertile regions of the Plainland with the Danube and with the major population centers in the western half of the empire.

These measures had an immediate and lasting effect on the agrarian economy. Prices of raw products, long depressed by the excessive costs of transportation, now corrected themselves. They increased approximately threefold within a single decade (1790-1799),[1] and

---

[1] At the grain exchange of Pest, the price of wheat rose from an average of .50-.66 Fls. (30-40 *Kreutzer*) per Hungarian (Pressburg) bushel to 1.98 Fls. in 1800-1801. Prices in "conventional" silver Florins: 1 Hungarian bushel = 1.74 American; 1 silver Florin (containing 60 *Kreutzer* or *Krajcár*) = $.48. (See Jerome Blum, *Noble Landowners and*

35

then, stimulated further by wartime demand, doubled again between 1800 and 1809.[2] These impressive price increases turned Hungary into a major producer of grain and wool, two items that, after 1800, replaced livestock as the chief source of cash for the average farmer.[3] To increase production for export markets, both inside and outside the customs area of the larger Habsburg realm, landowners expanded their acreage under cultivation by draining swamps and clearing forests, while at the same time they introduced new methods of cultivation. Especially on larger, aristocratic estates, we now encounter the systematic use of fertilizers, crop rotation, metal plows, and threshing machines. Suddenly, the rationalization (*pallérozás*) of agriculture became a popular slogan. In this spirit, a number of great landowners began to sponsor educational institutions in order to raise a generation of enlightened farmers. The most important of these institutions were the Georgikon Academy founded by Count George Festetich in 1797 at the city of Keszthely, the Farmers' Training School on Count Nákó's estate at Szarvas on the Plainland, and a School of Forestry and Mining, established on the domain of Prince Albrecht of Sachse-Teschen at Magyaróvár.

In the wake of these developments, "for the first time in history, financial gain became the acknowledged aim of farming,"[4] and the landowners, as one of them confessed with a touch of embarrassment, "acquired a taste for making money,"[5] not only by cultivating land, but also by engaging in a wide range of entrepreneurial activities only faintly related to farming. Some of the most prestigious landowners of the country led the way, but they were happily imitated by the owners of smaller feudal estates. The list of names and the diversity of the pursuits is impressive. Count George Károlyi set up glass fac-

---

Agriculture in Austria, 1815-1848 [Baltimore: Johns Hopkins University Press, 1948], p. 247.)

[2] From 1.98 Fls. in 1800-1801 prices rose to a monthly average of 4.49 Fls. in 1805-1806, leveling off to an annual average of 3.55 per bushel between 1807 and 1814. Budapester Handels- und Gewerbekammer, ed., *Beiträge zur Geschichte der Preise ungarischer Landesprodukte im 19. Jahrhundert*, p. xlix.

[3] In 1783 Hungarian landowners earned 5,060,000 Fls. from the export of livestock, 2,180,000 from the export of wool, and 3,040,000 from the export of cereals. In 1834 Hungary exported livestock in the value of 5,468,000 Fls., grain for 6,541,000 Fls., and wool for 19,036,000 Fls. See Robert Townson, *Travels in Hungary* (London: Robinson, 1797), p. 196, and Elek Fényes, *Magyarország statistikája*, I, 268.

[4] B. G. Iványi, "From Feudalism to Capitalism: The Economic Background of Széchenyi's Reform in Hungary," *Journal of Central European Affairs*, 20 (1960), 276.

[5] The words of Francis Kazinczy, landowner, poet, and distinguished philologist. Quoted by B. G. Iványi, ibid.

tories in his villages, Count Festetich and Duke Grassalkovich founded distilleries. Count Samuel Teleki started to manufacture bricks, while Count Sándor established a profitable lumber business. Count Casimir Batthyány, the owner of one of the largest herds of sheep in the country, engaged in diverse transactions on the commodity market: in 1804, for instance, he bought large quantities of coffee, tea, and colonial spices, to sell them a few years later at substantial profits at a time when the continental blockade was most effective.[6] Again others, among them Counts Almássy, Nádasdy, and Nicholas Eszterházy, together with several ecclesiastical landowners in Transdanubia, accumulated sufficient savings to provide short-term seasonal loans to their peers.[7]

The Napoleonic wars were followed by a continent-wide price depression that brought to a temporary halt the upward economic trend. This crisis looms large in the economic histories of Hungary, many of which describe it as an unmitigated disaster responsible for most of the future troubles of the landowning class. Indeed, from 1814 to 1819, the price of wheat declined by as much as fifty-five percent, and the price of livestock by about twenty-five percent.[8] But the fact of the matter is that by 1820 the economy began to recover, and within a few years both production and exports exceeded the levels that had been attained during the Napoleonic wars. Meanwhile prices held their own, or, as in the case of wool, were more than offset by increasing production. Thus while in 1808, at the height of the wartime boom, the country produced 60 million (Hungarian) bushels of grain, by 1834 this production figure had increased to 89.1 million.[9] The number of sheep, some ten million in the first decade of the century, doubled within twenty years, while the export of wool increased from 101,535 quintals (1816) to 248,491 quintals in 1845.[10] The cash value of wool exports increased commensurably, from 12.5 million convertible silver Florins (1802), to 27.5 million.[11] The cash

[6] For these examples see László Ungár, "A magyar polgári osztály kialakulásáról" [Formation of the Hungarian bourgeois class], *Századok*, 76 (1942), 306-308. Also, György Spira, "Egy pillantás a Hitel írójának hitelviszonyaira" [A glimpse at the credit record of the author of "Hitel"], *Történelmi Szemle*, 6 (1963), 350.

[7] See Ungár, ibid. Also, István Barta, "A magyar polgári reformmozgalom kezdeti szakaszának problémái" [Problems of the initial phase of the Hungarian movement of bourgeois reform], *Történelmi Szemle*, 6 (1963), 315.

[8] Budapester Handels- und Gewerbekammer, *Beiträge*, p. xx.

[9] Martin Schwartner, *Statistik des Königreichs Ungern* (Ofen-Buda: Gedruckt mit königlichen Universitätsschriften, 1809), I, 218. Fényes, *Statistika*, I, 122.

[10] Fényes, *Statistika*, I, 172, Blum, *Noble Landowners*, p. 101.

[11] Fényes, *Statistika*, I, 172 and 253.

value of grain, victuals, and livestock passing from Hungary to the Austrian half of the empire increased from 16.2 million Florins (1830) to 32.2 million in 1845,[12] and the cash value of the entire volume of exports (to Austria as well as to countries inside and outside the Habsburg realm) rose from its 26.4 million low in 1817, to 46.0 million in 1826, and to 61.7 million in 1838.[13]

What is quite remarkable to the casual observer is that, despite such obvious signs of economic vigor and rising cash incomes, the first half of the nineteenth century is not remembered as a period of well-being, material comfort, and agrarian self-confidence, but rather as an age of increasing pauperization, diffidence, and social malaise. To be sure, the Napoleonic wars created a flurry of excitement about the "abundance of cash" (*pénzbőség*), and left for posterity a number of literary works celebrating plentiful harvests of "rich golden sheafs" by a nobility happy "in its glorious temple of liberty."[14] The poets of the decade, Berzsenyi, Baróti-Szabó, Virág, and even the restless Csokonai, the plebeian son of the Calvinist Debrecen, "offered the best fruits of their labors to the noble lords,"[15] depicting the gaiety and quiet dignity of their lives. But this mood was relatively short-lived, and, after the Napoleonic wars, changed to one of deep gloom that would not lift even after the end of the recession of 1816-1817. Indeed, when Michael Vörösmarty wrote his "Summons" (*Szózat*) in 1836, he conjured up nothing less than the vision of the "magnificent death" of an entire nation. His prediction was echoed by Francis Kölcsey who in his "Second Song of Zrinyi" (*Zrinyi második éneke*) already saw "another people on the banks of our four rivers." A third poet, Joseph Bajza, in a popular elegy called the "Sigh" (*Sóhajtás*) recited by generations of Hungarian school children, could find "no joy in the past, no hope in the future." On a less cosmic scale, Alexander Petőfi recorded the demise of the landed nobility by creating the figure of Pál Pató, the Hungarian counterpart of Goncharov's Oblomov, the epitome of anomie, a bankrupt landowner presiding grimly over a dilapidated manor house and unproductive acres, too apathetic

[12] Blum, *Noble Landowners*, p. 92.

[13] Fényes, *Statistika*, I, 269. Commensurately, the taxes collected by the Treasury increased from 3.9 million silver Fls. in 1765 to 11.5 million in the 1780s, to 19.6 million in 1834, and 23.1 million in 1840. In relative terms, Hungarian tax revenues increased from 9.8 percent of the total revenues of the empire to 14.5 percent in 1834. Eckhart, *A bécsi udvar*, p. 21. Fényes, *Statistika*, II, 1.

[14] Dániel Berzsenyi, "Osztályrészem" [My share in life] in *Összes művei* [Collected works] (Budapest: Szépirodalmi Könyvkiadó, 1956), 25.

[15] Hóman and Szekfű, *Magyar történet*, V, 155.

to supervise his serfs or to have the roof of his house repaired.[16] The general tenor of public discourse was no less pessimistic. "If we look around in the country," the deputy of Torontál, Hertelendy, lamented at the Diet of 1840, "we cannot escape the sad conclusion that, before long, most of our fellow noblemen will become paupers."[17] To which the venerable Count Széchenyi added that "the majority of lesser noblemen [would] sooner or later be reduced to begging, or else forced to engage in the most menial occupations."[18]

While the reasons for this mood were multifold, all of them can be reduced to a single, overarching explanation, a continent-wide change in consumption patterns, and a concomitant redefinition of human needs and wants, stimulated by the first, successful spurt of the industrial revolution in a handful of western countries. Across the Continent, these changes were quite dramatic. They included improvements in housing, the availability of new manufactured household articles, articles of personal hygiene, seasonal fashions for both sexes, and the daily consumption of coffee, sugar, and tea. Many of these articles, such as eating utensils, perfumes, and soap had, of course, long been available to a selected number of consumers, the aristocrats and the very rich. But now, in the wake of the economic revolutions, these became available to the middle class, and often to the "average" consumer, not as luxuries, but as daily necessities that were integral parts of a "decent" or "civilized" life.

As elsewhere in Europe, these changes in consumption patterns began in the 1780s,[19] and were accelerated by the development of trade with the countries of the Occident. Thus, if noblemen throughout most of the eighteenth century were content to live in log cabins without glass windows, to wear the same items of clothing year around, and to make do without most of the household necessities of the modern age, the provincial landowners of the Napoleonic period already wanted to live in brick or stone houses, to conform to seasonal

[16] The pessimistic mood of the period is noted in Hóman and Szekfű, ibid., pp. 293-295.

[17] Gyula Mályusz, "A reformkor nemzedéke" [The generation of the reform period], *Századok*, 57-58 (1923-1924), 42.

[18] Antal Zichy, ed., *Gróf Széchenyi István hirlapi cikkei* [The newspaper articles of Count Stephen Széchenyi] (Budapest: 1894), II, 37.

[19] These changes are dramatically illustrated by figures pertaining to the consumption of cotton in Britain (in million tons): 1750: 1 m.; 1780: 3 m.; 1790: 15 m.; 1800: 56 m.; 1830: 112 m. A similar trend is observable in the consumption of wool: 1780: .8 m.; 1790: 1.5 m.; 1800: 3.8 m.; 1810: 5.0 m.; 1830: 12.3 m. See B. R. Mitchell, *European Historical Statistics, 1750-1950* (New York: Columbia University Press, 1975), pp. 427-429, 443-444.

fashions, to consume sugar, and to have tableware, clocks, perfume, soap, and whatever else had become part of daily life in biedermeier Vienna or empire Paris. "With the abundance of cash," wrote one contemporary disapprovingly,"people develop new tastes and wants every day. Silver, so far only seen in the houses of the rich, now appears in many households, not only on the dining table but in the bedrooms as well. Simple houses are being turned into stately mansions. . . . The watch, beforehand as rare as a white crow, has now turned into an article of necessity, so much so that even servants wear them."[20] The innocence and "biblical simplicity" of rural life were gone, replaced by more sophisticated urban styles of life and aspirations. Thus the gentry landowner not only wanted to have better housing in the country, he also began to dream about a "three-room apartment in the city, . . . no butlers, mind you, but a piano in the drawing room, and a language tutor for his adolescent daughters."[21] And even if such impulses were tempered, life itself had become more complex, requiring the expenditure of cash at every turn. Politics was a case in point. For centuries, the Diet had only sat for a few days at a time, while the attending noblemen would pitch their tents and roast their own calves and oxen. Now the Diet was in session for months, and living in a tent would have been too ridiculous to contemplate. It certainly would have made the delegates the laughingstocks of polite society in Vienna and Paris, which, consciously or subconsciously, the Hungarian nobles so much wanted to emulate. Consequently, the delegates rented quarters and paid for their board in cash, an expense heavy enough to dissuade some provincial notables from accepting the honor of representing their county at the assembly.

While it is tempting to describe these outlays as luxuries, a major part of spending was for items that by then were regarded as staples in the industrial nations. This becomes quite obvious if we examine the country's imports, 86.5 percent of which (1838) consisted of cloth, linen, cotton yarn, and fabric (the last two items accounting for 63 percent of the total).[22] Whether or not these were luxuries, the costs to the consumer were still prohibitive. For while in the countries of the industrial core new patterns of consumption had arisen as an integral part of an organic process of development, in Hungary, as in the other countries of the European periphery, they were grafted upon an underdeveloped economy. The result was that consumer

[20] Johann von Csaplovics, *Gemälde von Ungarn* (Pest: Hartleben, 1829), i, 254.
[21] Hóman and Szekfű, *Magyar történet*, v, 228.
[22] Fényes, *Statistika*, i, 268-269.

spending outstripped productivity, and eventually undermined it by cutting deep into the producers' margin of savings for reinvestment. The trend is well illustrated by the figures available on Hungarian foreign trade for the years 1817-1826 (the only complete set for the prerevolutionary period), during which time the volume of Hungary's major imports rose at a rate substantially higher than that of her exports (Table 4).

This tendency to overconsume and underproduce is also dramatically evident from the aggregate figures for the cash value of Hungary's foreign trade. Prior to 1815 this balance was, on the whole, positive. However, it began to deteriorate thereafter, and between 1816 and 1826 the country incurred an average per annum loss of 1,728,406 Fls.[23] This represented over a period of eleven years an aggregate of 19 million Fls. lost in trade with countries outside the western provinces of the Austrian empire. After 1827 Hungary also developed a deficit with her Austrian trading partner, the amount of which, according to two Austrian statisticians, reached thirty-four million Fls. in 1834, and a staggering forty million in 1838.[24] While these figures are "beyond doubt mistaken and exaggerated,"[25] there

TABLE 4
HUNGARY'S MAJOR EXPORTS AND IMPORTS,
1817-1826

	1817	*1826*	
	Amount	*Amount*	*% Change*
Imports			
Cloth, quintals	12,532	23,455	85.7
Cotton fabric + yarn	4,800	10,101	110.4
Linen	11,957	42,287	254.8
Exports			
Cattle, heads	107,872	122,543	14.3
Cereals, bushels	2,147,509	1,879,914	− 12.5
Wool, quintals	100,792	190,003	88.6

SOURCE: Fényes, *Statistika*, I, 252-263. Based on the Report of the Special Committee on Trade of the Diet of 1825-1827.

[23] Ibid., I, 248-249.

[24] Ibid., I, 270.

[25] According to Fényes (ibid., I, 271-272), the discrepancy is due to an overestimation of Austrian imports of cotton yarn and fabric, and an underestimation of Hungarian exports of wine and spirits to the Austrian provinces.

is no question that a substantial trade deficit did exist, and that it was financed by the export of coin and precious metals hoarded by noble families over generations, or else by contracting foreign debts at exorbitant interest rates.[26]

Among noble landowners, the class most affected by these economic trends was the noble middle class or the gentry. The personal consumption of the aristocracy, however conspicuous it may have been, was not increasing at the same rate as that of the middle-class families: watches, tableware, sugar, and coffee took less of a toll on higher than on lower and middle incomes. In addition, the sheer size of aristocratic estates provided a certain cushion against total and immediate ruin. But the gentry's smaller estates could not well absorb the costs of status consumption. Thus many of the gentry not only became indebted, but, given restrictions under the prevailing laws of entail, signed over their properties to creditors in the form of "leases in perpetuity." This is not to say that all of the gentry landowners were profligate consumers who were in debt or had lost effective control over their estates. But those who were not now felt desperately impoverished, and perceived themselves as experiencing downward social mobility. Their deprivations, in other words, were purely relative to the rising living standards of social classes in the Occident with whom they readily identified. But in a rapidly changing world, standing still, or not moving fast enough, is sufficient to turn one into a déclassé.

It was to avoid this fate that the younger generation of the noble middle class began to turn to the educational system, not only in search of gentlemanly pastime, as had been their wont in better times, but of a professional career to supplement or replace the dwindling incomes of their ancestral estates. From the 1820s onward, the number of students rapidly increased. Yet in the famous old Protestant colleges of Patak, Debrecen, Enyed, and in Hungary's only university, just recently transferred from Tirnau to Pest, most of the students lived in abject poverty, supporting themselves by manual labor or by the collection of alms. The truly vexing question was what, if anything, these students would accomplish by earning degrees? For while by 1846 there were some 33,000 people who qualified as college grad-

---

[26] Altogether, it has been estimated that Hungarian landowners contracted (and repaid) debts of no less than 300 million Fls. in the first half of the nineteenth century, and on the average owed 18 million Fls. per annum in interest. See László Ungár, "A magyar nemesi birtok eladósodása" [Indebtedness of the landholdings of the Hungarian nobility], *Századok*, 69 (1935), 48. Based on detailed information from the county of Pest, Ungár also argues that there was a substantial increase in the cases of insolvency after 1839 (ibid., p. 52).

uates, the country already had twice as many licensed attorneys per capita as the more developed, western provinces of the Habsburg empire.[27] The backward economy offered few alternatives. The young graduates would thus become lawyers without clients, scholars without academic chairs, and writers without a reading public, a marginal intelligentsia in quest of social status and economic security. Indeed, in the 1830s more and more of them delayed their entry into the professions. Instead, they turned into "practitioners forever," or else became the hangers-on of popular deputies in the Diet, forming the hard core of a rambunctious "parliamentary youth," as notable for its enthusiastic support for radical reforms as for its recurrent rows with the placid German burghers of the two capital cities Pressburg and Pest.

While the peasantry was not in the mainstream of these developments, in the long run it would not remain unaffected by expanding commercial and intellectual relations with the occidental countries. New habits and articles of consumption did, after all, penetrate rural society. This is clear from the structure and sheer volume of imports in the 1830s and 1840s. But in addition to factory-made linen and cotton fabric, the rural population had become familiar with wheat bread, simple household utensils, sugar, and, above all, better and more sanitary forms of housing. Here and there, the traditional mud and adobe hovels (*kuckó*) with their open fireplaces were replaced by more solid structures with chimneys and windows. In most cases, of course, this familiarity with new articles of consumption was not tantamount to possession, for few of the small peasant farmers had the wherewithal to increase the volume of their product, either by reclamation or by the introduction of mechanical implements. The plight of the peasants was further aggravated by persistent and often successful attempts on the part of noble landowners to increase rent, services, and above all, the local taxes to finance a plethora of new budget items, including expenditures for the maintenance of roads, the per diems of public officials,[28] and the costs of converting hitherto honorary posts into salaried administrative offices.

Faced with these increasing burdens and little prospect for improving their material standard, many marginal peasant farmers dropped out of the rural economy, and, in the absence of large urban

---

[27] Ervin Szabó, *Társadalmi és pártharcok az 1848-49-es magyar forradalomban* [Social and political conflicts in the Hungarian revolution of 1848-1849] (Vienna: Bécsi Magyar Kiadó, 1921), p. 52.

[28] Until 1836 when the Diet forbade the levying of taxes for the payment of the per diem of deputies and ordered these per diems either abolished or paid by the nobility of the country.

centers or a viable industrial economy, simply took to the roads, moving from one locality to another. The counties attempted to deal with the rising problem of vagrancy by establishing compulsory workshops, or by administering corporal punishment to discourage the entrance of indigents in the district under their jurisdiction.[29] Partly in response to these measures, then, many peasants sought refuge in the vast expanses of the Plainland or in the still dense forests of Transdanubia where they turned to a life of highway robbery. These subsequently much romanticized *betyárs*, like the *haiduki* of the Balkan countries, were in effect social bandits, breaking the law while still adhering to the fundamental codes of the peasant community. They appeared in the 1820s and multiplied so fast that on occasion the constabulary of the counties had to enlist the help of the military to restrain them. When caught, these unfortunate Robin Hoods of the Hungarian *puszta* were publicly executed, often in spectacularly cruel ways, though after 1830, largely at the behest of liberal reformers, the most brutal forms of execution (like the breaking of the culprit's bones on the wheel) were outlawed by the royal courts of appeal.

In any case, these measures could neither conceal nor remedy the obvious malaise of peasant society. Thus together with the appearance of poorhouses, vagrancy laws, and attempts to round up highwaymen, we now encounter persistent prophesies concerning the outburst of large-scale peasant violence. These prophesies turned briefly into a terrifying reality in 1831, when the peasant population of seven northeastern counties went on a bloody rampage, triggered by the outbreak of a cholera epidemic and the quarantine imposed by the authorities. In their blind fury, the rebels burned down manor houses, killed landowners and public officials, including officers of sanitation whom they accused of poisoning the wells and of plotting to exterminate the villagers. The uprising was entirely spontaneous, without plan, leadership, or even a list of grievances. The whole affair was thus much in the style of medieval *jacqueries*, devoid of political ideology or awareness. But even so, the spectre of an all-out peasant war continued to loom large, and, together with the pauperization of the nobility, served as an important catalyst for the ensuing movement of social, economic, and political reforms.

A Crisis of Identity

The impulse to reform and to modernize, however, cannot be solely understood in terms of these frustrations and fears. It must also be

---

[29] For a discussion of social disorganization and administrative response, see Z. Pál Pach, *Magyar gazdaságtörténet*, i, 312-317.

sought within the broader context of a collective crisis of identity, brought on by the technological advances of the Occident that culminated in the industrial revolution of the eighteenth century. These technological advances not only produced higher levels of nutrition and comfort, and hence a new, and constantly rising standard of living against which the majority of mankind could measure its own misery, but they also gave the technologically more sophisticated nations a critical edge in warfare over the "less developed" nations of the global periphery. If hitherto economically primitive, but morally and physically determined bands of nomads—like the Huns, the Mongols, or the Hungarians themselves in their day—could harass, plunder, and subjugate their more civilized neighbors, now, for the first time in history, even plundering required technology, along with a complex economy capable of sustaining and replacing it. (It was thus by no means accidental that General Montecuccoli's famous dictum concerning the three prerequisites of warfare—money, money, and more money—dates from the seventeenth century, as does the wisdom of mercantilism that related the power of the kings to the economic sophistication of their subjects.) Technology, in other words, became a key to both national power and popular welfare, and, as such, an object universally desired by elites anxious to maintain their integrity, and by masses of people keen on improving the condition of their daily lives.

It was by virtue of holding this key to national wealth and power that a handful of nations of the Occident emerged as the core of the rising modern world system, and as the global equivalent of a ruling class of might and privilege. Like all other elites, this global elite of powerful nation states was eager to surround its advantages with an aura of moral legitimacy, and proceeded to do so by setting aside the old medieval principles of divine providence and replacing them with a new secular theory to justify social and international inequality. If previously power and wealth were regarded as God given, now the successful pioneers of the first material civilization linked them to achievement by ingenuity, hard work, and purposeful endeavor, available to all who possessed the virtures of resolve and self-discipline. In terms of this formula, the Occidental nations of the "core" became a global elite of might as well as right, for so forceful was the experience of their success, and so persuasive their argument, that it was not only accepted by themselves, but also by the "backward" societies of the periphery. In this respect, there is a close resemblance between the proletarian nations of the time and the lower classes of Victorian England. Much like the latter, the former would not only accept the legitimacy of inequality, but would do so with a sense of shame and

45

guilt, which was accompanied by a firm conviction that the only way to improve their condition was by following the examples set by their betters. It was in this way that the experience of a few nations became the norm for "progress," and that this notion of progress would imply not only the transfer of technology, but also the transfer of institutions and patterns of social conduct.

In the Carpathian countries, the penetration of these ideas may be traced with a degree of accuracy to the end of the eighteenth century. Even before, of course, differences between Hungary and the societies of the Occident had been noted by travellers to and from the country, among them the many Protestants who studied at the universities of Holland, England, and Germany, or the professional soldiers who roamed the countries of the Continent in imperial service. But neither Hungarians nor westerners thought that Hungary was a backward country, or that the West was progressive by virtue of its material life. Rather, they saw each other's countries as separate and mildly exotic parts of the world, different, but not inferior or superior to one another. If Hungarians expressed any value judgments about this difference, it tended to be in favor of their own country and its heroic or bucolic qualities. Indeed, according to the popular motto of the nobility—*Extra Hungarian non est vita, si est vita, non est ita*—there was no life outside the boundaries of the country, or if there was, it certainly was not worth living. It was in the same spirit that the poet laureate of the eighteenth century, Baron Lawrence Orczy, would enjoin his countrymen to "leave deceitful trade" to Englishmen,[30] or that another poet, Joseph Gvadányi, authored a long satirical poem against those who showed preference for foreign dress and manner of speech.[31]

According to the historians Bálint Hóman and Julius Szekfű, whose monumental work examines this period with particular care, "the first Hungarian who was dissatisfied with just about every aspect of national life, and wanted to change it by following foreign examples,"[32] was a Lutheran minister from Pressburg, Mathias Bél, a graduate of the University of Halle and the author of an early work on the geography of Hungary. As a would-be reformer, Bél "constantly searched and probed to find out where people lived better or happier, and never tired of giving advice: Hungarians should work harder, should not

[30] "Tokajba való érkezés télen" [Arrival in wintry Tokaj], quoted in Marczali, *Hungary in the Eighteenth Century*, pp. 86-87.

[31] József Gvadányi, *Egy falusi nótáriusnak budai utazása* [The journey of a village notary to Buda] (Pozsony and Komárom: Weber Simon, 1791).

[32] Hóman and Szekfű, *Magyar történet*, v, 14.

be idle during the winter months, should use more efficient methods of plowing, harvesting and threshing."[33] His voice, however, remained a lone cry in the wilderness, and would not even be faintly echoed for another generation when a number of young writers, among them George Bessenyei and Paul Ányos, all of them members of the imperial-royal bodyguard, came into contact with the ideas of the French enlightenment. Their mode of literary expression was primitive and their social concepts, to say the least, confused—at times they attempted to integrate Voltairean thinking with the historical traditions of Hungarian feudalism—but like Bél they held up foreign models to their countrymen, lamenting that the erudition, culture, and civility of Paris and Vienna were largely absent from their native land.

These nostalgic writings were hardly more than inchoate and inconclusive literary prattle. But toward the end of the century, Hungarian men of letters discovered the disciplines of statistics and economics, and beginning with an anonymous *Dissertatio de industria nationali Hungariae* (1792), turned out a remarkable array of works, comparing the achievements of the Occident with the lack of progress in their own country.[34] The most important and erudite of these economists was Gregorius Berzeviczy, a scholarly nobleman of professed Jacobin sympathies who, in two major works, compared the economies of Austria and Hungary. He came to the disconcerting conclusion that not only the trade and industry of Hungary, but her agriculture as well, was lamentably backward. "Whether we compare the towns, the villages, the farms, or the entire way of life" [in the two halves of the Habsburg realm], he wrote in 1797, "we cannot fail to admit that the provinces of Austria are the more advanced ones. . . . Indeed, the condition of the Austrian peasant is often superior to that of many Hungarian nobles."[35] Berzeviczy offered three explanations for this state of affairs: the discriminatory tariff policies pursued by the Crown in favor of Austria, the antiquated institutions of the Hungarian economic system, and, not least of all, the "indolence" of all classes of Hungary's agrarian producers. These conclu-

[33] Ibid.

[34] Apart from the *Dissertatio*, these works included Lajos Mitterspacher, *Elementa rei rusticae* (Pest: Typis Universitatis, 1794); Károly Rumy, *Populäres Lehrbuch der Oekonomie* (Wien: Schaumburg, 1808); Ferenc Pethe, *Pallérozott magyar gazdaság* [Rationalized Hungarian farming] (Sopron: Nemzeti Gazda-Hivatal, 1805); Gregorius Berzeviczy, *De commercio et industria Hungariae* (Lőcse: Podhoranszki, 1797) and *De conditione et indole rusticorum in Hungaria* (Sopron: Joseph Máriássy, 1806). For a summary analysis of this literature, see Julius Kautz, *Entwicklungsgeschichte der volkswirtschaftlichen Ideen in Ungarn* (Budapest: Grill, 1876), pp. 64-110.

[35] Berzeviczy, *De commercio*, p. 63.

sions were echoed by a number of other economists, among them Francis Pethe and Albert Thaer who, like Berzeviczy, alternatively denounced the insidiousness of exploitative tariff policy and the "dumbness" of the Hungarian peasant, urging their compatriots to catch up with the more advanced provinces of the empire.[36]

For a decade or so during the Napoleonic wars these sober voices went largely unheard among a nobility dizzy with its momentary entrepreneurial success and the flow of easy cash into the country. But after the war came the crisis, and the idea of Hungarian backwardness rapidly gained currency among the educated public. The scholarly opinion of economists was often corroborated by stories of returning soldiers and travellers, most of whom gave rapturous accounts of the cleanliness of German cities, the paved roads of Austria, the bustling ports of Holland, or the literacy of Swiss peasants. In contrast, Hungary, once a proud tower of Christian civilization and an integral part of the Occident, now had become an "oriental" country of "dirty jackboots and stinking pipes."[37] A few traditionalists, like Joseph Dessewffy, pleaded that it was not right always to prefer the foreign to the domestic, and to sulk that "the gondoliers of Venice sang better than the boatmen of the Danube, that the British racehorse [was] superior to the Hungarian, that Como [was] more beautiful than Badacsony, and that Madeira [was] better than the wines of Tokaj."[38] But the majority of the educated public now sympathized with the editor of the fashionable quarterly, *Athenaeum*, who, reporting on his trip across the Hungarian plain in 1839, wrote derisively about the "tedious and prosaic countryside," where, "in the appropriate words of a foreign gentlemen . . . the highest point was the horn of an ox," about the "pathetic barges of the Tisza," and about "the sole roadside inn where the guests kept on their greasy fur coats," where "a group of oafish peasants entertained the guests by performing the swineherder's dance on cue from the jackbooted servant."[39] Before long, this orgy of foul smells would waft across the entire panorama, and envelop not only the roads and roadside inns, but also the institutions of the country. If roads were wretched, so was the institution of serfdom, if the inns were laughable, so were the privileges of the nobility. In time, even the glorious "ancient liberties" would be reduced to a

[36] Ferenc Pethe, quoted in Hóman and Szekfű, *Magyar történet*, v, 160.

[37] Gyula Szekfű, ed., *A mai Széchenyi* [Topical Széchenyi] (Budapest: Magyar Szemle Társaság, 1934), p. 83.

[38] József Dessewffy, *A "Hitel" cimü munka taglalatja* [A critique of the work "Credit"] (Kassa: Werfer, 1831), p. 3.

[39] Quoted in Hóman and Szekfű, *Magyar történet*, v, 309.

grotesque farce under the literary scrutiny of writers like Baron Eötvös or Alexander Petőfi, who would treat them more as so many blots on the national honor than as potential sources of national pride.

On the whole, the changing self-image of Hungarians paralleled a shift in foreign perceptions of their country. In the past, the centuries of Turkish wars and occupation had lent the place an aura of mystery,[40] and its image, bolstered by tales of natural wealth and beauty, had long remained positive, so much so that between 1729 and 1784 Hungary attracted nearly a million immigrants from over-populated Alsace, Swabia, and Lower Austria. But after these decades, the earlier fascination evaporated, and the tales of quaint, exotic charm soon gave way to matter-of-fact accounts of economic under-development.

In the last decade of the eighteenth century, most of these accounts were written by Englishmen travelling in pursuit of markets for the industrial products of their country.[41] Schooled in a tradition of pragmatism and utilitarianism, they were unfavorably impressed by the inefficiency of the economic system and returned to England disappointed because, despite its natural wealth, the country was not yet ready to offer adequate opportunities for trade. But if such Englishmen as Townson (1793) and Bright (1818) were "acid" and "irritable"[42] in their comments on Hungary, the Frenchman de Serres was downright contemptuous of the backwardness of the country which he squarely blamed on the character of its inhabitants. "The Hungarians," he wrote in 1814, "are naturally indolent and prefer pastoral to agricultural life. Although Hungary is a fertile country, the inhabitants have no idea how to extract the riches of the soil that is theirs to cultivate. Ignorant and superstitious, the Hungarians are bad agriculturists, and equally little attracted to trade."[43]

A few foreign observers, like Julia Pardoe and John Paget[44] (both of them romantically linked to Hungary), briefly rekindled the old images of chivalry and charm that would return during the subsequent years of reform, revolution, and the war of independence. Nonethe-

[40] Doreen Warriner, ed., *Contrasts in Emerging Societies* (Bloomington: Indiana University Press, 1965), p. 32.

[41] The two most important of these are Townson, *Travels in Hungary*, and Richard Bright, *Travels from Vienna to Lower Hungary* (Edinburgh: Constable, 1818).

[42] Warriner, *Contrasts in Emerging Societies*, p. 33.

[43] Marcel de Serres, *Voyage en Autriche* (Paris: A. Bertrand, 1814), III, 262.

[44] Julia Pardoe, *The City of the Magyars, or Hungary and Her Institutions in 1839-1840* (London: G. Virtue, 1840); John Paget, *Hungary and Transylvania* (London: John Murray, 1855).

less, among native Hungarians the image of backwardness remained deeply engraved for the decades to come, and the desire to overcome it provided a strong emotional component to the reform movements of the years 1825-1848.

THE ARISTOCRACY BETWEEN REFORM AND REACTION

A Progressive Design

The link between economic progress and institutional reform had been firmly implanted in the public mind ever since Gregorius Berzeviczy published his treatise on Hungarian agriculture in 1806. But the idea, however obvious, did not mature into a coherent social program until the country had been drawn into more extensive commercial relations with other countries, both inside and outside the empire, and until the call for reforms was taken up in the 1820s by one of the great magnates, Count Stephen Széchenyi. In Hungary, so popular wisdom would have it thereafter, neither reforms nor revolutions could be initiated save under the blessings of an aristocrat.

As an aristocrat, Széchenyi had impeccable credentials, for his family was among the dozen or so most prestigious in the country, and its members not only owned substantial tracts of land in western Hungary, but had long served Crown and Church with considerable distinction. Among them were a cardinal, several archbishops, a palatine of the country, and several soldiers, while Stephen's father Francis, a well-known patron of the arts, was the founder of Hungary's National Museum and Library. Following in their footsteps, young Széchenyi embarked early on the road to public service by joining the army during the Napoleonic wars. Subsequently, he saw combat at Leipzig, took part in the occupation of Paris, and then returned to the Congress of Vienna as one of the crowd of elegant bystanders. After the Congress, he rejoined his regiment briefly, only to resign his commission in order to devote himself to a life of study and travel.

Like so many of his countrymen, Széchenyi was deeply affected by his experiences in foreign countries, especially in Britain. He was as much impressed by the achievements of English trade and industry as he was by the country's agricultural progress, which in his view had preempted violent political revolution and had permitted the landed aristocracy to maintain its traditional position in society and politics. "What a happy country," he wrote to his father in 1816, "where so few are the unfortunate. We have to bow before her greatness."[45] In

[45] Gyula Viszota, ed., *Gróf Széchenyi István írói és hírlapi vitája Kossuth Lajossal* [Count

comparison to Britain, of course, Hungary was a rather bleak place, a "great fallow," or "wasteland," with "poverty, misery and filth everywhere."[46] In the place of the teeming ports, busy factories, and the prosperous landowning class of Britain, in Hungary he could only see the "mud and dust of Pest,"[47] bad roads, lazy peasants, and a haughty, but ignorant nobility. When he returned to these conditions Széchenyi experienced a genuine culture shock and crisis of identity, in the course of which he, like so many natives of backward countries, veered from one extreme to another, sometimes exuberantly praising the unique virtues of his countrymen, sometime cursing the sloth of his oriental race that after a thousand years could not find its proper place in the midst of the civilization of the Occident.[48] His personal crisis was aggravated by financial adversity. When after his father's death he came upon his inheritance, he was to find out that his substantial estate was deeply in debt, so much so that his Viennese bankers refused to issue further loans in his name. This rebuff no doubt acted as a catalyst for the publication of his first, and major, programmatic work, *Hitel* (*Credit*) in 1830, and adds a somber biographical note to it.

The program that would emerge from this crisis of identity in the thousands of printed pages of Széchenyi's works and in his personal correspondence was distinctly aristocratic, reflecting not only Széchenyi's experiences, but also his social background as one of the grandees of the realm. It is true, of course, that these pages are full of lofty references to the nation and the fatherland. But it is also true that Széchenyi could see no conflict or difference between the interests of the nation as a whole, and those of the aristocracy as its ruling class. Indeed, as he stated quite explicitly in 1831, the "continued preponderance of the landowning classes [was] the sole guarantee for the survival of the nation."[49] And even if his program was designed ultimately to benefit the entire community, the only class capable of carrying it out was the aristocracy. As Széchenyi would put it in a letter to the Transylvanian Baron Wesselényi: "Our most sacred duty is to change the condition of the fatherland with as little fanfare as possible, and, I believe, can only be accomplished at the Magnates'

Széchenyi's literary and journalistic polemics with Louis Kossuth] (Budapest: Magyar Történelmi Társulat, 1927), i, iv.

[46] István Széchenyi, *Világ* [Enlightenment], 1832, in *Széchenyi István Művei* [Collected Works] (Budapest: Tudományos Akadémia, 1903-1904), i, 86.

[47] Szekfű, *A mai Széchenyi*, p. 243.

[48] Ibid.   [49] Ibid., p. 180.

Table [of the Diet]."[50] The other classes of Hungarian society were quite clearly not suited to the task. The bourgeoisie was weak and foreign, the peasantry illiterate, while the gentry, in Széchenyi's aristocratic opinion, was a "coarse lot" (*eine unwissende rohe Bagage*), "the mixture of the Spanish grand, the French *garçon* and the lazy Hottentot."[51]

Although Széchenyi's program was presented at great length, and argued in a somewhat cumbersome manner, it still can be easily reduced to a few essentials. The first of these is simple and straightforward: Hungary was an underdeveloped country, a condition most strikingly manifest in the fact that her landowners "did not enjoy the level of well-being that they would be entitled to given their circumstances," and yet, they were unable to "bring their estates up to a higher standard."[52] By then, this observation, to be sure, was far from original, but Széchenyi's remedy was. For instead of exhorting his peers to be frugal and to accumulate capital by saving for reinvestment, he envisaged an agricultural revolution to be financed initially by foreign credit which, in his analysis, would start to flow into the Hungarian economy if only the restrictive laws of entail were abolished to permit mortgaging and sale of land. True, Hungarian landowners were also expected to do their share. Once foreign capital became available, they would have to take the next step by encouraging the cash commutation of labor services, and by accepting the liquidation of seigneurial rights over the serf's parcel. However, a pragmatist to the core, Széchenyi would convincingly argue that these reforms would not really involve a great sacrifice, for in the long run they would permit landowners to replace the inefficient labor of the serfs with more productive wage labor. Greater productivity would in turn produce greater incomes, and in view of these greater incomes, the landowning class could relinquish its traditional exemption from direct taxes without running the risk of financial ruin. By advocating this last measure, his program came full circle. The equalization of tax burdens among the population promised to increase the purchasing power of the small peasant farmer, and thus held out the prospect of a viable internal market capable of generating further economic development, including the eventual rise of an industrial economy.

[50] Béla Grünwald, *Az új Magyarország* [The new Hungary] (Budapest: Franklin, 1890), p. 145.

[51] Mályusz, "A reformkor nemzedéke," p. 40.

[52] István Széchenyi, *Hitel* [Credit], 3rd ed., Fontes Series (Budapest: Magyar Tudományos Akadémia, 1930), p. 17.

This program for economic development, however, was not to stand on its own, but was to be part of a more comprehensive program of modernization under the label of *polgárosodás*. This Hungarian word carries a triple connotation of civilization, citizenship, and *embourgeoisement*, and the program that emerged from the sequels to *Credit* aimed at these three interrelated objectives. First, it advocated the "advancement of public intelligence" and the "multiplication of cultivated human heads" (*kiművelt imberfő*),[53] to be achieved by expanding the educational system so that the lower strata of the population could become more efficient producers, capable of functioning in an economy of greater complexity. Secondly, the program set out "to secure the civic existence of all the inhabitants of Hungary"[54] by granting them equality before the law and thereby transforming them into fully qualified contractual partners in economic transactions. These two measures, increased education and legal emancipation, would open up avenues of social mobility for talent from all strata of society, and would not only revitalize the country's elite but would surround it with a new aura of legitimacy. In the process, Széchenyi realized, those who enjoyed their privileges solely by virtue of heredity would be doomed. But the industrious and enterprising members of the old ruling class would survive the test and, like the British aristocracy of Széchenyi's time, would emerge as a far more secure and firmly entrenched social and political entity.

These thoughts took shape, and were put in writing between 1831 and 1834, by which time the terms "citizen" and "civic existence" already subsumed the ideas of suffrage and political participation. Széchenyi was well aware of this, for by all accounts he had followed with some interest the electoral debates of England. He also conceded that, in the long run, such reforms might be enacted in Hungary as well, and that the rising classes of entrepreneurs and prosperous farmers would eventually have to be included in the political nation. But as a practical matter, such reforms would have to wait until the country became prosperous and "civilized." For the time being, Széchenyi had few political reforms to propose. Thus, in his *Stádium* (1834), he published a twelve-point agenda of priorities, only one of which may be construed as political. This was a modest proposal to the effect that the nobility of each country should elect two "tribunes" or public defenders" (following the Austrian model of the *Untertansadvokat*) to intercede on behalf of commoners in matters involving tax

[53] Hóman and Szekfű, *Magyar történet*, v, 265.
[54] Szekfű, *A mai Széchenyi*, p. 159.

assessments and disputes with their own landowners.[55] Over the years, he became even more cautious. Ten years after the publication of *Stádium*, in his *Adó* (*Taxation*), he discussed the principle of "no taxation without representation" at some length, only to conclude that it made little sense in a country where most taxpayers were illiterate and as yet devoid of civic responsibility.[56] In England, he pointed out ruefully, the extension of suffrage represented a step in the right direction, because there the public was not only prosperous, but mature. But in Hungary, there was no genuine public opinion, "only a set of vague ideas derived from conjectures and fallacies."[57] Under these circumstances, the idea of a constitutionally limited monarchy, much like the idea of the free press, was "right in principle," but in practice it was "like the torch in the hands of the arsonist."[58]

As an aristocrat and a political conservative, Széchenyi also remained highly ambivalent toward the idea of nationalism. It is true, of course, that his writings are filled with passionate expressions of loyalty and love toward the fatherland and nation, but these sentiments never led him to accept the notion of an independent or fully autonomous Hungarian state. Like most of his fellow aristocrats, his loyalty to the larger empire was unimpeachable. In private, he never referred to the monarch as king, but as emperor, and on his journeys abroad, he usually referred to himself as an Austrian subject.[59] It is also true that he was one of the foremost advocates of substituting Magyar for Latin as the official language of the country. Yet, unlike many of his contemporaries who regarded language as the mysterious essence of nationhood and argued their case emotionally on cultural and political grounds, Széchenyi merely regarded language as a medium of social communication. A living language was preferable to a dead one because it was more accessible to the masses of people who would inevitably enter the marketplace and the production process. And Hungarian was preferable to the other languages spoken in the country, not because it was inherently superior to them, but because it was already spoken by the single largest group of people. In

[55] Ibid., p. 160.

[56] István Széchenyi, "Az Adó," in Viszota, *Széchenyi vitája*, I, 656.

[57] Quoted from Gyula Szekfű, ed., *Három nemzedék és ami utána kővetkezik* [Three generations and whatever has happened after them], 3rd ed. (Budapest: Egyetemi Nyomda, 1935), p. 54. All quotes in the present volume are from the third, enlarged, edition of the work.

[58] Ibid.

[59] George Bárány, *Stephen Széchenyi and the Awakening of Hungarian Nationalism, 1791-1841* (Princeton: Princeton University Press, 1968), p. 83.

any case, "language was not the foundation of the building."[60] The building blocks of the modern state were "intellect, virtue and Christian morality."[61] When therefore in the 1840s the resistance of the non-Magyar nationalities to the introduction of the Magyar language became increasingly evident, Széchenyi reversed his earlier stance, counseling his countrymen against the imposition of an official language in the name of abstract and foreign ideas. His moderation was appreciated by the highest circles of the Viennese government. Thus, while at first he was regarded as a dangerous firebrand, later he was recognized for being what he was, an economic progressive and political conservative. In a secret report to the emperor drafted by the Hungarian Chancellor Reviczky, Széchenyi was described as a man who "wants to transform Hungary into a second England," but who "does not go along with the demagogic liberalism of the present age, . . . is devoted to the ancient constitution, respects, loves and praises . . . the supreme benevolence of His Majesty."[62]

Conservative Reality

Széchenyi's reform program was, in the first place, addressed to the aristocracy, and indeed a number of younger peers responded to the publication of *Hitel* by forming a progressive caucus at the Magnates' Table. But the caucus was small and its membership never exceeded thirty or thirty-five. After an initial flurry of enthusiasm, even this small membership began to dwindle. Upon Széchenyi's private initiative, however, a number of worthy causes were taken up: a National Casino was founded where the aristocracy could ostensibly mix with businessmen; the urban renewal of Pest got underway; a Danube steamship company was formed; and plans were made for building a permanent bridge between Buda and Pest. But the legislative record of the Diet remained nothing short of dismal. The celebrated "reform diets" of the period merely passed a few measures facilitating the litigation of commercial disputes, and added to these a handful of acts to firm up the use of the vernacular in the educational system. One should note, of course, that the Diet of 1832-1836 devoted hundreds of its sessions to the drafting of an Urbarial Act, designed to overhaul the entire structure of feudal relations between lord and peasant. But during the years of debate, the text of the original bill was gradually whittled down and in its final draft the idea of statutory

[60] From Francis S. Wagner, "Széchenyi and the Nationality Problem," *Journal of Central European Affairs*, 20 (1960), p. 295.

[61] Szekfű, *A mai Széchenyi*, p. 83.

[62] Bárány, *Széchenyi*, p. 175.

commutation was replaced by the principle of voluntary redemption, subject to bilateral agreements between landowner and serf and largely under terms set by the former.

The fact of the matter was that, by addressing his program to this fellow magnates, Széchenyi appealed to the wrong constituency. By 1830 or so, the entrepreneurial momentum of the aristocracy had all but spent itself. While landowners were still interested in increasing the volume of production on their estates, in view of the pressures of status consumption, they did not so much try to attain it by intensifying capital investment as by an increasing reliance on corvée. This is amply evident from statistics relating to the amount of land cultivated by serfs as opposed to other kinds of labor. Thus, if the census of 1787 found 217,198 statutory parcels enfiefed to serf tenants, in 1828 the number was 254,629, and in 1848 262,407, despite the fact that in the interim the Urbarial Act had been passed, ostensibly designed to encourage the cash commutation of feudal services.[63] Before the revolution of 1848, feudalism in Hungary had been on the rise rather than on the decline. This trend, of course, was common throughout all the countries of eastern Europe, though in the case of Hungary, the trend was clearly accelerated by the steady decline of wool prices after 1830. This decline induced landowners to revert to the production of grain, a process more compatible with serf labor than sheepherding and the production of raw wool.

Perhaps even more important was the fact that Széchenyi's program, while argued with impeccable logic, rested on a fatally flawed fundamental premise. For while Széchenyi envisaged a critical role for western bank capital in providing the initial stimulus for agricultural development, interest in assuming such a role was nowhere in sight among potential investors and the managers of international capital. It would not even materialize after 1848, when the laws of entail and seigneurial rights were abolished. The reasons for this must be sought in the laws of supply and demand of the contemporary world market, which continued to favor capital exports for transportation and industry over and above the agricultural enterprise of underdeveloped countries. The problem of agricultural credit in Hungary would thus remain acute for most of the century. And while Széchenyi's design for an agricultural revolution financed by foreign capital appeared to be more and more utopian with every passing year, the idea of a large imperial market, protected by a wall of ag-

---

[63] Fényes, *Statistika*, I, 117. Ignác Acsády, *A magyar jobbágyság története* [History of Hungarian serfdom] (Budapest: Faust, 1942), p. 372.

ricultural tariffs, began to take shape as a viable alternative. This would enable the great landowners to survive without modernizing their estates or abandoning the essentials of a serf economy. In this view, the aristocracy needed not capital but imperial goodwill. This could presumably be acquired by closing ranks behind the Crown, by surrendering some of the traditional prerogatives of the magnates, and by supporting more actively the integrity of the empire.

However, the alliance that was gradually taking shape between Crown and aristocracy did not rest on economic, but on political foundations. The imperial government, after all, had a long-standing interest in the modernization of Hungarian agriculture, and this interest was also maintained under Chancellor Metternich's regime. What worried the chancellor was the growing unrest and anti-imperial, nationalistic sentiment among the Hungarian gentry and the lesser nobility. In 1836, many of the deputies to the Diet were still wont to use old patriotic slogans, demanding the redress of traditional grievances. But by 1839, all this had changed. Thus when Metternich, an astute observer of Hungarian politics, came to the opening of the Diet, "this most tedious of constitutional comedies,"[64] he was stunned to discover that the "old opposition [had] almost completely disappeared," that "the lunatic opposition [had] gained tremendous momentum . . . and was now the most numerous of all parliamentary factions."[65] His dismay was shared by the aristocratic members of the Upper Table. Count Aurél Dessewffy complained bitterly that the "magnates [had] become the objects of hate," and that "the whole movement of reform [was] now nothing but a movement aimed at seizing the property of the aristocracy."[66] Others spoke of the rise of a "class of professional agitators" determined to destroy the aristocracy by "exploiting the tyrannical whims of majorities."[67] Indeed, Széchenyi himself was turning gloomy and pessimistic. In his words, "the lower estate [of the nobility] and the youth are dissatisfied with the progress of reform and demand more and more in their reckless intemperance. . . . In the counties, young and penniless agitators have appeared, whose fury and French sansculottism can hardly be restrained. . . . These agitators want to transform the eight-hundred-year-old kingdom into a modern French republic where the people represent the

---

[64] Clement Metternich, *Nachgelassene Papiere* (Wien: Braumüller, 1881-1884), VI, 306.

[65] Ibid., VII, 60.

[66] Aurél Dessewffy, *Elmélkedés a megnyíló országgyülés felől* [Thoughts on the forthcoming Diet] (Kassa: Werfer, 1839), p. 121.

[67] From Géza Ballagi, *A nemzeti államalkotás kora* [The age of building the national state] (Budapest: Athenaeum, 1897), p. 322.

highest forum, and where private property may become subject to redistribution."[68]

The rhetoric was inflated, but the fears were real, and led the imperial chancellor to enter into a political alliance with the Hungarian magnates. At first this alliance was informal, and entailed the appointment of a number of loyalist aristocrats as temporary "administrators" of the counties with instructions to influence the outcome of elections and of local politics. In 1843-1844, this mandate was carried out in many jurisdictions by organizing bands of thugs from the local lumpen-nobility to terrorize the county assemblies and to prevent the election of liberal deputies to the Lower Table. This new regime was described by frustrated opponents as the *bunkókrácia*, or the rule of the bludgeons (*bunkó* being the Hungarian word for a club widening at its end, now wielded by the paid agents of the aristocracy). This did produce some tangible results, inasmuch as it prevented the victory of the liberals at the elections for the new Diet and produced a relatively docile majority at the Lower Table of parliament. Metternich was satisfied. But both he and the more astute supporters of the established order realized that royal commissioners of dubious legality or the club-wielding members of the noble proletariat represented only temporary expedients and that, in the long run, the alliance between the Crown and the magnates would have to be formalized by establishing a political party that could serve both as an electoral machine and as a mouthpiece of the alliance in public life. The initiative was taken by Metternich himself in a confidential memorandum to his Hungarian counterpart, Royal Chancellor Count George Apponyi.[69] Copies of this memorandum were passed on to a number of influential peers, and, after prolonged negotiations among Metternich, Apponyi, and the leaders of the Magnates' Table at the Diet, a Conservative party made its debut in November 1846. In the words of its founders, the party was to have a nationwide political organization reaching down to the county level, "to unite the conservative element throughout the country, to integrate them into the political life of the nation, and to coordinate their activities in electing deputies and officers of local government."[70] With two exceptions, the signatories of this manifesto and the members of the steering committee of the party were secular or ecclesiastic peers, and were the members of the Upper Table of the Diet, among them

[68] Viszota, *Széchenyi vitája*, I, lxxxix.

[69] Mihály Horváth, *Huszonöt év Magyarország történetéből, 1823-1848* [Twenty-five years from the history of Hungary], 2d ed. (Pest: Ráth Mór, 1867), I, 197-198.

[70] Ibid., p. 198.

Counts Dessewffy, Majláth, Zichy, Keglevich, de la Motte, Cziráky, and Forgách, Barons Mednyánszky and Majthényi, the Archbishop Kopácsy, and Bishop Lonovich of Csanád.[71] Széchenyi, once the chief advocate of reforms, was asked to join, but refused. But in 1847 he accepted from the hands of the royal chancellor the office of high commissioner for transport, and in the fall of that year he ran on an essentially conservative platform for a seat at the Lower Table.[72] By then, Széchenyi had become a lonely and tragic figure, who would soon suffer a nervous breakdown and finish his life in a Viennese asylum.

The Conservative program, drafted by Count Anton Széchen (no relation to Széchenyi), was a document of profound political and economic traditionalism. It upheld the "ancient constitution" of the country, stressed the importance of "legitimacy, justice and loyalty," and castigated the "blind imitation of foreign examples."[73] In this spirit, the program rejected the idea of political reforms, save for some changes in the representation of royal free boroughs known to be friendly to Crown and aristocracy. While paying lip service to the idea of "progress"—by now a stock phrase in all political programs—in social matters it merely reaffirmed the lame stipulations of the Urbarial Act of 1836, adding cursory references to the need for improving the system of taxation. In reality, the magnates would have nothing to do with either the compulsory redemption of feudal obligations or the taxation of the nobility, and in the fall of 1847 they fought both measures tooth and nail at the stormy sessions of the last feudal Diet. True, in March 1848 the Magnates' Table voted unanimously for a whole spate of legislation abolishing the economic institutions of feudalism. But this act was less magnanimous than it has occasionally been presented to posterity, for the magnates passed the bills in question under duress,[74] with only seventeen of the more than

[71] Ibid., pp. 197-198.

[72] Unlike in Britain, this was consonant with constitutional law. Thus as Horváth notes (*Huszonöt év*, I, 141), in 1825-1827 there were four magnates sitting at the Lower Table as the delegates of counties; in 1847 there were eleven, including Széchenyi.

[73] Ervin Szabó, *Társadalmi és pártharcok*, p. 72.

[74] As Count Joseph Pálffy noted during the debate on the abolition of land tenure on March 18, 1848: "The main reason for the enactment of this article is that the Honorable Estates are worried about the possibility of an insurrection. . . . Since in such perilous times the protracted exchange of messages between the two Tables of the Diet is impractical, I accept the draft bill without further reservations." To this Count Széchen added that the bill reflected "extraordinary circumstances and that its acceptance was necessary to calm down the people." (Szabó, *Társadalmi és pártharcok*, pp. 74, 108-109.) Széchenyi's comment was: "The nonsense passed" (Szekfű, *Három nemzedék*, p. 54).

eight hundred voting members of the Table present on the historic occasion.[75]

THE GENTRY BETWEEN FREEDOM AND PROGRESS

Liberalism vs. Redress

In view of the retreat of the aristocracy into economic and political conservatism, the leading role of the gentry in the reform movements of 1825-1848 remains one of the rarely disputed facts of Hungarian historiography. To be sure, as all correlations between social class and political behavior, this one is far from perfect, for some of the gentry and the petty nobility sided with the conservative aristocrats in defense of their "ancient rights," while a handful of magnates—Louis and Casimir Batthyány, George Károlyi, the Protestant Count Zay, the Barons Eötvös, Wenckheim, and Wesselényi—stayed on the side of reform, if only to exert a restraining influence.[76] But even so, the association is impressive, and its existence is evident from the statistical information that emerges from an analysis of voting patterns. Thus, whether we examine the electoral results of 1832 or 1847 (Table 5), we will find that the reformist deputies hailed from the counties where the density of the common nobility was the greatest and where the holdings of the gentry were substantial enough to counter the economic influence of the Church, Crown, and aristocracy. In contrast, the conservatives were elected in the counties where the holdings of magnates, Crown, and clergy were dominant and where the number of common nobles, that is, the electorate, was small and susceptible to economic pressure and manipulation.

Unlike Széchenyi's reform initiatives, those of the gentry grew out of an ongoing movement of protest against arbitrary government and recurrent imperial attempts to curtail the powers of the Hungarian parliament. During the second half of the reign of Francis I, the Hungarian Diet was not convened for a period of fourteen years (1811-1825), while the autonomy of the counties was undermined by

---

[75] Árpád Károlyi, *Az 1848-diki törvénycikkek az udvar előtt* [The legislative acts of 1848 before the royal court] (Budapest: Magyar Történelmi Társaság, 1936), p. 35.

[76] Batthyány especially was seen to have accepted the chairmanship of the liberal caucus to "maintain the desirable preponderance of the magnates" on both sides of the political spectrum. (Horváth, *Huszonöt év*, III, 192.) This view was shared by many, among them *The Times* of London, whose obituary of Batthyány (upon his execution in October 1849) stated: "Although he had assumed the leadership of the opposition in the Diet, no man in the assembly of magnates was more jealous of the dignity of his order, or a more chivalrous champion of aristocratic power." (*The Times*, October 17, 1849.)

TABLE 5

CORRELATION BETWEEN POLITICAL AFFILIATION, NUMBER OF VOTERS, AND THE
DISTRIBUTION OF PROPERTY, 1832-1848

Political Affiliation	No. of Counties	Average No. of Voters	% of Land Owned By Magnates, Church, Crown	By gentry
A. 1832-1836				
Conservative	12	1,811.1	62.0	36.5
Uncommitted	14	3,879.9	55.1	40.1
Liberal	19	3,296.0	58.3	41.1
No Information	4	2,882.5	81.0	18.0
Total	49			
B. 1847-1848				
Conservative	20	1,272.5	72.1	23.8
Conservative Leaning	8	3,460.0	55.1	43.1
Liberal Leaning	7	3,584.7	48.7	51.3
Liberal	14	5,375.1	50.8	49.0
Total	49[a]	3,036.6	59.0	40.0

SOURCES: 1) Affiliation (in the absence of formal identification with parties): 1832-1836, Barta, *A fiatal Kossuth*, p. 173, with reference to materials in Hungarian National Archives. For 1847-1848, text of confidential report by Electoral Commissioner Földváry to Chancellor George Apponyi in Barta, ed. *Kossuth Lajos összes munkái*, IX, 220-223, 229-235; 2) Electorate: Danyl and Dávid, *Az első magyarországi népszámlálás, 1784-1787*. These figures were preferred to Fényes, *Statisztika*, I, 118, because they were more complete and because Fényes' figures are mere extrapolations from the nationwide census of fifty years before. One may point out that between 1787 and 1837 a shift in population (and probably in the common nobility) took place from the north-west to the southeast of the country. But the revised, and more accurate figures, would only make the proposed correlations more perfect, for all of the staunchly conservative counties lay in the area that experienced an outflow, rather than influx, of population. 3) Landholdings, see also *Az első magyarországi népszámlálás, 1784-1787*.
[a] Croatian delegates omitted.

the appointment of royal commissioners who used a variety of sub-terfuges to prevent the normal functioning of local government. When the Diet was finally convened in 1825, the seething frustrations of the lesser nobility exploded in demands for the redress of its griev-ances and for the impeachment of royal officials, many from the magnate class, for their misdeeds during the years of extra-parlia-mentary government. The sessions of the Diet and the meetings of the county assemblies now echoed with protests against governmental tyranny, and against the "haughty and greedy oligarchy . . . bent on destroying a nation of free men."[77]

[77] From Mályusz, "A reformkor nemzedéke," p. 57.

Such protests were, of course, well within the traditional bounds of feudal politics. But the stirrings of the nobility in 1825 and in the years thereafter had several new aspects that set them apart from the parliamentary movements of earlier decades and centuries. Unlike their predecessors, this generation of protesters had been exposed to liberal ideas emanating from England and France and, under their spell, sought not merely to restore but to change the balance of power in feudal society between king and country, Church and state, aristocrat and common nobleman. Thus as the counties were preparing for the elections of 1825 and 1830, their assemblies demanded institutional reforms in the name of popular sovereignty and representative government. To take a few examples: the counties of Zala and Szatmár proposed that the common nobility be given representation at the Magnates' Table; the county of Temes instructed its elected deputies to seek the abolition of aristocratic titles, while the county of Zemplén demanded outright abolition of the Magnates' Table and the establishment of a unicameral assembly with the exclusion of hereditary privilege.[78] And if the power of the magnates was to be curtailed by abolishing the hereditary branch of government, royal authority was to be made accountable through the constitutional device of a responsible ministry, whereby royal officials would become subject to parliamentary votes of confidence. This would have reduced the role of the king-emperor himself to that of a passive bystander. As to the Church, the counties revived some of their traditional grievances concerning the jurisdiction of ecclesiastic courts and the religion of children born of mixed marriages (whom the Catholic church habitually claimed as their own to the dismay of the Protestants and of other religious denominations). But here again, the demands of the counties went far beyond the traditional redress of grievances. A number of deputies wanted to introduce the institution of civil marriage. Others wanted to make priests (including the Cardinal Prince Primate) criminally liable for violating the rights of other denominations. The representatives of one county, refractory Bereg, demanded that the Catholic church sever its ties with Rome and pledge its loyalty to the Hungarian state.[79]

No less significant than the transformation of traditional protest into a modern movement of reform was the change of old-fashioned patriotism into modern nationalism. The term *natio*, of course, had been a stock phrase in the dictionary of Hungarian feudalism, and,

[78] István Barta, *A fiatal Kossuth* [The young Kossuth] (Budapest: Akadémia, 1964), pp. 133-138.
[79] Hóman and Szekfű, *Magyar történet*, v, 321-323.

like its nineteenth-century French counterpart, designated a political community, albeit one that was devoid of ethnic connotations. The old *natio Hungarica* (or, alternatively, *populus Hungaricus*) included all freemen, whether they spoke the Magyar vernacular or not. But now, under French influence, the nation became a political *and* ethnic community. At first, this was interpreted by some to mean that the non-Magyar element—among them the entire bourgeoisie, half of the aristocracy, and about one-fifth of the common nobility—was to be excluded from the exercise of political rights. Yet once they read the French authors more carefully, the leaders of the liberal nobility could not escape the conclusion that if the nation was truly an ethnic community, and if the Hungarian nation was to become an entity deserving the name, then political rights would have to be extended to the classes outside the bastions of traditional privilege. Thus, if as late as 1828 Paul Felsőbüki-Nagy could warn the Diet that any political concession to the commoners "would spell doom to the idea of liberty,"[80] in 1832-1836 almost all liberal counties made ringing pleas for extending political rights to part, or all, of the common people. The tone was set by Francis Kölcsey at the assembly of the county of Szatmár when he called for a "nation of ten million free men, instead of one consisting of seven hundred thousand demoralized souls."[81] Echoing Kölcsey, one of the assemblymen of Zemplén queried whether parliament should represent "thirty thousand pedigreed drones, or eight million industrious citizens?"[82] In response, one of his colleagues offered the enthusiastic opinion that the "Hungarian constitution should involve eight million people, instead of the one hundred thousand or, more properly, the thirty thousand who effectively participate in politics."[83] Somewhat more pragmatically, the assemblies of Békés and other counties instructed their deputies to seek voting rights for peasants who, pending legislation, would redeem their feudal obligations or else pay a certain amount of direct taxes.[84]

[80] Horváth, *Huszonöt év*, I, 234.
[81] István Barta, "A magyar polgári reformmozgalom," p. 330.
[82] Barta, *A fiatal Kossuth*, p. 102.
[83] Ibid., p. 108. The variation in the figures cited has no political significance. It merely reflects the ignorance about the actual number of inhabitants of the country at that time. The last official census had been taken in 1787 and found approximately 8 million inhabitants in Hungary, Transylvania, and Croatia-Slavonia. On the other hand, in the 1830s it was correctly estimated that the number of Hungarian subjects was closer to ten million. The 700,000 figure above refers to the estimated number of noblemen, burghers, and other freemen, while the 100,000 figure apparently refers to those adult males who had the right to vote.
[84] Ibid., pp. 158-159.

1825-1848

Liberalism: East and West

While the gentry's leading role in the quest for such reforms is a matter of historical record, questions remain concerning its collective motivation. Some historians of more recent times have been inclined to answer these questions in terms of historical analogies. According to these, the gentry, much like its English counterpart, was a class of agrarian entrepreneurs who rejected the antiquated feudal structure mainly because it hindered the expansion of the market and limited their economic opportunities.[85] The analogy is appealing, but tenuous, for even in the opinion of sympathetic observers the gentry was a class in decline, if not teetering on the verge of economic ruin.[86] This decline is not only evident from the cold figures relating to indebtedness and diminishing acres, but also from the perusal of private records and other biographical materials. From these, the leading public figures of the age emerge not as prosperous squires anxious to secure their share of the market, but as marginal landowners who were plagued by pecuniary problems and who devoted as much of their time to evading obstreperous creditors as they did to saving the fatherland. Among the major political figures of the age Eötvös had grave problems in making ends meet, and in one particular period of his life he was forced to move from the house of one friend to another because he was unable to afford a place of residence.[87] Szemere, a future prime minister of the country and member of a family whose lineage was presumed to go back to one of the ancient Magyar chieftains, "lived in oppressive and melancholy poverty."[88] The great Kossuth's finances were notoriously murky. "In one prolonged period of his life," one of his recent biographies states, "his personal docu-

---

[85] This analogy has been popular with writers of different methodological and ideological persuasion. Among conservatives it found favor with Hóman and Szekfű (*Magyar történet*, v), László Ungár ("A magyar polgári osztály"), and B. G. Iványi ("From Feudalism to Capitalism"). Among the Marxists and quasi-Marxists, Gyula Mérei, *Mezőgazdaság és agrártársadalom Magyarországon, 1791-1848* [Agriculture and agrarian society in Hungary] (Budapest: Teleki Pál Társaság, 1948), Erik Molnár et al., *Magyarország története* [History of Hungary] (Budapest: Gondolat, 1971), especially ı, 408-438; Z. Pál Pach, *Magyar gazdaságtörténet*, especially ı, 260-270. For a more critical view of the problem, see Mályusz, "A reformkor nemzedéke," and István Barta, "A magyar polgári reformmozgalom." Despite ritualistic references to the "bourgeois" character of the reform movement, this last essay shows remarkable insight into the methodological shortcomings of conventional historiography.

[86] Ballagi, *A nemzeti államalkotás kora*, p. 71.

[87] For Eötvös' finances in his early years, see Zoltán Ferenczi, *Báró Eötvös József* [Baron Joseph Eötvös] (Budapest: Tudományos Akadémia, 1903), pp. 47-48.

[88] Szekfű, *Három nemzedék*, p. 96.

64

ments contain nothing but evidence for financial difficulties. They consist of overdue promissory notes, and letters discussing overdue loans with impatient creditors."[89] At one time early in his career he had even been accused of misappropriating public funds, and though this charge was never proved, it continued to cast a shadow over his public life. Likewise, both Kölcsey and Deák experienced financial difficulties. Kölcsey was forced to seek salaried employment with his county, while Deák had to stay away from one Diet for lack of funds, even though he owned 810 acres of land, including 164 acres of the best Transdanubian vineyards.[90] Indeed, so nagging were the financial problems of most parliamentarians that it had become a standard practice of the Crown to rid itself of its most cantankerous critics by bribing them with public office or other emoluments. As cases in point, Thomas Ragály and Abraham Vay, after acting as key members of the opposition, accepted lucrative posts on the staff of the Royal Chancellor; and the fiery Paul Felsőbüki-Nagy, the scourge of royal tyranny, retired from politics in 1834 after having been appointed by the Crown to act as the executor of the huge Pálffy estate.[91] Thereafter, liberal deputies at the Lower Table decided to swear a solemn oath at the opening of each legislative session not to accept office or funds from the Crown during the tenure of the Diet, a custom that well attests to the financial plight and temptations that the leaders of the common nobility had to face.

The hypothesis concerning the entrepreneurial character of the gentry is also belied by the ways in which the liberal ideology of the West came to be reinterpreted in Hungary, after an initial burst of rhetorical enthusiasm. In the core area of Europe where it was born, liberalism did indeed originate with a class of agrarian entrepreneurs and merchants who, in their historical moment of success, wanted to be free to pursue their affairs without any outside protection or interference. The result was a doctrine built around the idea of personal freedom and the emancipation of the individual from the authority of the state. Not so in Hungary and in other societies of the European periphery, where liberalism became the ideology of a class desperately searching for alternatives to economic entrepreneurship. This class was ready to dispense with its erstwhile feudal privileges because they impeded this search. But at the same time, it wanted to strengthen rather than weaken the modern state, so that it could afford protection

[89] Barta, *A fiatal Kossuth*, p. 24.

[90] Zoltán Ferenczi, *Deák Ferenc élete* [The life of Francis Deák] (Budapest: Tudományos Akadémia, 1904), II, 226.

[91] Ballagi, *A nemzeti államalkotás kora*, p. 283.

65

against the vagaries of the market, and, as a last resort, provide the bankrupt landowner security of employment in its bureaucracy and political institutions. This is not to say that the issues of personal freedom and individual rights were irrevocably thrown overboard. But in the years to come, concern for these issues was overshadowed by a mounting interest in the unification of the state, its modernization, and its emancipation from foreign, imperial tutelage.

If one contrast between the liberals of East and West was in terms of the social character of the protagonists, another was in terms of the problems they faced in their respective societies. The societies of the West were, on the whole, advancing economically due to technological innovation and a self-sustaining process of saving and reinvestment. There, the chief problem for liberals was how to absorb the social consequences of economic change within the political institutions of the countries. In contrast, Hungary and her neighbors on the European periphery were economically backward countries where liberals faced the problem of creating a modern society and of generating economic change. Here, the classical liberal injunction of laissez-faire seemed to offer little practical guidance. Even so, for some time Hungarian liberals did profess to be disciples of Adam Smith, and their early economic programs merely echoed Széchenyi's pleas for the abolition of the laws of entail, serfdom, and the customs frontier between Austria and Hungary. But then matters changed. In 1841, Friedrich List published his *Das nationale System der politischen Oekonomie*, and this work, with its advocacy of protectionism and national autarchy, became an instant success in Hungary, so much so that in 1842 List visited Pest to receive an enthusiastic public welcome. Almost overnight, the liberals abandoned their earlier call for free trade and became the exponents of an autonomous customs area to protect Hungarian economic interests.

No less momentous was the fact that, under the influence of List, the liberals abandoned not only the principles of laissez-faire and the concept of organic evolution popularized by Széchenyi, but also his emphasis on the development of agriculture. As a student of English history, Széchenyi had not been against industrialization, but he firmly believed that industrial development had to be preceded by the rise of capital-intensive farming. Also, Széchenyi the landowner was deeply concerned that the reversal of these priorities might be damaging to the interests of his own class, while as a loyalist he was fearful that protectionism within the empire might embitter relationships between Austria and Hungary. None of this particularly concerned the liberals, who as representatives of a prospective political class had their eyes not only on economic development, but also on national independence, power, and prestige. "Anyone," wrote the liberal Kossuth in the ensuing round of public polemics, "who interprets the term 'nation' according to the criteria of the nineteenth century, must be aware of the fact that those who do not possess the independent levers of civilization are only a people, or race, but cannot be treated as a nation. Among these levers, the most significant ones are trade and the manufacturing industries. Without them one can exist as a country, but not as a nation. And we Hungarians want to be considered as a nation by standards set by the present century."[92]

Or, as he reminisced during his self-imposed exile some forty years later: "While in captivity [in 1837-1840, for an offense against the restrictive press laws], I was oft thinking about the prerequisites of social welfare. Already then I was convinced that a nation engaged in the cultivation of land only is a kind of one-armed being. Furthermore, the usefulness of this one arm is dependent on the caprice of the weather. . . . So, whichever way I looked upon the problem, I came to the conclusion that the development of industry was a burning necessity for our country, for its general welfare, indeed, for the prosperity of the agricultural economy."[93]

The full-fledged economic program of the liberals appeared in a lengthy memorandum submitted to the Commercial Commission of the Diet in 1843. The authors of this document, among them Louis Kossuth, repeated Széchenyi's complaints about their country's backwardness, but their analysis of its causes and the cure they proposed were quite different from Széchenyi's. The country's economic plight, they wrote, was mainly due to its "colonial dependence" on Austria, the absence of technically trained personnel, and "the existence of social and political institutions diametrically opposed to industrial interests."[94] In the cities, the memorandum continued, the growth of manufacturing industries was stifled by the selfishness of guild masters and by feudal law that prevented non-noble manufacturers from owning the property on which their factories were built. As a general solution, the memorandum suggested the "development of a national industry by all the social and political means available," then added

---

[92] *Hetilap*, No. 1 (1846). Quoted in Endre Arató, "A magyar nacionalizmus kettős arculata" [The two faces of Hungarian nationalism] in Erzsébet Andics, ed., *A magyar nacionalizmus kialakulása és története* [Formation and history of Hungarian nationalism] (Budapest: Kossuth, 1964), p. 89.

[93] *Pesti Napló*, No. 97 (February 21, 1885).

[94] Mihály Futó, *A magyar gyáripar története* [History of Hungarian manufacturing industries] (Budapest: *Magyar Gazdaságkutató Intézet*, 1944), p. 189.

seven specific recommendations: that factories in royal free boroughs be exempt from guild regulations; the assessment and levy of taxes on industrial property be made uniform throughout the country; new factories be granted subsidies; that a polytechnical institute be established at Pest; skilled workers be recruited from foreign countries; a patent law be adopted by parliament; and that industrialists be granted the same status in civil courts as the nobility of the country.[95]

When, as expected from the beginning, these proposals foundered on the resistance of the Crown and the Table of Magnates, Kossuth and his associates organized the first Hungarian boycott of Austrian manufactured goods. "Under different conditions we would have resorted to the instrument of the protective tariff for the advancement of national welfare. However, under the present conditions, our only hope lies in the tenacity of our fellow citizens. Since we cannot establish customs protection on our borders, we will have to set up ramparts at the thresholds of our own homes."[96] These words by Maurice Szentkirályi at the county assembly of Pest introduced the so-called Protective Association (Védegylet), whose members were expected to pledge themselves not to buy foreign manufactured articles for a period of six years. Within a few months, the founders collected over one hundred thousand pledges. This number was too low to have a genuine impact on foreign trade, but high enough to worry the Austrian government, and justly so, for the association united different factions of the liberal nobility under the respectable slogan of economic development. "It is incomprehensible to me," wrote Kossuth in the fall of 1844, "how anyone could refuse to support such harmless, and purely economic objectives."[97] Metternich was of a different opinion. In a memorandum to the emperor he wrote that the admitted objective of the association was absurd, while its concealed purpose amounted to high treason.[98]

If backwardness transformed the economic doctrine of liberalism, the ethnic fragmentation of Hungarian society made a shambles out of the original liberal formula for the relationship between the nation and the state. This formula emerged from the historical experiences of France, where the state was the product of nationhood in that it had come into being in its broad outlines from a desire for unity on the part of a multitude of Frenchmen living under the jurisdiction of different feudal entities. The process of building the modern state was thus more or less tantamount to the unification and centralization

[95] Ibid.   [96] Horváth, Huszonöt év, III, 8.
[97] Kossuth, "Open Letter to the Public," in Futó, A magyar gyáripar, p. 206.
[98] Clement Metternich, "Aphoristische Bemerkungen" in Rudolf Sieghart, Zolltrennung und Zolleinheit (Vienna: Manz, 1915), p. 160.

of these provinces, all of them inhabited by people speaking the same language. This formula was eagerly embraced by the liberals of Germany and Italy, as well as of the smaller Slavic and Rumanian communities of southeast Europe, mainly because in each of these areas the application of the ethnic principle to political organization held out the prospect of a larger, more populous, and powerful territorial entity. In Hungary, too, liberals boldly adopted the slogan of national unification, and defined it as the administrative unification of Transylvania, Croatia-Slavonia, and the Military Frontier with the Kingdom of Hungary proper. They did so even though the liberal formula was of little relevance in Hungary, for here the historical state was a multinational entity, a small empire itself within the larger imperial unit. The problem was that the unification of these hitherto autonomous territorial entities would have diminished, rather than increased, the ethnic character of the national state. Conversely, the strict application of the ethnic principle would have reduced the population, territory, and international prestige of the state. This created an obvious dilemma for Hungarian liberals, especially because they were members and representatives of a prospective political class whose interests and identity were closely intertwined with the power and prestige of the territorial state. As a "state bourgeoisie" in the making, the liberals could not well be expected to preside over the diminution or truncation of the territorial unit whose management would provide them with social status, purpose, and security. In their bewilderment, some Hungarian liberals merely engaged in wishful thinking about a unitary state that the Slavic and Rumanian populations would accept "in gratitude" for the legal and political rights to be bestowed upon them by liberal reforms.[99] But others were more realistic, and from their realism there emerged gradually the outlines of a new formula that assigned historical primacy to the state over the nation, arguing that the state was not so much a product as a producer of national sentiment. By 1841, when Széchenyi challenged the country to a grand debate on nationality, for most liberals the question was not whether the state should be an instrument for building the nation, but whether it should function as a cultural, or as an administrative and coercive instrument.

Moderates and Radicals

From its inception until some time after 1848 the Hungarian liberal movement failed to acquire coherent structure and internal discipline.

---

[99] Ferenc Pulszky, *Meine Zeit, mein Leben* (Pressburg and Leipzig: C. Stampfel, 1883), II, 283.

The very term "liberal" was loosely applied,[100] and competed with the politically more neutral "patriotic" and "progressive" designations. True, in 1839, some members of the Diet formed a Reform Club (so named after its British counterpart), and the parliamentary caucus was broadened into an Opposition Circle in 1847, with a common platform and a steering committee to coordinate the campaign of liberal candidates for the forthcoming elections. But in both caucus and circle, there remained conspicuous divisions, between a dwindling number of moderates and an increasing number of radicals whose changing fortunes largely reflected the pauperization and mobilization of the nobility in this age of explosive socioeconomic change.

The moderates, who dominated the movement during its first decade, drew their leaders from an established local squirearchy which for centuries had taken a leading role in the affairs of the county and of the Lower Table of the national Diet. Steeped in the traditions of feudal constitutionalism, these leaders—among them Francis Kölcsey, the Calvinist Baron Wesselényi (who, by virtue of the location of his estates was the leader of the Transylvanian movement), and the impressive Francis Deák, the pride of the nobility of western Hungary—never ceased to warn that the purpose of reforms was "not to destroy the nobility, but to elevate the masses,"[101] that the "new laws should combine the interests of all estates,"[102] and that they should not merely reflect numerical majorities but also a consensus among the parties to the original social contract, the Crown, the aristocracy, and the common nobility. But more important than tradition was the fact that their constituents continued, however tenuously, to maintain their grip on their estates, and at this particular historical moment they still had something to lose, which made them reluctant to take undue political risks. Indeed, although they were ready to embark on the road to institutional reform, they were as fearful of antagonizing the Crown as they were of provoking a peasant rebellion, by either irresponsible agitation or signs of dissension among the ranks of the nobility. Their dilemmas and fears were well expressed in a letter written by Deák to the poet Vörösmarty on the eve of the opening of the Diet of 1832:

> What will the forthcoming Diet bring us? This question is on the minds of all who dare to think and are able to do so. Some are

[100] As Pulszky notes, while the term "liberal" had been widely used "until 1840 it had only meant that one was at loggerheads with the government, gave up the hope of holding public office, exposed oneself to harassment and denunciations, and had difficulty in obtaining a passport." Ibid., I, 207.

[101] From Barta, "A magyar polgári reformmozgalom," p. 330.

[102] From Barta, A fiatal Kossuth, p. 165.

stubbornly defending the ossified privileges of an oligarchy, and would rather see nine million people live in continued misery than accept even the slightest change in our institutions. Others have become so frightened by recent events [the cholera rebellion] that they are willing to promise anything, or more than what they can ever hope to deliver. They do great harm because out of their promises the common folk build golden castles of hope, and when these hopes are disappointed, for they can only be disappointed by the Diet, they will take up arms once again.[103]

The radical faction first gained national visibility at the Diet of 1839, and continued to grow as political awareness increased among the 100,000, or so petty noblemen. If beforehand this petty nobility had participated in politics mainly as clients and retainers of big land-owners, now these relationships between patron and client were shaken loose by social decay, economic development, and the rudiments of education among this class of privileged freeholders and landless noblemen. "Hitherto," wrote the liberal deputy Pálóczi-Horváth in the 1830s, "the petty nobility had accepted the lead of large landowners. But now, they are often ready to make common cause with the taxpaying people, appear in the assemblies on their own, and influence the proceedings by exercising the *ius vocis publicae*."[104] The validity of this observation seems to be corroborated by a number of political pamphlets after 1840 concerning the "sandalled," "pipe-smoking" (*pipás*), and "seven-plum-tree" (*hétszilvafás*) nobles, and by steady reports of their rambunctiousness in and out of the county assemblies.[105]

The backbone of the radical faction nevertheless consisted of the rising noble intelligentsia, of those *gens de lettres et de lois* who so frequently occupy the center of the political stage at dramatic moments of history. The two most conspicuous figures of the faction, Louis Kossuth and Joseph Eötvös, certainly fit this designation, for the one was a lawyer who earned his fame as a journalist, while the other was an impoverished baron who made his living as a poet, novelist, and pamphleteer. Both were members of a rising class of professional politicians, who now began to converge on the city of Pest, trans-

---

[103] Ibid., p. 119.

[104] From Mályusz, "A reformkor nemzedéke," p. 52.

[105] A good example for this literature is Ábrahám Szücs, *A pipás nemesek véleménye az adó, háziadó, örökváltság, hitel, ősiség, és a magyar nyelv iránt* [The opinion of pipe-smoking nobles on matters of taxation, the house tax, redemption, credit, entail, and the use of the Magyar language] (Kecskemét: Szilády, 1844). For references to this literature and some of the incidents, see Ballagi, *A nemzeti államalkotás kora*, Hóman and Szekfű, *Magyar történet*, v, 346-347.

forming it into a center of national culture and public opinion. Among their supporters, we find the segment of the noble middle class that had already lost its nexus with land, and was now seeking refuge in the professions, the arts, and in the few salaried positions of the county. In the words of Aurél Dessewffy, a distinguished observer of the contemporary scene: "The radical faction is weaker than its voice seems to indicate. The clergy, the aristocracy and even the substantial [common] nobility stay away from it and . . . in view of this the leading role in the party is played by 1) the magistracy of the county, i.e. those who, by virtue of their office are always present at the assemblies; 2) those landowners who aspire to gain public office; 3) nobles whose livelihood is already provided by public office; 4) the lawyers; 5) the gallery, i.e. the youth of the county."[106] For obvious material and social reasons, this element had little patience with the gradualism of Kölcsey or the nitpicking legalism of Deák, and, instead of seeking to secure the consensus of all the estates, they were ready to change the political order, in Kossuth's oft quoted words, "with or without, if need be against,"[107] the will of the Crown and the aristocracy. Instead of the cautious, step-by-step approach of the moderates they wanted to see reforms "now or never," and raised their voices to an angry crescendo, sometimes threatening, sometimes cajoling, sometimes conjuring up the image of an all-engulfing peasant *jacquerie* to intimidate their opponents. So it seemed that with their entry onto the political stage, Széchenyi's hopes for a "silent reform" were dashed forever. In the place of quiet parliamentary arguments, the country was now treated to denunciations of "damnable" (*átkos*) Austria, of greedy magnates, and of intractable national minorities who resisted liberal efforts to introduce Magyar as the official language of the country.

With the growing desperation of the reformers, not only the volume and the tone but also the substance of public discourse changed. The moderates and Széchenyi were always proud to have addressed themselves to the mind, by appealing to reason and the enlightened self-interest of their constituents. It was in this spirit that Széchenyi had argued with his peers "to reform while we can of our own free will,"[108] or that Deák had exhorted the landed middle class to save itself by making prudent concessions to the lower estates of the population. In contrast, the leaders of the radicals made a point to "speak to the heart," that is, to appeal to the moral sensibilities of their audience,

[106] Aurél Dessewffy, *Elmélkedés*, p. 204.

[107] István Barta, ed., *Kossuth Lajos az utolsó rendi országgyülésen* [Kossuth at the last Diet of the estates] (Budapest: Akadémia, 1951), p. 332.

[108] Széchenyi, *Hitel*, p. 463.

playing on the themes of guilt and shame. True to this principle, Kossuth's articles in *Pesti Hírlap* (*The Pest News Herald*) were full of gruesome reports of public floggings and other indignities inflicted upon the common people, often coupled with dire warnings that it was by such practices that the civilized world was judging Hungary. "The whiplash has long been abolished even in the colonies," he exclaimed in one of his famous editorials. "Are we going to remain more backward than Jamaica?" he queried, adding petulantly: "How long are we going to wait?"[109] The writings of Eötvös, likewise, were impassioned pleas for change that used the technique of hyperbole to evoke a sense of embarrassment or fear. While one of his novels, *The Notary of the Village*,[110] is a sardonic comment on the backwardness of Hungarian public institutions that made the country the laughing-stock of the civilized world, another, *Hungary in 1514*,[111] is a blood-curdling story of lordly injustice, culminating in the great peasant uprising of the sixteenth century and the torture execution of the peasant leader Dózsa by an insanely vindictive nobility. These novels are bluntly political. Indeed, in many ways, they are the literary extensions of Eötvös' pamphlets devoted to the many causes célèbres of the age (if not of liberals of all ages): the political emancipation of the masses, the legal equality of religious minorities, the rights of tenants (in Hungary and in Ireland), the abolition of corporal punishment, and the reform of penitentiaries.[112] As such, Eötvös' novels may well be regarded as forerunners of Chernyshevsky's "critical realism," if not the "socialist realism" of an even later day. As in the latter, the characters are neatly divided between the good and the evil, and if the good are not always flawless—like the serf Viola in the *Notary*, who was forced to become an outlaw by a corrupt local administration—they are victims of an unjust social order that leaves them with few real choices in life.

These shrill voices were not merely the products of frustration,

---

[109] *Pesti Hírlap*, No. 26 (March 31, 1841).

[110] József Eötvös, *A falu jegyzője* [The notary of the village] (Pest: Hartleben, 1845).

[111] József Eötvös, *Magyarország 1514-ben* [Hungary in 1514] (Pest: Heckenast, 1847). For an English language comment on Eötvös' novels, see Paul Bödy, *Joseph Eötvös and the Modernization of Hungary, 1840-1870* (Philadelphia: Transactions of the American Philosophical Society, 1972), pp. 44-45.

[112] Apart from his major programmatic statement, *Die Reform aus Ungarn* (Leipzig: Köhler, 1846), Eötvös wrote the following political pamphlets: "Vélemény a fogházjavitás ügyében" [An opinion on the improvement of jails], *Báró Eötvös József összes munkái* [Eötvös' collected works] Budapest: Révai, 1904), xii, 3-37; "Szegénység Irlandban" [Poverty in Ireland], pp. 38-108; "A zsidóság emancipátiója" [The emancipation of Jewry], ibid., pp. 109-158; and the series "Teendőink" [What is to be done?] published originally as six articles in *Pesti Hírlap* between May 13 and November 25, 1847.

anguish, and status desperation. They were part of an overall radical design to mobilize the public in the struggle for political reform. To woo the public, the Crown and the conservatives were using money and patronage, commodities that the radical intelligentsia did not possess. So they countered with a barrage of words, delivering their message through pamphlets, novels, and the press, which was fast becoming an effective political instrument. The most conspicuous example of the use of this medium was the daily *Pesti Hírlap* which, under Kossuth's general editorship, acquired 5,000 regular sub-scribers and reached an estimated 100,000 readers,[113] an impressive number in a country where the number of literate people was under a million and the electorate numbered 136,000 voters. And if the more sophisticated segment of the public was to be reached via the press, the message was delivered to the less sophisticated, in Széchenyi's exasperated words, "by peddling it from county to county."[114] Kossuth proudly acknowledged this charge, adding that in a single year (1842) "the country had seen more rallies than all the meetings and political banquets of Great Britain."[115]

The term "public," however, carried different connotations for dif-ferent people, and those differences not only set Kossuth and Eötvös apart in the political arena, but made them into bitter rivals. For Kossuth, a man of supremely pragmatic bent, the public meant above all the electorate, the 136,000 voters whom he wanted to mobilize in the service of the liberal cause. In order to accomplish this task, he did what comes naturally to all professional politicians, and attempted to win their confidence by playing on their hopes and fears. Thus, to the chagrin of many latter-day radicals, Kossuth not only cajoled and threatened, but also heaped extravagant praise on the nobility, prom-ising to protect their lives, limbs, and vital interests. The essence of Kossuth's message to his peers was that while the nobility would have to surrender its traditional political monopoly, it would be allowed to maintain its corporate identity and to play an important role in the life of the nation. The nobility, Kossuth never tired of reiterating, could not be the "lord and master," but it could be the leader of the nation,[116] not only figuratively but in reality as a class of professional politicians. For, as Kossuth would reassure his followers in 1848,

[113] Ballagi, *A nemzeti államalkotás kora*, p. 510.

[114] Viszota, *Széchenyi vitája*, I, cxv.

[115] Lajos Kossuth, *Felelet Gróf Széchenyi Istvánnak* [Response to Count Stephen Széchenyi] (Pest: Landerer és Heckenast, 1842), pp. 40-41.

[116] István Barta, ed., *Kossuth Lajos összes munkái* [Collected works of Kossuth] (Bu-dapest: Akadémia, 1951), IX, 334.

"while the plebeians would be given the right to vote," they would, "much like in ancient Rome, continue to send patricians to the legislature."[117]

If Kossuth spoke incessantly *about* the people but *to* the nobility, Eötvös was inclined to do the very opposite. For whatever personal reasons, Eötvös was a man deeply alienated from his peers, and instead of raising their political consciousness, he attempted to carry his message to the oppressed people directly. This message, replete with charges of noble corruption and degeneracy, found favorable reception among a handful of young writers—some of them, like Petőfi, commoners; others, like the future novelist Maurus Jókai, noblemen who were ready to drop their titles inspired by Eötvös' lofty humanism. But the large majority of the electorate was hostile, while the "masses" were uncomprehending. Indeed, from a practical political point of view, their very existence was a figment of the imagination, a misplaced analogy from the experience of France and England. The bourgeoisie was foreign in culture, the peasantry still illiterate, and decades away from the most rudimentary elements of political awareness. This became painfully clear in the summer of 1848 when the vast majority of newly enfranchised voters either stayed away from the polls, or else exercised their rights under instructions from priests and landlords.[118] But even before, there were ominous signs of political isolation. When, in 1844, after intricate legal, financial, and political maneuvers, the editorship of *Pesti Hírlap* passed from Kossuth to Eötvös, within a year the paper lost not less than 90 percent of its subscribers and readers.[119] Hungary, quite obviously, was not yet ready for popular radicalism.

The political chasm between Eötvös and Kossuth further deepened on account of their respective views of the nation and the national state. For Kossuth, of course, ethnicity was a quintessential component of nationhood, a definition Eötvös rejected on the grounds of higher principles. Not that Eötvös would accept Széchenyi's traditionalist view of the nation as a moral and religious entity. Rather, under the in-

[117] *Pesti Hírlap*, No. 24 (April 19, 1848).

[118] "Even in Pest," complained *Pesti Hírlap* in June 1848, "the gathering place of the country's intellect, only one-third of all eligible voters registered" (*Pesti Hírlap*, No. 95, June 22, 1848). In the countryside, indifference was even greater. In Félegyháza, only 95 of the 1,508 voters appeared at the polls. In Cegléd, an estimated 2,200 were eligible; 772 registered and 310 voted. In nearly one-half of the constituencies elections were unanimous, mainly because the voters followed the advice of the priest. See György Spira, *A magyar forradalom 1848-49-ben* [The Hungarian revolution in 1848-1849] (Budapest: Gondolat, 1959), p. 209.

[119] Bödy, *Eötvös*, p. 38.

fluence of his personal friend de Tocqueville, Eötvös was inclined to see the nation as a perfectly rationalized form of human association, sustained not so much by primordial solidarities as by the enlightened self-interest of its members. And if Kossuth accepted the nation as the highest form of political organization to which the individual owed his loyalty, Eötvös tried to accommodate national loyalties with loyalties to a larger, supra-national community. Such a community, Eötvös seems to have believed, would either arise out of the legacy of the French Revolution, or else could be created by rationalizing the structure of the Habsburg empire. This is the idea that would preoccupy Eötvös for most of his career after the abortive revolution of 1848.[120]

If these ideas did not endear Eötvös to his contemporaries, his views on the state struck the final blow to his prospects as a national political leader and earned him his reputation for political dogmatism. At issue here was the idea of a centralized and bureaucratized system of public administration, inspired by the example of contemporary France. The French system of public administration, to be sure, was popular with many Hungarian liberals, not least of all because it promised vastly expanded employment opportunities based on education and merit, rather than election, connections, or heredity. But if many favored a system of bureaucratized administration over and above the dilettantish governance of the county with its lay assessors and elected administrators, in the short run most liberals still defended the old system on the time-honored ground that it was the most important line of defense against dynastic encroachments on constitutional government. Consequently, the majority of reformers was in agreement that, however important an issue, the modernization of public administration would have to wait until such time as Hungary became an independent country, or, more plausibly, until her constitutional status was further clarified within the larger Habsburg realm.

This tactical argument did not appeal to Eötvös, who regarded the county as the very symbol of "medieval barbarism" (and made it the prime target of his ire in his *Notary of the Village*). In his opinion, the abolition of the county was not only one of many progressive measures, it was the precondition of any further progress, since a modern, centralized bureaucracy was not merely a neutral, administrative instrument, but also a political instrument for defending the rights of common people against subversion by insidious traditional and re-

---

[120] See especially Joseph (József) Eötvös, *Die Garantien der Macht und Einheit Österreichs* (Leipzig: Köhler, 1859). For a short summary of this work, Robert Kann, *The Multi-National Empire* (New York: Columbia University Press, 1950), II, 93-99.

gional interests. Much like American liberals of another century, Eötvös was deeply concerned with the influence of wealth over numbers, and, alternately, with the oppression of minorities by local majorities. In fact, some of the arguments between the "municipalists" and the "centralists" could easily be mistaken for the civil rights debate in the United States during the 1950s and 1960s. As in the latter, there were occasional references to bureaucratic tyranny, a danger to which Eötvös was not entirely oblivious. He did treat the subject somewhat lightly, though, by assuring his audience that bureaucratic overbearance could be effectively checked by vigorous civic associations, parties, and a politically mobilized public.[121] As a general proposition, this argument was valid. But in backward Hungary, it would be a long time before such organizations and a politically aware public would arise. In their absence, Eötvös would live long enough to witness how a professionalized and politicized administrative system would preempt the development of a civic polity.

THE BOURGEOISIE: OLD AND NEW

The Decline of the Old

What was quite remarkable, but by no means inconsistent with the overall context of backwardness, was that the crisis of the agrarian classes was accompanied by a similar crisis of the commercial and industrial classes in the traditional urban communities. Indeed, while the Hungarian landowning classes had their moment of entrepreneurial glory during the Napoleonic wars, the decline of the urban bourgeoisie continued unabated as the "solid" and "industrious" burghers, with their particular religious and economic tradition, ignored new economic opportunities, and themselves fell prey to the styles of life that were ruining the gentry. Thus in 1807, at the height of the Napoleonic boom, when scores of noble families could easily match the amount, only eight members of the established merchant and manufacturing guilds had incomes in excess of 20,000 Fls.,[122] and no one in the guilds of Pest earned more than 15,000 Fls.,[123] even though the city was the center of the new, burgeoning wool and grain trade. Not surprisingly, economic stagnation was accompanied by demographic decline and by a steady flow of population from the cities to the counties. If in 1787, 5.78 percent of the population lived

---

[121] Eötvös, *Die Reform aus Ungarn*, especially pp. 112-113.
[122] Schwartner, *Statistik*, I, 41.
[123] Budapester Handels- und Gewerbekammer, *Beiträge*, p. xix.

in the royal free cities, in 1837 this proportion was only 5.09 percent.[124]

Many of those who left the cities followed in the footsteps of the younger generation of the nobility, and sought livelihood in the professions, the sciences, and the arts, a step which in their case was more agonizing because it raised the need for linguistic and cultural assimilation. Nevertheless, as one distinguished German intellectual noted in 1830: "For some time now, a hundred or so young men graduate from our gymnasia who speak flawless Magyar, and are imbued with a Hungarian patriotism that might soon affect the entire [ethnic] character of the fatherland."[125]

There was, of course, a native German culture in the country. But the educated public and the growing nationwide audience for the arts and literature were outside the narrow confines of the walled cities, a prospect not lost on young, and upwardly mobile, urban residents. Thus while traditionally the makers of Magyar culture and the practitioners of the sciences and arts had been ethnic Hungarians, many of them from the Calvinist communities, from the 1830s onward we encounter a new social phenomenon, a creative intelligentsia drawn from the Lutheran and other German communities. By 1840, the list of names was already in the hundreds.[126] It included, to name but a few well remembered by posterity, the writer Francis Toldy (Schedel), the historians Feszler and Henszlmann, the economist Andrew Thaisz, the professors Gustav Stencker, Békefi-Biegelbauer, and Palotai (Purgstaller) at the University of Pest, the composers Mátray (Rothkrepf), Szerelemhegyi (Liebenberger) and, not least of all, Franz Liszt, who prefaced the announcement of his first performance at Pest with the proud, if self-conscious words, "I am a Magyar."[127]

While the young, assimilated intelligentsia generally followed the leadership of the liberal gentry, the older generation that stayed behind in the cities retreated into a sullen economic and political conservatism, pleading for the protection of the Crown against the vagaries of the market and against the encroachments on their rights planned by the liberal nobility. In economics, the deputies of the cities were a perennial, and occasionally successful, lobby for the rights of the guilds, while in politics they were the staunchest opponents of institutional reform (save for periodic attempts to gain the same voting

[124] For 1787, see Danyl and Dávid, *Az első magyarországi népszámlálás*, pp. 50-51; for 1837, Fényes, *Statistika*, I, 118.

[125] Béla Pukánszky, *Német polgárság magyar földön* [German bourgeoisie on Hungarian soil] (Budapest: Franklin, 1936), p. 60.

[126] Ibid., pp. 32-61.

[127] Ibid., p. 45.

rights as enjoyed by the counties). This conservatism pitted the bourgeoisie not only against the Magyar gentry, but also against the young, assimilated intelligentsia, creating a deep conflict between generations that was most poignantly described in one of Toldy-Schedel's autobiographical novellas. In it the writer juxtaposed two cities, traditionalist Buda, the city of the German fathers, and progressive Pest, the city of the sons. Pest was the gathering place of the assimilated intelligentsia whose rashness the author condemned, but whose victory over German culture, specifically over the German theater of Buda, he described as inevitable.[128]

The Rise of the New

The retreat of the older generation of burghers into economic conservatism and the escape of the younger generation from entrepreneurship created a social vacuum. As is so frequently the case in backward societies, this vacuum was gradually filled by immigrants who were free from the social norms, pressures, and expectations that had ruined the classes raised on local soil. In Hungary and in several other countries of the European periphery, these immigrants were Jews who, from the last years of the eighteenth century, began to move into the lands of the Hungarian Crown in substantial numbers. Thus, whereas the census of 1787 found only 75,089 persons of Jewish faith (representing less than one percent of the population), in 1805 their number was already 127,816, and in 1842, 241,632, or 2.5 percent of the inhabitants of Hungary and Transylvania.[129]

Jewish immigration to Hungary followed two different routes. The large majority of immigrants came from the Polish provinces, whence the flow of people was facilitated by the Austrian annexation of Galicia in 1772-1775. Barred from the cities, most of the newcomers settled in villages in the northeast and central parts of the country, following closely the riparian and overland routes of the grain and wool trade.[130] At the same time, a much smaller but economically far more significant group entered the country from the western provinces of the empire. They brought with them not only entrepreneurial skills, but also capital and connections with the great banking houses of Vienna. In the following decades, this small group of money-managers would handle the short-term credit needs of large estates, and the long-term financial needs of the rising milling industry and transportation system of the country.

---

[128] "Buda és Pest," in Pukánszky, *Német polgárság magyar földön*, pp. 46-48.

[129] Fényes, *Statistika*, I, 82.

[130] Szekfű, *Három nemzedék*, pp. 157-159.

The rise of this new class of non-native entrepreneurs quite obviously did not go unnoticed by the native classes. Indeed, by 1830 or so it became one of the most salient public issues. As on all other great issues of the time, public opinion was divided, and these divisions more or less followed the political and ideological cleavages we examined in the previous pages.

Not surprisingly, perhaps, the stiffest resistance to the new immigrants came from the old bourgeoisie of the privileged, royal free cities. Most of these cities, of course, were German, but the antipathy of the bourgeoisie tended to transcend ethnic and religious boundaries. It was as evident in Catholic Pressburg as it was in Lutheran Kronstadt, or in the Calvinist and Magyar Debrecen. From all these places anxious voices were raised lest the economic competition of Jews, and the abolition of residential restrictions in the cities, result in the material ruin of the inhabitants. In the words of a frightened burgher, should the Jews be granted permission to settle in the cities, "they would, in no time, seize all the sources of well-being, own all the houses, and make the other merchants into their serfs."[131] However, the burghers were not alone in these anxieties for they were shared by all who dreamed of transforming the landed class into a class of entrepreneurs. Among this group we find Széchenyi, whose anti-Semitic pronouncements were numerous.[132] He warned repeatedly that if the Jews were emancipated and given the right to acquire land, the economically inexperienced and heavily indebted landed classes would lose their holdings to them.[133] In Széchenyi's views, the Jews were highly useful auxiliaries in advanced societies like England and France that already possessed entrepreneurial classes of their own. But in a backward country, like Hungary, they would monopolize the economy, and hence undermine its national character.[134]

If Széchenyi was opposed to both emigration and emancipation, the majority of his fellow aristocrats, including some of the most vociferous conservatives, were indifferent to the problem. Their intellectual leader, Count Aurél Dessewffy, "did not fear the Jews, and did not believe that they would threaten the interests of the nation."[135]

---

[131] Jenő Zsoldos, ed., *1848-1849 a magyar zsidóság életében* [1848-1849 in the life of Hungarian Jewry] (Budapest: Neuwald, 1948), p. 11.

[132] See Bárány, *Széchenyi*, pp. 357-360.   [133] Ibid.

[134] As he rather tersely explained in one of his oft quoted metaphors, in large countries Jews were like a drop of ink in a lake, but in Hungary they were like the same drop in a glass of water. See Antal Zichy, ed., *Széchenyi István beszédei* [Speeches of Stephen Széchenyi] (Budapest: Történelmi Társaság, 1887), p. 352.

[135] Béla Bernstein, *A magyar szabadságharc és a zsidók* [The Hungarian war of independence and the Jews] (Budapest: Franklin, 1898), p. 12.

Some aristocrats may have harbored personal grudges, but on the whole the great landowners saw Jews as performing useful economic functions as moneylenders, innkeepers, bailiffs, or accountants on the large estates. Yet the solution they envisaged to the problem was quintessentially feudal: instead of emancipation, they advocated the bestowal of corporate rights, and the recognition of the Jews as a separate estate.[136]

Among the liberals, there were a few who shared Széchenyi's suspicions and antipathies. Thus Kölcsey in his historic speech on the "State of the Taxpaying People of Szatmár," one of the rhetorical landmarks of the age, "could see no greater single cause for the impoverishment of the peasantry, than the rapid increase in the number of Jews."[137] Much like Széchenyi, he concluded that "the place of the Jews [was] in large and prosperous states, and not in small and poor ones, for while in the former they enhance[d], in the latter they retard[ed] the development of public diligence."[138] Gabriel Klauzál, among others, favored emancipation but wanted to couple it with new legal barriers against further immigration. Yet the vast majority of the liberals had more interest in political than in economic entrepreneurship, and thus felt relatively little concern about Jewish advances in trade, finance, and property ownership. Far from condemning these advances, they felt that Jewish economic skills and capital might provide a shortcut to economic modernization in the country. But apart from such economic considerations, the liberals also showed sympathy toward the Jewish immigrants because of their readiness to learn the Magyar language, and their apparent eagerness to be a part of the national culture. In the words of Charles Zay, one of the earliest apostles of forcible cultural and linguistic assimilation, "the Jewish people show[ed] daily and glorious examples of quick adaptation to the Magyar nation."[139] This eagerness compared favorably with the reluctance and traditional isolation of certain segments of the German bourgeoisie. Thus, the "real Jews," one radical journalist argued in 1848, were not the new immigrants from Poland, but the *Spiessbürger* who had come from Württemberg and Saxony centuries before, and during all this time had not "taken the trouble" to learn the language of the "sweet motherland."[140] Confronted with a choice between a Jewish and a German bourgeoisie, most of the liberals had no hesitation to opt for the former. "Watch your way, cousin!" a

[136] Zsoldos, *A magyar zsidóság*, p. 10.

[137] Ferenc Kölcsey, *Minden munkái* [Collected works] (Pest: Heckenast, 1866), IV, 51.

[138] Ibid.   [139] Bernstein, *A magyar szabadságharc*, p. 22.

[140] Zsoldos, *A magyar zsidóság*, p. 23.

popular pamphlet fulminated during the anti-Jewish riots of the German bourgeoise in 1848, "If the nation has to choose between the two of you, it will damn well know what to do and, before long, will send you packing back to Germany." The rest of the pamphlet is a single flow of abuse, showing how philosemitism could serve as a vehicle for expressing anti-German, nationalist sentiment. The author, Ignatius Benedek, called the burghers "uneducated Swabian louts, murderers, blood-suckers, hyenas, who attempt to murder the honor of the reborn fatherland in its very cradle, . . . godless heathens they, who harass the poor Jew in his life, and would deny him rest even in his grave."[141]

If ideology, economy, and nationalist raison d'être all combined to make the liberals sympathetic, this sympathy was expressed in the patronizing language of the age, accompanied by expectations of a certain quid pro quo. Thus while Kossuth argued for granting the Jewish inhabitants of the country the full rights of citizenship, he also added that in order to be fully accepted into the nation Jews would have to reform their religion, cast out its "antiquated" and obscurantist elements, and abandon those tenets of Mosaic law that might "conflict with the vital interests of a modern economy and state."[142] At the same time, there was an easily discernible undercurrent of feeling that, in exchange for citizens' rights and all the potential advantages of economic participation, Jews should renounce not only part of their cultural heritage but should also keep out of politics and administration, spheres reserved for the declining landed middle classes. The opponents of emancipation appealed to this sentiment when they conjured up the images of Jewish deputies and county magistrates. Even some of the protagonists of emancipation expressed the opinion that "since the Jews were born for trade, they should continue to sell their leather, wool and feathers, but should leave public administration alone, lest they antagonize the common citizen."[143]

Notwithstanding such ambivalence, the time seemed to be ripe for emancipation. The liberals were in favor, and the conservatives, with a few exceptions, were either indifferent or not actively opposed. Thus, as early as 1839, a committee of the Lower Table put a Bill of Jewish Rights on the agenda of the legislature. The draft of the bill was succinct. It consisted merely of an eloquent preamble and two brief articles. The first of these proposed the abolition of the traditional tolerance tax; the second stated that Jews should be granted all

[141] Ibid.
[142] Bernstein, *A magyar szabadságharc*, pp. 18-19.
[143] Zsoldos, *A magyar zsidóság*, pp. 19-20.

the legal rights already enjoyed by the non-noble inhabitants of the country. This bill was accepted by an overwhelming majority, forty counties voting for, twelve counties and most of the the cities voting against. The same bill was then introduced to the Magnates' Table by Aurél Dessewffy, and was cleared after some debate and certain textual changes specifying a number of the rights to be granted, among them the right to settle behind the walls of royal free cities and the right to be tenants of both urbarial and allodial parcels. (The ownership of rural property, we ought to remember here, had as yet been reserved for the members of the nobility and for corporate entities invested with noble rights, such as the Catholic church and the governing bodies of the cities.) Once the bill was passed, however, it was vetoed by the king after persistent lobbying from the cities, and was sent back to the Diet with specific royal recommendations. These recommendations were incorporated into the original bill, and while the final version (enacted as Public Law xxix/1840) retained many of the earlier stipulations, it banned Jews from seven particularly depressed mining cities, and left the issues of residency and property rights to the discretion of the councils of individual municipalities.

III.

Bureaucratic State and Neo-Corporatist Society, 1849-1905

HISTORICAL BACKGROUND

Revolution and Institutionalization

After more than twenty years in opposition the representatives of the liberal gentry and intelligentsia did at last establish themselves as a leading force in parliament during the deliberations of what turned out to be the last Diet of the Estates in 1847-1848. True, even then the liberals fell short of a clear-cut majority, and their ascendancy was not so much due to electoral success as to persistent fears of a peasant rebellion during the long and hungry winter of 1847, and, ultimately, to the news of the revolutions of Paris and Vienna in February-March, 1848.[1] On March 15 demonstrations took place in Buda and Pest and under their spell the Estates passed, and the king signed into law, an impressive array of acts (Public Laws II-xxx/1848) designed to change the economic, social, and political profile of the country.

Under the leadership of Kossuth and the liberals the Diet quickly dismantled the legal and economic structure of Hungarian feudalism as its very first order of business. In one giant sweep, six legislative acts (to be promulgated as Public Laws vIII-xIII/1848) abolished the corvée, the tithe, the tax exemption of the nobility, and the entailment of feudal estates, making the former serfs tenants of urbarial parcels (though not the cottage tenants on the *demesne*) owners of the lands they had held in fief from their masters. Communal grazing lands were divided between the seigneurs and the villages, while the *demesne* proper remained in the hands of the previous owners, more than half of the total acreage in the form of large and medium-sized estates.[2] For all expropriated land the former owners were to receive just compensation, though under the pressures of the moment no attempt

---

[1] For an excellent description of the panicky mood of the times, see Szabó, *Társadalmi és pártharcok*, pp. 108-109.

[2] In 1895, almost fifty years after the revolution, land in Hungary was distributed as follows:

84

was made to fix the mode and exact amount beyond placing future payments "under the protective shield of national honor."

The bulk of the legislation, however, addressed itself to political matters and was designed to modernize the institutions of the Hungarian state. The most important of these acts, Public Law III, abolished the Royal Chancellery and the Residential Council, replacing them with a cabinet headed by a prime minister (or minister president) and responsible to parliament. The same act dissolved the Diet of the Estates and replaced it with a bicameral National Assembly (*országgyűlés*) consisting of a House of Lords (*főrendiház*) and a House of Representatives (*képviselőház*). The former inherited the membership of the old Magnates' Table, though not all of its constitutional powers, for henceforth most important legislation, including all money bills, were to originate in the lower chamber, with the Lords retaining the rights of rejection and review. The structure of the lower chamber meanwhile underwent significant transformations. While the old Lower Table had been a motley gathering of delegations representing the counties, the royal free cities, and the lower orders of the Catholic clergy, the membership of its successor was elected uniformly from 466 (later 413) single member constituencies across the country. As to suffrage, Public Law V granted the right to vote to all male citizens over twenty years of age provided that they met at least one of the following qualifications: ownership of at least one-quarter session (6- 10 acres) of land or other property in the value of 300 Fls.; payment of at least 10 Fls. in direct taxes on their property or money income; completion of ten years of education or more; proof that they, or their patrilineal ancestors, had voted in any of the elections prior to 1848. This last census qualification produced a substantial, though ever dwindling, category of voters by "ancient right."[3] Altogether, some 600,000 citizens, or an estimated 6.5 percent of the general

Size of Property	Of All Land	Of All Proprietors
-5 (cadastral) acres	5.8%	53.4%
5-20	23.6	36.3
20-100	29.9	9.3
100-1000	15.4	.8
1000+	32.3	.2

See Mihály Kerék, *A magyar földkérdés* [The land problem in Hungary] (Budapest: Mefhesz, 1939), p. 63.

[3] In 1874, about one-fifth of the total number of voters, or 168,921, were registered by such right. (Országgyűlés, Képviselőház. *Napló* [Proceedings of the House of Representatives of the Hungarian National Assembly], 1874, XI, 373. From here on, cited as *Napló*.) By 1878 this number had declined to 101,600, and by 1900 to 32,752, due

population, became enfranchised. This figure, on par with the one for contemporary Britain, was subsequently (1874) reduced to 5.8 percent by raising the tax census for the owners of single dwellings. Thereafter, the proportion of voters to the general population remained more or less stationary with the owners of land forming the single largest category among them.[4]

The third, but by no means least significant, category of laws was enacted to unify the Hungarian state and to redefine its relationship to the other countries of the larger Habsburg realm. Public Laws VI and VII merged Transylvania and Hungary under a single government (leaving, for the time being, the status of Croatia and the Military Frontier regions undefined and somewhat ambiguous). The articles of Public Law III increased the autonomy of the Hungarian state vis-à-vis the larger imperial unit by establishing separate Hungarian ministries of Defense and Finance. Even more important than the letter of this law was the construction put on it by the cabinet of Louis Batthyány and its Minister of Finance Kossuth, who together with other ministers claimed jurisdiction over all military units stationed on Hungarian soil, demanded the right to issue currency through a Hungarian National Bank and the right to conduct the foreign affairs of Hungary.

Such an interpretation of Public Law III was in contravention of the stipulations and spirit of the Pragmatic Sanction of 1722 and was immediately challenged by the royal rescript of March 28, 1848. In it King Ferdinand took exception especially to the authority claimed by the Hungarian Ministry of Defense. In response, there were angry demonstrations all over the country, and a sharp note of protest from the Hungarian Diet. In view of these, as well as of the impending war in Italy and the rebellious mood of Vienna, the note was hastily withdrawn. But the Hungarian ministries of Defense and Finance remained insufferable thorns in the imperial flesh, and as the fortunes of war (in Italy) and of politics (in Austria proper) began to favor the Crown, and as the revolutionary mood of the Continent began to subside in the summer of 1848, the "camarilla" of dynastic legitimists

---

to changing values, fading memories, and the relatively cumbersome procedure involved in proving that one's ancestors had been lawfully registered to vote. *Annuaire Statistique Hongrois*, Nouveau Cours, VIII (1900), 389, and XIX (1911), 438.

[4] By 1905 the total number of voters had grown to 1,056,800. Of these, 63.9 percent were registered as owners of land, 4.09 percent as owners of houses, 20.26 percent as taxpayers possessing business and money income, 7.31 percent under the educational qualifications, 3.09 percent by ancient right, and 1.19 percent on "other grounds." See *Annuaire Statistique Hongrois*, XIX (1911), 438.

set out to win back the concessions made to the obstreperous Hungarians, first by fomenting an armed rebellion among the Serbian, Croatian, and Rumanian inhabitants of the country, then by dismissing the revolutionary government and by ordering the dissolution of the Hungarian parliament.

The ensuing conflict and war of independence need not be described here in particular detail. Suffice it to say that the Hungarian parliament defied the royal rescript of dissolution, and while Premier Batthyány's moderate cabinet resigned, its place was taken by a Committee of National Defense headed by Louis Kossuth and manned by the radical wing of the national party. With considerable skill and energy this committee put in the field a sizeable army which, between November 1848 and April 1849, not only repressed the rebellion of the nationalities, but also forced the retreat of the imperial army from the territory of the country. Inspired by such military success, Kossuth called for the dethronement of the House of Habsburg, and a rump parliament complied on April 14, 1849 by declaring the country's independence from Austria. Thereafter, however, the fortunes of war rapidly changed. General Radetzky defeated the Piedmontese and his regiments were soon redeployed in Hungary, to be joined by a large Russian expeditionary army sent by Tsar Nicholas I in defense of the principle of dynastic continuity. Vastly outnumbered and outgunned, the Hungarian main force retreated to the south of the country where it eventually surrendered to Prince Pashkievich, the commander in chief of the Russian expeditionary army.

Absolutism and Compromise

The surrender of the Hungarian national (*Honvéd*) army on August 13, 1849 was followed by months of harsh repression under the military administration of Baron Julius Haynau, the personal representative of the new emperor, Francis Joseph I. Kossuth and several members of the revolutionary government, together with five thousand officers and civilians, escaped the country and found refuge in the Ottoman empire. Of those who stayed in the country, some one hundred and fifty, including Prime Minister Batthyány and thirteen commanding generals, died on the gallows or before firing squads. Another 1,765 individuals were given stiff prison sentences to be served in Austrian dungeons. All junior officers of the national army and some 45,000 of its members were forcibly enlisted in Austrian regiments.[5] The rest of the population was subjected to various in-

---

[5] Sándor Márki, *Az 1848-49-ik évi szabadságharc története* [History of the war of independence of 1848-1849] (Budapest: Athenaeum, 1898), p. 343.

dignities: prominent individuals, among them several ladies of high society, were whipped in public for nationalist sympathies; public gatherings and theater performances were banned; the display of national colors, the wearing of national costumes, and even the sporting of Kossuth-style beards became punishable offenses.

In the summer of 1850 Haynau's military administration was dissolved and the former kingdom of Hungary was incorporated into the unitary administrative system of the empire. The Hungarian constitution was rescinded on the grounds that the nation had forfeited its historical rights by its act of disobedience. The territories of the Hungarian Crown were divided into four separate provinces—Hungary, Transylvania, Croatia-Slavonia, and a newly created Serbian Voivodina—and each of these in turn, was divided into a number of regions and districts superseding the old territorial divisions of the counties. The assemblies and officers of local government were dismissed. In their place came professional administrators recruited mainly from the German and Bohemian regions of the empire. The official language of the country became German with some concessions to the vernacular in each of the provinces and districts.

The new political order was bluntly autocratic or, in its own idiom, "absolutist" in character. The principles of this new order were set forth in a terse cabinet rescript (*Cabinetschrift*) in 1849, and were elaborated in somewhat greater detail in the Basic Charter of 1851. According to these two documents parliamentary institutions were to be abolished throughout the empire, the organs of government were to be solely responsible to the monarch, and the nine-member Reichsrat, called into being by imperial decree, was granted purely consultative functions. Emperor Francis Joseph, who fashioned these principles, took an active interest in the affairs of state. He closely supervised the conduct of both civilian and military affairs, presided over the cabinet meetings, and, after the death of Premier Felix Schwarzenberg in 1854, did not name a successor but assumed the duties of the office himself.

The counterrevolution destroyed the feeble beginnings of modern parliamentary government, but it did not attempt to reverse the trend toward social and economic reform. On the contrary, the policies associated with the name of Schwarzenberg and his Minister of Interior Alexander Bach were designed to raise Hungary to the level of Austria and the empire as a whole to the level of the West European countries. Thus in retrospect, even such an implacable critic as the socialist Karl Renner would later observe that "the years after 1850 were a period of sweeping administrative reform and comprehensive social legislation. Bach's organizational concept had only one, albeit fatal, weakness: it had been created by counterrevolution and not revolution, not democracy but bureaucracy was its instrument."[6]

Ironically, perhaps some of the most urgent tasks faced by this government concerned the implementation of the legislation passed by the revolutionary Hungarian parliament. First and foremost, the new regime had to arrange for the orderly transfer of titles from the old to the new landowners, and to work out a system of compensation whereby the Treasury assumed responsibility for the peasants' debts and paid landowners 310,000,000 Fls. (an average of 525 Fls. per urbarial parcel), to be delivered not in cash, but in inflated state bonds.[7] Simultaneously, the government implemented the revolutionary legislation concerning the reform of the tax system: the complex maze of feudal levies was abolished and replaced by a uniform system of land, house, and income taxes, together with an excise levied on tobacco, salt, and spirits, raising the revenues of the Treasury tenfold within a period of eight years.[8] Last but not least, the government undertook to reform the judicial and administrative systems by introducing the principles of the Austrian civil, administrative, and penal codes. Much despised by the Hungarian gentry, this system was nevertheless acknowledged to be more equitable than its predecessors even by embittered nationalist historians. "Under this system," wrote one of them, "not only the lords but the peasants, too, could find redress for their grievances."[9]

Such equitable handling of the public's business, however, contributed little to the overall popularity, legitimacy, and stability of the autocratic regime. In Hungary not only the gentry but the aristocracy and the smallholding classes, too, resented the foreign administrative system and the loss of constitutional government. The Slavs and Rumanians were hardly less resentful for, as a bitter adage of the times

[6] Rudolf Springer (Karl Renner), *Grundlagen und Entwicklungsziele der österreichischen Monarchie* (Vienna and Leipzig: F. Deuticke, 1906), pp. 37-38.

[7] This was clearly inspired by political considerations for in the Austrian parts of the empire one-third of the compensation was to be paid by the peasants themselves directly to the landowner in cash. See Gyula Bernát, *Az abszolutizmus földtehermentesítése Magyarországon* [The land redemption policies of the absolutist government in Hungary] (Budapest: Egyetemi Nyomda, 1935), pp. 29-30, 64-127. Also, Albert Berzeviczy, *Az abszolutizmus kora Magyarországon* [The age of absolutism in Hungary] (Budapest: Franklin, 1922), ii, 374.

[8] Karl Czoernig, *Österreichs Neugestaltung, 1848-1858* (Augsburg and Stuttgart: Crotta, 1858), pp. 530-532.

[9] Gusztáv Beksics, *I. Ferenc József és kora* [Francis Joseph I and his times] (Budapest: Athenaeum, 1896), p. 431.

had it, these peoples got as their reward what the Magyars had been given as their punishment, that is, membership in a large imperial unit that did little to acknowledge collective aspirations for nationhood and self-government.

Even so, during the 1850s there were few signs of open defiance to the regime. The most important of its opponents, the Magyar landowning class, withdrew to its estates and resisted "passively" by refusing to speak German, by growing illegal tobacco, and by accumulating substantial arrears in taxes. But in 1859 Austria became embroiled in a new war with Italy, and during that ill-fated campaign there were alarming signs of popular alienation and outright disloyalty. On the battlefields there were defections from the Magyar troops. A Magyar legion fought on the Italian side, while at home the public was openly rejoicing over Italian victories. And while the Magyars rejoiced and fantasized about the arrival of armies of liberation, the non-Magyar peoples displayed only apathy toward the ultimate fate of the empire.

The experiences of the Italian campaign led directly to a series of constitutional experiments, in the course of which the emperor attempted to save the centralized administrative structure of the empire by making concessions to the principles of representative government. Thus the Hungarian Diet, together with other diets and regional assemblies throughout the empire, was reconvened to select a delegation of representatives to a newly established all-imperial legislature. The Hungarians refused to comply. Their recalcitrance led to the collapse of the constitutional experiment and ushered in another period of absolutism (1861-1865) followed by yet another military defeat (1866), this time at the hands of Prussia. This latest of humiliations only underscored the glaring weaknesses of the imperial edifice, and accelerated negotiations between the emperor and the representatives of the Hungarian political establishment.

The *Ausgleich*, or Compromise, of 1867 that emerged from these negotiations was a compact between the emperor of Austria and the Hungarian nation, as represented by its parliament. In terms of this document (promulgated as Public Law xii of 1867), the territorial and constitutional integrity of Hungary was restored, the Austrian empire was transformed into an Austro-Hungarian Monarchy with its ruler, Francis Joseph I, assuming once again the separate titles of Austrian emperor and Hungarian king. The Hungarian state regained its freedom of action, except in matters pertaining to defense and foreign relations. The administration of these "common affairs," and of finances pertaining to them, was entrusted to three ministries, responsible neither to the Austrian nor to the Hungarian parliament, but to delegations representing both legislative bodies. Meanwhile, commercial policy, tariffs, the monetary system, railways, and the levy of indirect taxes were designated as "affairs of common concern," subject to decennial negotiations between the Austrian and the Hungarian governments. If the delegations could not agree, the conflict was to be arbitrated by the monarch. The customs frontier between the two halves of the Austro-Hungarian Monarchy, and the independent Hungarian National Bank (established during the revolution) were not restored, but they were designated as negotiable items. State debt and common expenditures were to be divided between Austria and Hungary by a ratio of seven to three, but this ratio, or quota, was to be renegotiated every ten years to reflect the relative economic potential of the two countries. In order to please the Magyars, in both halves of the Monarchy a token force of a few regiments (the *Honvéd* in Hungary and the *Landswehr* in Austria) were to remain under the jurisdiction of separate ministries of national defense. Otherwise, the imperial and royal army remained under the effective control of the common Ministry of War and of the monarch in his capacity as commander in chief.

As the Magyars demanded, Transylvania, the Voivodina, and the districts of the Military Frontier were integrated with the territory of Hungary proper. Relations between Croatia and Hungary were made subject to bilateral negotiations which, in 1868, produced a separate Hungarian-Croatian compromise modeled closely on the terms of the Austro-Hungarian agreement. This document provided for Croatian home rule, but designated finances, postal, and railroad administration as matters of common concern between Croatia and Hungary. Croatian contributions to Hungarian finances were to be renegotiated periodically. Legislative powers over local affairs were vested in a provincial assembly, while common affairs were to be handled by the Hungarian parliament, augmented for this purpose by a delegation of Croatian deputies with full voting rights. The Croatian chief executives, or *banus*, would be appointed by the king upon the advice of the Hungarian premier. These provisions granted the Croats a somewhat special status among the peoples of Hungary, analogous to the status enjoyed by the Poles of Galicia in the Austrian half of the Monarchy.

Institutions and Realities

The compromise of 1867 also restored the status of domestic, political, and social institutions largely to what it had been under the provisions of the constitutional legislation of 1848. Once again the country was to be governed by a cabinet under a prime minister, appointed by the king but responsible to a parliament consisting of a House of Lords and House of Representatives. The latter would be elected under a franchise that was narrow, but not much out of line with the electoral systems of other European countries. Indeed, the institutions and the rights of the citizenry followed closely certain foreign models, though they were also thoroughly consonant with local tradition, so much so that few constitutional lawyers or politicians of the time saw them as anything but the fruits of a prolonged process of organic development.

Nevertheless, these institutions—parliamentary government, the electoral system, equal property, and personal rights—were imposed on a society whose economic structure was relatively undifferentiated, whose members had expectations shaped by the experiences of the advanced nations, and whose elite had a teleological commitment to the idea of catching up with the material, intellectual, and administrative progress made by other European societies. These structural differences, expectations, and commitments would soon become the source of considerable strain, producing social, economic, and political outcomes that had been little anticipated in or before 1848. Thus instead of leading to political democracy, a capitalist market economy, and a society based on equal rights, in Hungary they resulted in a bureaucratic polity, a pseudo-market, and a neo-corporatist society in which rights continued to be commensurate with social function, while social function was less frequently assigned by merit than by heredity. The principal actors in this neo-corporatist society—the politicized bureaucrat, the neo-traditionalist landowner, and the ethnic entrepreneur—provide the chief points of contrast with the western social and political experience. At the same time, they provide the chief points of analogy between Hungary and the other societies of the European and extra-European periphery.[10]

BUREAUCRACY ASCENDANT

The Rise of Bureaucracy

The Compromise of 1867 not only restored the constitutional autonomy of Hungarian governments, it also opened up the way for the

---

[10] For ethnic entrepreneurship, the pseudo-market, and the bureaucratic polity, see especially Fred W. Riggs, *Administration in Developing Countries*, and Riggs, *Thailand, the Model of a Bureaucratic Polity* (Honolulu: East-West Center, 1966); for forms of cor-

creation of a modern and independent system of national administration. To this opportunity the Hungarian governments responded eagerly and as a matter of high priority. The motivation for doing so was twofold. First, there was a need to create an administrative infrastructure for the more complex and sophisticated society that was expected to arise under the aegis of national governments. Second, there were pressures for accommodating those segments of the landowning class and the educated public that had consistently supported the leadership of the liberal faction in politics.

The pressures of accommodating the economically marginal classes had been latent all through the age of reform, but they burst into the open instantly during the revolution of 1848. The first independent ministries had hardly hung out their shields when the newspaper *Március Tizenötödike* [Fifteenth of March] took note of "hundreds of jobhunters roaming the streets of the capital."[11] In reality, this number was not in the hundreds but in the thousands. On April 1, the Ministry of Finance already had 1,350 applications on file for about fifty new positions.[12] For a similar number of job openings, the office of the prime minister received no less than 1,642 applications.[13] Sympathizing with the plight of the applicants, the radical press coined the slogan "bread to the people, jobs to the lawyers,"[14] and demanded the screening of candidates for proper—liberal and radical—political credentials. Under the circumstances only a few of these candidates were accepted in the civil bureaucracy. The vast majority had to be satisfied with commissions in the newly formed National Guard, and, later, in the *Honvéd* army. "Where did all the radicals go?" one of their number, Paul Vasvári, mused in June 1848. "I'll tell you: some of them went into the bureau to take care of the affairs of the country. Others returned to their earlier pursuits and await better days. Yet others joined the army."[15] Four weeks later, Vasvári himself found a position

---

poratism in the modern world, see Philippe Schmitter, *Interest Conflict and Political Change in Brazil* (Stanford: Stanford University Press, 1971), and by the same author, "Still a Century of Corporatism," *Review of Politics*, No. 85 (January 1974); for instances of what has been referred to here as "neo-traditional" landownership, see Barrington Moore, Jr., *Social Origins of Dictatorship and Democracy*; for a classical treatment of the same problem: Constantin Dobrogeanu-Gherea, *Neoiobagia* [Neo-Serfdom] (Bucharest: Socec, 1910).

[11] *Március Tizenötödike*, April 17, 1848.

[12] Márki, *Az 1848-49-ik évi szabadságharc*, p. 31.

[13] Gyula Kéri, *A magyar szabadságharc napi krónikákban* [A day-by-day account of the Hungarian war of independence] (Budapest: Franklin, 1899), p. 296.

[14] György Spira, *A magyar forradalom 1848-49-ben*, p. 185.

[15] *Életképek*, No. 24 (June 4, 1848).

in the bureaucracy. At first he aspired for an adjunct professorship at the University of Pest, but Eötvös, the minister of education, remonstrated. Thus instead of the professorship, Vasvári was given a minor post in Kossuth's Ministry of Finance, in recognition of his past political services as one of the leaders of the "parliamentary youth."[16]

The same tumultuous scenes were repeated in 1867 upon the restoration of the constitutional government. Once again, thousands made their way to Buda and Pest, among them the former officers of the *Honvéd* army, political prisoners of the absolutist regime, emigrés, and invalids, together with a number of educated Hungarians who had had no chance to be employed in the bureaucracy of the absolutist state. The government was sympathetic, and opened the doors of administration to new personnel. Thus while the national government had inherited some 16,000 officials from the Austrians (many of whom were dismissed or repatriated to Bohemia or German Austria), in 1872 we already find 22,000 and in 1875, 32,000 civil servants.[17] Thereafter the number of bureaucrats increased by leaps and bounds: from 60,776 in 1890 to 97,835 in 1900 to 119,937 in 1910.[18] However, these numbers only relate to persons employed by the central administrative apparatus of the state. The total number of public employees (including the salaried employees of municipalities and the enterprises of the state) was 265,447 in 1904 and 387,922 in 1914.[19] These figures represented roughly 3.5 percent of the active labor force. In terms of this ratio Hungary was on par with, if not slightly ahead of, some of the most advanced industrial societies of the Continent.[20]

The model for the new national administration was the one proposed by the Centralists before 1848. True, throughout the absolutist period the county was wistfully remembered as one of the bastions

[16] Szabó, *Társadalmi és pártharcok*, p. 121.

[17] Károly Keleti, *Hazánk és népe* [Our country and people] (Budapest: Ráth Mór, 1889), p. 55.

[18] *Annuaire Statistique Hongrois*, ix (1901), 80, and xix (1911), 93.

[19] László Buday, *A megcsonkított Magyarország* [Dismembered Hungary] (Budapest: Pantheon, 1921), p. 44.

[20] In Germany the number of administrators was 635,000 in 1913, representing some .9 percent of the population, while the total number of people employed in the public sector was 924,786 (1920), or 1.5 percent of the population. Statistisches Reichsamt, *Statistik des Deutschen Reiches*, No. 402, *Berufaufzählung* (Berlin: Reimar Habbag, 1929), pp. 41 and 224. In Great Britain the number of public employees in the civilian sector was 309,432 (1920), or .8 percent of the population of the country. Great Britain, Census Office, *Census of England and Wales, 1931*, Occupation Tables (London: H.M. Stationery Office, 1934), p. 679.

of ancient liberty, and as late as 1865, Premier-designate Andrássy ventured that in a choice between the county and the parliament he would unhesitatingly choose the former.[21] But in 1867 the age of absolutism had passed, and since the Hungarian ruling classes had conquered the state for themselves they had little use for the instruments of local self-government. Eötvös and Trefort, two leading members of the old Centralist faction, became members of Andrássy's cabinet, and it was under their auspices that legislative work began to refurbish the administrative structure of the country.

In the first bills drafted after the Compromise, the centralizing intent was concealed behind a design to rationalize and modernize the administrative system. Thus Public Law IV/1868 was ostensibly designed to separate the administrative and judicial functions of the county, but in doing so the bill established district courts and placed them under the jurisdiction of the Ministry of Justice. Similarly, Public Law XLII/1872 was aimed at improving local government by replacing the unwieldy general assemblies with more efficient and smaller bodies, elected partly under the general franchise and partly by a college of the most substantial taxpayers of the county. However, reduction of the size and membership of these bodies also made them more vulnerable to manipulation by government representatives. In much the same vein, the first legislative acts of the Tisza cabinet (Public Laws VI, XX, XXIII/1876) seemingly aimed at standardizing the administration of the country by abolishing special jurisdictions and by redrawing the boundaries of the counties. But the same legislation was also used to abolish a few obstreperous counties and the majority of the old royal free cities inhabited by Germans, while it guaranteed continued autonomy for a number of Magyar cities, among them the now united Budapest (designated as the "residential-capital city" of the country).[22]

Far more direct, however, were the provisions of the ensuing legislative acts of 1878 and 1886. The former (Public Laws XX-XXIII/1878) reduced the county and municipal assemblies to largely ceremonial functions by vesting most of their powers in permanent executive committees. These committees were to consist of twenty members—ten elected and ten *ex officio*—and were to be presided over by the lord lieutenants, that is, the chief local representatives of the central government. And if this legislation "divested the assemblies

---

[21] Gusztáv Gratz, *A dualizmus kora* [The age of dualism] (Budapest: Magyar Szemle, 1934), I, 92.

[22] A good summary of this legislation is to be found in Robert W. Seton-Watson, *Racial Problems in Hungary* (London: Constable, 1908), pp. 240-242.

of much of their power, reduced popular representation to a minimum, and strengthened the hold of the central government over local affairs,"[23] the provisions of Public Laws xx-xxi/1886 destroyed these autonomies altogether by reducing the elective principle to a sham. For while the chief administrative officers of local government (the city mayors, the deputy lord lieutenants, high sheriffs, county attorneys) remained elective, candidates for these offices were to be nominated by a special committee consisting of the lord lieutenant, three of his appointees, and three persons elected by the county assembly. To restrict the electoral principle even further the law stipulated that only candidates screened by this committee could be lawfully elected, and that once elected, their tenure was subject to review by the minister of the interior, who could exercise this power upon the request of a minority in the assembly. A similar system was introduced at the level of the communes whose officials—the notary, the judge, the coroner, the jurymen—were to be elected by the village council. But the power to nominate the candidates was given to the high sheriff (*szolgabíró*) of each district within the county, while a right of veto over appointments was vested in the lord lieutenant.

The Politics of Bureaucracy

Whatever the original motivations behind it, the decision to create a centralized and professionalized administrative system had significant and only barely anticipated consequences. The most important of these was the accumulation of power in the presumably neutral administrative bureaucracy. Once an administrative system was created, its members were under pressure to justify themselves. Partly in an attempt to do so and partly in blind imitation of foreign examples, they began to introduce, interpret, and enforce literally thousands of new regulations[24] concerning sanitation, licenses, housing, transportation, and economic transactions of all kinds. At the same time, members of the administration became the assessors and collectors of taxes. These powers of taxation and regulation gave local bureaucrats and their superiors in Budapest considerable leverage over an illiterate or semi-literate class of peasant smallholders. In the

[23] Ibid., p. 241.

[24] Excluding appropriations bills and routine legislation the Hungarian parliament passed 871 bills between 1867 and 1887, most of them in this area. See Rezső Rudai, "Adalék a magyar képviselőház szociológiájához, 1887-1931" [Notes on the sociology of the Hungarian House of Representatives, 1887-1931], *Társadalomtudomány*, xiii (1933), 216. Meanwhile the number of cases handled by the bureaucracy increased from 244,793 to 1,140,832 per annum. See *Annuaire Statistique Hongrois*, xix (1911), 445.

occidental countries, this bureaucratic leverage was successfully resisted by powerful classes of urban and rural entrepreneurs. But in
Hungary, where the traditional economic elite was in decline and
where the entrepreneurial class was foreign and still in an embryonic
state, administrative leverage was quickly transformed into political
leverage through pressure put on the electorate to cast ballots for
candidates favored by the bureaucracy. And if the selective assessment
of taxes and fines was not enough to encourage electoral conformity
under the prevailing system of open suffrage, local authorities could
resort to still more effective administrative means, such as manipulating the voting register, putting recalcitrant villagers under a health
quarantine, or declaring bridges unsafe for passage to prevent the
voters of the opposition from reaching the appointed polling place.[25]

Electoral corruption—the purchase of votes, the use of forgery, and
intimidation—had been known in Hungarian politics before. But in
the last quarter of the nineteenth century, such methods of influenc-
ing electoral outcomes were institutionalized and became routine.
Under the premiership of Coloman Tisza (1875-1890), the parliamentary Liberal party (founded in 1875) and the administrative bureaucracy were welded into a single, powerful machine in which the
bureaucracy was charged with "making" the elections and perpetu-
ating the Liberal majority, while parliament and the party would lend
an aura of legitimacy to bureaucratic policies and provide a forum to
articulate bureaucratic interests. As part of this standing arrangement
some 160 constituencies, inhabited mainly by Slovaks and Rumanians,
turned into "rotten boroughs" under bureaucratic tutelage. From
these boroughs the candidates of the incumbent party were returned
with monotonous regularity, frequently with no opposition at all.[26]
In return, much of the membership—sometimes as many as one-
third—of this "Government party" was recruited from the bureaucracy,[27] to form the nucleus of a perennial majority and the hard core
of the prime minister's "mameluke guard."

[25] For a detailed description of these methods of fixing elections, see Robert W. Seton-
Watson, *Racial Problems*, pp. 249-274, and *Electoral Corruption and Reform in Hungary*
(London: Constable, 1911).

[26] These and other figures pertaining to electoral results are based on Ferenc Fodor,
"A magyar képviselőválasztások térképe, 1861-1915" [Maps of Hungarian parliamentary elections, 1861-1915 in Hungary], Hungarian Ministry of Foreign Affairs, *Hungarian Peace Negotiations: The Hungarian Peace Delegation in Neuilly* (Budapest: Horánszky,
1922), IIIB, Annex VII.

[27] See Table 17. In addition we may take note of the fact that 14.6 percent of the
deputies had held at one time or another elective local office, 6.4 percent had been
judges, and 4 percent had served as professional officers in the army. Figures based

In order to further enhance the power of the political machine, in 1885 Tisza moved to reduce the influence of the hereditary branch of government, the House of Lords, over which the administration could exercise no electoral control. According to the provisions of the Parliament Act of that year, no less than 469 peers were excluded from the upper chamber, and the membership was provisionally fixed at 369. This number included 205 hereditary peers, 83 church dignitaries (including the heads of the Protestant, Orthodox, and, after 1895, the Jewish religious communities), and, as a new feature, 81 life members. Henceforth, aristocratic titles no longer automatically carried membership in the House of Lords. Rather, such membership had to be conferred separately upon the recipient of an aristocratic title. While the awarding of aristocratic titles remained a royal prerogative, both hereditary and life peerages were to be awarded upon the advice of the prime minister who, in case of emergency, could seek the appointment of new members to secure the passage of a particular piece of legislation. In the political argot of the day, this device was known as the *pairschub*—from the French word for peer, and the German word for shift—and while this was actually never resorted to, the threat itself was sufficient to keep the lords in line. Though they were often at loggerheads with the government, after 1885 they turned down only a single bill, involving an ecclesiastic matter. And even in this case the peers eventually reversed themselves under royal and ministerial pressure.

By manipulating elections and emasculating the hereditary branch of government, the political machine emerged as the single most important actor on the Hungarian political stage. But while clearly dominant in public affairs, this machine was far from omnipotent, for in this liberal day and age it would labor under a number of significant constraints imposed upon it by the international environment. To put it differently, while the bureaucracy had a vested interest in maximizing the power of the state, it was also interested in maintaining its international respectability. It thus had to abide by the rules of "civilized conduct" then prevalent in the advanced countries of the European continent. While these rules were broken time and again, such breaches would exact a certain moral and political price, which not only put a damper on bureaucratic arbitrariness, but also forced the governments of the day to engage in a degree of give-and-take with interest groups and the public at large.

---

on analysis of biographies in semi-official *Országgyűlési Almanachok* [Parliamentary almanacs] of 1887, 1897, 1910.

In the first place, the desire to adhere to civilized rules of international conduct put definite limits on electoral corruption and on the amount of open violence that the bureaucracy could use to manufacture electoral results. While the bureaucracy could herd the docile or indifferent Slovak and Rumanian voters to the polls to elect the candidate of the government without much resistance, it would usually fail to do so in the Magyar constituencies of the Plainland and Transylvania where the Calvinist gentry and smallholders were stubborn enough to resist pressure, even physical intimidation, and cast their ballot for the candidates of their own choice. And if these constituencies were "open" by default, others—among them the electoral districts of Budapest and other urban areas—were open by design to serve as models of political probity, and to prove to all the world that the political system was genuinely competitive. Altogether these 200 or so "open boroughs" gave public opinion a chance to leave its imprint on electoral results, all the more because by tacit convention prominent political figures, including the premier, were to run in these constituencies to provide proof of their personal popularity and the popularity of their government. It was not unusual therefore for party leaders to emerge as losers from electoral contests. The great Coloman Tisza, prime minister and the architect of the entire political edifice, was himself defeated twice, once in 1878 at the zenith of his political career when he sought reelection in the Calvinist Magyar city of Debrecen, and again in 1901, when as a venerated elder statesman of his party he stood for one of the electoral districts of Budapest.[28]

The bureaucracy was similarly hamstrung in another fifty or so constituencies. Here the electorate may have been small and politically indifferent, but a substantial number of them were the tenants, clients, or other dependents of the owner of a single large estate whose economic influence matched or even outweighed the administrative influence of the bureaucracy.[29] Much as in the rotten boroughs of the

---

[28] Not all Hungarian statesmen abided by this rule of the game, however. Stephen Tisza, Coloman's son and successor to the premiership (1903-1905, 1912-1917) represented the Vizakna constituency, a rotten borough with a handful of intimidated Rumanian voters. But his choice, no doubt, contributed further to his lack of popularity and to the downfall of his government in 1905.

[29] The electoral process in one such district is described by Albert Apponyi in the following manner: "Edmund Zichy, the owner of the Árva estate that spread over most of the constituency, offered me to stand for election. The largest estate thus stood behind me and so did the priesthood. . . . I had to learn a short diction in the Slovak language and made a ten-day tour in the splendid Carpathian winter. I enjoyed the trip—and was elected unanimously." Albert Apponyi, *Ötven év* [Fifty years] (Budapest: Pantheon, 1922), pp. 71-72.

bureaucracy, elections in these pocket boroughs were unanimous or predictable, guaranteeing the presence of a large and politically independent aristocratic contingent on the benches of the House of Representatives. Thus while the wings of the hereditary aristocracy had been clipped by successive institutional reforms, the corporate identity and interests of great landowners were still adequately recognized by the political system (Table 6).

As a result of these constraints the bureaucracy could fix elections, but could not do so by tricks and force alone. While the machine could count on 160 or so safe seats from its rotten boroughs, a parliamentary majority required another 50, a safe majority another 80-90 seats. These would have to be won either by humoring the great landowners or by capturing a number of seats from the open boroughs. In other words, the machine could hold its own against the great landowners if it had a measure of public support, or defy public opinion in alliance with the aristocracy, but it could not hope to survive in the face of opposition from an outraged public and an alienated aristocracy. This was the case in 1905, the one and only time in modern Hungarian history when the incumbent government failed to attain a majority in the House of Representatives. The effective conduct of government therefore entailed bargaining, payoff, cooperation, and a degree of responsiveness to the public mood. Conversely, the opposition parties and pressure groups could protect their own interests by setting conditions for electoral cooperation, or else, between elections, by raising the prospect of secession from, or fusion with, the Government party. Indeed, at times these secessions and fusions were so frequent that some observers were inclined to see them as an effective substitute for a working two-party system.

A detailed description of these parliamentary maneuvers would require a separate volume. Here we can list only some of the most significant instances when the aisle was crossed to and from the Liberal party: in 1876, sixty-eight deputies defected on account of disagreements with the government's handling of fiscal negotiations with Austria; in 1884, sixteen deputies defected to join the conservative Mod-

TABLE 6
ARISTOCRATS IN THE HOUSE OF REPRESENTATIVES, 1875-1905
(by percentage)

1875: 10.8	1884: 12.8	1896: 13.4
1878: 11.0	1887: 13.3	1901: 13.6
1881: 12.4	1892: 16.4	1905: 14.4

SOURCE: Ernő Lakatos, *A magyar politikai vezetőréteg, 1848-1918*, p. 26.

erate Opposition group; in 1892-1894, twenty-eight deputies left the Liberal party on the issue of civil marriage and church-state relations—some of these defectors eventually returned to the fold, others formed their own Catholic People's party; in December 1898, thirty-eight deputies, almost all of them landowning aristocrats, crossed the aisle in protest against Premier Bánffy's handling of appropriations; in 1899, nearly the entire conservative opposition fused with the Liberal party only to leave it again the spring of 1904, while in November of the same year two dozen more deputies left the Liberal party to form a new Constitution party. During the thirty years of unbroken Liberal rule (1875-1905) the Government party lost, and eventually regained, at least 250 of its parliamentary deputies. The threat of secession always hung over the party, and to counter it prime ministers had to consult their back-benchers regularly. At critical junctures they had to ask for votes of confidence in party caucus, and the frequently debilitating results forced changes in the policies of the government. Coloman Tisza himself was far from immune to such pressures. At the time of the budget crisis of 1877, for instance, he polled the parliamentary membership of his party: 181 deputies voted for his appropriations bill, 69 against, while 94 abstained.[30] Subsequently two of Tisza's successors—Bánffy in 1899 and Khuen-Héderváry in 1903—were thrown out of office by back-bench rebellions, the latter by a formal vote of the rank and file of the Liberal party.

The autocratic tendencies of the system were further mitigated, and its pluralistic tendencies enhanced, by a number of habits, conventions, and quasi-institutions that operated as correctives in the absence of free competition and represented built-in restraints on the arbitrary exercise of power. In the last analysis these restraints derived from the norms prevailing in the international system, but they were also supported by the traditions of the ruling class, and as such they were most effective in protecting the personal and political rights of the members of the establishment: the gentry and the aristocracy. But, as much by default as by design, they were also instrumental in blunting the harshness of the bureaucratic regime towards the lower classes and the national minorities.

Politically, the most significant of these correctives was the practice of parliamentary obstruction. Just as in the leisurely days of the feudal Diet, the parliamentary rules of procedure were lax. There were no restrictions on the time allotted to individual speakers, and such devices as the "kangaroo" or the "guillotine" used in the British House

[30] Gratz, *A dualizmus kora*, I, 159.

of Commons to curb debate were yet unknown in Hungary. One deputy could challenge the accuracy of the minutes, and only twenty signatures were needed to force a roll call. These liberal rules of procedure naturally invited filibustering, especially because the opposition parties justly felt that they had little chance to overthrow the government at the polls. Thus when the minority was confronted with a bill that it regarded as deleterious to its vital interests, it either held marathon speeches or else resorted to the tactic of "technical obstruction" by raising innumerable challenges to the minutes or demanding roll calls on petty matters of procedure. In one famous instance the House of Representatives decided in a midnight vote that the debate should have ended at noon. On another occasion the record of the previous session was challenged twenty-one times, and over each challenge the roll was called. Parliamentary obstruction prevented not only the passage of regular bills, but of routine measures and appropriations as well. To avoid the embarrassment of an "ex-lex" (a period without regular budget appropriations), prime ministers were often forced to enter into deals with the heads of the opposition. Prime Minister Széll, for instance, concluded a formal pact with them after becoming the head of the government in 1899. In this pact the opposition pledged not to obstruct the election of a new speaker of the House and to permit the passage of four bills, including the appropriations bill for the year. In exchange, the prime minister guaranteed the "cleanness" of the forthcoming elections—that is, no electoral interference in the open boroughs—and agreed to submit legislation to the House to extend the jurisdiction of the High Court of Justice over electoral complaints.[31]

The authoritarian features of the regime were further tempered by the existence of a press that was politically and financially independent from the government. Indeed, by the turn of the century there were hundreds of independent daily newspapers and periodicals: in Budapest alone 21 daily papers were published, averaging 400 printed pages and a weekday circulation of one million.[32] Although most of the papers of the country were printed in the Magyar language, the minorities did not go unrepresented; in 1909, 150 newspapers were published in German, 11 in Slovak, 44 in Rumanian, and 1 in Ruthenian.[33] And while the press had a distinctly bourgeois flavor in that it catered to the tastes of the urban propertied classes, the

[31] Ibid., I, 397.

[32] Zoltán Horváth, *Magyar századforduló* [The turn of the century in Hungary] (Budapest: Kossuth Kiadó, 1961), pp. 162-163.

[33] Oscar Jászi, *The Dissolution of the Habsburg Monarchy*, p. 282.

politically outcast socialists had no less than 24 regular organs, including the daily *Népszava* with a circulation of 25,000.[34]

On paper, the freedom of the press was curtailed by the provisions of the very press law (Public Law XVIII of 1848) passed to abolish the hated institution of censorship, for the act outlawed advocating the overthrow of the constitutional order and incitement to committing a common crime. To these provisions the Penal Code of 1878 added incitement against class, nationality, and religion, and upheld the provision of the original press law that called for a security deposit of 10,000 Fls. by each editor against which cash fines for libel could be assessed by the courts. "Incitement through the press" became a misdemeanor under the law to be punishable by up to two years in prison. Although these provisions did lead to several trials in the 1890s, they did little to dampen the muckraking enthusiasm of the press, particularly when it came to uncovering bureaucratic excess or the peccadillos of the high and mighty. Once again such muckraking was not the sole prerogative of the establishment press, but was shared by the socialists whose organs excelled in merciless and vituperative attacks against leading political figures. Thus when *Népszava* started to run a daily column on the caucus of the parliamentary majority, the editors titled it "News from the Nationalist Pigsty." The author of the column referred to the government as a "criminal gang," and spoke of the minister of justice as "that brainless constable." The same newspaper announced Stephen Tisza's appointment to the premiership by saying that "this chief of brigands had come to his filthy parliament on money stolen by his predecessor [ex-premier Leslie] Lukács," and thereafter made a habit of referring to him as a "knave," "murderer," and "criminal" without ever being tried for libel or incitement.[35]

The chief guardian of these freedoms was a judicial system whose institutions provided the ultimate check on the incipient authoritarianism of the bureaucratic regime. Many of these institutions, of course, had deep roots in the local soil, but after 1848 they were brought up to prevailing international standards: laws were codified, courts were separated from the other branches of government, and juries were drawn from the voting registers rather than from the ranks of the local nobility. In subsequent years these juries proved to be of great political importance, for in disputes between the citizen and the state their members tended to be kindly disposed toward their peers, giving them every benefit of the doubt. It was for this very

---

[34] Horváth, *Magyar századforduló*, p. 140.
[35] For all quotations, ibid., p. 337.

reason that "in political and libel cases acquittal was very frequent."[36] The disposition of the courts of appeal was no less flexible. In 1912 the High Court reversed the sentence of Julius Kovács, a deputy who fired five shots at Stephen Tisza, on the grounds that the assailant had acted in the defense of the constitution. Another celebrated case was the libel suit brought by Prime Minister Lukács against the Deputy Zoltán Désy who had publicly described him as the greatest swindler in Europe, accusing him of the misappropriation of public funds for political purposes. Désy was found guilty in the first instance, but his sentence was reversed by the High Court in a case that sent shock waves through the body politic and forced the resignation of the prime minister. Apart from such "freedom of expression" cases, the High Court also offered a measure of protection against electoral abuse. Thus, pursuant to appropriate legislation between 1899 and 1914 the court investigated sixty-five electoral complaints.[37] In sixteen of these sixty-five cases the court ordered new elections on the grounds that voters of the opposition parties had been prevented from reaching the polling place, or were otherwise grossly mistreated by the gendarmes or local administration.[38]

There is no question, of course, that the courts were far more favorably disposed toward Magyars than toward members of the national minorities, and more lenient toward the members of the establishment than toward such political outcasts as the Social Democrats and Agrarian Socialists. Thus the same juries that indignantly defended the freedom of their peers had no difficulty convicting Slovaks and Rumanians or sending socialist agitators to jail. The same High Court that reversed electoral results in Magyar constituencies was reluctant to review complaints by representatives of national minorities. Nor was the court sympathetic to the Agrarian Socialist leader Andrew Achim, whose election had been annulled on the flimsy pretext that it had been obtained by seditious means. And yet, the very fact that political cases were tried in public and in full observance of certain procedural norms served at least to blunt the repressive intent of the authorities. Thus reading about the political trials of the period one is first struck by the great number of cases in court, then by the relative leniency of the sentences. According to the documentation provided by Robert Seton-Watson, in one critical decade (1898-1908) 503 Slovaks were indicted on charges ranging from incitement to riot

---

[36] Ibid.

[37] According to the *Reports* of the Committee on Credentials. To be found in the record of the first session of the House in *Napló*, 1901, 1905, 1906, and 1910.

[38] Ibid.

to abusing the Hungarian flag, and in 81 separate trials they drew a total of 79 years and six months. During the same period 216 Rumanians were sentenced to 38 years and nine months.[39] The aggregate figures are impressive, but a division of years by sentences yields averages of 1.6 and 2.2 months. In most cases the terms were to be served in the nominal captivity of "state confinement" (*államfogház*). Longer sentences were usually reduced or suspended by executive clemency. In one of the best-known trials of the period, sixteen authors of a Rumanian memorandum to the Crown were sentenced in May 1894 to a total of twenty-nine years. The sentences were appealed and upheld in the higher courts, but on September 17, 1895 all the defendants were released from confinement.[40] Similarly, the records of the socialist movement, published by one of its leading members, show that 916 of its members stood trial in the pre-World War I decade and drew a collective sentence of twenty-four years and eleven months, or an average of twelve days per person.[41] These sentences spread bitterness without arousing genuine alarm or terror. Hamstrung by restraints, the governments could temporarily stem the tide of national and social protest, but could not reshape or mobilize society and thus resolve its ever increasing problems.

The Economics of Bureaucracy

In developing a modern bureaucracy the Hungarians followed the model of France and of other core countries. The problem was that while in the latter bureaucratization had been an organic process that went hand in hand with certain economic changes—the rise of an industrial and market economy[42]—in Hungary the bureaucracy and the apparatus of the modern state were imposed on a backward economy. This economy had yet to attain the capacity for generating large amounts of surplus for financing social overhead. As a result, the economics of bureaucracy soon turned into the economics of fiscal stress, perennial scarcities, and recurrent budgetary crises.

The gap between economic base and bureaucratic superstructure became evident shortly after the restoration of constitutional govern-

[39] Seton-Watson, *Racial Problems*, pp. 448-466.

[40] See *Budapest Hírlap*, news items on September 18 and 20, 1895.

[41] Vilmos Böhm, *Két forradalom tüzében* [In the crossfire of two revolutions] (Vienna: Bécsi Magyar Kiadó, 1923), p. 19.

[42] "Though by no means alone," writes Max Weber, "the capitalist system has undeniably played a major role in the development of bureaucracy. Indeed without it, capitalist production could not continue." Max Weber, *The Theory of Social and Economic Organization* (Glencoe: The Free Press, 1964), p. 338.

ment. True, the absolutist government left the treasury in a reasonably sound state. But the condition of public finance deteriorated rapidly as the Hungarian governments started to hire new bureaucratic personnel and felt obligated to remunerate it at levels comparable to prevailing Austrian pay scales.[43] To make matters worse, parliament refused to raise the tax rate or vote new revenues on the ground that however inadequate the aggregate amount was, Hungarian farmers were already taxed at a rate three to four times higher than their British and French counterparts.[44] Under these circumstances the government was forced to raise revenue by reassessing property values across the country and by organizing quasi-military campaigns (adószedési hadjárat) to collect the taxes. Most notorious was the campaign of 1869, in the course of which gendarmes and revenue officers raided villages and went from house to house terrorizing reluctant taxpayers, sequestering their livestock, furniture, and household equipment.[45] This campaign, which embittered the rural population, raised revenues by a mere eleven percent. Altogether, within a seven-year period (1868-1875) the expenditures of the state increased by 58.5 percent, tax revenues by 21.8 percent (Table 7). To make up for the difference, and to finance the costs of constructing railroads, the government floated bonds. However, international confidence in the new Hungarian state was so low that the bonds sold at 55-75 percent of their face value on the European money markets.[46] National debt soared. As a result, the years between 1868 and 1875 are usually remembered in Hungarian history as a period of fiscal mismanagement and crisis.

The finances of the Hungarian state were consolidated under the premiership of Coloman Tisza. By the means described above, Tisza had established such a firm bureaucratic grip over parliament that Finance Minister Coloman Széll could raise revenues that earlier parliaments had failed to countenance. Thus within three years revenues

[43] In the years 1867-1872 bureaucratic personnel increased 200 percent, their salaries 238 percent. Alexander (Sándor) Matlekovits, *Das Königreich Ungarn statistisch und wirtschaftlich dargestellt* (Leipzig: Duncker and Humblot, 1900), II, 915.

[44] According to some estimates the land tax amounted to as much as 24.5 percent of the income of the average Hungarian farmer, in contrast to 6.75 percent and 7.5 percent paid by British and French farmers respectively. Gyula Bernát, *Az új Magyarország agrárpolitikája, 1867-1914* [The agrarian policy of the new Hungary, 1867-1914] (Pécs: Egyetemi Könyvkiadó, 1938), p. 49. The student of comparative taxation, however, should also note that in Japan the same tax took approximately 33 percent of the farmer's income. William Lockwood, *The Economic Development of Japan* (Princeton: Princeton University Press, 1954), p. 98.

[45] Erik Molnár, *Magyarország története*, II, 79.

[46] Matlekovits, *Das Königreich Ungarn*, I, xxx.

TABLE 7

REVENUES, EXPENDITURES, AND NATIONAL DEBT, 1868-1875

(1,000 Fls.)

Year	Revenues	Expenditures	National Debt
1868	154,067	147,451	254,345
1869	152,517	161,995	241,740
1870	171,224	199,947	378,761
1871	179,577	215,116	384,632
1872	186,627	237,439	421,912
1873	181,707	251,057	475,670
1874	190,294	250,127	552,322
1875	192,850	233,349	623,472

SOURCE: Alexander Matlekovits, *Das Königreich Ungarn volkswirtschaftlich und statistisch dargestellt*, II, 867-869.

from the land tax increased twenty-five percent, from the house tax twenty-seven percent.[47] In addition, Széll introduced an income tax supplement together with a number of special excises, among them taxes on hunting licenses, firearms, jewelry, wine, and meat.[48] By 1880 these revenues made possible the balancing of the budget and had created enough international confidence in the state for Hungarian bonds to sell at close to face value.[49]

However, the effectiveness of these measures was only temporary, for the state apparatus appeared to be insatiable while further increases in property and income taxes threatened to undercut the profitability and competitiveness of agricultural enterprise on the continental grain market. In other words, the fiscal managers of the country had to develop a tax system that could provide adequate revenue for the bureaucracy while permitting a degree of capital accumulation and technical innovation in the agricultural economy, particularly in the larger grain-producing units on which the country's export revenues were dependent. The solution, first explored under Széll's successor Julius Szapáry, was to shift the tax burden from the large toward the small production unit, from rural to urban taxpayers, and, finally, from the propertied to the wage-earning classes.[50]

This reform of the tax system had been designed by Alexander Wekerle, a career bureaucrat who would eventually become minister of finance (1887-1892) and then three times prime minister.[51] It was under his fiscal regime that the land tax became de facto regressive,

[47] Ibid., pp. 854-856.   [48] Ibid.

[49] 92.6 percent of their nominal value. Ibid., I, xxx.

[50] For Szapáry's fiscal policies, ibid., pp. 857-858.

[51] The great importance attached to revenue collection is reflected in the fact that

for under the new system of assessments large estates of 1,000 acres were taxed at a rate of approximately nine percent of their income to maintain their profitability and to enhance their export potential, while small farms under fifty acres were taxed at a rate as high as thirty percent.[52] In addition, urban taxpayers, and the owners of houses, workshops, and factories were taxed at a rate fourteen percent higher than the owners of farms.[53] Last but not least, it was under Wekerle's tenure in office that the tax system shifted decisively from direct to indirect taxation by means of levies on tobacco and spirits as well as on such staples as kerosene, flour, and salt. Altogether, the Wekerle ministry raised income and property taxes thirty percent above the 1880 level, but raised revenues from excise by 330 percent.[54] As a result, the average urban wage earner contributed ten percent of his income to state revenue while the average rural laborer contributed fifteen to eighteen percent,[55] a substantial amount in a society where close to seventy percent of family income was spent on comestibles alone.[56]

By creating this tax system Wekerle put the finances of the Hungarian state on a sound basis. From 1880 to 1895 public revenue more than doubled—from 247.3 million Kronen to 501.9 million—without commensurate increases in the national product.[57] The state was rescued from bankruptcy, and the bureaucracy could be paid at a "decent" and "civilized" standard.[58] In so doing the Tisza-Wekerle system of public finance saved Hungary from the curse so common to other backward societies: the spread of petty corruption as a means of closing the gap between bureaucratic expectations and salaries. Not that corruption was totally absent. But it did not become the rule, for unlike most of their Balkan counterparts, Hungarian public servants did not routinely shake down shopkeepers or extort payments from

---

Tisza himself occupied the portfolio of finance temporarily in 1877 and 1887, and that all three of his ministers of finance—Coloman Széll, Julius Szapáry, and Alexander Wekerle—proceeded from the Ministry of Finance to the office of the prime minister.

[52] Bernát, *Az új Magyarország*, p. 49.

[53] Calculated from information in *Annuaire Statistique Hongrois*, VIII (1900), 449.

[54] Matlekovits, *Das Königreich Ungarn*, I, xxx, and II, 921.

[55] József Szterényi, *Die Ungarische Industriepolitik* (Wien: Hofverlag, 1913), p. 27.

[56] According to most available estimates, 66 percent of the income of agrarian workers and 40-60 percent of that of industrial workers was spent on comestibles. See Bernát, *Az új Magyarország*, p. 254.

[57] Matlekovits, *Das Königreich Ungarn*, I, xxx.

[58] In 1906, 3.5 percent of the active labor force were state employees; their share in the national income was about 7 percent (Molnár, *Magyarország története*, II, 176). However, this income was unevenly distributed and skewed toward the higher brackets of the "ministerial" bureaucracy.

clients who passed through their offices. By the standards of other east European bureaucracies, then, the Hungarian bureaucracy was relatively clean. Yet for the average taxpayer this cleanliness only implied a greater efficiency in syphoning off resources from the private to the public sector. Thus, in the last analysis this efficiency only aggravated the social and economic consequences of bureaucratization, for the lower classes were deprived of a greater amount of cash than they would have been from the random pilferings of gendarmes and railroad conductors. Indeed, this tax system not only depressed the living standard of wage earners, but in the long run also prevented the rise of a domestic market for the products of the budding national industry. To a large extent it was as a result of the Tisza-Wekerle system that the Hungarian economy developed an excessive reliance on foreign markets for both its agricultural and industrial products, and hence became extremely vulnerable to the global movement of prices.

The Sociology of Bureaucracy

The premature rise of the bureaucracy had not only political and economic but social consequences as well, for the national administration was not only the locus of public power and spending, but also an important target of mobility for the talented, the ambitious, and the socially dislocated. In this respect once again the forces of backwardness were at work. For while in the Occident economics had come before politics, in Hungary and in other countries of the periphery politics was in command. The bureaucratic machine was surrounded with an aura of power and authority.

Not surprisingly, the first recruits into the national bureaucracy came from the gentry. For one thing, in the 1860s and 1870s most educated men in the country were members of this class. For another, the government of Coloman Tisza made the rescuing of the declining nobility an explicit objective of its social policy. "In the seventies and eighties," writes one social historian, "the best recommendation for an administrative position was a shining name. . . . At first came the impoverished members of illustrious families, then the lesser noblesse, and finally the educated offspring of the sandalled peasant nobility." As a result, "no other age in Hungarian public life came to be so completely identified with the gentry as were the years of Coloman Tisza's premiership."[59]

[59] Zoltán Lippay, *A magyar birtokos középosztály és a közélet* [The Hungarian landed middle class and public life] (Budapest: Franklin, 1919), p. 98. For a similar observation see László Tóth, *A gentry társadalomtörténetéhez* [Notes on the social history of the gentry] (Budapest: Turul, 1939), pp. 6-7.

However, even in the heyday of the Tisza regime the gentry fell short of monopolizing either politics or bureaucracy. In the first place, there were the ubiquitous aristocrats in government, parliament, and, to a lesser extent, in administration. Then there were the educated commoners, some of them inherited from the Austrians and retained because they possessed rare skills and technical competence. Their numbers were apparently diminishing until 1885, but in that year a new Civil Service Act tightened the merit system by introducing new educational qualifications for promotion and hiring. Thus, in spite of all the built-in nepotism, the members of the gentry class were forced to compete with outsiders, especially in the more "technical" fields of commerce and finance. As Table 8 shows, in 1890 the gentry (and the lesser nobility) still occupied 56.7 percent of the higher positions in four key ministries. But within the next twenty years this proportion would decline to 45.9 percent; in the Ministry of Finance it fell to 38.6 percent. These figures pertain to the membership of the small and exclusive executive class (fogalmazói kar). The proportion of commoners was most certainly higher in the lower echelons of the administration. Although the percentage of commoners was lower among cabinet ministers and the members of parliament, signs of social mo-

TABLE 8
SOCIAL COMPOSITION OF THE HUNGARIAN BUREAUCRACY, 1890 AND 1910
(Four ministries, executive class)

| | Percentages | | | |
	Aristocrat	Gentry[a]	Commoner	Don't Know
1890				
Office of P.M.	—	67.5	23.2	9.3
Interior	1.8	64.1	24.5	9.6
Commerce	1.2	51.6	39.2	8.0
Finance	6.6	43.8	40.0	9.6
Average of Above	2.4	56.7	22.7	9.2
1910				
Office of P.M.	4.1	50.0	37.6	8.3
Interior	—	47.6	42.8	9.6
Commerce	3.5	47.4	40.1	9.0
Finance	6.5	38.6	45.3	9.6
Average of Above	3.5	45.9	41.5	9.1

SOURCE: Hungary, Statisztikai Hivatal, *Magyarország tiszti cim- és névtára* [Official directory of Hungary] (Budapest: Pátria Nyomda, 1890 and 1910). Titles of nobility either indicated or checked against information in Béla Kempelen, *Magyar nemesi családok* [Hungarian noble families] (Budapest: Grill, 1911-1936), I-XI.

[a] Includes other "common" nobles.

110

bility are evident even here. For between 1887 and 1910 at least one-third of the representatives (see Table 8) and one-fourth of the cabinet ministers (Table 9) had no family connection with the "historical classes," but entered the political establishment from the outside by virtue of education or technical expertise.

A substantial number of the latter, perhaps as many as seventy percent of those in the "commoner" category, were members of the erstwhile German bourgeoisie which, with the exception of the inhabitants of a few stubborn Saxon communities, was ready en masse to give up economics for public service. And if by virtue of tradition, education, and middle-class status, the German bourgeoisie was next in line to the gentry on the ladder of social mobility, other ethnic groups—Slovaks, Croats, and Rumanians—would soon follow in their footsteps as the offspring of a few well-to-do farmers and horse traders began to graduate from institutions of higher learning. The governments in turn were ready to embrace them on condition that they renounce their language and ethnic identity. Indeed, after 1890 it became a tacit policy of the governments to encourage the entry of the upwardly mobile non-Magyar element into bureaucracy, so as to deprive the increasingly restless minorities of an educated elite of their own. Toward the end of the century the bureaucracy, together with the educational system, would not only serve as an avenue of social mobility, but also as an instrument of assimilation and acculturation. As a Magyar nationalist—himself a recent convert to Magyardom—aptly observed, the schools and the system of public administration were two parts of one big machine into which "one feeds a Slovak child on one side, and on the other out comes a Hungarian gentleman."[60]

TABLE 9

KEY MINISTRIES OCCUPIED BY STATUS GROUPS, 1875-1918

(Number of months)

	Total	P.M.	Interior	Commerce	Finance
Aristocrats	585	112	138	237	98
Gentry[a]	995	317	331	194	153
Commoners	484	87	47	85	265
Total	2,064	516	516	516	516

SOURCE: Based on Statisztikai Hivatal, *Magyarország tiszti cim- és névtára*, 1938, pp. 4-7. Peerages and titles granted during the period were not counted.

[a] Includes other "common" nobles.

[60] Béla Grünwald, *A felvidék* [The highlands] (Budapest: Ráth Mór, 1878), p. 140.

This trend and purpose were well reflected in the changing ethnic composition of public administration in the country. Thus while at the turn of the century 92.9 percent of all local officials, 95.6 percent of the ministerial bureaucracy, and 96.9 percent of all judges listed themselves as Magyars in the official census,[61] an analysis of family names (Table 10) suggests that at least one-third of these, and almost half in the Ministry of Finance, were of non-Magyar origin, with their numbers steadily increasing from 1890 onward. A similar analysis does not exist with respect to the composition of parliament, but there is some evidence to show that there, too, the same trend prevailed. Thus, according to the observations of R. W. Seton-Watson, in 1906-1910 375 members (91.0 percent) of the House of Representatives listed themselves as Magyars in the official census, but 114 (or 27.5 percent) had been recently assimilated, 26 of them with newly Magyarized names.[62]

The flight of the German bourgeoisie from commercial and industrial pursuits deepened the ethnic division of labor that had been taking shape in the pre-1848 period, for the Germans were replaced by Jewish immigrants whose numbers steadily increased. In 1910 the

TABLE 10
ETHNIC ORIGIN OF HUNGARIAN BUREAUCRATS,
1890 AND 1910
(Four ministries, executive class)

	Percentages		
Ministry	Magyar	German	Other
1890			
Office of P.M.	76.5	17.6	5.9
Interior	79.2	16.9	3.9
Commerce	70.8	23.2	6.0
Finance	60.9	37.1	2.0
Average of Above	71.8	23.7	4.5
1910			
Office of P.M.	66.6	16.7	16.7
Interior	61.9	23.8	14.3
Commerce	58.1	26.4	15.5
Finance	57.7	39.0	3.3
Average of Above	61.0	26.4	12.6

SOURCE: Statisztikai Hivatal, *Magyarország tiszti cim- és névtára*, 1890 and 1910. Percentages based on names alone.

[61] Hungarian Ministry of Foreign Affairs, *Hungarian Peace Negotiations*, I, 236-237.
[62] Seton-Watson, *Racial Problems*, p. 188.

Jewish population reached close to one million or 5.1 percent of the entire population of the country (Table 11). Since residential restrictions had been eliminated, more than half of this population now lived in larger urban centers, 220,174 of them in Budapest where they made up 23.5 percent of the city's inhabitants.[63]

The position of this ethnic community was regulated as much by formal legislation as by tacit understandings. On the one hand, the Emancipation Act of 1868 granted Jewish citizens equality before the law, opening to them all avenues leading to economic entrepreneurship and participation. On the other hand, the informal social contract that now took effect barred members of the Jewish faith from politics and public life. To be sure, Jews did have the right to vote. Like other Hungarian citizens they exercised this right, sometimes freely, sometimes under duress, but usually in support of the Government party whose members in turn included an occasional Jewish deputy as an act of what today would be described as "tokenism."[64]

The prevalence of this ethnic division of labor is clear from a variety of occupational and religious statistics. Thus if we examine the "virilists," the list of the highest class of taxpayers throughout the country, we will find that in 1887, 20.05 percent of those who paid more than 1,000 Fls. in direct taxes were Jewish, including 62.2 percent of all businessmen, 64.6 percent of all tenants of estates, and 12.5 percent of landowners, but only .6 percent of all officials who fell into this particular income bracket (Table 12). At the same time (1883), there were only ten Jews in the entire ministerial apparatus, none in the counties, and only five in the two houses of parliament.[65] This situation, as we will see, changed around the turn of the century for the census of 1900 already listed Jews in public employment. But the

TABLE 11[a]
THE JEWISH POPULATION OF HUNGARY, 1842-1910

1842	241,636	1890	730,342
1869	553,641	1900	846,254
1880	638,314	1910	938,458

[a] Quoted from official census figures in Péter Ujváry, *Magyar zsidó lexicon*, p. 553.

[63] *Annuaire Statistique Hongrois*, XIX (1911), 17-18.

[64] In 1868, for instance, leaders of the governing Deák party made a point of having a Jewish representative from the prestigious Fifth District of the capital city. The choice was between Moritz Wahrmann and Maximilian Falk. Deák's personal choice fell on the former on the grounds that, as the son of a rabbi, and as a banker, he was "more authentically Jewish" than the thoroughly assimilated Falk, a writer by profession. See, William O. McCagg, *Jewish Nobles and Geniuses in Modern Hungary* (Boulder and New York: East European Quarterly and Columbia University Press, 1972), pp. 151-152.

[65] *Egyenlőség* (Budapest), February 11, 18, 25, 1883, ibid., p. 185.

TABLE 12
HIGHEST CLASS OF TAXPAYERS (VIRILISTS) IN EIGHTEEN COUNTIES, 1887

Occupation	Gentiles	Jews	Total
Landowners	2,145	305	2,450
	87.5%	12.5%	100.0%
Tenants	105	192	297
	35.4	64.6	100.0
Business	226	362	588
	37.7	62.3	100.0
Lawyers, judges	438	26	464
	94.4	5.6	100.0
Doctors, pharmacists	173	28	201
	86.1	13.9	100.0
Officials, clerics	319	2	321
	99.4	0.6	100.0

SOURCE: *A megyei adófizetők statisztikája* [Statistics of the taxpayers of counties] as it appears in Censor, *Társadalmunk és társadalmi hivatásunk* [Our society and calling] (Budapest: Published by the author, 1887). The sheer volume of names and tables made it necessary to restrict this analysis to eighteen counties randomly selected from a list of sixty-four.

majority of the Jewish citizenry and educated class remained closely identified with the modern economy. The statistics show that 54.0 percent of the owners of commercial establishments (66.2 percent in Budapest), 85.0 percent of the directors and owners of financial institutions (90.3 in the capital), together with 62.1 percent of all employees in commerce were Jewish, as were 12.5 percent of all industrialists (31.6 percent in Budapest).[66] However, these figures alone do not tell the entire story for they include both the humble artisans and shopkeepers, as well as the members of the twenty or so "grand" families—the interlocking clans of the Kohner, Ullman, Herzog, Deutsch, Mauthner, Goldberger, Wodianer—who, much like the Japanese *zaibatsu*, controlled among themselves some 90 percent of Hungary's modern banking system and industrial plants. This relationship worked both ways for not only was the majority of the bourgeoisie Jewish, but the majority of Jews was bourgeois rather than proletarian, 57.2 percent of them being owners and salaried employees of enterprise, 17.9 percent professionals, and only one-fourth (24.9 percent) of them wage earners.[67]

What is quite remarkable in comparison to other European coun-

[66] Alajos Kovács, *A zsidóság térfoglalása Magyarországon* [The ascendancy of Jewry in Hungary] (Budapest: Kellner, 1933), pp. 41-43.

[67] Ibid., p. 42. The last set of figures refers to the territory of "rump" Hungary in 1920.

tries is that in Hungary Jewish entrepreneurship was not restricted
to commerce, banking, and industry, but also made deep inroads into
the agricultural economy following the gentry's flight into bureaucracy. It is true, of course, that the largest latifundia were still owned
by the members of the magnate class. But at the same time, 19 percent
of all estates between 200 and 1,000 cadastral acres were under Jewish
ownership, as were 139 of the 687 estates (or 19.9 percent) over 1,000
cadastral acres.[68] Among the latter there were quite a few substantial
ones: the holdings of the Popper family extended over 47,000 acres,
Sigismund Schossberger's farms over 26,000 acres, and the properties
of Albert Wodianer over 30,700 acres.[69] Put together, these holdings
made up 14.6 percent of the arable land in the country. But Jewish
involvement in the agricultural economy went farther than ownership,
for apart from these proprietors we will find that 73.2 percent of all
big tenants were Jewish (1910), together with 26.6 percent of all salaried employees in agriculture, including agronomists, superintendents, and accountants.[70] With these figures in mind the statement of
one anti-Semitic author that 37.5 percent of Hungarian agriculture
was "controlled" by Jewish interests may be exaggerated but not altogether farfetched.[71]

Just as prior to 1848, so after 1867 the immigration and embourgeoisement of Jews was on the whole welcome by the Hungarian social
and political elite. True, as in the earlier period, the landowning
classes remained somewhat ambivalent. For while the large landowners would profit from the skill and meticulousness of Jewish tenants
and farm managers,[72] the lesser landowners would resent their indebtedness to Jewish creditors or fear the loss of their property to
them. But if the landowners were ambivalent, the bureaucratic state
reached out its arms and embraced them, in Coloman Tisza's words,
"as the most industrious and constructive segment of the Hungarian
population."[73] For one thing, Jews were creators of a modern economy
that the political machine needed for survival, status, power, and

[68] Ibid., p. 40.
[69] McCagg, *Jewish Nobles*, p. 132.
[70] Kovács, *A zsidóság*, pp. 44 and 72.
[71] This is the conclusion reached in Géza Petrassevich, *Zsidó földbirtokosok és bérlők Magyarországon* [Jewish landowners and tenants in Hungary] (Budapest: Stephaneum, 1904).
[72] As a conservative deputy stated in parliament with remarkable bluntness: "The truth is, gentlemen, that if you have a gentile for a tenant he will come at the end of the year and appeal to your Christian brotherhood and mercy. On the other hand, you can be sure that your Jewish tenant will pay the rent even if his wife and children will freeze or go without eating." *Napló*, 1890, xix, 301.
[73] *Napló*, 1882, v, 64.

prestige. For another, they would provide revenues not only to the state but to those individual members of the political elite who would act as fixers, intermediaries, and brokers between the business community and the bureaucratic-parliamentary machine. While the Hungarian establishment was untainted by the petty corruption that was so much a part of the Balkan political scene, its members were not entirely above collecting pecuniary reward as legal advisors, lobbyists, or members of the board of banks and industrial enterprises. The extent of this practice may well be gauged from a deposition to the House of Representatives in 1896, according to which 55 members of the parliamentary Liberal party held 77 jobs with railroads and transportation companies, while another 86 held 193 positions with banks and various industries.[74] For obvious reasons the exact figures on salaries and fees are impossible to establish. But one may get some idea of how lucrative these jobs were from a report in the daily *Budapesti Hírlap*, according to which thirty-five members of the Liberal party collected an annual two million Kronen in retainer fees alone.[75]

The relationship between the Jewish businessmen and the native elite comes close to the pattern of "pariah entrepreneurship"[76] that we are familiar with from the experience of other backward societies. As relative newcomers to the country, Jews could not expect protection and favors as a matter of right, but had to purchase them from the men close to the centers of political power. But if so, we must also remember that in Hungary this relationship had yet another dimension which was at least as important as material gain, one which set Hungarian Jews apart from other Jews in East Europe, and from other ethnic entrepreneurs in developing countries. This dimension had a great deal to do with the complex ethnic structure of the country in which Jews were not only seen as the allies of the Magyars, but as their most important allies against the other nationalities. For after 1880 or so their linguistic and national identification provided the critical five-percent margin that made the Magyars the majority rather than the minority in their own country. For this reason the governments of the day not only defended the profit margins of Jewish enterprise, but made an ostentatious philosemitism the hallmark of the liberal era, so much so that in the years to come the words "liberal" and "philosemitic" came to be nearly synonymous in Hungarian common parlance. Nor was this a matter of sheer rhetoric. When in the 1880s an irritating and abusive anti-Semitism swept the countries of

[74] *Napló*, 1896, xxi, 305.   [75] November 25, 1900.

[76] For the term and concept see Riggs, *Administration in Developing Countries*, pp. 188-193.

central Europe, Tisza not only denounced it as "shameful, barbaric and injurious to the national honor,"[77] but proceeded to use his machine to undercut the electoral support of the rising Anti-Semitic party. More than that, in response to this flare-up of anti-Semitism, Tisza's successors introduced legislation in parliament designed to put the finishing touches on the work of emancipation. Thus, at the very time when the anti-Semitic Christian Social party was sweeping to electoral victory in Austria, in Hungary the Jewish communities were granted representation in the House of Lords and equal rights with the Catholic and Protestant denominations.

The patronage and protection of official Hungary was paid back with interest. In politics, the great financial oligarchs provided money for the manipulation of electoral campaigns, while the rank and file of the bourgeoisie dutifully cast its ballots for the candidates of the Liberal party. In Budapest, where one out of every four inhabitants and every other voter was Jewish, Liberal deputies were elected with impressive majorities, even at times when the voters of other constituencies revolted. It was this loyalty that earned the lavish praise of liberal Hungary, while prompting Austrian anti-Semites to quip derisively about the nation of Judeo-Magyars and the city of Judapest.

Even more important than electoral and political support was the fact that the immigrants adopted their country with such considerable enthusiasm that within a generation they became overwhelmingly Magyar in language and culture. In 1880, 58.5 percent of all Jews gave Magyar as their mother tongue; in 1910, 77.8 percent.[78] This newly assimilated element "was often more loyalist than Apponyi, more chauvinistic than Ugron; they composed Magyar songs, wrote romantic poems, and when they founded new factories they did so 'for the benefit of the fatherland.' "[79] In the provinces inhabited by the minorities, the bourgeoisie became the outpost of Magyar culture. In the Rumanian and Slovak villages Jewish shopkeepers and country doctors were often the only persons who spoke the Magyar language among the inhabitants. Hence they tended to become the natural allies of the notaries, the gendarmes, and other officials representing the government in Budapest. As a Jewish member of parliament stated in 1895:

> Statistics prove that the Jews of the districts inhabited by nationalities carry on regular missionary work. Statistics also prove that

[77] *Napló*, 1882, v, 65.

[78] Hungarian Ministry of Foreign Affairs, *Hungarian Peace Negotiations*, i, 107.

[79] Horváth, *A magyar századforduló*, p. 56. Apponyi was one of the leaders of the conservatives; Ugron was the leader of the National Independence party.

where for miles around not a Magyar word is to be heard—in Rumanian, Slovak or German districts—it is a Jewish family living in the most modest circumstances which not only cultivates the Magyar language in its own circle, but also does its best to inoculate its children with the Magyar language and culture. We see that he who in the non-Magyar districts wishes his children to learn the Magyar language sends them to the Jewish school.[80]

The linguistic and cultural assimilation of Jews and their strategic position between the Magyar and non-Magyar nationalities did not make them full-fledged members of the Hungarian nation, but it certainly raised them above the status of pariah entrepreneurship. Rather than being pariahs in the conventional sense of the word, the Hungarian Jews of the period were a feudal estate in disguise, a corporate entity within the main body of the nation, endowed with privileges commensurate to its social function, but barred from the levers of political power by the traditional criteria of religion and heredity. This anomaly of an ostensibly liberal age was ignored and accepted in the nineteenth century. But in the twentieth it would become an irritant, and one of the major sources of tension in Hungarian society.

POLITICAL DYNAMICS

Agrarian Predicament

From a purely economic point of view the quarter-century between 1850 and 1875 will be remembered on the Continent as an age of agricultural prosperity. All over Europe grain prices were high. A bushel of Hungarian wheat that had brought a scant 2.19 Fls. in the years 1840-1849 sold for 4.16 Fl. in 1850-1854, 4.48 in 1854-1859, and 4.77 in 1860-1864.[81] The favorable trend continued well after the restoration of constitutional government. Thus in 1864-1869 the price of wheat stood at 4.69 Fl.; in 1870-1874 at 4.57; and in 1875-1879 at 4.65 per Hungarian bushel.[82] Adjusted to inflation (and calculated in constant, 1930 Pengő), prices throughout the third quarter of the century exceeded those of the second quarter by about 200 percent.[83]

---

[80] Seton-Watson, *Racial Problems*, p. 188.

[81] Budapester Handels-und Gewerbekammer, *Beiträge*, xli.

[82] Ibid. Also, Károly Rege, *A magyar buza áralakulása és termelési költségei* [Price and production cost of Hungarian wheat] (Budapest: Pátria, 1931).

[83] 1850-1854: 179.9; 1855-1859: 206.8; 1860-1864: 184.2; 1865-1869: 191.8; 1870-1874: 190.0; 1874-1879: 211.5. Rege, *A magyar buza*, passim.

In response to the favorable trend in grain prices, Hungarian sheep farmers abandoned the now faltering wool market, and within a decade or so almost four-fifths of arable land was planted in cereals.[84] Compared to the prerevolutionary decade the amount of cereals produced tripled, and the volume of exports increased from 4.5 million metric quintals to 14.7 million.[85] By the standards of the times these advances were so spectacular that the attention of foreign economists, businessmen, and governments turned to Hungary. "The external world suddenly discovered our extraordinary opportunities and tried to establish economic relations with us,"[86] a contemporary related in retrospect. According to the Viennese Professor Bontoux, "Hungary, a country barely known a decade ago but endowed with immense riches [would] soon be able to take a commanding position in the economy of Europe."[87] To which he added in the preface of the second edition of his work seven years later: "What was a probability in 1861 has now become a reality."[88] This no doubt was an overstatement. But the German economist Max Wirth likewise wrote of the hopeless position of Hungary's competitors (including Russia and North America) in the Austrian, Swiss, and German markets.[89] The Bavarian government, alarmed at the prospect of dumping, sent the economist Henrik Ditz to Hungary to investigate the situation and to suggest measures for the protection of German agricultural interests.[90]

However, just as in the pre-1848 period, the production and price boom did not translate into a sense of general well-being. Indeed, the very opposite was the case, for in spite of the favorable movement of prices and bumper crops in all but three years, the economy of the period was still habitually described as "barren," "accursed," and "woeful" by all classes of the agrarian population,[91] so much so that more recently historians have begun to question whether there really

[84] In 1867 wheat, rye, barley, or oats were planted on 78.1 percent of all arable land. Alexander (Sándor) Matlekovits, *Die Landwirtschaft Ungarns* (Leipzig: Duncker and Humblot, 1900), p. 95.

[85] Ferenc Eckhart, *A magyar közgazdaság száz éve, 1841-1941* [One hundred years of the Hungarian economy, 1841-1941] (Budapest: Posner, 1941), p. 55. The metric quintals used since 1854 equal 100 kg.

[86] Sándor (Alexander) Matlekovits, *Wekerle Sándor emlékezete* [Eulogy of Alexander Wekerle] (Budapest: Magyar Lapkiadó, 1922), p. 7.

[87] Eugen Bontoux, *Ungarn und die Ernährung Europas* (Wien: Waldheim, 1861), p. 3.

[88] Bontoux, *Ungarn*, 2d ed. (Wien: Waldheim, 1868), p. xi.

[89] Max Wirth, *Europa und die Bodenschätze Ungarns* (Leipzig, 1868), p. 31.

[90] One of the results of Ditz's mission to Hungary was his valuable study on the agriculture of the country, *Die Landwirtschaft Ungarns* (Leipzig, 1866).

[91] Eckhart, *A magyar közgazdaság*, p. 55.

was a "grain boom" at all.[92] The answer still ought to be affirmative, for during these years production, exports, prices, and land under cultivation were increasing. The problem was that these increases could barely keep pace with the rising costs of production (up 329 percent between 1848 and 1867) and taxes (up nearly 1,000 percent)[93] stimulated by the costs of labor and social overhead, and, in the last analysis, by rising consumer expectations. Thus, notwithstanding the glowing accounts of foreign observers and obvious increases in gross farming income, the net income of agrarian producers and of the population at large continued to stagnate. As before, improvements in technology and the consumption of industrial goods were financed by short-term credit, until outstanding debts reached 1.4 billion Fls. in 1881 (or 72 percent of the market value of all land under cultivation).[94] The number of bankruptcies increased. In 1890, 14,978 farms were foreclosed, and in 1900 the figure rose to 19,228. Over the thirty-year period between 1876 and 1906 some 118,000 farmers lost their holdings in toto.[95] Most of these auctioned-off properties were the minuscule holdings of "dwarf" or strip-farmers. But the major losers were still the owners of medium sized estates. Between 1867 and 1895 holdings in the 200- to 1,000-acre category, the type most closely associated with the gentry, declined from 6,600,000 to 4,260,000 acres, or from 16.8 to 9.1 percent of all arable land in the country.[96] In 1809, the general conscription of the nobility listed 27,000 landowners in the middle-income category.[97] In 1875, there were 13,748 landowners who qualified as such, but in 1890 there were only 9,592,[98] of whom not more than two-thirds were descendants of the original seigneurial proprietors.

If in the eyes of contemporaries the seventies were "barren," the eighties and the nineties were seen as years of agrarian depression and unmitigated economic disaster. Due to sudden improvements in transportation technology—the building of railroads across the North

[92] John Komlós, "The Efficiency of Serf Labor: The Case of Austria-Hungary," paper presented at the Ninth Annual Meeting of the American Association for the Advancement of Slavic Studies, Washington, D.C., October 1977.

[93] Eckhart, A magyar közgazdaság, p. 26; Czoernig, Osterreichs Neugestaltung, p. 531; and see above, n. 8.

[94] István Bernát, Tanulmányok az agrárpolitika és a magyar agrármozgalom köréből [Studies on agrarian policy and the Hungarian agrarian movement] (Budapest: Pátria, 1927), p. 237.

[95] Speech of William Mezőffi. See Napló, 1907, xiv, 263.

[96] Pál Sándor, A XIX. századvégi agrárválság Magyarországon [The agrarian crisis of the end of the 19th century] (Budapest: Akadémia, 1958), p. 153.

[97] See Chapter i, n. 23.

[98] Annuaire Statistique Hongrois, xix (1911), 80.

American Plain and the expansion of commercial steam shipping—cheap overseas grain gained ground rapidly on the Continent, putting great pressures on the agrarian producers that supplied Central and Eastern Europe. In 1860 European countries had imported only a negligible 200,000 metric quintals of grain from overseas. But this amount increased to 10 million quintals in 1870, and to 40 million in 1878, or three times the amount exported from Hungary.[99] As a result of these imports grain prices on the free market fell by thirty-six percent in the 1880s and by forty-eight percent in the 1890s.[100] In absolute terms this decline merely meant a return to the pre-1848 price levels. But given the production cost of Hungarian grain—nearly thirty percent above the costs in the United States[101]—Hungarian farmers rapidly lost their ability to sell their product on the West European markets, and even closer to home they were seriously threatened by foreign competition despite a valiant, and partly successful, effort to increase the volume of production without further increasing the area under cultivation.[102]

Agrarian producers of different classes sought different remedies to their continued predicament. At one end of the social spectrum, petty proprietors retreated into a semi-subsistence economy: only eleven percent of the farmers produced for the market, the remaining eighty-nine percent consumed their produce[103] and tried to cover their cash needs by working as seasonal laborers on large estates or as day laborers on railroad construction projects. The members of the agrarian middle class—the gentry and the lesser nobility—abandoned their farms and sought refuge in the bureaucracy and in public life. Only the large landowners were strong enough to resist the downward economic trend, and they did so by political means. These landowners formed the nucleus of an agrarian pressure group whose aim was to subvert the forces of the market and to restore the institutional supports of traditional landownership.

Liberalism and the Political Class

By entering the bureaucracy, the gentry and the German bourgeoisie rapidly transformed themselves from marginal economic classes

[99] Pál Sándor, "Die Agrarkrise am Ende des 19. Jahrhunderts," *Studien zur Geschichte der Österreichisch-Ungarischen Monarchie, Studia Hungarica*, 51 (1959), 168.

[100] Roland Kühne, "Geschichte des Getreidehandels und der Getreidepreisbildung in Ungarn" (Ph.D. dissertation, Moson-Heidelberg, 1910), p. 63.

[101] Gyula Rubinek, *Vámpolitikai kérdések* [Problems of tariff policy] (Budapest: Stephaneum, 1904), p. 7.

[102] See Chapter iv, p. 153n.

[103] Reported to the House of Representatives by Joseph Hortoványi. *Napló*, 1892, iii, 19.

into a full-fledged and more or less homogeneous political class with a vested interest in the supremacy of the national state and in the integrity of its institutions. To be sure, for decades a nostalgic air of traditional conviviality continued to linger over public life as the members of this political class adjusted themselves to their new social role and identity.[104] But the new administration produced more than its share of dour and faceless bureaucrats, who went about their business in the ministries with single-minded dedication,[105] while in the cabinet the two Tiszas and some of their associates were models of puritanical sobriety and devotion to the *raison d'état*, urging all classes of society, including the landowning class, "to succumb to [its] grandiose imperatives."[106] In the years after 1875 the welfare of the state was to take precedence over the welfare of society, though the pursuit of the common good was still subject to legal and institutional restraints. In brief, the ideology of the class could be reduced to the principles of legalism and secular etatism for which the liberal theories of the age provided a convenient political language.

These etatist credentials of the political class were seemingly compromised by the terms of the settlement of 1867 and the limitations

---

[104] Nowhere was this spirit of conviviality more evident than in various forms of conversation and address. All members of the party and the senior bureaucracy were expected to use the cordial "te" (corresponding to the German "du") when addressing each other and it was not unusual for senior officials to address their subordinates as "son" (*fiam*) or "younger brother" (*öcsém*), to be addressed in turn as "uncle" (*bátyám*). The use of "Mister" and the third person singular, *maga*, or any impersonal form of address, were regarded as slightly derogatory and mainly reserved for one's social inferiors. For an excellent description of these mannerisms and the etiquette of the bureaucratized middle class, see János Makkai, *Urambátyám országa* [The country of urambátyám] (Budapest: Singer és Wolfner, 1942). The term *urambátyám* is untranslatable and in itself most characteristic of the milieu, for it had been coined from two words: *uram* (my sir) and *bátyám* (my uncle). This term was generally used by the younger members of the privileged caste in addressing their seniors. For a sympathetic account of the mores of the Hungarian upper middle class, see John F. Montgomery, *Hungary: The Unwilling Satellite* (New York: Devin-Aldair, 1947); for a thoroughly unsympathetic view, Rusztem Vámbéry, *Hungary: To Be or Not To Be* (New York: Ungar, 1946).

[105] The names that come readily to mind are those of four men—Alexander Wekerle, Alexander Matlekovits, Leslie Lukács, and Joseph Szterényi-Sterk—who were most directly responsible for Hungary's economic and fiscal policies from the 1880s to the First World War. All of them were assimilated Magyars. They made their marks as top civil servants in the ministries of finance, commerce, and industry, and were later elevated to cabinet rank. Nothing in the recollections about these men suggests either flamboyance or dilettantism.

[106] István Tisza, *Magyar agrárpolitika* [Hungarian agrarian policy] (Budapest: Athenaeum, 1897), p. 18.

they placed on national sovereignty. Tisza's machine and the Liberal party nonetheless upheld them, not as an act of subservience or loyalty to the dynasty, but as an act of pragmatism and shrewd calculation. No less ardently patriotic than their ultra-nationalist critics and opponents, the Liberals could argue with justification that the partnership with Austria, while falling short of contemporary models for the national state, had tangible economic advantages, and, in addition, gave Hungary a disproportionate influence in European politics. The protagonists of this partnership could always point to Andrássy's tenure in office as the foreign minister of the Monarchy and to his success in promoting policies inspired by Magyar fears of panslavism and Russian domination. Indeed, an independent Hungary with her sixteen or eighteen million inhabitants (half of them unfriendly national minorities) could hardly have hoped to make similar excursions into great power diplomacy. Moreover, the Hungarian ruling circles had a dynamic view of the dualist arrangement in that they entertained the hope that one day the center of power in the Monarchy would shift from Vienna to Budapest. In the last decades of the nineteenth century these hopes were kindled as much by the Magyarophile sympathies of the Empress Elizabeth and the Crown Prince Rudolph as by the turmoil of Austrian domestic politics which so conspicuously contrasted with the stability and predictability of the Hungarian bureaucratic regime. In the meantime, Liberal governments jealously guarded the country's constitutional autonomy and prerogatives. The Austrian imperial anthem was de facto banned in Hungary, and the slightest hint of Austrian intervention into Hungarian politics was met with immediate rebuttal. Thus when the Austrian premier Kroeber once ventured an opinion on Hungarian constitutional law, his counterpart in Budapest dismissed it as the dilettantish view of a "distinguished foreigner." The Hungarian governments also doggedly resisted Austrian attempts to modify the quotas for common expenditures established by the Compromise. Between 1867 and 1890 the Hungarian quota increased by a mere 1.5 percent despite considerable increases in the sources of public revenue. In 1897 an irate Austrian delegation demanded a new 42—58 division of expenditures, but Hungarian obduracy forced them to settle at 32.5 to 67.5.[107] Far from being satisfied with the role of subservient junior partner, the Hungarian political class tried to make the best of the arrangement by bickering for new advantages at every turn.

[107] Arthur May, *The Habsburg Monarchy, 1867-1914* (Cambridge: Harvard University Press, 1960), pp. 348-349.

If one component of this liberal etatism was the struggle against foreign tutelage, another was the struggle against the tutelage of the established Church. At issue here were the very legitimacy of the national state and a conflict of prerogatives in such matters as education, family life, and the free practice of religion. These issues had preoccupied Hungarian liberals from the very beginning of the reform movement. But before 1848 the liberals were too weak to challenge the powerful Church, while in 1848 they had their hands full with other, more pressing matters. It was only after 1867 that they were well enough entrenched in power to press for the rights of the state over the Church. They did so first by demanding, unsuccessfully, the right of veto over clerical appointments (traditionally exercised by the monarch rather than parliament) and, further, by undercutting the dominant position of the churches in the realm of public education.[108]

However, as elsewhere in contemporary Europe, the major friction between Church and state arose from conflicting claims of jurisdiction over matters of civil law. Before 1867, marriage, divorce, the religion of children from mixed marriages, and conversion from one faith to another were all regulated by Catholic canon law. This state of affairs was particularly controversial because half of the population were members of different denominations whose own practices became subject to Catholic jurisdiction in case of conflict. To eliminate this irritant in the relationship between churches, in 1868 parliament passed a law regulating the religion of children born of mixed marriages, but the law was openly flaunted by the Catholic clergy and further attempts at regulation were frustrated by a veto of the House of Lords in 1883.[109] Undaunted, the government introduced stiff penalties for the violators of the earlier legislative act. When a papal encyclical urged clerical disobedience to the decree, the liberal government took up the gauntlet by submitting new, and more extensive anti-clerical legislation to the two houses of parliament. After bitter

[108] In 1868 the state had not yet controlled a single institution of learning, but by the end of the century 19.7 percent of the primary schools, 26.3 percent of the secondary schools, and the University of Budapest became state institutions, while the rest of the institutions of higher learning were placed under effective curricular control by uniform educational standards that were legislated for all the schools of the country. See Matlekovits, *Das Königreich Ungarn*, ii, 808; and Lajos Lóczy, *A magyar szentkorona országainak leirása* [Description of the countries of the Hungarian Crown] (Budapest: Kilián Frigyes, 1918), p. 221.

[109] For this and other details of the Church-state conflict, see Gábor Salacz, *A magyar kulturharc története* [History of the Hungarian culture struggle] (Pécs: Egyetemi Könyvkiadó, 1938), pp. 35 ff.

and prolonged debate, punctuated by demonstrations in the gallery and the streets, parliament passed three bills (Public Laws XXXI-XXXIII/ 1895). These bills introduced civil marriage and divorce proceedings, effectively terminated Catholic authority over the affairs of other denominations, and eliminated the last vestiges of discrimination against Jews by permitting conversion to the Judaic faith, and by seating the representatives of Jewish religious communities in the upper chamber. The Church was far from being demolished, but in a legal confrontation it had proved no match for the secular, bureaucratic state.

Far more inconclusive and vexing was the confrontation between the state and the national minorities of the country. This was especially so because liberal theory provided no doctrinal guidance and the age of reform set no precedents apart from insisting that the modern state should have a unitary character. The events of 1848-1849 demonstrated the inadequacies of this formula, and in the next decade Hungarian liberals—Eötvös in Hungary and Kossuth as an emigré—attempted to revise it by leaning toward the ideas of regional autonomy and federation. By 1867, however, these ideas seemed dated and impracticable, and the Hungarian elite returned to the unitary concept of the national state, though without totally ignoring the ethnic pluralism of the country. Thus while the Nationalities Act of 1868 once again spoke of a "single, indivisible Hungarian nation," it also acknowledged that "this nation consisted of different nationalities," and that "all nationalities—Magyars, Slovaks, Rumanians, Serbians and Ruthenes—[had] equal rights."[110] Specifically, any group that made up twenty percent of the population in any county was granted the right of using its native tongue in the county assembly, before the courts, and in petitioning the government. Once more, private organizations and churches were declared free to determine the language of instruction in any school supported by them, while in state-supported schools instruction was to be offered in the language of the majority of the local population. Francis Deák, the chief sponsor of the bill, also suggested the establishment of one Serbian and two Rumanian counties but this failed to win the support of the parliamentary majority. Similarly, his motion to provide state subsidies to a Serbian national theater in Ujvidék (Novi Sad) lost on the floor of the House in November 1868.[111]

The well-known fact about the Nationalities Act is that while the

[110] Gábor Kemény, *A magyar nemzetiségi kérdés története* [History of the nationalities problem in Hungary] (Budapest: Gergely, 1946), pp. 53-54.
[111] Ibid.

majority of Magyar politicians regarded it as exceedingly generous, the leaders of the other nationalities rejected it as thoroughly inadequate, even as a basis for further legislation. Yet no further concessions to national minorities were forthcoming. Between 1868 and 1878 new national states emerged on the Balkans that made the Magyars even more wary of their minorities. At the same time, the character of Hungarian politics was changing. In 1868 parliament was still made up of country gentlemen, but by 1875 it was already under the sway of a bureaucratic machine whose members refused to compromise the territorial and administrative integrity of the unit that provided them with prestige, livelihood, and identity. Thus instead of further expanding minority rights, the Tisza government introduced a regime of repression by outlawing "national agitation" and by institutionalizing the rotten borough system, actions that deprived the non-Magyar ethnic groups of effective political representation. Even more significantly perhaps, Tisza and his successors transformed the unitary state from a political into a cultural concept, for not only did they expect the ethnic minorities to obey the law of the state but enjoined them to become Magyar in language and custom. "Since patriotism is inconceivable without a common language," pontificated one of the members of the Liberal party, "our task must be to create one," and then he added: "What we expect from them is not only that they speak the Magyar vernacular but that they start to feel like Magyars themselves. This we demand from them, and if they reject our outstretched hands we will have to use methods which, in the short run, will not endear us to them, but which in the long run will produce beneficial results."[112] A few politicians of the old school remonstrated that this was the height of folly. But the majority were ready "to conquer for Magyar supremacy . . . by any means save for immorality and outright brutality."[113]

The governments for their part went about this task by passing one educational bill after another—the Educational Act of 1879, the Secondary School Act of 1883, and the Nursery School Act of 1891—each of which was designed to increase the number of subjects taught to non-Magyars in the Magyar language. And if these measures had, in Seton-Watson's appropriate observation, an element of bluff about them,[114] the bureaucracy nevertheless was more effective in gaining control over the school system by using the resources of the budget.

---

[112] József Sándor, *Az EMKE megalapítása* [The founding of the Transylvanian Hungarian Cultural League] (Kolozsvár: EMKE, 1910), pp. 83-84.

[113] Ibid.

[114] Seton-Watson, *Racial Problems*, p. 219.

A system of subsidies gave authorities the right of veto over curricula and appointments in any educational institution that received more than 200 Kronen (100 Fls.) in public funds. By using this leverage, the bureaucracy was able to convert some 1,200 impoverished Slovak schools, and 280 Rumanian schools into predominantly Magyar-language institutions, so that by the end of the dualist period 78.5 percent of the 16,496 grade schools and 90.5 percent of the 186 gymnasia had a predominantly Magyar instructional character.[115] These figures speak of less than full success, and, in the last analysis, these cultural policies produced only mixed results. On the one hand, they succeeded in capturing the potential intellectual elites among certain ethnic groups—above all among Germans and Slovaks[116]—and reversed the earlier 45-55 ratio between Magyars and non-Magyars in favor of the former.[117] On the other hand, in spite of all effort and expense, in 1910, 32.2 percent of the population, or 77.8 percent of the minorities, were still totally ignorant of the Magyar idiom,[118] while the rest certainly fell short of Magyar expectations of loyalty and patriotism.

Liberalism and Development

As a political class living off public revenue, the liberal elite of Hungary had a vested interest not only in economic stability but in the steady development of the country's economy. The bureaucracy was constantly expanding, and its rising needs could not be satisfied by a stationary economy. In addition, the political position of the national state, inside and outside the dual Monarchy, largely depended on its ability to close the economic gap between itself and the other European states. Finally, as many Hungarian statesmen well

---

[115] Oscar Jászi, *The Dissolution of the Habsburg Monarchy*, p. 329; *Annuaire Statistique Hongrois*, XVIII (1909), 377.

[116] In general, between 1869-1910, the rate of assimilation was highest among Germans whose proportion among the general population was down 21.6 percent. They were immediately followed by Slovaks (−21.0 percent). The Rumanians and the Serbs lagged behind with respective proportionate losses of 8.6 and 6.6 percent, while the proportions of Ruthenes remained stationary. The principal variable here was apparently religion shared or not shared with the Hungarians. While Catholicism, and, to a lesser extent, Lutheranism made ethnic groups susceptible to assimilation, Greek Orthodoxy apparently made them resistant. Percentages based on figures in Hungarian Ministry of Foreign Affairs, *Hungarian Peace Negotiations*, I, 139.

[117] In 1869 the number of Magyars was 6.117 million, the number of non-Magyars (excluding Croatia-Slavonia) 7.391 million. In 1910 the respective figures were 9.869 vs. 8.225. Ibid., I, 139.

[118] Lóczy, *A magyar szentkorona*, p. 175.

realized, the policy of nation-building by assimilation was contingent on the ability of the economy to provide material incentives to potential converts.

If on these grounds the commitment of Hungarian elites was unswerving, the strategies of development varied with economic exigencies and opportunities. In the decade following the Compromise of 1867 the economic outlook was bright and the governments of the day could reasonably trust the autonomous forces of the market to propel agricultural growth, and, indirectly, to stimulate the development of an industrial economy from the savings of agriculture. Under these circumstances the incipient mercantilism of the 1840s was abandoned, and, instead of protecting the producer, the substantial legislation of the period was designed to remove potential obstacles to a free market in produce, land, and labor. It was in this spirit of laissez-faire that in 1871-1872 guilds were finally abolished, that laborers were given statutory rights to bargain over their wages, and that the last restrictions on the sale of rural property (established by the Imperial Edict of 1854 to protect the peasant homestead) were lifted with the avowed purpose of permitting the transfer of land from the less to the more efficient producer.[119] Otherwise, the role of the state was to be confined to building an infrastructure, by promoting the construction of railroads and by laying down the foundations of universal education (1868) in order to create a literate and sophisticated labor force for the economy of the future.

This liberal trend in economic policy was gradually reversed after 1878 in the wake of the continent-wide agricultural crisis. Even beforehand there were pressures to change the policy on the part of conservatives representing marginal producers. But with the collapse of grain prices the protection of agriculture became not only an economic but a political concern for a government anxious to maintain the country's export potential on which the whole structure of public finance and the design for industrialization hinged. Thus while in 1880 Tisza still grumbled about those who "wanted to turn the state into a trafficker in grain"[120] by burdening it with regulatory and entrepreneurial functions, his closest associates were already charting a new course for the Hungarian economy. "The individual should be active, the whole society should be active, but the state should not remain inactive either," wrote Tisza's minister of commerce in a significant memorandum to the cabinet and parliament, and he added: "The principle of laissez-faire is justified only as long as natural growth

[119] Bernát, *Tanulmányok*, p. 51.   [120] *Napló*, 1880, xi, 363.

is possible. Once the process of natural progress is stalled, economic liberalism has only a paralyzing effect on national vigor."[121] Alexander Wekerle, at that time still a faceless member of the fiscal bureaucracy, described his economic principles in a similar vein: "The most important task of the state is to remove roadblocks to economic progress. But today the spirit of enterprise is sagging. Agriculture is unable to intensify production. The population is increasing and the excess can be absorbed only if the state is ready to intervene."[122]

For the moment, the intervention of the state was most needed to salvage agrarian exports and to raise the sagging profit margins of the agrarian economy. It was to this effect that the liberal governments became the spokesmen of agrarian interests, lobbying hard for protective tariffs for the joint Austro-Hungarian customs area. But if the liberal government, party, and bureaucracy undertook to lobby for protective tariffs, in doing so they had their own etatist concerns that went beyond the agricultural producer's narrow concern for an adequate profit margin. Specifically, the bureaucracy and the government tried to avoid placing excessive pressures on the urban standard of living, at least as long as the industrial economy was weak and, in the words of a modern economist, just about to "take off."[123] Thus while the joint tariff agreement negotiated with Austria in 1882 set import tariffs for cereals and flour, up until 1902 these tariffs raised the local price of grain only barely above the levels prevailing on the unprotected European market[124] (Table 13).

But the fifty-percent drop in agricultural prices had to be borne by someone, and, as in the other countries of the European periphery, a disproportionate share of the economic burden wound up on the shoulders of the lowest, and politically most helpless, classes of agrarian wage earners. This was accomplished gradually by a string of labor-repressive measures passed by the Hungarian parliament. First in the long line of these was the Domestic and Farm Servants' Act of 1878, a law that imposed humiliating conditions on seasonal laborers by exempting their masters from legal liabilities for "minor acts of

---

[121] Jenő Zichy, *Emlékirat a magyar ipar fejlesztése érdekében* [Memorandum concerning the industrial development of Hungary] (Budapest: Pesti Könyvnyomda, 1880), p. 16.

[122] Matlekovits, *Wekerle*, p. 15.

[123] Walt W. Rostow, *The Stages of Economic Growth*, especially pages 17-35.

[124] The tariff agreement of 1882 imposed 1 Krone (.50 Fl.) duty per metric quintal of wheat, .50 K. on other cereals, and 3 K. on flour. The tariff agreement of 1892 raised these amounts threefold, from eight to twenty-two percent of the free market value of these products. See Bernát, *Az új Magyarország*, pp. 172-180, and Rubinek, *Vámpolitikai kérdések*, p. 21.

TABLE 13
THE AVERAGE PRICE OF WHEAT IN LONDON AND VIENNA, 1878-1899
(in Austrian Kronen)

Year	London[b]	Vienna[c]	Year	London	Vienna
1878	25.7	23.6	1889	16.5	17.4
1879	24.2	24.6	1890	17.6	17.8
1880	24.5	26.8	1891	29.4	21.4
1881	25.0	26.8	1892[a]	16.8	19.4
1882[a]	24.9	24.2	1893	14.5	17.2
1883	23.0	22.0	1894	12.7	15.4
1884	19.7	19.6	1895	12.7	15.0
1885	18.1	18.0	1896	14.6	15.6
1886	17.2	18.6	1897	16.8	21.6
1887	17.9	18.2	1898	19.0	24.8
1888	17.6	16.4	1899	14.5	20.1

SOURCE: Roland Kühne, "Geschichte des Getreidehandels und der Getreidepreis-bildung in Ungarn," p. 63.

[a] Tariff rates increased.
[b] Free market.
[c] Protected market.

violence," and further, by stipulating that farm and domestic servants could not sue for damages on account of "expressions of opinion about their conduct . . . normally regarded as offensive to personal honor."[125] At the same time, the Penal Code of 1878 effectively undercut the provisions of the earlier liberal labor code inasmuch as it defined "gatherings for the purpose of extracting wages" as illegal assembly, "interference with the work of others" as an attack on private property, and "violent argument for the furtherance of wage claims" as a form of criminal assault.[126] This was followed by further legislation, ministerial decrees, amendments to the labor code, and finally by the Agricultural Labor Act of 1898. The quintessence of labor-repressive legislation, this act explicitly outlawed agricultural strikes, made agricultural laborers criminally liable for breaches of seasonal contracts, and further provided that fugitive laborers be returned to their place of work by the gendarmerie.[127] In neighboring Rumania similar measures evoked the label of "neo-serfdom."[128] In Hungary, contemporaries dubbed Public Law II/1898 the Slave Law (*rabszolgatörvény*). Whatever the label, the net result of such legislation in both countries was a return to a pre-capitalist mode of production

[125] Molnár, *Magyarország története*, II, 126.

[126] Ibid., II, 99.

[127] Julius Bunzel, *Studien zur Sozial-und Wirtschaftspolitik Ungarns* (Leipzig: Duncker and Humblot, 1902), p. 47.

[128] See Constantin Dobrogeanu-Gherea, *Neoiobagia*.

and the depression of the standard of living of the rural wage-earning classes.[129]

By 1880 or so, therefore, the exponents of the liberal political philosophy had come to agree with several conservative spokesmen on the need to protect the profit margin of large agricultural production units in order to maintain the country's grain exports and to sustain the accumulation of domestic capital. In this respect, Hungarians were influenced by the Viennese economist Bontoux, especially because his theories seemed to be corroborated by the production record of their own smallholders. But if there was agreement on this principle, the political and the landowning classes had conflicting views on the most desirable kind of proprietorship. On the one hand, the liberals argued that "it made no difference who owned the land as long as he produced and paid his taxes conscientiously."[130] Indeed, they did not hide the fact that they preferred the new, often Jewish, landowners to the traditional proprietors because they saw them as rational and more efficient farmers. On the other hand, the conservatives argued that some higher principle should prevail over the principles of the market, and that agrarian production units should stay in the hands of the nobility whose sense of mission and continuity was the sole guarantee of the integrity of national politics.

The conservative argument had made hardly a dent on liberal policy in the 1870s (one of the reasons why aristocratic landowners at first refused to enter Tisza's Liberal party and preferred to form their own conservative caucus). But in 1880 the issue was raised with a new sense of urgency, leading to a prolonged public and parliamentary debate, out of which a well-crafted compromise emerged between the polar liberal and conservative perspectives. By the terms of this compromise the outright and wholesale entailment of agrarian properties was avoided. But under the provisions of an ancient and rarely used law (Public Law IX/1687) members of "historical" families were now encouraged to apply individually to the Crown for the right to turn

---

[129] Whether this resulted in a depression or mere stagnation of the rural standard of living has not yet been firmly established by social and economic historians. Bernát speaks of a decline of 37.5 percent, comparing the years 1874-1883 with those of 1894-1903 (*Az új Magyarország*, p. 195). Bunzel on the other hand calculates that average rural cash earnings declined by 10 percent (from 200 Fls. to 180 Fls.) in a twenty-five-year period, without adjusting these cash earnings to the rate of inflation (Bunzel, *Studien*, p. 97). Another, more recent writer provides an extensive analysis of wages in both cash and kind, and his tables show a slight increase in both during the years of the agrarian depression. In sum, while the nutritional standards and housing of the rural population did not substantially deteriorate, its ability to buy manufactured goods certainly did. (See Sándor, *A XIX. századvégi agrárválság Magyarországon*, pp. 300-302.)

[130] Bernát, *Tanulmányok*, p. 51.

part of their estates into *fidei commissa*, or inalienable trusts, to be inherited through primogeniture. While the term "historical" was not so defined, in practice it nearly always applied to aristocratic families, for all but four of the ninety-two estates eventually so favored were the properties of old magnate clans, among them the Eszterházy, Festetich, Széchenyi, Andrássy, Batthyány clans, and other grandees whose names are familiar from these pages.[131] Between 1880 and 1910 altogether 1,806,648 acres were so entailed.[132] Thus while the clock was not completely turned back on capitalist agriculture, some two-thirds of the acreage of large holdings (about one-sixth of all arable land in the country) was transformed into neo-traditional estates protected from the vagaries of the market.

If the protection of agriculture was a matter of economic exigency, the protection of industrial enterprise was a matter of nationalist and etatist priority, based on the quest for national prestige and independence. However, in this respect Hungary's problems were what they had been in 1842, for while the Compromise of 1867 made the issue of customs a negotiable item, it forbade the unilateral imposition of tariffs by either the Hungarian or the Austrian parties. And even if the imposition of tariffs had not been banned by law, common wisdom would have counselled against it, for by the mid-eighties Austria had virtually become the sole "foreign" market for Hungarian agricultural exports, absorbing 91.7 percent of Hungary's wheat, 90.7 percent of her cattle, and 80.7 percent of the flour sold outside the administrative boundaries of the country.[133] Under these circumstances the Hungarian state could resort only to indirect means of protection by developing an elaborate system of subsidies through the provisions of the successive Industrial Acts of 1881, 1884, and 1890. According to the provisions of these acts the Hungarian state: 1) granted tax exemptions to newly established factories; 2) reimbursed firms for the duties on factory equipment imported from outside the dual Monarchy; 3) exempted new enterprises from stamp duties and other administrative fees; 4) provided credits and cash grants for particular industries; and 5) gave preferential treatment to Hungarian industrial products when making public purchases.[134]

---

[131] Dénes Sebess, *Magyar agrár evoluciok* [Hungarian agrarian evolutions] (Budapest: Egyetemi Nyomda, 1933), pp. 141-142.

[132] Ibid., p. 137; Bernát, *Tanulmányok*, p. 295. In 1910, the total number of acres entailed was 2,270,000; 463,352 acres, however, had been so protected before 1880.

[133] Matlekovits, *Das Königreich Ungarn*, II, 509-512.

[134] Ibid., I, 27-31; Gratz, *A dualizmus kora*, II, 224. Futó, *A magyar gyáripar*, pp. 275 ff.

These largely technical provisions were supplemented by measures of a broader political significance, designed to make Hungarian industry profitable, competitive, and attractive to foreign investors. Production costs played a significant role and the government was instrumental in keeping them down by ensuring greater "labor peace" than in neighboring Austria and Germany. While labor repression in industry was never practiced on the same scale as in agriculture, the provisions of the penal code were on occasion applied to discourage strikes and attempts at collective bargaining. This, however, was only part of an overall attempt to create a generally favorable business climate in which investment capital could count on protection not only from the unrest of the labor force, from agrarian excess, but also from the demands of great landowners for higher tariffs, the abolition of the grain exchange, the prohibitive taxation of profits, a moratorium on the repayment of agrarian debts, and for the expropriation of "vagabond" capital. The agrarians, to be sure, made inroads into the formulation of public policy by using their institutional and social leverage. But much of their design was emasculated by the political class, in part because of their direct involvement in the profits of banks and interests, in part because of their nationalist and ideological commitment to industrialism as a "higher" form of economic organization. In retrospect this commitment has often been underestimated and Hungarian liberalism dismissed as a "mere figleaf of agrarian feudalism."[135] In reality, the elite of nineteenth-century Hungary was, like the elites of today's "emerging nations," an interest group in its own right with an ideology of development, though given the institutional and international restraints under which it operated, it could not simply destroy its adversaries. It could only strike an even balance among their conflicting interests. That the Liberals did so is amply evident from their tariff policies between 1882 and 1902, from the respective budget appropriations for agriculture, commerce, and industry (Table 14), and from their policies of taxation whose burdens, in the last analysis, fell more heavily on agriculture than industry (though not on the owners, but on the labor force). True, after the turn of the century when the bureaucratic regime began to weaken under a multitude of pressures, landed interests made new inroads into public policy. But in the penultimate year of the old century the Budapest Chamber of Commerce—an organization less given to advertise its good fortunes than its adversities—could still state in its *Yearbook* that the "wisdom of the parliamentary majority . . . had saved

---

[135] Vámbéry, *Hungary*, p. 46.

TABLE 14
State Expenditures by Sector, 1868-1894
(percentages of budget)

Year	Railroad Building	Ministry of Commerce and Industry	Ministry of Agriculture
1868	—	12.51	2.43
1875	6.39	9.13	4.27
1880	6.85	9.13	3.43
1885	5.81	15.55	4.41
1890	4.73	16.72	4.38
1894	3.98	21.91	4.84

Source: Matlekovits, *Das Königreich Ungarn*, ii, 911.

the country from the kind of agrarian reaction that [had] gained the upper hand in Germany and in the Austrian half of our Monarchy."[136]

Independence and the Political Counterclass

In 1867 the Hungarian gentry and the rest of the educated public accepted the terms of the Compromise not only because under the circumstances this seemed to be the wisest course of action, but also because those terms established an institutional framework that promised to absorb the gentry and educated classes into the state apparatus. Consequently, at the time of the settlement only 7 of the then 446 members of the Lower House voted against the act. The rest either supported it, or accepted it with minor reservations.

However, the expectations of the gentry and the educated classes concerning the new institutional framework remained in part unfulfilled. For while tens of thousands of positions were created in the civil service, the expansion of the bureaucracy could not keep pace with the rate at which the landed middle class became pauperized. As we have seen, between 1867 and 1890 some 60,000 people entered public administration. But at the same time an equal, or perhaps even greater, number of potential recruits remained outside the state apparatus with limited means of support. Economically and socially superfluous, this free-floating element gradually emerged as an embittered political counterclass of "outs" whose members shared the fundamental philosophical premises of the "ins," but who wanted to get their share of the spoils of the state, and hoped to accomplish this by changing the terms of the Compromise of 1867.

[136] *Budapesti kereskedelmi és iparkamara, évkönyve* [Yearbook of the Hungarian Chamber of Industry and Commerce] (Pesti Könyvnyomda, 1898), pp. 15-16.

The marginality and social disillusionment of the déclassé emerge from the pages of countless "gentry novels" with their feckless and nostalgic heroes, whose images are still deeply carved into the collective memories and consciousness of Hungarians. The image varies somewhat with the sympathies of the individual authors: in the novels of Coloman Mikszáth (*The Noszty Boy*) and Francis Herceg (*The Gyurkovics Boys*) the heroes are lovably indolent; in Margaret Kaffka's *Colors and Years* and Julius Krúdy's *Sinbad* they are aimless and exude *Weltschmerz*, while in the novels of Sigismund Móricz (*Gentlefolk's Fun, Frankie Kerek*) they are always on the verge of self-destruction, social and physical. It would be, of course, an obvious exaggeration to say that each and every member of the provincial landowning class and landless noble intelligentsia conformed to these literary images. But if one can catch an occasional glimpse of old social virtues in individuals, there is no doubt that collectively the landed gentry, and with it the old urban bourgeoisie, had reached the end of a road that began with the naive optimism of the 1800s and led through the growing pessimism of the 1840s.

If the social life of this class now revolved around nightlong card games and revelries in provincial homes and coffeehouses, its public life centered around the activities of a nationalist opposition represented by the Party of Forty-Eight and the Party of Independence. Founded in 1868 and 1874, respectively, these two parties occasionally merged under the name of National Independence (1848) party, only to split up again and again into two or more separate factions whose combined electoral strength over the years reflected the changing economic fortunes of the country and of the landed gentry. Thus in the years 1872-1878 when economic conditions were still tolerable and when expectations concerning the dualist state were still high, the nationalist opposition commanded the support of only some eight percent of the deputies. But then economic conditions deteriorated, the pauperization of the landed classes accelerated, and competition for public employment increased. So the number of deputies elected on the various platforms of the nationalist opposition increased, too, until in 1905 they captured 40.9 percent of the electoral districts or practically all the open boroughs inhabited by ethnic Hungarians (Table 15). This last election led to the temporary demise of the Liberal party, and to the formation of the ineffectual "Coalition" government of 1906-1910.

The social dynamics behind the fortunes of the Independents and Forty-Eighters is amply evident from an analysis of the composition of their parliamentary factions. On the one hand, the bloc of nation-

TABLE 15
PARTY COMPOSITION OF THE HOUSE OF REPRESENTATIVES,
1875-1905

Year	Liberals		Conservatives[a]		Nationalists[b]		Other[c]		Total	
	Seats	%	Seats	%	Seats	%	Seats	%	Seats	%
1875-78	330	79.9	39	9.5	36	8.7	8	1.9	413	100
1878-81	237	57.4	100	24.2	76	18.4	—	—	413	100
1881-84	225	54.5	100	24.2	88	21.3	—	—	413	100
1884-87	242	58.6	96	23.2	75	18.2	—	—	413	100
1887-92	261	63.2	71	17.2	81	19.6	—	—	413	100
1892-96	243	58.8	78	18.9	92	22.3	—	—	413	100
1897-1901	290	70.2	61	14.8	62	15.0	—	—	413	100
1901-05	276	66.8	29	7.0	98	23.8	10	2.4	413	100
1905-06	159	38.5	73	17.7	169	40.9	12	2.9	413	100

SOURCE: Gratz, *A dualizmus kora.*

[a] Independence and Forty-Eight parties, splinter groups.

[b] Includes non-party deputies identified with Conservatives.

[c] Includes representatives of Slovak, Serb, Rumanian National parties, Agrarian Socialists, Republicans.

alist deputies, like any other in parliament (indeed more so than the Liberal party), was closely associated with the gentry and the erstwhile common nobility. On the other hand, the aristocratic contingent that graced the benches of the other parties (Tables 16 and 17) was absent, hence the landowners of the faction were far less prosperous than those appearing in the Liberal and Conservative columns. Not surprisingly, the group of ex-civil servants among them was less numerous (and hardly any of them had a background in the ministries).[137] And while a substantial number of the deputies were practicing lawyers, these were not the Budapest "fat cats" serving large banks and industrial corporations, but provincial attorneys whose clientele consisted of smallholders and artisans. All in all, we have to agree with one of the students of Hungarian elites that the Forty-Eighters were not only a group of "outs" facing the "ins," but also a party of have-nots resentful of the haves of the Liberal party.[138]

The division between Independents and Forty-Eighters more or less mirrored the division between nationalist moderates and radicals in pre-1848 days. Of the two parties the Independents were more moderate, content to fight for changes that would have given them periodic chances to share in the public largesse. Thus while the In-

[137] Eighty-eight percent of the few public officials in the parties of the nationalist opposition were elected officials of counties rather than ex-members of the ministerial bureaucracies. See Rudai, "Adalék," p. 224, and Lakatos, *Politikai vezetőréteg,* p. 56.

[138] Lakatos, *Politikai vezetőréteg,* p. 84.

TABLE 16
SOCIAL COMPOSITION OF THE HOUSE OF REPRESENTATIVES,[a]
1887-1910

Party	Commoner	Noble	Don't Know	Total	Arist.	Gentry	New Noble[b]	Old Noble
					Breakdown of Noble Category			
Liberal	203	489	48	740	122	367	66	423
	27.4%	66.1%	6.5%	100%	16.6%	49.6%	8.9%	91.1%
National Independent	67	137	29	233	11	126	5	132
	28.8	58.8	12.4	100	4.7	54.1	2.1	97.9
Conservative[c]	21	58	9	88	15	43	1	57
	23.9	65.9	10.2	100	17.0	48.9	1.1	98.9
Catholic	14	16	3	33	3	13	0	16
	42.4	48.5	9.1	100	9.1	39.4	0	100
The House	326	693	102	1,121	155	538	72	621
	29.1	61.9	9.0	100	13.6	48.3	6.4	93.6

SOURCES: Albert Sturm, ed., *Országgyűlési Almanach* [The Almanach of the National Assembly] (Budapest: Pester Lloyd, 1887 and 1897); Ferenc Végváry and Ferenc Zimmer, eds., *Országgyűlési Almanach* (Budapest: Pester Lloyd, 1910) and Kempelen, *Magyar nemesi családok.*

[a] Includes deputies from the years 1897-1892, 1897-1901, and 1910-1918. Each deputy appears only once even though he may have served more than once.

[b] New noble refers to those whose titles date after 1867.

[c] Because of constant secessions and fusions the conservative column turns out to be rather unrepresentative.

dependents criticized the Compromise, they did not want to abrogate it outright, but advocated a "constructive dialogue" with the purpose of exacting piecemeal revisions. "Common affairs are a reality," wrote the Transylvanian deputy Nicholas Bartha in 1898. "They are here to stay. They can be reformed gradually but not abolished overnight. The way to reform them is to win a parliamentary majority and to become the government of His Majesty."[139] In the same vein, the official program of the Party of Independence started out with a pledge of loyalty to the Crown, lamenting only the absence of a Hungarian royal court "in which our magnates could feel at home and would not be treated as alien intruders."[140] In other matters the party was content to advocate such reforms as the modification of the imperial escutcheon to include the Hungarian coat-of-arms, the adop-

[139] *Ellenzék* (Kolozsvár), September 23, 1898.
[140] Gyula Mérei, *Magyar politikai pártprogrammok* [Platforms of Hungarian political parties] (Budapest: Egyetemi Nyomda, 1935), p. 114.

TABLE 17
OCCUPATIONAL BACKGROUND OF MEMBERS OF THE HOUSE OF REPRESENTATIVES,[a]
1887-1910

Party	Landowner	Public Employee	Attorney	Professionals and Teachers	Total
Liberal	226	227	136	76	740
	30.6%	30.7%	18.4%	10.3%	100 %
National Independent	69	28	66	18	233
	29.8	12.0	28.2	12.2	
Conservative	38	17	21	10	88
	43.0	18.8	24.4	11.0	
Catholic	13	2	6	12	33
	38.0	6.6	17.3	34.9	
House	381	300	251	126	1,121
	34.0	26.8	22.4	11.3	

SOURCE: As above, Table 16.

[a] Since the lists of occupations and parties are incomplete, neither horizontal nor vertical columns add up to totals.

tion of national colors for Hungarian regiments, and Hungarian consular representation in foreign countries.[141]

Unlike the more moderate Independence faction, the radical Forty-Eighters wanted more than a political system that would merely permit the alternation of "ins" and "outs" in government. While they shrank back from the open advocacy of secession from the Monarchy, over the years they developed a program for expanding the scope and function of the Hungarian state to the point where it could absorb in toto the derelict gentry and the educated classes. Thus, instead of access to the "pork barrel" the Forty-Eighters wanted to see the restoration of the constitution of 1848: a separate Hungarian diplomatic corps (with its opportunities for high-status employment), and, most significantly, an independent Hungarian army "without which all the institutions of the national state [were] mere Potemkin villages."[142] In the view of the radicals such an army could serve a number of inter-related purposes. First, it could act as a shield of the nation (presumably against the recalcitrant minorities) to be used at the discretion of the Budapest government rather than of the despised Ministry of War in Vienna. Second, it could serve as a genuine "school of the nation" on the Prussian model, i.e., as an instrument for acculturating the peasantry and the minorities. Third, it could offer attractive career

[141] Ibid., pp. 121-124.　　　　[142] Napló, 1902, viii, 192.

opportunities from which the nationalist gentry had been effectively barred by the hostility and supranational spirit of the imperial corps of officers, and would at last permit the rise of a genuine Hungarian *Junker* class, next to the civil bureaucracy of the state.[143]

The economic policy of the Forty-Eighters was closely related to this nationalist program. Declaring themselves the true heirs of Louis Kossuth—who lived until 1894 but remained an emigré in Italy—the leaders of the joint parliamentary faction were wont to describe Hungary as a "mere colony, destined to provide primary products for a more powerful nation."[144] From the very beginning they denounced laissez-faire principles for, in the words of Irányi, the leader of the Forty-Eight party in 1873, "trade between unequal parties always favors the stronger and hence does not deserve the designation 'free.' "[145] Two years later Irányi's deputy and would-be successor put the party on record in favor of industrialization by means of setting up an autonomous Hungarian customs area and an independent National Bank.[146] These demands, echoed by two generations of nationalist leaders, were most starkly summarized in one of Francis Kossuth's parliamentary speeches: "There is no sacrifice that the country should not make for economic development. Economic development may be attained only through industrialization, and industrial growth is anomalous in the absence of economic independence. The independent customs territory and National Bank are, therefore, not only political abstractions but the preconditions of economic growth."[147]

The declarations of such economic principles were received with angry and frightened objections by the ruling Liberals who reminded the radical nationalists of the powerful leverage industrial Austria held over Hungarian agricultural exports. In response, the Forty-Eighters spun a web of imperialistic fantasies about the rise of a "greater Hungary" and of new markets for both her industry and agriculture. Thus according to a number of writers close to the nationalist opposition, Hungary would gather sufficient strength in the twentieth century to impose her will on the neighboring countries and re-emerge as a European great power on her own. "Today the Hungarian nation is still in a transitory stage," wrote the nationalist deputy and journalist Paul Hoitsy in 1902. "She is strong enough to resist

[143] For a programmatic statement of the Forty-Eighters, see *Napló*, 1892, II, 14-15.

[144] The parliamentary statement of Francis Kossuth, Louis' son, upon his election as president of the National Independence (1848) party. *Napló*, 1901, I, 38.

[145] *Napló*, 1873, IV, 368-369.   [146] *Napló*, 1875, I, 351.

[147] *Napló*, 1911, III, 429. For similar authoritative statements, see also *Napló*, 1906, I, 30-31 and II, 127, 259; *Napló*, 1901, I, 104; 1902, II, 192, 247.

encroachments coming from the outside, but not strong enough to embark upon the road of conquest."[148] However, according to Hoitsy, Hungary would shortly annex Bosnia, Dalmatia, and the other smaller territories that had been her tributaries in the Middle Ages. "She may or may not annex Serbia," but in any case, "the future generations will live to see Hungarian supremacy over Bulgaria and hear Hungarian spoken on the streets of Sophia."[149] Rumania's fate would be the same as Bulgaria's, for her people did not possess the true qualities needed to create and sustain an independent state. These territorial conquests would not only ensure markets needed for the Hungarian industry yet to be developed, but would also require large numbers of military and administrative personnel, thus providing the unintegrated gentry and would-be bureaucrats with a sense of hope, pride, and purpose in life.

While nurturing these grandiose dreams of mercantilist imperialism, the political counterclass still had to depend on the goodwill of an electorate of artisans and smallholders whose immediate, daily concerns were bound to influence the rhetoric of their parliamentary deputies. Thus the parliamentary and electoral speeches of the period abound with ringing declarations of intent to protect the interests of the "small man"—the artisan and the peasant farmer—together with scathing attacks on big industry, big landholdings, and big capital, whose role was becoming ever more conspicuous after 1890. In this vein, the Forty-Eighter deputies demanded subsidies not for big factories but for the small village craftsman,[150] the "protection of the hundreds and thousands of Hungarian windmills scattered across the countryside . . . instead of the protection of the interests of the three or four big milling companies of Budapest."[151] By the same token, the big banks were urged to grant credit not to the great landowners but to the small farmer pressed by innumerable burdens. But this loud—sometimes populist, sometimes agrarian—rhetoric remained just that. For when the nationalist opposition had its brief stint in power (1906-1910), it followed the economic policies of its predecessors to the letter, and even used the same technical personnel (Wekerle, Szterényi) to execute these policies. It continued to protect the

---

[148] Pál Hoitsy, *Nagymagyarország* [Greater Hungary] (Budapest: Lampel, 1902), p. 7. It should be noted here that Hoitsy (Hojca), like the other chief protagonist of "Hungarian imperialism" Eugen Rákosi (Kremser), was a first generation Magyar.

[149] Ibid., p. 102.

[150] See, for instance, G. Hellebronth in the appropriations debate of 1901. *Napló*, 1901, I, 104. Also Mérei, *Pártprogrammok*, p. 119.

[151] Julius Endrey, *Napló*, 1894, XXI, 7.

interests of big estates at the expense of the small ones, it quadrupled the amount of state subsidy to heavy industry,[152] but providentially placed 22,000 of its own adherents into the executive bureaucracy, and another 111,000 or so in the employment of the state.[153]

In that enlightened day and age when religious tolerance was still regarded as the hallmark of civilized conduct by the international community, the majority of Independent and Forty-Eighter deputies not only accepted the etatism and legalism of the ruling Liberals, but also their positive view of Jewish entrepreneurship, and their overall concept of developing the Hungarian economy, so to say, by proxy. But in the seventies and eighties there were sporadic flareups of anti-Semitic sentiment in the Hungarian countryside, fueled as much by the xenophobic superstitions of the peasantry as by the resentment of petty landowners whose acres—unprotected by the device of the *fidei commissa*—often wound up in the hands of Jewish landowners. Thus while the aging Kossuth denounced this anti-Semitism from abroad as "a German idea . . . an odious foreign import,"[154] and the leaders of the parliamentary opposition Irányi, Ugron, and Helfy (a converted Jew) concurred wholeheartedly with the assessment, a dozen or so deputies from the Independence and Forty-Eight parties teamed up to form an anti-Semitic parliamentary club, and ran on an anti-Semitic platform in the elections of 1881, 1884, and 1887.[155]

By opponents and historians alike this movement has been generally described as an incipient rebellion against capitalism and the market economy. In reality, the impulse and momentum for the movement were more complex and contradictory, lacking the ideological coherence that the anti-Semitic movements developed in the twentieth century. For one, if we look at the electoral map of the country we will soon discover that the movement had two separate geographical and

[152] By the provisions of Public Law III/1907. See Eckhart, *A magyar közgazdaság*, p. 123. It should be noted here that in 1907 the Hungarian parliament liquidated earlier tariff agreements with Austria and set up an autonomous customs territory. This law, however, was not to take affect until 1917, at which time changes in the prevailing tariff rates were further postponed.

[153] László Buday, *A megcsonkított Magyarország* [Dismembered Hungary] (Budapest: Pantheon, 1921), p. 259. A public reference to the character of the spoils system under the "coalition" of the parties of the nationalist opposition by Julius Berki, in *Napló*, 1921, x, 388.

[154] A letter of Kossuth read in the Hungarian parliament. Quoted in Klaus Schickert, *Die Judenfrage in Ungarn* (Essen: Essener Verlag, 1943), p. 173.

[155] The president of the club, Victor Istóczy, was a member of the Liberal party, but all other members of the club were Forty-Eighters or Independents. For a recent history of the movement, see Judit Kubinszky, *Politikai antiszemitizmus Magyarországon, 1875-1890* [Political anti-Semitism in Hungary, 1875-1890] (Budapest: Kossuth, 1976).

141

cultural centers: one in Catholic Transdanubia in the heart of the Hungarian *Vendée*, the other in Protestant eastern Hungary around the great Calvinist center of Debrecen.[156] In these two areas the anti-Semitic idiom may well have had two separate meanings. While in the Transdanubian districts the Jew was the symbol of a new economic order characterized by the incomprehensible fluctuations of the market, in eastern Hungary he was merely a more efficient competitor, presumably manipulating and subverting the market principle to his own advantage. These contradictory preceptions were reflected in the public statements of the parliamentary deputies of the faction: while their program was replete with demands for the restoration of certain traditional institutions (such as the guild, residential requirements, and the medieval confessional oath), they also used many of the liberal-progressive code words of the day. Nowhere was this contradiction more evident than in the writings and speeches of Iván Simonyi, one of the founders of the Hungarian anti-Semitic movement. In a German language pamphlet Simonyi lambasted not only Jewish economic domination, but also the "farce" of parliamentarism and the "culturally alien" concept of Roman law.[157] Yet at the same time, Simonyi treated parliament to a remarkable historical treatise cast entirely in the secular-progressive frame of reference of the age in which he argued that the evolution of western civilization must be understood as a sequence of four great historical revolutions: that of Christ against the pharisees, of Luther against the Catholic church, of the bourgeoisie against absolutism, and, lastly, the revolution of the producer against the Jewish subversion of the rational principles of the market.[158]

Property vs. Professional Politics: The Conservatism of the Aristocracy

In contrast to the middle classes of traditional society whose members gradually transformed themselves into a political class and counterclass vying for the proprietorship of the state, the aristocracy of Hungary on the whole succeeded in maintaining its identity as an economic class and as such remained the chief and most effective

---

[156] In 1884 sixteen constituencies elected anti-Semitic deputies. Five of them (Cegléd, Fülöpszállás, Hajdúnánás, Hajdúböszörmény, and Orosháza) were predominantly Protestant constituencies, eleven of them (Magyaróvár, Mosony, Pincehely, Somogycsurgó, Somogyszil, Szakcs, Szempe, Szenc, Tapolca, Verbó, Zalaegerszeg) predominantly Catholic constituencies. See Kubinszky, *Politikai antiszemitizmus*, pp. 208-212; Zoltán Bosnyák, *Magyarország elzsidósodása* [The Judaization of Hungary] (Budapest: Held, 1937), pp. 137-138.

[157] Iván Simonyi, *Judaismus und die parlamentarische Komödie* (Pressburg: Published by the author, 1883), quoted in Schickert, *Die Judenfrage in Ungarn*, p. 157.

[158] *Napló*, 1882, VI, 324.

exponent of property rights vs. the rights of the bureaucratic state. To be sure, during the years of absolutism the voices of this lobby were muted, for the aristocracy, like all the other classes, was reduced to either subterranean bickering with bureaucrats or to pleading its case in high places without any genuine political leverage. But in 1867 the constitution was restored and the aristocracy regained some of its earlier political influence, in part through its dominant position in the House of Lords, in part through the ever present aristocratic contingent in the House of Representatives with its political base in the pocket boroughs. This contingent maintained its leverage over the governments of the day by playing the game of periodic secessions and fusions, which over time produced a number of independent formations on the benches of the opposition heavily identified with great landowners: The Conservative party of Baron Sennyei (1875-1884), the Moderate Opposition (1884-1892), the National party of Count Albert Apponyi (1892-1899), and the Constitution party of Julius Andrássy, Jr. (1904-1910).

Irrespective of label and affiliation the members of this aristocratic contingent were the mainstay of an agrarian lobby whose principles were most succinctly summarized by the astute and cynical Count Alexander Károlyi: "What is good for agriculture is good for the country. We must judge all policies by this standard for three-quarters of the population derive their livelihood from agricultural production. If industry serves the purposes of agricultural development it should be subsidized. If it is detrimental to agrarian interests it should perish."[159] But the conservatism of the aristocracy did not merely imply lobbying for higher tariffs, lower taxes, and subsidies for agrarian enterprise, for "agrarianism" was only part of a broader and more comprehensive attempt to restore the structure and institutions of traditional society. Thus while the Conservative Manifesto of 1876 stopped short of openly advocating the restoration of feudalism, it denounced the reform legislation of 1848 as detrimental to the harmony and stability of social relations. Above all, these reforms were said to have reduced land to a "mere commodity," thus depriving it of its "ethical character" and hence of its proper social and political weight,[160] while the institutionalization of equality "made masters defenseless against the insolence of their servants," and threatened to subvert the natural order of society.[161] To remedy this situation

---

[159] *Napló*, 1895, xxi, 236.

[160] István Bernát, *Das verpfändete Ungarn* (Budapest: Europa, 1896), p. 46.

[161] János Asbóth, *Magyar conservativ politika* [Hungarian conservative policy] (Budapest: Légrády, 1876, p. 113.

the manifesto urged the re-entailment of land, curbs on the "profit-eering of the new 'finance oligarchy,' " and, finally, the restoration of corporal punishment ("to save the poor from heavy fines and imprisonment that threaten the integrity of family life").[162]

The agrarian interests that shaped this conservative social philosophy were also instrumental in shaping the magnates' attitudes both toward the dual Monarchy and toward the national state. The magnates of the country owed their wealth and rank to the past benevolence of Habsburg king-emperors, and these traditional ties of loyalty and the sense of gratitude were strengthened by the knowledge that without the protected Austrian and Bohemian markets the great landowners of Hungary could barely have survived the depression of the eighties and the nineties. For this reason, conservative agrarians continued to extol the advantages of the empire, and, at the same time, showed considerable ambivalence toward the supremacy of the national state. In theory, conservatives juxtaposed the ideas of religious and national communities, emphasizing the primacy and moral superiority of the former over the latter. In practical politics, these principles translated into active opposition to the secessionist schemes of the Forty-Eighters and indifference to the policies of assimilation promoted by the Liberals. If in fact the conservatives threw few obstacles in the way of aggressive cultural and national policies, they rarely used their collective power and prestige to promote them actively.[163]

The resentment the great landowners felt regarding the economic and national policies of the political classes was further deepened by the prevailing practices of machine politics and the nature of the political system. True, the aristocrats in parliament did not strenuously object to the narrow suffrage and other limitations on the political rights of the lower classes, but they resented the high-handedness of the two Tiszas and the encroachments of the bureaucracy upon their local spheres of influence. Acting as a traditional *fronde* against the modern, bureaucratized state apparatus, the conservatives denounced the practices of Coloman and Stephen Tisza not from the viewpoint of democracy but of oligarchy. In politics as in economics, the conservative magnates did not want "progress" but a return to the practices of previous ages, that is, to the freewheeling electoral contests of pre-1848 times over which their class exercised considerable influ-

[162] Ibid., p. 26.

[163] Some exceptions must be noted, though, among them that of Count Albert Apponyi, one of the chief architects of assimilationist policies and sponsor of the Educational Act of 1907.

ence. In the Hungary of the late nineteenth century the landowning classes could argue with some justification that tyranny was modern and liberty traditional. Therefore it is not surprising to find that the protagonists of the most reactionary economic and social programs— Albert Apponyi, Julius Andrássy, Jr., Paul Sennyei—were also those who continued to plead for "political liberties" and for a "government based on covenants, laws and equity."[164] These pleas became particularly vocal around the turn of the century when, under the pretext of suppressing agitation among the national minorities, Premiers Bánffy and Stephen Tisza attempted to smash some of the electoral strongholds of aristocratic conservatism. In response, the aristocratic *frondeurs* founded the Puros movement consisting of conservative deputies from all major parties. The movement was designed to restore "integrity and honesty in public life," and to end the "one-party system, the odious institution of the Government party with its predictable majorities that kill courageous and free political discussion."[165] In the nineties this group exercised some influence in public life. They blocked the government's attempt to destroy the last vestiges of municipal autonomy by the "etatization of administration." They campaigned for greater fairness of electoral practices, sponsored a parliamentary code of ethics, and were instrumental in extending the jurisdiction of the High Court of Justice over electoral irregularities. Yet at the same time they used their political weight to maintain the highly restrictive electoral census that excluded some three-quarters of the adult male population from the exercise of the franchise. Like the great Whig dukes of England a few generations before, they defended the political rights of a landed class against the overbearance of the central administration, but they had little sympathy for the idea of popular government.

In 1867, and for at least two decades thereafter, political conservatism seemed to be an exclusively aristocratic affair. The leader of the Conservative party in parliament, Baron Sennyei, warned repeatedly that "we" (meaning the aristocracy) "should not let leadership pass from our hands."[166] While some members of the party were wondering aloud whether anyone but a titled aristocrat should qualify for full-fledged membership[167] in view of the fact that a few truly

[164] Gratz, *A dualizmus kora*, I, 211.

[165] Ibid. For a similar speech by Count Apponyi condemning "majority . . . by divine right to which we must unquestioningly bow without regard to the means by which they secured this delegation of the national will," see Seton-Watson, *Racial Problems*, p. 190.

[166] Mérei, *Pártprogrammok*, p. 33.   [167] Gratz, *A dualizmus kora*, I, 146.

grands seigneurs—Princes Paul Eszterházy and Tassilo Festetich among them—were content to send their lawyers, estate superintendents, and other retainers to represent them among the "plebeians" in the lower house of the parliament.[168]

In the 1880s this small group of conservative deputies won a number of significant concessions from the government and succeeded in stabilizing the position of the great landowners in economics as well as in politics. But the effects of these victories were only temporary, for in the 1890s agrarian prices continued to fall raising the need for further protectionist and labor-repressive measures, while the bureaucratic state continued to press for its prerogatives, this time at the expense of the Catholic church, a major ally of the landowning aristocracy. The narrow political base of the pocket boroughs seemed to be inadequate to meet these challenges. It was in an attempt to widen this base that a number of pragmatic aristocratic politicians founded a Catholic People's party in 1894 as an instrument for drawing peasant smallholders and rural artisans into conservative politics under the leadership of a village intelligentsia of priests, pharmacists, and elementary schoolteachers.[169]

Mindful of this constituency, the program of the party was designed to capitalize on the grievances of the small entrepreneur whose fortunes had been severely tested not only by agrarian depression but also by the competition of the rising, modern manufacturing industries. Thus while the earlier conservative programs had urged protection for the "historical classes," this one demanded credits for the small farmer, protection of the peasant homestead, and subsidies for the village craftsmen.[170] In addition, the program inveighed against usury, unearned profits, and the disorganization of rural society which it proposed to stem by a tighter control of liquor licenses, the banning of child and woman labor, and by compulsory church attendance on religious holidays.[171] But these measures were temporary expedients

[168] Lakatos, *Politikai vezetőréteg*, p. 79.

[169] In 1897 the party had eighteen members in the House of Representatives: seven of them were landowners, two of them priests, another two pharmacists, six persons were elementary schoolteachers. In 1906, at the height of its popularity, the party had 34 members in the House. Twelve were landowners (five of them aristocrats), seven Catholic priests, five schoolteachers, two small shopkeepers, and five lawyers (three of them legal advisors of bishoprics). In terms of occupation and social origin the party's deputies were indeed more plebeian than those of any other party in the contemporary parliament. See Lakatos, *Politikai vezetőréteg*, p. 60; also Tables 16 and 17.

[170] Mérei, *Pártprogrammok*, pp. 164-168.

[171] Ibid.

meaningful only within a broader indictment of liberal capitalism and within the larger design for the reordering of priorities on a continent-wide, if not on a global, scale. Thus wrote one of the chief ideologues of the People's party at the turn of the century: "The pathology of the contemporary world is not due to the illness of its constituent parts. We deal instead with a venereal disease spread over the entire organism that cannot be cured by amputation. We will have to restore the natural order of societies that has been uprooted by liberalism and capitalism."[172]

In this general indictment of capitalism, the chief culprit responsible for "uprooting the natural order" of the world and of societies was the mechanism of the market. In the words of another conservative politician in 1902: "In the struggle for wealth, the stronger trampled upon the weaker and the less shrewd. Only usurers are benefiting from the artificial principle of equality. Unrestricted economic competition is also detrimental to true patriotism for it is bound to destroy loyalty to king and country. What [we] want is the restoration of the ethics of the previous ages, above all, in production and social relations."[173]

But the destruction of harmony was not the only charge raised against contemporary capitalism. The problem with the latter was not merely that it had fostered unrestrained competition among individuals and nations, but that it rewarded risk-taking and "speculation" rather than achievement by hard labor: "Differences in wealth, education and culture in today's society are not due to productive labor but to interest rates and the false theory of the productivity of capital. Instead of a society of enrichment by capital investment we will have to create a social order in which the prosperity of the individual is proportionate to his own work.[174]

And if the economics of capitalism destroyed the harmony and natural equilibrium of societies by debasing productive work, the politics of liberalism did its own damage by repudiating traditional religious doctrine concerning the divine origins of political authority: "The modern state has become the legal source of its own existence. All of its actions are judged by purely utilitarian standards. This has

[172] Sarolta Geöcze, "Konzervativizmus és keresztény szocializmus" [Conservatism and Christian socialism], *Huszadik Század*, 9 (1904), 272.

[173] Sándor Károlyi, "A gönczi levél" [Letter from Göncz], quoted in Antal Balla, *A magyar országgyülés története* [History of the Hungarian parliament] (Budapest: Légrády, 1927), p. 182.

[174] Ottokár Prohászka, *Produktív e a pénz?* [Is money productive?] (Budapest: Szent-istván Társulat, 1898), p. 52.

led to a ruthless competition for benefits that threatens to destroy those who had failed to stoop to this standard of political morality and egotism."[175]

As a corollary to this critique, the party was critical of the ethnic state, viewed as another product of the liberal age that fostered selfishness not only between man and man, but between one Christian nation and another. In this spirit the party expressed sympathy for the plight of Hungary's ethnic minorities, and professed a "perfect understanding of their grievances"[176] concerning the excesses of the government's nationalist policies. And while recognizing the nation as a legitimate political entity, the new conservatives of the People's party, much like the old conservatives of the grand aristocracy, believed in the moral supremacy of Christian commonwealths of which the Habsburg Monarchy seemed to be the foremost contemporary example.

Coherent as this critique was it did not take the party very far in parliamentary politics. No sooner did it enter the political arena than it felt the iron grip of the bureaucratic machine which, presided over by Premier Bánffy, made the elections of 1896 the most repressive in the entire parliamentary history of modern Hungary. But the party's electoral fortunes were not much brighter in subsequent elections either, for while the bureaucracy resolutely defended its own bailiwicks, including most of the Slovak and Swabian constituencies, the Magyar electorate of the "open" boroughs, including a disproportionately large number of Calvinist and Jewish voters, remained largely unreceptive to the "clerical" party with its professed sympathies for national minorities. Thus while its Austrian counterpart, Lueger's Christian Social movement, captured election after election in the western half of the Monarchy, the People's party of Hungary remained but an appendage of aristocratic politics in the shadow of a powerful bureaucratic machine.

[175] János Molnár, in *Napló*, 1897, v, 230.
[176] Mérei, *Pártprogrammok*, p. 161.

IV.

The Revolution of the Left (1906-1919)

ECONOMIC DEVELOPMENT AND POLITICAL CRISIS

Economic Progress, 1867-1914

Propelled by the policies of sympathetic governments and by the vigor of immigrant entrepreneurs, the Hungarian economy made considerable progress during the age of Austro-Hungarian dualism. In the years between 1867 and 1914 the gross national product of the country is estimated to have increased five to sixfold.[1] By conservative estimates, thus, the Hungarian economy was developing at an annual rate of 3.8 percent over the fifty-year period, though this rate was somewhat unevenly distributed between the first and second twenty-five years. For while in the seventies and eighties annual growth most likely hovered around 2.5 percent, in the eighties this figure rose to 6-7 percent, and shot up to an annual 8.5 percent in the fifteen years after the turn of the century.[2] By gaining such momentum, Hungary left behind the lesser economies of the European periphery, and moved ahead with the same speed as such major developing countries as Russia and Japan.[3]

[1] According to Molnár (*Magyarország története*, II, 176), the increase was fivefold, a figure extrapolated from partial information available on industrial and agricultural income, from changes in the tax revenues of the state, and from increases in the Hungarian quota of the common expenditures of the Austro-Hungarian Monarchy. In any case, the first systematic attempts to calculate the national income of Hungary were made only in this century. The most authoritative of these, by Friedrich Fellner, put Hungary's national income in 1906 at 6,500 million Kronen. Another study, by Béla Katona, estimated the national income of the country at 12-13,000 million Kronen in 1913, a figure drawn almost entirely from the industrial statistics collected that year. While the country had experienced explosive growth in the intervening years, this last figure seems exaggerated. See Frigyes Fellner, *Magyarország nemzeti jövedelme* [The national income of Hungary] (Budapest: Akadémia, 1916); Béla Katona, *Die Volkswirtschaft Ungarns* (Budapest: Légrády, 1913); for a more recent assessment, see Iván T. Berend and György Ránki, "Nemzeti jövedelem és tőkefelhalmozódás Magyarországon, 1867-1914" [National income and capital accumulation in Hungary, 1867-1914], *Történelmi Szemle*, 9 (1966), 187-203.

[2] Frederick Hertz, *Economic Problems of the Danubian States* (London: Gollancz, 1947), p. 25.

[3] According to the various sources cited above, in the years immediately preceding

Much of this growth, probably as much as two-thirds of it, was due to the industrialization of the country. This process took place in two separate spurts. The first and more modest one of these was encouraged by the agricultural price boom of the sixties and seventies, and resulted in the establishment of numerous breweries, flour mills, sugar refineries and other food processing plants. Then, in the 1890s, the industrialization of the country took off in earnest, stimulated by the influx of large amounts of foreign—mostly Austrian and German, but also English and French—bank capital.[4] Financed by this capital, new factories were mushrooming. From 1899 to 1913 the horsepower capacity of industry increased from 262,070 to 929,868,[5] while the gross value of industrial output rose from 1,366,000,000 Kronen to 3,314,000,000.[6] The fact that between 1890 and 1910 the population dependent on agriculture decreased from 82 to 62.4 percent,[7] while the number of those dependent on industry increased from 12.4 to 24.2 percent is even more telling.[8] To be sure, independent craftsmen or workers employed by small businesses made up a substantial part of this labor force. But even so, by 1910 there emerged a substantial class of factory workers employed in large production units (Table 18), more than half of them in Budapest, a city whose population

---

the First World War twenty-six to thirty-three percent of the Hungarian GNP was produced by industry. In contrast, the contribution of the industrial sector to the GNP of southeast European countries (Rumania, Bulgaria, Serbia) was fourteen percent or less. Meanwhile, the respective figures for Russia and Japan were 28.0 and 30.5 percent. For the Balkans, see Iván T. Berend and György Ránki, *Gazdasági elmaradottság* [Economic backwardness] Budapest: Közgazdasági és Jogi Könyvkiadó, 1979); for Russia, see P. Lishchenko, *History of the National Income of Russia* (Moscow: International Publishers, n.d.), p. 697; also Alexander Gerschenkron, "The Rate of Growth in Russia since 1885," *Tasks of Economic History*, 7 (1947), 145; for Japan, Okhawa Kazusi, *The Growth Rate of the Japanese Economy since 1878* (Tokyo: Kinokiniya, 1957), especially pp. 7 and 248.

[4] In 1900, about 60 percent of the capital stock of industries was controlled by non-Hungarians. By 1913 this figure had declined to 36.6 percent. See Iván T. Berend and György Ránki, *Magyarország gyáripara, 1900-1914* [The manufacturing industries of Hungary] (Budapest: Akadémia, 1955), p. 106.

[5] Louis (Lajos) Lóczy, *A Geographical, Economic and Social Survey of Hungary* (Budapest: Kilián, 1919), p. 107.

[6] Ibid., p. 108.

[7] For comparison, during the same period the agrarian population of Japan declined from 84.8 to 61.5 percent, in Russia from 88.8 to 82 percent, and in Austria-Hungary as a whole, from 67.1 to 56.8 percent. See Colin Clark, *The Conditions of Economic Progress* (London: Macmillan, 1940), pp. 192-205.

[8] Dezső Pap, *A magyar szociálpolitika a világháborúban* [Hungarian social policy during the World War] (Budapest: Grill, 1934), p. xlvi.

TABLE 18
STRUCTURE OF THE ACTIVE INDUSTRIAL LABOR FORCE,
1900 AND 1910

	1900		*1910*	
	Number	*%*	*Number*	*%*
Independent Craftsmen	301,026	33.7	330,975	29.5
Workers of Small Enterprises 1-20 Employees	361,665	40.5	375,166	33.4
Factory workers 20+ Employees	230,641	25.8	416,543	37.1
Total	893,332	100.0	1,122,684	100.0

SOURCE: Dezső Pap, *A magyar szociálpolitika a vilagháborüban,* p. xlvi.

increased prodigiously from 270,000 to nearly a million in the half-century preceding World War I.[9]

From a structural point of view, the industrialization of Hungary bore many of the marks of finance capitalist development in peripheral societies.[10] For one thing, the ownership of modern industry was highly concentrated. In 1900, five holding banks controlled 57.4 percent of the capital stock of modern industry, and had substantial interests in 225 of the 250 largest companies in the country.[11] Likewise, the labor force was not only heavily concentrated around Budapest, but also in a handful of mammoth enterprises. In 1907, 25 percent of the labor force was employed by 25 enterprises[12]; half of the machine and metal workers were employed in nine plants, 97 percent of steelworkers in three factories.[13] For another, the finance capitalist route and the global division of labor were amply evident in the differentiation of Hungarian industries, specifically in the rapid shift from light to heavy—metal, machine-tool, and chemical—industries. Thus by 1899, the joint percentage share of these industries was second only to food processing with respect to annual output, and first with respect to the number of workers employed (Table 19).

[9] Molnár, *Magyarország története,* II, 178.

[10] For this pattern of development, see Alexander Gerschenkron, *Economic Backwardness in Historical Perspective* (Cambridge: Harvard University Press, 1962), especially pp. 5-30.

[11] Berend and Ránki, *Magyarország gyáripara,* pp. 34-35.

[12] Statisztikai Hivatal, ed., *Ungarisches Statistisches Jahrbuch,* 15 (1907), 155.

[13] Ibid., p. 156.

TABLE 19
STRUCTURE OF HUNGARIAN INDUSTRIES BY BRANCH,
1899 AND 1907[a]

	Annual Output (Million Kronen)		No. of Workers		HP Capacity	
	1899	1907	1899	1907	1899	1907
Food and comestibles	646	940	40,718	72,019	70,011	120,414
Iron and Metal	182	267	46,131	52,857	72,892	89,374
Machine-tool	171	219	39,364	54,916	46,985	115,484
Wood	96	173	29,288	22,243	20,298	23,492
Chemical	84	162	13,178	49,027	9,870	99,861
Textile	53	133	14,285	32,535	12,675	30,302
Magnesium, gypsum, glass	51	77	32,523	51,612	15,785	32,038
Leather	31	72	4,933	8,440	1,949	5,228
Clothing (confection)	20	45	3,820	14,070	248	1,665
Paper	16	40	5,761	10,015	10,625	18,863
Other	17	30	6,566	9,345	1,232	2,702
Total	1,367	2,158	236,567	377,079	262,570	539,423

SOURCES: Hungary, Központi Statisztikai Hivatal, *Statistisches Jahrbuch für Ungarn* (Budapest: Athenaeum, 1900), VIII, 141-142, 145-146. Louis Lóczy, *Survey*, pp. 107-108.
[a] Factories employing twenty workers or more.

Meanwhile textiles remained one of the weakest branches of industry. This apparently was a feature common to all economies experiencing delayed industrialization in this historical period.[14] But in Hungary this weakness became even more pronounced given the country's special relationship with Austria, the great competitive advantages of the established Austro-Bohemian textile industry and its political influence over the tariff policies of the Dual Monarchy. After 1900 the government in Budapest attempted to remedy the situation by channeling sixty-five percent of all government subsidies into textiles. This was done secretly, given the great political sensitivity of the issue,[15] and resulted in only a small measure of success.

While the achievements of Hungarian industries are well recognized, and have often been described in glowing terms, Hungarian agriculture is generally dismissed as a total failure, as the victim of the profligacy of its owners, or of the great agrarian depression of 1878-1906. There is, of course, some truth to these negative assessments and explanations. But the adverse impact of the crisis and the

[14] See especially Gerschenkron, *Economic Backwardness*, p. 209.
[15] Eckhart, *A magyar közgazdaság*, p. 123; Berend and Ránki, *Magyarország gyáripara*, p. 28.

extent of agrarian profligacy appear to have been grossly exaggerated by agrarian conservatives and radicals alike. The fact of the matter is that even at the height of the crisis some credit was available for agriculture, otherwise farmers simply could not have piled one loan upon another, increasing the aggregate amount of their indebtedness decade after decade. And if the gentry and the aristocracy did not fully appreciate investment opportunities, we ought to keep in mind that by the end of the century close to one-half of the total acreage was owned, rented, or managed by new ethnic entrepreneurs, who were fully cognizant of modern methods of estate management and applied them, at least within the limitations of the overall institutional context. It was most likely for this reason that despite the prevalence of depressed prices, some improvements were made in the technology[16] of production, and that, as a result, per-acre productivity,[17] the amount of grain harvested, and the gross income of farmers continued to increase even in the face of economic adversity. Thus between the years 1871-1880 and 1901-1910, the production of wheat rose from an annual 16.64 to 40.93 million metric quintals, while the gross income of wheat farmers increased from 455.3 to 916.9 million (calculated in 1930 Pengő adjusted to inflation; see Table 20).

This is not to say that all was well with Hungarian agriculture. For while both gross production and income increased by over 200 percent during a thirty-year period, this income did not keep pace with the continent-wide rise of industrial prices.[18] Furthermore, part of the

TABLE 20
AVERAGE ANNUAL VOLUME AND VALUE OF WHEAT PRODUCED, 1871-1910

Year	Million Metric Quintals	Million Pengő[a]
1871-1880	16.64	455.28
1881-1890	31.62	665.28
1891-1900	37.49	744.48
1901-1910	40.93	916.91

SOURCE: Rege, *A magyar buza.*
[a] 1930 Pengő adjusted for inflation.

[16] Molnár, *Magyarország története*, II, 174.

[17] Between the periods 1871-1875 and 1901-1915 the per (cadastral) acre production of wheat increased from 4.1 metric quintal (mázsa) to 7.1; rye from 3.8 to 6.8; corn from 5.3 to 9.9; potatoes from 17.2 to 46.9; sugar beets from 83.8 to 136.7. Molnár, *Magyarország története*, II, 174; Eckhart, *A magyar közgazdaság*, p. 96.

[18] A. R. Prest, *Consumers' Expenditures in the United Kingdom, 1900-1918* (Cambridge: The University Press, 1954), pp. 5-10.

cash income that shows up in the statistics was not the result of improvements of method, but of protectionist measures. Finally, throughout these years the morale of the agricultural labor force deteriorated rapidly. All in all, by the first decade of the new century it was abundantly clear to all intelligent observers that the system of production had been pushed to its limits, and that no further increases in productivity could be attained short of major changes in existing political and social institutions. On the Left and the Center, this realization provoked a number of designs and experiments for the reorganization of society and the political order, while on the Right it was the cause of further retrenchment among agrarian conservatives, and one of the contributing causes of the political crisis of 1905-1910.

In sum, from a purely economic point of view "development" in Hungary was a reality, and the rates of growth attained measure up well against the contemporary record of both the core countries and those of the periphery.[19] From a social and political point of view the question is, of course, how such changes in gross national product affected the life of the population at large. In the Hungarian case the purely statistical answer is easy to find, for during the fifty years when national income increased fivefold, the population increased by a mere 34.1 percent.[20] Using elementary arithmetics we can thus conclude that during the half-century under consideration per capita income rose by approximately 272 percent, largely during the years 1900-1913. More accurately, while in 1901 income per head in the country was 185 Kronen ($37.30 at the prevailing rate of exchange), in 1907 it was already 325 Kronen ($65.65), and it may have increased to as much as 550 Kronen in 1913 (unadapted to inflation).[21] Indeed, according to the calculations of Colin Clark with respect to relative living standards, per capita income in Hungary increased from 250 to 427 international units.[22]

One should hasten to add that per capita income figures, whether in dollars or in international units (IU's), only partially reflect conditions of life among the general population. This is especially true

[19] This appears to be especially the case with respect to the rate of industrialization. Between 1885 and the outbreak of World War I, the average industrial growth rate was 4.49 percent in Germany, 2.11 in the United Kingdom, 5.26 percent in the U.S., and 6.55 in Sweden. League of Nations, ed., *Industrialization and Foreign Trade* (Geneva, 1945), pp. 132-134.

[20] *Annuaire Statistique Hongrois*, xix (1911), 57.

[21] 1 Krone = U.S. $.202. Figures from Fellner, *Magyarország nemzeti jövedelme*, quoted in Molnár, *Magyarország története*, ii, 176. See also, Katona, *Die Volkswirtschaft*, pp. 104-105.

[22] Clark, *Conditions of Economic Progress*, p. 131.

in peripheral societies where the distribution of income is highly uneven. Hungary was no exception to this rule, for, according to the best available estimate, one-third of the national income was received by seven percent of the population, another third by twenty-seven percent, while the last third was shared by sixty-six percent of the people.[23] But even within these groups further inequities existed: between the 3.5 percent of public employees (who had access to about 7 percent of the national income) and the roughly 3.5 percent of owners and entrepreneurs who reaped approximately 26 percent of the total[24]; between the urban and the rural labor force whose income differential was approximately 2.5:1[25]; between skilled and unskilled workers (Table 21); and finally among industrial workers of various skills and trades, whose wages responded to different demands on the global labor market (Table 22).

The Crisis of Mobilization

If the economic policies of Hungarian governments helped along the industrialization of the country, their cultural policies became an important factor in the rise of a system of popular education. Initially, these policies were motivated by the desire to create a sophisticated, or, at any rate literate, labor force in anticipation of the complexities

TABLE 21
WEEKLY EARNINGS OF INDUSTRIAL LABOR FORCE,
1901-1910

| | Percentages | | |
	1901	1906	1910
Less than 10 K.	29.1	22.7	18.8
10-14 K.	23.1	22.1	20.5
14-20 K.	21.4	24.9	26.1
20-30 K.	14.9	18.6	19.9
30-40 K.	4.8	7.7	8.8
40-50 K.	1.6	2.6	3.8
50 + K.	0.7	1.1	2.0
Don't know	4.4	0.3	0.1

SOURCE: Központi Statisztikai Hivatal, ed., *A magyar birodalom gyáriparának üzemi és munkásstatisztikája* [The statistics of Hungary's manufacturing industries and laborers] (Budapest, 1910), p. 114.

[23] Molnár, *Magyarország története*, II, 176.
[24] Ibid.
[25] Based on comparisons in Bunzel, *Studien*, pp. 5 and 84; also Nicolaus Sándor, "Die Lage der ungarischen Landarbeiter," Ph.D. Dissertation, Leipzig, 1911, p. 96.

TABLE 22
AVERAGE ANNUAL WAGE OF WORKERS
BY INDUSTRY, 1910

Industry	Kronen
Machine-tool	1,445
Printing	1,247
Metal	1,085
Leather	863
Chemical	841
Clothing	785
Food	748
Textile	589

SOURCE: Központi Statisztikai Hivatal, *Üzemi és munkásstatisztika*, 1910, p. 42.

of a commercialized and industrialized economy. But almost from the beginning, these policies became enmeshed with considerations of status and international prestige in a world that regarded education as a mark of "culture" and "civilization." Such motivations were present in all of the backward societies of eastern Europe, and tended to accelerate the process of educational development. But in the case of Hungary, this process was further stimulated by the desire to create an ethnically homogeneous society, and by the conscious use of the school system as an instrument of national integration. For this reason, Hungary's educational "revolution" was one of the most far-reaching of the countries of the European periphery. In the fifty years between 1849 and the end of the century enrollment in primary schools alone increased sevenfold, from 324,000[26] to 2,546,649,[27] while the number of literate people, a bare 10 percent of the adult population in 1842, rose to 34.4 percent in 1870, 61.4 percent in 1900, and 68.7 percent in 1910.[28] The number of literate males (over the age of seven) came close to 80 percent.[29]

The spread of mass education, however rudimentary it may appear by today's standards, had a number of significant social and political consequences. First of all, through the medium of the educational system large numbers of people became exposed to the images of the outside world, and through these images, began to develop "insights into the real functioning of society."[30] As a corollary, the ability to

[26] Fényes, *Statistika*, I, 66 and 99.
[27] Matlekovits, *Das Königreich Ungarn*, I, xii.
[28] Hungarian Ministry of Foreign Affairs, *Hungarian Peace Negotiations*, IV, 4.
[29] Ibid.
[30] Mannheim, *Man and Society*, pp. 44-45.

156

read and write made more people available for mobilization by political elites. The literate public was accessible to communication, organization, and indoctrination in ways more effective than the face-to-face, personal relationships that had been necessary to bring into motion the medieval *jacquerie*. In the 1825-1848 period it was the petty nobility that became so mobilized as a political resource. Now, toward the end of the century, insights into the social mechanism penetrated deeper, and edged far beyond the narrow circle of property and privilege into the ranks of common laborers in the countryside and the cities.

This "entry" of the masses into politics has a familiar ring from the history of western societies. Even there, of course, this process was agonizing. But in Hungary and in the other countries of the global periphery the process created far greater stress because it was far more abrupt, and because the masses emerged as political actors in an arena of far greater scarcities, in a society that had not yet completed the structural transformations associated with successful agrarian and industrial revolutions. Moreover, this stress was aggravated by a pervasive sense of relative deprivation generated by the international demonstration effect of the material achievements of the advanced societies of Europe. This is to say that while the Hungarian economy was developing at a respectable rate—and by 1907 the Hungarian per capita income figure of $66.65 (or 427 IU's in 1913) compared quite favorably with the $52.50 (306 IU's) for Russia,[31] the 250 IU's per head in the Balkans, or the 192 IU's per capita for Japan[32]— it was pathetically low when compared to the 1,066 IU's for Great Britain, the 881 IU's for Germany, or the 814 IU's for France.[33]

Even more significant than these abstract indicators of social welfare were differences in wages and income distribution between the core and the peripheral countries. To examine the validity of this proposition let us start by observing that in 1913 the wage of the average industrial worker in Berlin was measured at 5.17 RM (U.S. $1.23, 6.09 Austro-Hungarian Kronen),[34] an amount that translates into U.S. $338.25 per annum, per wage earner. At the same time, in Budapest the average industrial wage was 3.14 Kronen per day, or 857.22

[31] One hundred and two rubles per capita. See Serge Prokopovicz, *Histoire économique de l'URSS* (Paris: Flammarion, 1952), p. 372. Clark, *Conditions of Economic Progress*, p. 91.

[32] Clark, *Conditions of Economic Progress*, p. 98.

[33] Ibid., pp. 83-91.

[34] International Labor Office, ed., *Wages in Germany 1800 to the Present*. Studies and Reports, Series No. 15 (London, 1945), p. 28.

157

Kronen per annum, the equivalent of U.S. $173.15.[35] This wage differential is commensurate to the differences in the national incomes per head in the two countries. Indeed, the Hungarian industrial wage earner had a slightly larger slice of the national income than his German counterpart.[36] Moreover, Hungarian industrial wages compared quite favorably with the $125.97 (244.61 rubles) wage of the average Russian,[37] and the $95.61 (192 yen) per annum wage of the Japanese industrial worker.[38] The trouble was, at least from the point of view of the Hungarian and other peripheral elites, that such global comparisons were never made by contemporary observers, whether they were foreigners or natives to the periphery, whether they were intellectuals or manual workers. Thus when a critic of Hungarian conditions like the German Julius Bunzel wrote his caustic comments on the condition of the Hungarian laboring classes, he drew *all* his comparisons from conditions prevailing in Austria, Germany, France, and England.[39] Likewise, when the venerable Samuel Gompers visited Budapest in 1910, he was quick to conclude that the condition of the Hungarian working man was one of the worst in the world.[40] Neither Bunzel nor Gompers were much concerned with comparing Hungarian conditions to those in neighboring Balkan countries, where the economy was developing at half the rate, while the population was increasing at thrice the Hungarian rate, producing a steady deterioration of living standards despite a far more equitable distribution of land and social resources than in Hungary. Domestic critics, and especially the Social Democratic party with its deeply ingrained Austro-German perspective, adopted the same standard. Seen in this light, the condition of the Hungarian laboring classes was indeed atrocious, apt to fill the privileged with guilt and the underprivileged with rage and despair.

However, as we compare the process of social mobilization and the entry of the masses into politics in Hungary and the Occident, we will find not only quantitative but qualitative differences in the emerging social patterns. In both Hungary and the West, social mobilization implied the rising political awareness of the masses. But in the West

[35] The aggregate figure is based on an average work year of 273 days. Pap, *A magyar szociálpolitika*, p. 41.

[36] 266 percent vs. 232 percent. The figures—derived by dividing the average industrial wage by per capita national income—for Russia and Japan were 239 and 289 percent respectively. Apparently, the less developed the country, the higher the relative earnings of the industrial worker.

[37] Prokopovicz, *Histoire économique*, p. 372.

[38] Clark, *Conditions of Economic Progress*, p. 255.

[39] See Bunzel, *Studien*.

[40] Samuel Gompers, *Labor in Europe and America* (New York: Harper, 1910), p. 92.

this mobilization was accompanied, if not preceded, by another significant experience, the rise of a market economy and of a society within which the individual had a chance to develop a sense of personal autonomy and efficacy. In the West, the rising mass consisted of small producers and wage earners who had learned to live in a world of give-and-take, and to fend for themselves without the emotional support of the traditional *Gemeinschaft*, of kinship groups and extended families. The mass, in other words, had been rationalized before it was mobilized, it had been acculturated to the norms of the impersonal *Gesellschaft* before entering the political stage.

Not so in Hungary and in the other societies of the European periphery, where the market penetration of society, and especially of rural society, was limited, where land and labor never turned into genuine commodities to be bought and sold in response to the laws of supply and demand, and where only one in ten agrarian proprietors produced regularly for the market rather than for home consumption. Here the images of the modern world were dispensed through an educational system, but they were not corroborated by actual social experience. The result was a lopsided process of rationalization and a fragmented view of reality. The lower classes, among them the lower classes of agrarian society, began to develop certain insights, above all insights concerning the political vulnerability of elites. But these insights were not accompanied by attitudes and orientations that we associate with the ideal model of the modern *Gesellschaft*. To put it differently, these masses became modern politically but not socially, for while they became available for mobilization, they did not possess the attitudes and patterns of behavior that are essential to the effective functioning of a civic polity.

This fragmentation of attitudes is readily discernible in the works of rural sociologists of a more recent age,[41] as well as in the programs of agrarian socialists around the turn of the century. In both, chiliastic fundamentalism coexisted uneasily with talk about universal suffrage, and a fervent desire for enfranchisement was coupled with incomprehension of the subtleties of representative government. Deeply mistrustful of aliens, the agrarian socialist movements were almost exclusively led by local prophets and petty charismatic characters,[42] whose search for social justice was in the name of brotherhood, and

[41] For this literature see Chapter VI, especially notes 8-16.

[42] In 1901 twenty-eight agrarian socialists ran for election. Their occupations are listed as shoemaker, worker, carpenter, locksmith, machine operator, mason, agricultural laborer, journalist, and private employee. See Zoltán Bodrogközy, *A magyar agrármozgalmak története* [History of agrarian movements in Hungary] (Budapest: Egyetemi Nyomda, 1929), p. 77.

159

often cast in the language of a xenophobic nationalism. The split personality of the peasant exasperated the establishment liberal, but even more so the urban socialist who suspected the anti-capitalism and revolutionary zeal of the agrarian proletariat. In the words of an editorial in the social democratic daily *Népszava* in 1907: "The peasant is opposed to capitalism. But his opposition is different [from that of the urban worker]. . . . Revolutionary in appearance, the peasantry is reactionary in the true sense of the word. It wants to restore the subsistence economy and the handicrafts, and return to the 'good old days.' "[43] Be that as it may, the city and the countryside had no common language, and the Left gradually abandoned the agricultural proletariat more in frustration than in anger.

The political consciousness of the laboring classes was first evident among the urban proletariat whose members formed a German *Arbeiterverein* in 1869, and an ethnically more neutral and politically more militant Party of Non-Voters in 1876. However, these beginnings were relatively feeble, and the labor movement did not gain ground until the rise of a class of factory workers employed in the sprawling heavy industrial plants of the capital city. Thus it was only in 1890 that effective working-class organizations—a Social Democratic party with loosely affiliated trade unions—made their appearance. But after that date both the party and the unions rapidly acquired membership and muscle. In 1897 the unions organized an illegal but successful series of strikes in the capital. In 1901 the party put up fifty-eight candidates for election, none of whom were returned to parliament under the highly restrictive franchise. But even without parliamentary representation the socialists became a force to be reckoned with. At the turn of the century, the party had 72,790 members, while the trade unions enlisted 130,000 in the factories.[44] This membership was the largest any organization had ever had before in Hungary. Moreover, this membership was merely the militant hard core, with whose help the socialists could easily mobilize 150 to 200,000 people on short notice for the purposes of street demonstrations and later for political strikes. Some of the most notable of these occurred on October 10, 1907, on September 12, 1911, March 4, 1912, and on the "bloody Thursday" of May 12, 1912, when hundreds of thousands of demonstrators clashed with the military in front of the house of parliament. "Until the mid-nineties," a conservative historian of the period

[43] *Népszava*, July 26, 1907. See *A magyar munkásmozgalom történetének válogatott dokumentumai* [Selected documents of the Hungarian labor movement] (Budapest: Kossuth, 1955-1959), ɪv, 548-549. From here on *MMTVD*.

[44] Böhm, *Két forradalom tüzében*, p. 20.

notes, "it was the university youth who organized the demonstrations at times of great political excitement. However, in and after 1896 the Social Democrats monopolized the streets. . . . They and only they could call out the masses."[45]

While the urban proletariat had shown early signs of its restlessness, the Hungarian countryside remained quiet and seemingly complacent for more than twenty-five years after the Compromise of 1867, notwithstanding the depressed condition of living. As late as 1890, a member of the Party of Independence in parliament could favorably compare the peasant with the urban proletariat and extol the traditional virtues of the former: "He does not organize meetings. He does not chant the International. He works if he has a job. If he does not have a job he goes out and finds one. And if he can't find one he goes without eating and does not complain. No one in this country is more honest and patient than the agrarian laborer."[46] But this calm was deceptive. While on the surface little appeared to have changed, deep down there had been a substantial erosion of traditional values. Many peasants no longer believed in the inevitability of social inequality. After 1867 literacy spread in the villages, and the railroad network brought to the peasants new images of the world and of themselves. Conditions during the crisis years had created a great deal of pent-up discontent which was soon to burst into the open. In 1891-1892 there were bloody riots in the county of Békés where large crowds besieged the seat of the local administration. In the next few years the political situation further deteriorated. In some parts of the country, Bunzel reports, it was not safe for landowners to walk around even in broad daylight.[47] In 1894 one of the agrarian leaders, John Szántó-Kovács, was arrested and his trial in the district court triggered another wave of violence that resulted in the imposition of martial law. In 1897-1898 ill-organized agrarian unions struck the grain harvest and fought pitched battles against imported strikebreakers and the military units brought in for their protection. The authorities prevailed, but a National Union of Agrarian Laborers could still enlist 48,616 members,[48] and within a few years the agrarian socialists succeeded where the industrial proletariat had failed. They elected two deputies—the socialist William Mezőffi, and the populist socialist Andrew Achim—to the House of Representatives.

For the students of political science these movements should be

[45] Gratz, *A dualizmus kora*, I, 351.
[46] Baron Andreánszky, *Napló*, 1890, XVI, 183.
[47] Bunzel, *Studien*, p. 19.
[48] Nicholaus Sándor, "Die Lage der ungarischen Landarbeiter," p. 149.

particularly interesting because they arose not in the most impoverished, but in the most prosperous regions of the country, in the Tisza-Maros triangle that subsequently was dubbed the Stormy Corner (*Viharsarok*). It was here in the rich black belt of the Hungarian plain that the socialist deputies were returned, that the riots and strikes occurred, and that the National Union of Farm Laborers recruited most of its members. Indeed, in an apparent paradox, the incidence of rural violence and political action was highest in the counties where statistics show the best wages and the most even distribution of land. Whereas wages in the Carpathian Highlands ranged between .50 - .68 Kronen per day, and in quiescent Transdanubia between .90 and 1.15 Kronen, in the three counties of the Stormy Corner (Békés, Csanád, and Csongrád) they ranged between 1.83 and 2.07 Kronen (in 1890, prior to the first outbreak of violence).[49] And while in "feudal" Transdanubia large estates occupied 50-75 percent of the arable land, in Békés small proprietors owned 63.7 percent of the acreage in parcels of less than fifty acres.[50]

This anomaly was not lost on the political commentators of the day, who were also quick to discover the nexus between social communication and political activism. Commenting on the causes of agrarian radicalism, the Liberal deputy Louis Návay stated that "the material conditions of the laborers on the Plainland [were] far superior to those elsewhere in the country," hence "the origins of the movement [were] not economic but social. . . . Its causes [had] to be sought in the values and ideas of the workers."[51] The conservative deputy Gideon Rohonczy explained the unrest in the following terms: "Twenty years ago we had social peace. But twenty years ago we had no railroad and telegraph. The peasant went about his business and associated with his own kind. For advice he had his lord and priest, and he listened to them."[52] The leaders of the riotous peasants interpreted the causes of the upheaval in similar terms. Thus appearing before the investigating committee of the local lord lieutenant, one Albert Szilágyi stated: "The rightful demands of the laborers increased because the people of the land study more, know more, see more. How can you blame us? We have learnt how to read and write. We would now like

---

[49] Pál Sándor, *A XIX. századvégi agrárválság*, p. 149.

[50] *Magyar Statisztikai Szemle* [Hungarian Statistical Review], 24 (1900), 64.

[51] Lajos Návay, "Az alföldi munkáskérdés" [Labor problems on the Plainland], *Budapesti Szemle*, 84 (1895), 36 and 39.

[52] *Napló*, 1898, xii, 392.

to wear better clothes, eat like human beings and send our children to schools."[53]

The crisis of mass politics was further aggravated by the national fragmentation of the country and by the prevalence of ethnic minorities hostile to the Hungarian state. Ironically, for decades after the dualist compromise these minorities were quiescent, so much so that their few representatives withdrew from public life in quiet despair. This was the case until the very educational system that was designed to convert them to Magyardom raised their political consciousness, and made them "available" for mobilization by their own elites. From the mid-nineties onward the Slovak, Rumanian, and Serbian press began to reach large peasant constituencies, and its successful agitation laid the groundwork for the return of the national parties to public life in 1901. The hitherto docile Slovak and Rumanian voters now resisted administrative pressures and were ready to fight pitched battles in order to be able to exercise their political rights.[54] More frequently than not the authorities prevailed, but only at an exorbitant political price, for the ugly sight of repeated electoral violence created a public outcry abroad, and established an image of Hungary as the prison of oppressed peoples.

Political Response

All over then, the entry of the masses into politics created a new situation to which the governments at first responded with a string of threats and coercive measures. "Are you industrial workers?" the minister of the interior inquired curtly from a visiting delegation in 1875. "If so, then work industriously. You do not have to bother with anything else. You need no associations, and if you mix into politics, I will teach you a lesson that you will never forget."[55] Subsequently, the workers' organizations were harassed, their leaders hauled into courts, and their members placed under police surveillance or house arrest. The movements of the peasants and the national minorities were treated even more harshly. Riots were put down by gendarmes and soldiers firing into the crowds or charging them with fixed bayonets. This type of violence reached its peak under the premiership

[53] Andor Vadnay, *A Tiszamellékről* [Report about the Tisza region] (Budapest: Budapesti Hirlap, 1900), p. 27.

[54] This small coalition of parties won six seats in 1901, ten in 1905, twenty-five in 1906, and ten again in 1910.

[55] Baron Wenckheim, quoted in Bunzel, *Studien*, p. 94.

of Desider Bánffy (1895-1899) during which, according to a recent source, 51 persons were killed and 114 wounded in confrontations between demonstrators and the law enforcement authorities.[56]

However, as we argued earlier, the system was not set up to handle such massive violence. Indeed, the Bánffy "terror" created a parliamentary outcry that brought down the unpopular government, and ushered in some of the more foresighted members of the ruling class. This element in the Liberal party realized that the wave of radical protest they were witnessing was neither an aberration, nor an ephemeral phenomenon, but one of the side effects of the progress that they had attempted to bring to their country. One of the major proponents of this view was August Pulszky, a university professor and one of the chief ideologues of the parliamentary majority. In his words, socialism was "an illness, to be sure," but it was an illness "produced by industrialization," a price that any civilized nation [had] to pay for economic development."[57] Stephen Tisza was of the same opinion. "The problem of workers," he stated in response to conservative critics, "was not created here in parliament, but by the growth of the manufacturing industries in our country. The rise of the working class is an inevitable concomitant of industrialization, and is a problem common to all contemporary societies."[58] Moreover, while Tisza was convinced that the antagonism between labor and capital was irreconcilable, he also believed that "a class raised to decent human standards [would] be less dangerous than a morally and materially frustrated mass of humanity that had nothing to lose."[59] In this spirit, the Hungarian parliament began to enact a series of measures designed to improve the condition of factory workers, including laws providing for extensive medical and accident insurance to cover much of the urban labor force. But even more significant were measures that restored the right of workers to strike and to bargain collectively. Stephen Tisza advocated this for the first time in 1897[60] and it was under his subsequent premiership that the Ministry of Interior issued its Decree No. 55-154-1904, suspending the anti-strike provisions of the Penal Code of 1878. This measure was portentous in that it represented a significant departure from the earlier, unconditional support of the entrepreneur by the Liberal party. Now, under the threat of social rebellion the Liberals inaugurated a new policy of paying off the workers at the expense of the bourgeoisie and the peasantry. For while the

[56] Molnár, *Magyarország története*, ii, 149.
[57] Quoted in Zoltán Horváth, *Magyar századforduló*, p. 97.
[58] *Napló*, 1891, xxii, 45.   [59] *Napló*, 1897, iii, 258.
[60] Ibid.

bourgeoisie was to pay higher wages, the peasantry was to pay still higher prices for certain industrial commodities.

Payoffs, however, represented only one aspect of Tisza's larger social design, for he firmly believed that the economic carrot should be accompanied by the political stick. Thus while he was a vigorous proponent of measures "to oil," in the Bismarckian fashion, "the social machinery," he was a rigid opponent of admitting the lower classes or the national minorities into the political community of the nation. As a political theorist he believed "that the individual should be free from coercion as a private person." But from this principle it did not follow "that he should also be free to participate in the exercise of state authority."[61] In Hungary especially universal suffrage was impracticable, for as he stated with considerable bluntness in 1905: "Entire regions of the country would be lost to the national cause and fall easy prey to anti-Magyar subversion colored by socialism. 2-300 Magyar deputies would face 150-200 non-Magyars, and a certain part of the former bloc would be controlled by the agents of the internationalist socialist movement. The rural constituencies would be swept by a demagoguery of the worst kind. The serious, responsible representatives of a national policy would be reduced to a handful."[62]

But this was not all, for Stephen Tisza, now Count Tisza, not only opposed the extension of political rights, but he set out to curtail still further the powers of the parliament. In this respect, his words and deeds appear at first sight contradictory. On the one hand, Tisza continued to extol parliament as "the greatest treasure of the nation" and the "only guarantor of its continued existence."[63] On the other hand, he proceeded to emasculate the opposition by attempting to do away with the filibuster, the last effective political weapon of the parliamentary minority. In reality, there is no contradiction between Tisza's words and deeds, rather we are dealing here with a particular view of parliamentarism and national politics. Even more so than his father and predecessor, Count Tisza was committed to the goal of economic progress, but faced with the unrest of the masses he became convinced that he could attain this progress only by reducing the leverage of special interests, including that of the landed aristocracy, over the political process. Yet Tisza, however authoritarian and etatist in his conception of politics, was not an aspiring totalitarian dictator. For while ready to discard the institutional restraints of parliamen-

[61] Béla Barabási-Kun, ed., *Tisza emlékkönyv* [Tisza memorial] (Debrecen: Egyetemi Nyomda, 1928), p. 84.

[62] *Budapesti Hirlap*, October 3, 1905.

[63] On November 18, 1905. See Barabási-Kun, *Tisza emlékkönyv*, p. 45.

tarism, he was still a firm believer in the idea of the *Rechtstaat*, and the restraints of publicity on a potentially arbitrary government. To put it differently, he defined parliament not as an institution that reflected public opinion or converted it into coherent public policy, but one that exposed politics to the glare of publicity, and hence forced the state to obey its own laws.

While this design did not lack logic and internal consistency, some of its premises were seriously flawed, and these flaws eventually made it counterproductive in terms of the very goals it was created to accomplish. For one thing, the peasantry had already been squeezed hard enough. To squeeze it more the government would have had to resort to coercive and terrorist measures that were clearly antithetical to the idea of the *Rechtstaat* and limited government. For another, the urban working class was not easy to "pay off" from available resources, for it was not only demanding its fair share of the meager national product, but it was clamoring for that "decent" human standard shaped by the benefits available to the industrial workers in the more advanced countries. In any case, the impressive increases in real wages and per capita income in 1901-1913 made hardly a dent on popular discontent: the political demonstrations of the working class were far more vociferous in 1912 than they had been at the turn of the century. And if the urban labor force experienced improvements in the condition of its life, this was to a large extent at the expense of the profit margins of the bourgeoisie. A certain cooling thus began in the relationship between the state and the entrepreneur,[64] and this process of cooling could not be reversed even by Tisza's bold move to open up the political machine to the educated sons of the Jewish middle class. But the most immediate stumbling bloc to these policies was the landed aristocracy, who bitterly resented this etatist design of improving the living standard of one class at the expense of others, as well as Tisza's repeated efforts to reduce the powers of the parliament vis-à-vis the bureaucratic machine. In vain did Tisza argue that, in the long run, his policies served the aristocratic interest. In 1904-1905 the great landowners abandoned him, and it was as a result of this abandonment that the bureaucratic regime failed to win a parliamentary majority in 1905. Five years later, Tisza

---

[64] This was evident from the results of the elections of December 1905, when two overwhelmingly Jewish constituencies in Budapest, traditionally Liberal, went to William Vázsonyi's Democratic party. The same conclusion was drawn by Interior Minister Kristóffy who, in a memorandum to the king in 1906, wrote about the bourgeoisie as one of the classes that deserted the Liberal idea of the state. For the latter see Gratz, *A dualizmus kora*, II, 106.

was back at the helm of the majority party, now re-labeled the National Party of Work. Some aristocrats were contrite, but others continued to resist and obstruct the legislative work of the parliament until June 4, 1912. On that day, they were bodily ejected from the chamber, and in their absence, at long last, the majority changed the rules of procedure, making it impossible for the opposition to tie up the proceedings of parliament. For the moment Tisza's triumph was complete. Yet his was a pyrrhic victory, for the ruling class was now deeply divided, and as such weaker than ever to resist growing popular opposition and the vicissitudes of the forthcoming World War.

A World in Crisis

To sum up the aforesaid, the predicament of the Hungarian elites was due to the politicization of the masses—generated by a ubiquitous international demonstration effect—in the context of relative scarcities. But if the international demonstration effect thus explains the prevalence of social tensions and the free-floating frustrations of the proletariat, both agrarian and industrial, it does not quite explain how these frustrations were woven into an ideological cloth and turned into full-fledged political movements. In order to understand these political developments, we will have to go beyond the study of the Hungarian social structure and examine the dimensions of yet another crisis, the crisis of the global society at the beginning of the present century.

One dimension of this crisis was ideological and stemmed from a growing tension between the legitimizing and the operational principles of the liberal-capitalist world system. Ever since the inception of the latter, its inequalities had been justified by ideas that had their roots in the religious ethic of a few societies of northwest Europe, ideas that placed a great emphasis on the importance of self-denial and self-reliance in the broader scheme of human affairs. These ideas had a worldwide appeal, for while they tended to justify the supremacy of the Occident, they still held out the prospect for the nations of the periphery of one day joining the global elite by the fastidious application of these particular principles. Unlike the traditional universe, this new one was flexible, not fixed by divine or hereditary right.

The problem with this ideology was that it ran counter to the true spirit of capitalism, a system founded not on self-denial but on risk-taking. This contradiction had long been sensed but never more acutely perhaps than in the last quarter of the nineteenth century, when the ebbs and flows of the grain market punished or rewarded the producer, quite often irrespective of dedication or hard work.

Conversely, the market seemed to reward many who were not conspicuously industrious, but who possessed an uncanny insight into the
workings of the market, and acquired wealth merely by investing at
the right time and the right place. This conflict between industry and
risk-taking, expenditure of effort and entrepreneurship, was most
intense in the countries of central and southeastern Europe, where
the rise of the modern economy was not the result of cycles of saving
and reinvestment but rather of the large-scale management of "mobile" capital by the banking system. It was thus here in the heartland
of finance capitalism that the critique of the market principle flourished and became politicized by the ideologues of the Right who
denounced "speculation," and by those of the Left who cried "exploitation." Thus while the former denounced the market as a giant
fraud and its profits as the evil gains of dishonesty, the latter described
wealth as the result of coercion, theft, or plunder. And if these stark
formulations do not do perfect justice to the various complex theories
of money and surplus value, they certainly capture the rhetorical
essence of the objections of the Right and Left and explain their
appeal to the various classes of the dispossessed.

However, the crisis of the world system was not only a crisis of
abstractions and theories, but a crisis of domination by the occidental
powers. This domination lasted for at least three centuries, and was
remarkable mainly because it was accepted by the rest of the world
not only on the grounds of naked power but on the grounds of moral
superiority. In these centuries of unchallenged primacy, the western
nations radiated a collective charisma as superior civilizations, aided
by their ability to keep internal and international conflicts within manageable bounds. The industrial society of the West, as Herbert Spencer
explained to appreciative audiences, was not only materially but culturally superior to the crude "military" societies of the agrarian past
and present, one that left behind the barbaric worship of battles and
heroic accomplishments in favor of technological and scientific ingenuity. This view was immensely popular in the eighties and nineties,
but toward the turn of the century the competition among industrial
nations was intensifying, and a number of astute observers, among
them Hobson and Lenin, began to sense that this competition might
well be the harbinger of a devastating war among the most powerful
nations. When this war came in 1914-1918, it destroyed half of a
continent and with it the Spencerian myth. It also tarnished the global
image of the Occident. If before 1900 the intelligentsia of the periphery almost uniformly looked to the West expecting *ex occidente lux*,
after 1914 many of them turned *ad orientem*, seeking political inspi-

ration from the revolutions of the periphery. In doing so, it rejected not only capitalism and the market, but also the liberal idea of restraint that the Occident had brought into the modern world. Henceforth revolutionaries not only wanted to restructure their environment in their own image, but laid claim to total freedom in their choice of means, and justified their actions with the chiliastic grandeur of their designs.

This crisis of legitimacy was closely intertwined with the crisis of modernization. To be sure, the term itself was rarely, if ever, used in that day and age. But the nineteenth century had a boundless faith in progress by means of technological innovation, and the belief was general that backward countries, if sufficiently determined, could advance by acquiring the most recent, i.e., modern, technologies. By the end of the century this optimism began to fade, for while some of the peripheral nations, among them Hungary, did make considerable progress, the nations of the industrial core did not stand still either. Indeed, the relative development of continental countries did not change at all during the century. In 1900, just as a century before, England, the Low Countries, northern France, and western Germany represented the center of global material civilization, while the economic standards of other European countries declined in proportion to their geographical distance from the center of the industrial world. Whether we take per capita income, the production of steel or wheat,[65] England was more "developed" than France or Germany, Germany more developed than Austria, Austria more advanced than Hungary, and Hungary more advanced than Russia or the Balkan countries. This pattern, of course, was apt to raise further doubts about the hypothesis that related progress to moral character, for the distribution of virtue followed too neatly the geographical variable. But even more significantly, this pattern gave rise to doubts as to whether development within the context of the nation state was a feasible answer to the many questions posed by the problems of the periphery. Thus the grand designs of the century—Marxism, populism, and fascism—arose not as ideologies of modernization, but as designs to restructure the international system. The populists dreamt of a global peasant village without the evils of the market and the industrial

[65] This is especially noteworthy because the pattern prevailed irrespective of climatic conditions. Thus in the years 1906-1913 we find the following amounts of wheat produced per hectare and country: England, 33.4 metric quintals; Denmark, 28.2; Belgium, 24.3; Germany; 20.1; Austria, 14.8; Hungary, 13.4; Rumania, 11.6; Russia, 10.4. See Molnár, *Magyarország története*, II, 174; David Mitrany, *The Land and the Peasant in Rumania* (New Haven: Yale University Press, 1930), p. 316.

169

economy, while the Marxists and later the fascists rejected the notion of a free market, but retained the idea of industrialism. And if populists and Marxists envisaged a world of equality beyond the nation state, the fascists began their advocacy of a more perfect hierarchy of peoples, sustained by coercion and the primordial solidarity of the superior races of the European continent.

INTELLIGENTSIA AND POLITICAL CLASS

Sources of Alienation

If one of the significant developments of the period was the politicization of the masses, another was the rise of a new political class, consisting mainly of a disgruntled and frustrated intelligentsia. These two developments were closely related, for it was the emergence of an available mass constituency that provided the alienated intellectuals with a new identity and an opportunity to lead the dispossessed into rebellion against the inequities of the neo-corporatist and bureaucratic order.

The political alienation of the intellectuals is often attributed by historians and sociologists to the "overproduction" of university and high school graduates in relation to the opportunities available in the economic system. This quantitative explanation of the phenomenon is frequently a valid one. But in the Hungary of the late nineteenth century, it can be accepted only with certain qualifications, for while the system of popular education was rapidly increasing, the system of higher education remained relatively elitist, and, until the very last decade of the dualist period, its rate of growth did not exceed that of the economic system. While the gross national product increased five- or sixfold between 1867 and 1914, the number of students enrolled in high schools quadrupled, while university enrollments merely trebled. And while the two figures are not strictly comparable—we may note that in 1840 the country had 33,000 "college graduates"—the statistics of 1910 found only 73,745 persons in possession of diplomas and higher degrees from universities.[66] At the same time, the number of high-school graduates was 251,534.[67] Students enrolled in high schools numbered 138,232, those at universities 11,893 (excluding the technical university),[68] a mere fraction of a population of 20 million.

[66] Hungarian Ministry of Foreign Affairs, *Hungarian Peace Negotiations*, III, 217.
[67] Ibid.
[68] Dezső Laky, ed. *Statistique des étudiants des universités hongroises* (Budapest: Pátria, 1933), p. 17.

These figures clearly indicate that in 1900-1910 the chief problem was not that too many graduates were chasing too few jobs, but rather that the majority of jobs available in economic life were not meaningful enough, that is, they carried too little power and prestige. Indeed, if we run down the list of the leading radicals of the period, we will have little doubt that many of them could have found employment in banks and factories by virtue of family connections or even parental ownership. But most of these young men aspired to more important positions, and "more important" in that day and age still translated into professional politics.[69] Yet professional politics, too, was an arena of scarcity, overrun by thousands with proper familial or political connections.[70] But now the masses had appeared as a political factor, and their presence provided the outsider with a romantic, revolutionary alternative to the dullness of the bureaucratic machine.

While the average educated person may have been troubled by the scarcity of political opportunities offered by the bureaucratic state, the creative intelligentsia of the country—the writers, poets, composers, painters, scientists, philosophers, and sociologists—were more frustrated by the lack of a "cultured" audience in the country. This is not to suggest that the Hungarian establishment was disinterested in literature or in the arts. But from the intellectuals' point of view they were not interested in the right kinds of books, poetry, paintings, and music. While the creative intelligentsia was part of a global avantegarde, the public, whether the rural gentry, the bureaucrat, or the members of the rising commercial class, had maintained a somewhat provincial and philistine taste. It was not that they were actively hostile to symbolism, futurism, modernism, impressionism, Freudian psychology, or German sociology, only that they were slightly baffled and uncomprehending. Thus when Szinnyei-Merse, Hungary's foremost impressionist, opened his exhibit at the National Gallery, members

[69] This becomes obvious from the fact that law, the principal avenue to administrative or political careers, remained most popular throughout with as many as fifty-five percent of all students enrolled in it, 1906-1910. See Laky, *Étudiants des universités hongroises*, p. 17.

[70] Following the usage common in this period, the term "intelligentsia" (*értelmiség*) encompassed both high school and university graduates. Of the approximately 320,000 individuals who fell into this category in 1910, statistics are available on 300,676 persons. Of the latter 118,918 were in public service. Another set of data is available on 185,734 high school and university graduates who paid at least 18 Kronen per annum in direct taxes. Of this group 56,547 were in "production" (meaning the economy), 66,471 in the civil service, and 62,716 in the "free" professions (including teaching, journalism, and writing). It was from this last group that much of the radical intelligentsia of the time was recruited, though obviously only a small fraction of the latter were, in fact, radical.

171

of the country's social and political elite attended, less out of deference to his talent than to his illustrious family name. But they were overheard grumbling about one of their own, a gentleman, painting such ludicrous pictures.[71] Likewise, when Bartók's first opera was performed, the critics of the establishment press expressed the same bafflement, and the high official in charge of the state's opera budget could only mutter a few embarrassed words about the composer's strange predilection for Rumanian folk music.[72] To such incomprehension and unerudite taste the intellectuals responded with frustration and rage. Bartók himself complained bitterly in a letter to his fellow composer Kodály about this "Hungarian herd of cattle (*marhák*)," and concluded intemperately: "From now on I won't bother with them. Let asses be asses. Let them drown in their Merry Widow, and let us take all culture out of this country."[73] To which Kodály responded sympathetically that the "roast pheasant [was] not for the donkey. . . . If we try to stuff it down his throat, he will only get sick."[74] Meanwhile Ady, the foremost symbolist poet of Hungary, a Verlaine and Rimbaud combined, expressed his disappointments in verse. His "Poet of the Steppe" is an allegory about himself, and a case study of the alienation of the "westernized" intellectual in a backward, peripheral society:

> He was a Cuman lad with open eyes
> Tormented by his many sad desires
> He herded cattle on the endless steppe
> And dreamed around the nightly herdsman fires.
>
> . . . .
>
> A thousand times he thought of wondrous things
> He thought of death, of wine, of women-lure—
> In any other country of the world
> He could have been a saintly troubadour
>
> But when he saw his many filthy friends,
> His feeble-minded comrades and his herd
> At once he buried all his many songs
> And sadly whistled or spat a vulgar word.[75]

There are such alienated intellectuals in all backward countries. But Hungary, with its western culture and non-western social reality, pro-

---

[71] Horváth, *Magyar századforduló*, pp. 35-37.
[72] Ibid.   [73] Ibid., p. 253.   [74] Ibid.
[75] Joseph Grosz and Arthur W. Boggs, eds. and trans., *Hungarian Anthology*, 2d ed. (Toronto: Pannonia Press, 1966), p. 101.

duced more than its fair share. Indeed, this remarkable generation included, among others, Karl and Michael Polányi, Bartók and Kodály, Karl Mannheim, Georg Lukács, the psychologists Alexander Ferenczi and Franz Alexander, together with the budding scientific geniuses of Theodor von Kármán, George Hevesy, and Leo Szilárd. Of these geniuses many who had internationally marketable scientific skills left for German academic chairs, and later for American ones. Others, like the poet Ady, went into temporary and self-imposed exile in Paris "to be away from the braggart Danube . . . with its horde of loud-mouthed *pandurs*."[76] But for the time being, most of them remained in the midst of the "Magyar fallow," determined to change it and to take revenge on the social, economic, and political establishment by siding with the socially dispossessed whose very existence was a living condemnation of the rulers of the country. Their state of mind was pungently described by Ady in one of his early newspaper articles: "We are bitter, restless, litigious people full of bile who get up every day on the wrong foot. There are few things that please us, and social conditions here please us least of all. We believe and teach that these conditions are intolerable. We think and teach that Hungarian society, in as much as one can speak of one at all, is superstitious, uneducated, sick, and in need of change."[77]

Social Composition of the New Political Class

The political class of the 1900s was not only new because it turned away from bureaucracy and embraced the idea of mass politics, but also because its members were recruited almost entirely from outside the traditional social establishment, the gentry and the aristocracy. True, there were a few notable exceptions to this rule among the creative intelligentsia—Ady, for instance, who was quite proud of his noble origins—but their presence is statistically insignificant. If we examine the names associated with the leadership of the organized Left, we will find at most three percent on the list who were born into noble families (among them the six members of the National Independence party who show up as members of the National Council of the October Revolution). The rest came from urban or small-town environments and were heavily identified with the business and professional classes of Budapest and of the provincial cities.

Statistics on parentage are notoriously hard to gather, so we may

---

[76] Horváth, *Magyar századforduló*, p. 252. The *pandurs* were the constables of the feudal county.

[77] *Nagyváradi Napló*, April 2, 1902.

regard ourselves as quite lucky to have access to such data, collected by the members of the radical Galileo Circle from among their fellow students who were in sympathy with their cause[78] (Table 23). The members and sympathizers of this circle were later heavily involved in the Radical, Socialist, and Communist parties, so that the results

TABLE 23
COMPOSITION OF THE STUDENT BODY.
PARENTAL OCCUPATION AND FIELD OF STUDY, 1910

	Percentages	
Occupation	Official Statistics (Student Body)	Galileo Statistics (Radicals)
Smallholder	10.1	4.2
Landowner	4.7	5.0
Business (industry + commerce)	22.3	37.0
Schoolteacher	13.0	8.1
Intellectuals	13.4	18.8
Public Employees	14.8	9.5
Salaried Employees (private)	6.6	6.6
Physician, Lawyer, Engineer	7.5	6.6
Military	.8	.2
Other	2.2	—
Don't know	4.6	4.0
Total	100.0	100.0
Faculty		
Law	55.0	41.8
Medicine	15.2	21.1
Philosophy	14.1	7.7
Engineering (science)	11.8	18.6
Other	3.9	7.2
Don't know	—	3.6
	100.0	100.0

SOURCE: Tömöry, *Új vizeken járok*, p. 200.

[78] Such sympathy may be inferred from the circumstances under which the information was collected. For while the Circle did not identify itself on the questionnaires, they were passed out by its members. No attempt was made to reach the entire student body or to make the sample representative. Consequently, the 800 answers (from a student body of 11,298 in 1908) show significant deviations from the statistics pertaining to the entire student body. For the conduct of the survey, see Márta Tömöry, *Új vizeken járok: A Galilei kör története* [On unchartered waters: History of the Galileo Circle] (Budapest: Gondolat, 1960), pp. 55-56.

of the survey may be also taken to reflect on the composition of the intelligentsia in these political organizations.[79]

Whatever the methods of collection, these statistics tend to corroborate the overall impressions of historians and contemporaries concerning the structure of left-wing movements. Among the radical students we find 37.0 percent whose parents were businessmen (a significant deviation from the 22.3 percent of the official statistics), 18.8 percent who were children of professional families (against 13.4 percent for the entire student body). At the same time, children of public officials were underrepresented (9.5 vs. 14.8 percent). In both the official and the Galileo Circle survey we find approximately five percent whose parents were landowners (100 acres or more), but since neither of the two statistics differentiates between "old" and "new" landowners, we may only guess that most of the radicals in this category come from families of "new" agrarian entrepreneurs.[80] What is truly remarkable, however, is the apparent inability of the radicals to attract students of peasant and rural smallholder background, a category that by now made up 10.1 percent of the student body. In contrast to this figure, the radical sample shows only 4.2 percent, which means that of about 1,150 students of peasant background, not more than 45 or 50 supported or sympathized with the radicals. This finding corroborates the general impression that most students from the villages supported the Catholic and Independence parties. After 1920 they and their younger brethren also would become radicals, but their radicalism would be of a different color.

The Galileo Circle study is also illuminating with respect to the breakdown of the radical intelligentsia by profession and training. To begin with, as we compare the Galileo sample with the more general statistics on higher education, we find that in both law students oc-

[79] The composition of the student body is reflected, albeit imperfectly, in the social composition of the elites of the Soviet Republic of 1919. Of the forty-five people's commissars of the Republic, eighteen held university degrees, with two doctors (Guth, Hamburger), two engineers (Kelen, Hevesi), two economists (Varga, Rákosi), and several lawyers among them. But this elite, indeed the rising political class, did not consist only of university graduates. Thus, among the commissars we find fourteen who held high school diplomas, while thirteen others were self-educated skilled workers who entered professional politics through the party and trade union bureaucracy of the social democrats. See William O. McCagg, "Hungary's Jewish Commissars and Ministers, 1905-1924," paper presented at the Berkeley Conference on the Hungarian Soviet Republic, March 1969; also Schickert, *Die Judenfrage in Ungarn*, p. 201; and Péter Újváry, *Magyar zsidó lexicon* [Hungarian Jewish encyclopedia] (Budapest: Pallas, 1929).

[80] Such speculation is warranted by the small percentage of nobles and by the high percentage of Jews among the radicals. See below.

175

cupied the number one place, although their proportion was much lower among radicals than among university students at large. On the other hand, medical students were overrepresented among the radicals. This fact, surprising as it may be to the contemporary western reader, should not be entirely unexpected in the Hungarian context where the medical profession had a relatively low prestige, and was regarded by many as an avenue of advancement for dedicated young men of low economic or ethnic status. Finally, what is equally remarkable in terms of our more recent experiences with student radicalism is the fact that in Hungary engineers were overrepresented among radical political activists, while philosophy students were underrepresented. Striking as it may appear at first, this contrast seems to be explicable in terms of differences in social situations. While modern western radicals function in the context of a super-industrialized society whose very existence and identity are closely interwoven with the idea of technology, the Hungarian radicals of the time lived in a backward socioeconomic environment, where technology had had as yet no chance to develop fully. While after 1900 technology was regarded less and less as a panacea in and by itself, it still attracted many an adventurous mind, in contrast to philosophy and the letters which in the particular environment were regarded as conservative "academic" disciplines, more dedicated to classification than innovation.

The Ethnic Dimension

Of the diverse characteristics of the new political class, however, none was more striking, and more frequently commented upon, than its identification with the country's Jewish minority. In statistical terms this identification is indeed conspicuous, and at least as close as the nexus between the liberal political establishment and the "historical" classes of the country. As in the case of the former we are dealing with a group that made up only five percent of the general population. Yet whether we examine the leadership of "bourgeois radicals" social democrats, socialist reformers or revolutionaries, the proportion of persons of Jewish parentage among them is never less than forty, and sometimes as high as sixty, percent (Table 24).

The high proportion of Jews in the rising radical movements reflects Hungary's backwardness in more than one way. For one, as a backward country, Hungary relied on a class of ethnic entrepreneurs to lay down the foundations of its commercial and industrial economy. In the first half of the century, these entrepreneurs were newcomers who engaged in their pursuits with the single-minded determination

TABLE 24
JEWISH MEMBERS OF LEFT RADICAL ELITES,[a] 1900-1919

Members	Total		Jewish		Non-Jewish		Possibly Jewish	
Delegates to								
Socialist Congresses	175	100.0%	73	41.7%	66	37.7%	36	20.6%
Galileo Circle								
Officeholders								
1908-1918	100	100.0	46	46.0	34	34.0	20	20.0
National Council								
November 1918	20	100.0	8	40.0	10	50.0	2	10.0
People's Commissars								
Soviet Republic, 1919	45	100.0	27	60.0	11	24.4	7	15.6
Central Committee[b]								
and Committees of the								
CC of Communist Party								
Nov. 1918, March, 1919	117	100.0	53	45.3	47	40.2	17	14.5
Names analyzed	457	100.0	207	45.3	168	36.8	82	17.9

SOURCES: Delegates, *MMTVD*, III, 599-623; Galileo, Tömöry, *Új vizeken járok*, Appendix XXVIII, 273-277; National Council, Újváry, *Magyar zsidó lexicon*; Commissars, McCagg, "Hungary's Jewish Ministers and Commissars, 1905-1924"; Central Committee, Tőkés, *Béla Kun and the Hungarian Soviet Republic*, Appendix F, pp. 242, 245.

[a] Jewish here means, "of Jewish ancestry on the paternal side." Where no biographical reference, figures derive from first and last names, which in this period provide reasonable guidance.

[b] The figure includes eleven persons (10.3 percent) co-opted explicitly as representatives of non-Hungarian nationalities.

of the immigrant, and they turned their businesses to considerable profit for themselves and for the country as a whole. But by the second half of the century, the immigrants were well settled, and had not only acquired the status aspirations of the indigenous population, but also the means to pursue them effectively. Just as the German bourgeoisie sent its offspring to the institutions of higher learning in the 1840s, and to the bureaucracy in the 1880s, so the sons of successful Jewish entrepreneurs were sent to acquire education in the 1860s, and were ready to enter professional politics by the turn of the century (Table 25).

The extent of Jewish educational and professional mobility was impressive,[81] and, quite clearly, will have to be taken into consideration when attempting to explain the phenomenon of Jewish radicalism. But once again, the quantitative relationship between demand

[81] By 1910, 48.9 percent of doctors, 45.2 percent of lawyers, 42.2 percent of journalists, and 37.2 percent of engineers were of Jewish origin. See Kovács, *A zsidóság*, 42.

TABLE 25
JEWISH STUDENTS, 1853-1913

Year	High Schools		Universities		Law		Medicine	
	No.	% of Total	No.	% of Total	No.	% of Total	No.	% of Total
1853-1854	846	5.5	122	9.7	9	1.2	94	26.3
1863-1864	3,514	9.6	402	10.3	135	4.8	239	36.7
1873-1874	5,135	15.2	549	12.3	280	8.8	163	26.2
1883-1884	7,354	19.6	1,302	27.6	428	17.8	589	50.0
1893-1894	10,159	21.2	1,516	27.1	633	19.7	470	44.7
1903-1904	15,847	23.6	3,242	30.3	1,773	27.5	420	46.8
1913-1914	18,943	22.5	3,858	28.6	1,069	18.6	1,646	46.7

SOURCE: A. Kovács, A zsidóság, pp. 32-35.

and supply will not tell the entire story, especially not in view of significant changes in the status of the Jewish minority at the turn of the century, or, rather, pursuant to Stephen Tisza's first premiership in 1903-1905. For reasons already mentioned, Tisza launched a discreet but determined effort to co-opt into his machine the upwardly mobile members of Jewish families, and he did so with conspicuous results. Within a single decade the percentage of Jews in the administration of the country jumped from practically zero to 5.2 percent.[82] But even more dramatic were the results at the more visible and commanding heights of government: if before the elections of 1905 there were only a few token Jewish deputies in the House of Representatives, between the years 1905 and 1910, this number increased to 102.[83] In "Tisza's" parliament of 1910 alone there sat 84 deputies of Jewish parentage (22 percent of the total),[84] and even in the parliament of 1906, elected as it was under the auspices of the Independence party (ever so slightly tainted with the reputation of anti-Semitism), there were at least 26 deputies of the same category.[85] Meanwhile, at the very apex of the political pyramid, we find six, or perhaps eight,[86] Jewish ministers, and nine state secretaries of sub-

[82] Kovács, A zsidóság, p. 43. This figure relates to members of the Jewish faith only and does not include any persons of Jewish parentage who had converted to one of the Christian faiths.

[83] McCagg, Jewish Nobles, p. 185.

[84] Ibid.

[85] Seton-Watson, Racial Problems, p. 188.

[86] Although McCagg lists six Jewish cabinet members, he, as well as R. W. Seton-Watson, hints strongly that Minister of Justice Géza Polonyi (1906-1907), previously Pollatschek, was also of Jewish origin. In addition, an anti-Semitic ditty from 1903 suggests that Defense Minister Alexander Nyiri (1903-1905) was of Jewish parentage. See McCagg, "Hungary's Jewish Commissars"; Seton-Watson, Racial Problems, p. 188.

ministerial cabinet rank.[87] There were now also sixteen Jewish members of the House of Lords, and Francis Heltai, the Lord Mayor of Budapest (1913), likewise had his roots in the country's Jewish community.[88]

The opening up of the machine, however, was only part of a general scheme to co-opt the upper echelons of the Jewish bourgeoisie into the country's social system and elite. Above all, the appointment of Jewish ministers and other high officials was accompanied by a massive campaign for ennoblement. The award of titles to Jewish families, of course, was not an entirely new phenomenon—there had been 126 documented instances of this practice throughout the nineteenth century[89]—but now the government put its full weight behind Jewish applicants, and wangled from the Crown another 220 titles for Jewish citizens, 105 alone during the four years of Tisza's second premiership.[90] Mainly as a result of these interventions, by 1918 there were 346 noble families of Jewish origin in Hungary, 318 of them recipients of the knighthood (common nobility), 26 of them of the more prestigious baronial title.[91] To a great measure, of course, this represented political pragmatism on the part of the country's traditional leaders. Yet such accelerated Jewish mobility cannot be attributed to cold calculation only, for on the heels of Tisza's affirmative action program (as it might be called today) followed numerous signs of greater receptiveness on the part of the indigenous society. The hitherto exclusive great clubs (the National and Countrywide) began to admit Jews to membership,[92] while intermarriage between the two groups increased substantially between 1900 and 1918.[93] These marriages were especially important because they involved not only the lower and the middle classes, but some of the country's foremost families, so that one anti-Semitic writer of later years could ruefully identify no less than twenty-six wearers of ancient aristocratic titles who married brides from Jewish families.[94] Among the many others who did so were two prime ministers of the period, Baron Géza Fejérváry and Leslie Lukács.[95]

Given this shift in public attitudes, the radicalization of the Jewish

[87] McCagg, "Hungary's Jewish Commissars."

[88] Schickert, *Die Judenfrage in Ungarn*, p. 125.

[89] McCagg, *Jewish Nobles*, pp. 135-137.

[90] Ibid.   [91] Ibid., p. 25.

[92] Ibid., p. 35.

[93] 393 in 1900, 864 in 1910, and 1014 in 1920. Kovács, *A zsidóság*, p. 26. Bosnyák, *Magyarország elzsidósodása*, pp. 24-25.

[94] Schickert, *Die Judenfrage in Ungarn*, p. 141.

[95] McCagg, *Jewish Nobles*, p. 36.

intelligentsia would be something of a puzzle, had it not been for certain conditions that its members were expected to fulfill in exchange for upward mobility. One of these conditions—that the newcomers adopt the social styles and mannerisms of the native upper classes—was uniformly applied to all newcomers, and was not difficult or morally degrading to comply with. However, in the case of Jews, this condition was accompanied by the tacit but firm expectation of religious conversion to one or another Christian denomination. This expectation was, of course, not unique in contemporary Europe. But in neo-corporatist Hungary it was more rigorously applied, and was applied in connection with the most desirable status positions in society. Thus if we examine closely the impressive list of occupants in high political and social positions, we will soon find out that most of the "Jews" on the list were persons of Jewish ancestry who, at one point or another, had converted to a Christian denomination. While a perfect accounting here is impossible, it appears that at least three-quarters of the deputies listed above were converts,[96] as were all the other high officials with the exception of one minister (Vázsonyi) and one state secretary (Vadász), the latter's case to be treated as another example of rank tokenism.[97] Likewise, membership in the great prestige clubs of the elite, or marriage to a "genuine" Hungarian count or baron had invariably been preceded by conversion. The same convention prevailed in the case of ennoblement, though after 1904 a few exceptions were made, especially when the title was conferred upon a "mere" banker or businessman.[98] A similar rigor was applied in the case of academic appointments for, according to one source, seventeen of the twenty-six "Jewish" professors at Hungarian universities in 1910 had been born or raised in the Jewish faith but converted prior to their appointment.[99]

While on the surface rather trivial, the condition of conversion created severe strains on Hungarian middle-class society. For one thing, it kept the devout traditionalist out of the mainstream of national life in a society that prided itself on its blindness to religious matters. For another, and even more important matter, it raised bar-

[96] This conclusion is suggested by a comparison of figures in McCagg, *Jewish Nobles*, p. 185, and Újváry, *Magyar zsidó lexicon*, p. 911.

[97] Upon Vadász's appointment the radical *Huszadik Század* wrote the following ironic comment: "Tisza maintains that he is blind to religious denomination. This is patently untrue. He considered religion very carefully when making this appointment, and Leopold Vadász owes his august office precisely to the fact that he has not yet rectified his religious status." "Zsidó államtitkár" [Jewish secretary], *Huszadik Század* 26 (1913), 642.

[98] McCagg, *Hungarian Jewish Nobles*, pp. 172-173.

[99] Schickert, *Die Judenfrage in Ungarn*, p. 129.

riers to the mobility of the agnostic, the secularized, and the enlightened in this thoroughly scientific age in that it confronted them with a bizarre dilemma: they had the opportunity to become members of a liberal, even anti-clerical, establishment, but only by taking the clerical route, through the ritual of baptism. To some the choice was clear and easy: refusal rather than joining in a travesty of common sense. To others, "Paris was worth a mass," though subsequently the decision often produced an acute crisis of identity. In either case, however, the secularized Jewish intelligentsia faced a serious crisis, which it eventually resolved by embracing internationalist ideologies, above all the ideology of radical socialism. In the words of a recent writer: "In contrast to those who bought themselves into baronies . . . leaders of the counterculture, and the Jewish intelligentsia within it, did not seek assimilation by artificial means, but rather sought to create an order in which the whole issue of assimilation was irrelevant,"[100] and to build a political community based on universalist criteria, rather than on the "tribal" particularism of the national state. For this reason, the members of the counterculture not only decried "the *junker* nationalism of the Magyar ghetto,"[101] but all other forms of ethnic identity, including the ethnic identity of the traditionalist Jew entrapped in his superstitions and false consciousness. Indeed, if we leaf through the radical literature of the period, in it we will find more attacks on Judaism and Jewish identity than in the press of the political Right. Even such a mild-mannered humanist as Oscar Jászi (himself a convert to Calvinism) railed mercilessly against the "cowardly wearers of the yellow patch, who still stand trembling in front of the military nobility,"[102] and in 1917 he circulated a questionnaire to expose what he later described as "the defects of the Jewish character ingrained by centuries of ghetto life."[103] In the same year the socialist Peter Ágoston-Augstein, subsequently Béla Kun's deputy commissar for foreign affairs, published a tract similarly offensive to both the traditionalist and the assimilationist bourgeoisie whom the author accused of war profiteering and usury.[104] And if the rhetoric of prewar and wartime radicalism was abrasive and went out of its way to offend

---

[100] György Litván, *Magyar gondolat—Szabad gondolat* [Hungarian thinking—free thinking] (Budapest: Magvető, 1978), p. 67.

[101] József Diner-Dénes, "A magyar junker" [The Hungarian *junker*], quoted, ibid., pp. 75-76.

[102] Oszkár Jászi, "Obstrukció es választójog" [Filibuster and suffrage], quoted, ibid., p. 97.

[103] Oszkár Jászi, *Magyar kálvária, magyar feltámadás* [Hungarian calvary and resurrection], 2d Hungarian ed. (Munich: Aurora, 1969), p. 155.

[104] Péter Ágoston, *A zsidók útja* [The Jewish way] (Nagyvárad: TT, 1917).

all who refused to rid themselves of the false consciousness of an ethnic identity, the young extremists of the Soviet Republic of 1919 turned metaphor into terrifying reality as they attacked both Magyar and Jewish nationalism, and sought out traditionalist Jews with special ferocity as targets of their campaigns of terror.[105]

VARIETIES OF RADICALISM

Reformers and Revolutionaries

From the discussion on the preceding pages there emerge certain common denominators in the views of the new political class. First and foremost perhaps, the members of this class were united in their opposition to the political and economic institutions of the neo-corporatist society of Hungary with their barriers to human fulfillment and social mobility. Second, they all shared a profound distaste for the particularism of ethnic nationalism that was woven into the fabric of all European societies, including, of course, the society of Hungary. But if such consensus existed among them as to the evils of society, they were deeply divided as to potential remedies. For while some of them believed in the development of the productive forces of society, others wanted to change the entire structure and rules of the global system. And while one part of the political class maintained its commitment to the institutional heritage of the Occident, another was ready to throw this tradition to the wind and pursue its design free from awkward restraints. Vague and uncertain at first, these divergent perceptions of reality became in time expressed in organization and formal ideology, and it is in terms of the latter that we can distinguish between "bourgeois" and socialist reformers, and, later, between reformist and revolutionary socialists.

The backbone of the "bourgeois," or more properly citizens' (*polgári*)[106] reform movement, consisted of a group of sociologists, journalists, and philosophers, both academic and free-lance, who on the first day of 1900 got together to form an Association for the Scientific Study of Society (*Társadalomtudományi Társaság*, or TT), and to found the journal of *Huszadik Század* [Twentieth century], an organ that subsequently was to play a significant role in crystallizing the

---

[105] 7.4 or 11.9 percent of those executed (depending on whether we accept the larger or smaller estimate of victims), and 18.4 percent of those imprisoned during the Republic were Jews. Ujváry, *Magyar zsidó lexicon*, pp. 220-221.

[106] It will be well to recall here that the Hungarian word *polgár*, like its German counterpart *Bürger* from which it derives, denotes both the residents of cities—and, by extension, the commercial-industrial classes—and an emancipated citizenry.

thinking of a whole generation of radicals. However, the beginnings of the association and the journal were innocuous enough, for the avowed purpose of both was merely to engage in the scientific analysis of social problems, with membership open to all who subscribed to this purpose. Accordingly, next to a number of academic intellectuals, the roster of the association's officers also included such prominent members of the establishment as Count Julius Andrássy, Jr. and Lóránt Hegedüs, future conservative members of diverse Hungarian cabinets. Even so, from its inception, the association tilted toward the Left. Its journal repeatedly denounced "medieval feudalism, Magyarizing chauvinism and agnostic [sic] clericalism,"[107] and attacked prevailing conditions with such vehemence that by 1906 the representatives of the establishment had no choice but to resign from membership. The radicals now were left to their own devices, but for some time analysis still prevailed over advocacy. It was only in 1910 that a number of intellectuals gathered around the figure of Oscar Jászi and founded a Citizens' Radical party. While never much more than a brain trust of "intellectual laborers" (a term its members preferred to the more tainted "intelligentsia"), this party would serve as an important link between the socialists and the small left-wing faction of the parliamentary Independence party and as such play a crucial, if ultimately ill-fated, role in the short-lived democratic republic of November 1918-March 1919.

The philosophy of the party unfolds from the writings of Jászi, its chairman, founder, and one of the charter members of the Association for the Scientific Study of Society. Like so many of his confreres, Jászi was an early convert to socialism, and as late as 1904 urged all radical intellectuals to join the Social Democratic party. But in 1905, for the first time in his life, he made a pilgrimage to France, and, like so many of his friends, was beguiled by Paris and the entire ambiance of "bourgeois" society.[108] Compared to backward Hungary, Zola's France seemed to be a country of freedom and riches with institutions that were well worth preserving and emulating. True, even then, Jászi did not abandon the idea of socialism. But in his own half-Spencerian,

[107] Oszkár Jászi, quoted in Tibor Süle, *Sozialdemokratie in Ungarn* (Köln: Böhlen, 1967), p. 22.

[108] For Jászi's personal and political development, and his road to and from socialism, see Litván, *Magyar gondolat*, pp. 35-43; Horváth, *Magyar századforduló*, pp. 313-315; Süle, *Sozialdemokratie*, pp. 165-166; as well as two of his own works: Oszkár Jászi, "Az új Magyarország felé" [Toward the new Hungary], *Huszadik Század*, 15 (1907), especially pp. 3-5; and Oszkár Jászi, *A történelmi materializmus állambölcselete* [The theory of the state in historical materialism] (Budapest: Társadalomtudományi Társaság Könyvtára, 1908), especially pp. 124-125.

half-Marxist scheme of human history, he envisaged socialist society as the final product of a prolonged evolutionary process that must be preceded by the liquidation of feudalism, militarism, and the entire edifice of Hungarian neo-corporatism.

The premise of the party's program was that "the chief sources of Hungary's difficulties [were] to be found in the backward state of political freedom and individual liberty."[109] As a first priority, therefore, this backwardness would have to be remedied by institutional reform, including the introduction of universal suffrage and the abolition of the House of Lords. Such reforms were not only desirable as ends in themselves, but also as the means of creating a new institutional framework for economic development, within which the market could be freed from the tentacles of the *fidei commissa*, protectionism, and finance capitalism. Above all, a democratic parliament would be able to introduce a sweeping land reform—expropriate estates over 300-500 acres[110] and distribute them among peasant farmers—a measure with deep political and economic implications. Politically, land reform would end the influence of the "feudal" classes over public policy, while economically it would create a prosperous smallholding class, a domestic market for the industry, and a cycle of savings and reinvestment that would terminate the country's dependence on large holding banks and foreign capital. The effectiveness of this program, of course, hinged on the assumption that the small farm would be more productive than the large estate. This was a tenuous proposition, and the Radicals were not impervious to the risk that in a free market large concentrations of land and capital might undermine the independence of the small producer. But the risk was worth taking, for as Jászi pointed out in one of his articles:

> Even if the feudal latifundia give way to a system of landowning dominated by banks, this development should be welcome, because the new concentration will not be agrarian-feudal, but industrial-capitalist in character. It would derive from economic activity and not from plunder or treasonable services to the foreign dynasty; and this is an enormous difference, for the new economic concen-

[109] "A Radikális Párt programmja" [Program of the Radical party], *Világ*, June 7, 1914, p. 5.

[110] The exact limit was a matter of debate. The symposia of the Galileo Circle and the TT usually worked with 300- to 350-acre figures. On the other hand, the People's Law of 1918, passed by the democratic republic (Public Law XVIII) as an edict, expropriated estates over 200 acres, but permitted individuals and institutions to acquire land up to 500 acres. Tömöry, *Új vizeken járok*, p. 156; Böhm, *Két forradalom tüzében*, p. 135.

184

tration will replace militarism with capitalism: together with the latifundia will also perish the medieval House of Lords, the inequitable tax system, the rule of prelates and counts. In their place there will be a bourgeois Hungary in which the proletariat can gradually gather political strength.[111]

If Jászi's thinking about society and politics was obviously influenced by Spencer and Marx, his thinking about the national state was inspired by a source closer to home, Julius Pikler, a professor of jurisprudence at the University of Budapest, whose relativist views and dialectical reasoning scandalized conservative opinion and nationalist circles. The essence of Pikler's teaching was that nationalism did not stem from a deep human instinct but was merely a reflection of the needs and exigencies of a particular period, and hence the national state was doomed to pass when these needs and exigencies no longer existed.[112] This teaching appealed to Jászi who by instinct and preference was an internationalist, but who, as a rational political observer, understood the strength of national sentiment in contemporary eastern Europe. Thus while the ultimate objective was internationalism, the "road to it led through the nation state."[113] The conclusion drawn from this observation was that at the "prevailing stage of historical development" the nation state, like capitalism, should not be abolished but humanized.[114] This could be accomplished by stripping the nation's heroic appeal to primordial solidarities, and by transforming it into a rationalized human association sustained by the self-interest of its members. In the particular Hungarian context this required blunting the edge of Magyar nationalism, the termination of assimilationist policies, and the recognition of the cultural and administrative autonomy of the national minorities of the country.[115]

In more specific, programmatic terms, Jászi and the Radicals wanted to give Hungary a Swiss-type constitution, while maintaining the ter-

[111] Oscar Jászi, "A latifundium elleni küzdelem" [Struggle against the latifundium], *Huszadik Század*, 16 (1907), 478.

[112] Gyula Pikler, *Az emberi egyesületek, különösképen az állam keletkezése és fejlődése* [The origins and development of human associations, and especially of the state] (Budapest: Társadalomtudományi Társaság Könyvtára, 1905). A detailed discussion of Pikler's work and its influence on Jászi in Horváth, *Magyar századforduló*, pp. 119-123.

[113] "A Társadalomtudományi Társaság Pulszky vitája" [Pulszky symposium of the TT], *Huszadik Század*, 1 (1901), 311.

[114] See especially Oszkár Jászi, *A nemzeti állam kialakulása és a nemzeti kérdés* [The rise of the national state and the national question] (Budapest: Társadalomtudományi Társaság Könyvtára, 1912), p. 532.

[115] Ibid.

ritorial and political integrity of the existing unit. Relationships to Austria were to be decided later. For the moment, the oppressed national minorities reacted favorably, and in 1912-1914 there emerged the broad outlines of an alliance between them and the Radicals of Budapest. But Hungary, alas, was neither Switzerland nor the United States (another frequently mentioned model), and when in the fall of 1918, Jászi attempted to put his program into effect as minister of nationalities, he was rebuffed by the minorities, unwilling to settle for less than their own national states. Within the national states the same primordial sentiments would reign as in old Hungary, but this time to the disadvantage of the Magyars and their political classes.

If the "bourgeois" radical was willing, at least within the context of the given historical setting, to accept the nation state and use it as an instrument of economic development, the socialist tended to be hostile to any such design. For one thing, he regarded incremental increases in productivity as less important than the global expropriation of the means of production. For another, he viewed the nation state as a bourgeois instrument that mainly served to prolong class rule by pitting the proletariat of one country against that of another. For these reasons, the public pronouncements of the Social Democratic party contained very little that could pass as a coherent economic program apart from the reiteration of the collectivist commitment. Yet these pronouncements were replete with vulgar denunciations of the nation state that could not but offend the sentiments of a considerable segment of society. In these years, the party banned the national anthem and colors, refused to celebrate national holidays, and lost no opportunity to point out that the proletariat had no fatherland. Indeed, its leaders publicly vowed "to teach their children to hate [this] fatherland,"[116] denounced the "bourgeois" Kossuth and the "vulgar bravadoes" of 1848.[117]

Such inflammatory rhetoric, notwithstanding, the party leaders rapidly retreated to a more cautious stance, and within only a few years of the party's founding were content to fight for better wages, the freedom of organization, and, on a larger scale, for universal suffrage. Indeed, the militants who had founded the party in 1890 under the auspices of the Second International turned into functionaries with truly amazing speed, betraying little taste for political adventurism lest they risk their meager economic and organizational achievements. After 1899, the party leadership openly sided with the revisionists of

[116] Horváth, *Magyar századforduló*, p. 601, n. 1.
[117] Ibid., p. 242.

the international movement, and subsequently made the struggle for parliamentary representation the centerpiece of its political program. If the great demonstrations for universal suffrage occasionally turned into violent confrontations with the police, this was not so much by design, but because of the failure of the leaders to control their more volatile followers. As far as the leadership was concerned, "the Hungarian proletariat [stood] on the principle of peaceful evolution and [was] merely clamoring for universal suffrage, because it [was] the precondition of such peaceful evolutionary process."[118] In this respect, the "old guard" of the socialist leaders had their eyes fixed firmly on the German and Austrian models.

While rent by petty factionalism, the party did seem to be united on strategy, at least until 1903-1905 when radical students from the universities began to join the ranks in substantial numbers. Thus while in 1896 the careful eyes of the researcher could detect not more than eighteen socialist students, by 1902 this number had grown to about 150.[119] These students, together with other young intellectuals, soon turned out to be the young Turks of the party, who led the struggle against antiquated party statutes—among them, the 1889 statute of the Austrian Social Democratic party—challenged the "opportunism" of old guard functionaries, and, more importantly, rejected the relevance of the Austro-German model in favor of alternative models.

One alternative to the Austro-German model with its emphasis on universal suffrage was suggested by the syndicalism of the Mediterranean countries. This syndicalism, together with the recently published works of Michels, Sorel, Ostragorski, Pareto, and Mosca, was brought to Hungary by Ervin Szabó, a brilliant and well-trained social scientist, who subsequently synthesized this mélange of voluntaristic anti-parliamentarian theories into a single, coherent argument against the party's quest for representation. According to Szabó, the institutions of representative governments were subversive of the ideals of democracy, for given the special skills that the politician was required to have, parliamentarism inevitably led to a dictatorship of the professional over the politically uninitiated masses. To forestall such a development, which Hungary had fortunately not yet experienced, Szabó argued that the Social Democratic party (SDP) should cease its agitation for universal suffrage, and instead strive to establish direct democracy by self-governing councils, in both the country and the party proper. Such a policy would not only prevent the concentration

[118] Desider Bokányi, in *MMTVD*, ii, 642.
[119] Bunzel, *Studien*, p. 104.

of power in the hands of professional politicians and party bureau-crats, but would also create a splendid opportunity for the education of the backward masses. These masses of Hungary, together with the broad masses of other peripheral and semi-peripheral countries, could then take a leading role in the struggle for the global victory of socialism.[120]

A second political alternative was presented to the Hungarian SDP by Julius Alpári, a young man who, in 1902, at the age of twenty surprised the great Eduard Bernstein as much with his precocity as with his dedication to the principles of Marxist orthodoxy.[121] Thus if Szabó was worried that parliamentarism might subvert democracy, Alpári was concerned with the parliamentary corruption of socialism. In this connection Alpári argued that in the societies of eastern Europe, including, of course, Hungary, not even the freest of elections could give the proletariat more than a handful of seats, while the bulk of the political benefits would accrue to the peasantry, the petty bourgeoisie, and other reactionary elements. In view of this, Alpári and his colleague Arnold Dániel quite openly and explicitly argued for the relevance of the "Russian model." While they fell short of achieving the coherence of the Leninist synthesis, they entertained little doubt that the victory of the socialist revolution in this part of the world would require more, rather than less, of the *stramme Disziplin* that Szabó and the syndicalists rejected.[122]

From the inception of this dispute the entrenched leadership of the SDP responded with ad hominem attacks on the "youngsters . . . who tried to save the working class from itself."[123] The old guard dismissed Szabó and Alpári as impractical dreamers and armchair revolution-aries, frequently citing August Bebel's contemptuous phrase about "gad-fly, upstart academics" (*hergelaufene Akademiker*). They grumbled about the coming of the "dictatorship of the intelligentsia," and were willing to confess to one tactical error only, to wit, that they had admitted this "gang of students" to the party.[124] This chagrined ver-biage, however, portended graver things, for in 1904 Szabó was issued a serious reprimand, while some of the young orthodox intellectuals

[120] See Ervin Szabó, *A munkásmozgalom 1903-ban* [The labor movement in 1903] (Budapest: A Huszadik Század Kiskönyvtára, No. 2, 1904); also Horváth, *Magyar századforduló*, pp. 388-394.

[121] Bernstein met Alpári at the Stuttgart Congress of the Second International and greeted him with the words: "So jung und schon so orthodox." Süle, *Sozialdemokratie*, p. 196.

[122] Ibid., pp. 195-196. For the "Russian" model, see the recollections of Karl Polányi, onetime president of the Galileo Circle, in Tömöry, *Új vizeken jarok*, p. 174.

[123] Ibid., p. 70.   [124] Ibid., p. 108.

were fired from the editorial board of the socialist daily *Népszava*. But the war of words continued and climaxed in 1910 when the dissidents, including most of the leading intellectuals of the party, were expelled from the SDP by a vote of the leadership of 101 to 50. For the time being the old guard was victorious, while the "Jacobins" and the "Russians" of Hungarian socialism became politically homeless. By the good graces of the establishment Szabó found a job in the City Library of Budapest and retreated into scholarship (until his death in September 1918). Alpári found consolation in lecturing to the young radicals of the Galileo Circle who, like himself, became increasingly convinced of the incompatibility of democracy and revolution, and were searching for a formula to resolve the conflict between the two classical commitments of the socialist movement.

The Communist Party

The homeless of the socialist Left eventually found political refuge in the Communist party, whose Leninist ideology provided the formula for which they were searching. According to this well-known formula, the revolution would indeed need a dictatorship free from awkward institutional restraints, but this would be a dictatorship of a special kind, exercised on behalf of the working class over a recalcitrant or unreconstructed minority of the population.

The Communist party of Hungary (CPH) was founded twice, first on November 4, 1918 when a number of sympathetic prisoners of war from Hungary gathered in a Moscow hotel and established a temporary Central Committee under the auspices of the Russian Bolshevik party. The members of the committee, then, took the train to Hungary, rented quarters in Budapest, and invited their leftist friends to a meeting on November 20. The result of this meeting was the second, now official, founding of the party with a leadership that included people from the entire spectrum of the "homeless" Left. Among them were six ex-prisoners of war (Kun, Rabinovics, Seidel, Vántus, Pór, Nánássy), four ex-members of the Social Democratic party (Vágó, László, Rudas, Szántó), and three members of assorted revolutionary syndicalist and "technocrat" groups (Helfgott, Kelen, Hevesi). In addition, there were a number of students who came via the Galileo Circle (Duczynska, Korvin, Sallai, and Rákosi, the latter both a former Galileist and a prisoner of war in Russia).[125] Finally,

---

[125] Molnár, *Magyarország története*, II, 299. The "technocrats" were engineers by profession who turned to the revolution in the first place because they hoped it would permit the development of technology for the benefit of all mankind. See Gyula Hevesi, *Egy mérnök a forradalomban* [An engineer in revolution] (Budapest: Europa, 1959), p. 103.

there were Alpári, Pogány, Landler, and the later famous Eugene Varga, who only joined the party after some hesitation in February 1919, but remained a dedicated party member to the bitter end and even thereafter. The same was true of George Lukács and a number of "revolutionary humanists," who were at first deemed unreliable, but were later accepted for membership and gained considerable prominence in the Soviet Republic.[126]

Examining the relatively terse program of the new party and the editorial of the first issue of *Vörös Ujság* (*Red News*) on December 7, 1918, we are informed that the communists were an international party that had emerged in response to the moral and material crisis of capitalism. Its historical mission was to save mankind from the anarchy of the market, and from an otherwise inevitable regression into barbarism.[127] The party's ultimate objective was nothing less than world revolution, while its proximate goal was to revolutionize Hungary for this historical purpose. In addition to these lofty goals, the official proclamations of the party and its numerous programmatic statements between November 1918 and March 1919 alluded to the need for the socialization of land and other means of production, and for the improvement of the lot of the proletariat by the distribution of the amassed wealth of the bourgeoisie. But however carefully we read these documents we will find no mention of industrialization or national independence, the well-established trademarks of communist programs of more recent years. For the time being, the emphasis was on the strategy and the tactics of winning power in Hungary and in the rest of the world. And insofar as these tactics were not explicitly formulated and publicized, they became readily evident from the behavior of the the party, above all, from its role in the illegal seizure of land and factories, in instigating inordinate economic demands on the government, and in staging demonstrations against the efforts of the democratic Republic to protect the territorial integrity of the country.

THE SOVIET REPUBLIC

Antecedents

At this point in our narrative we must place the rise and activities of the Communist party in the context of the times, specifically in the

---

[126] For an excellent description of the founding of the party and of its leadership see Rudolf Tőkés, *Béla Kun and the Hungarian Soviet Republic* (New York: Praeger, 1967), pp. 83-99.

[127] December 7, 1918, p. 1. Facsimile in *MMTVD*, v, 352-353.

context of the democratic revolution that Hungary had experienced in October-November 1918. On October 31, spontaneous demonstrations took place in Budapest. King Karl IV appointed Michael Károlyi—the "red count," and the leader of the left wing of the Independence party in parliament—prime minister of Hungary. On the same day Count Tisza was assassinated by marauding soldiers. A day later a twenty-member National Council was formed, and by the vote of this organ, Hungary severed her ties with Austria and sued for a separate armistice. Fifteen days after these events a Republic was proclaimed with Michael Károlyi as its president.

The National Council and the cabinet of the Republic drew its members from three parties—the left wing of the Independence party, the Social Democrats, and Jászi's Radicals—and from the representatives of assorted radical groups, among them the "press" (three representatives in the National Council) and the feminists (one representative). The old parliament was dissolved, and by decree the National Council introduced universal suffrage (though it refrained from holding elections under the statute). The government also lifted all wartime restrictions on the freedom of the press and assembly, and made earnest preparations for the distribution of land among the peasantry. Such good intentions, however, produced few tangible political benefits for the government, for the democratic coalition was facing long pent-up demands on the part of diverse groups which the backward and war-torn economy could not fulfill. The bitterness over unfulfilled expectations was exacerbated by Communist propaganda that pointed to the existence of continued economic inequalities in the country, and instigated both the rural and urban proletariat to take matters in their own hands. In the face of such attacks the government generally took a defensive and diffident posture for fear that it might be labeled as counterrevolutionary. But when the Communists staged a bold attack on the editorial offices of the socialist *Népszava* and killed several policemen defending the building, the government ordered the arrest of the entire Central Committee and their confinement in the Central Prison of Budapest.

However, a far more serious, and eventually fatal, threat to the government was posed by the behavior of the victorious Entente powers. The leaders of the democratic coalition, above all Károlyi and Jászi, were well known for their pro-French sympathies, an attitude that the French government and the commander of its Balkan expeditionary army, General Franchet d'Espèrey, reciprocated with open contempt. Worse still, this pro-Entente government of Hungary was not privy to wartime agreements among the allies that stipulated the transfer of two-thirds of Hungary's territory to Rumania, Yugoslavia, and Czechoslovakia. Nor were the clauses of these secret agreements revealed at once on November 1, when Hungary was suing for an armistice. Rather, they were communicated to the government piecemeal in the form of periodic diplomatic notes, each one requiring the cession of new, and ever larger, territories. By January 1919, the Károlyi regime decided to resist these demands by force. But there the government was hamstrung by its pacifist credentials, and, once again, by a relentless Communist propaganda against the "bourgeois" war of "territorial integrity." The final blow to the government was dealt on March 19, 1919 when the head of the Entente mission in Budapest handed his final note to Károlyi designating the postwar boundaries of Hungary. These boundaries were as unexpected as they were unacceptable to the Hungarians, but with morale low and material resources limited, Károlyi resigned and handed over power to the Socialists.[128] The latter in turn purged themselves of their own traditional leadership, and so rejuvenated, offered an alliance to the imprisoned Communists. A pact was signed, and a Revolutionary Governing Council of People's Commissars was formed with the Socialists retaining numerical preponderance. Nominally, the president of the council was the Socialist Alexander Garbai, but from the first to the last day of the regime, the commanding figure of the government was its Communist commissar for foreign affairs, Béla Kun, whose name became synonymous with the entire revolutionary experiment. However, at this point labels were less important than the division between moderates and all-out revolutionaries that cut across all traditional party lines. Between these two groups the balance of power favored the revolutionary side, for a majority of Socialist commissars were just as radical as the Communists. Eventually, as emigrés, such "old" Socialists as Bokányi, Hamburger, Haubrich, Lengyel, and Landler joined the Communist party, or worked for the Third International.

The Left-Socialist-Communist alliance proceeded to unite the two parties—first under the name of Socialist Party of Hungary, later under the Socialist-Communist Workers' party label—and, at the same time proclaimed a Republic of Councils (*Tanácsköztársaság*), or Soviet Republic. Within a matter of days after its proclamation, this Republic achieved what its predecessor had been incapable of achieving: revolutionary legitimacy in the eyes of the working classes. This legitimacy enabled the Revolutionary Governing Council to silence obstreperous

[128] Károlyi's own story in "Die Geschichte meiner Abdankung," *Arbeiterzeitung* (Vienna), July 25, 1919. His version has been criticized by detractors who claim that he knew about the plans to incorporate the Communists into the new government.

pressure groups,[129] and to institute a far-reaching program of socialization, including the socialization of all landholdings over 100 acres. Even more remarkably, the new Republic successfully mobilized the urban working class by transforming overnight the "bourgeois war of territorial integrity" into a "revolutionary war." Using this slogan they organized a Red Army that not only put up a creditable defense, but mounted a temporarily successful counteroffensive against the Czech and Rumanian armies.

Revolutionary Dictatorship

The political institutions of the new Soviet Republic in part reflected the still muddled thinking of the radical Left, in part the institutional model that the prisoners had brought back from Soviet Russia. In form, these institutions were democratic and were built on the principles of popular sovereignty and participation in government. Thus as one of its first measures, the Republic issued a temporary constitution,[130] whose provisions enfranchised citizens over the age of eighteen irrespective of sex or other qualifications. The only exception to this rule was that priests, former exploiters, and a vaguer category of potential criminal and political offenders were specifically excluded from the exercise of political rights. Participation in the affairs of the state was to have been through a hierarchy of councils that ascended from the grass roots to the highest level, that is, to a National Congress of Councils, designated as the supreme repository of the popular will. The Revolutionary Governing Council of the People's Commissars was to be accountable to this body, and it was in consultation with the congress that the commissars were supposed to act on appropriations and other legislative business. Next to these institutional provisions for political participation, the constitution guaranteed broad civil and political freedoms to "all working people," including the freedom of speech (Article 8), and assembly (Article 9), together with the right to a free education and to diverse social and cultural benefits. In the spirit of democracy and internationalism, the constitution recognized the multi-ethnic character of Hungary in that it granted broad linguistic and cultural rights to all minorities. Over and above these

---

[129] For months Kun had urged returning veterans to demand a severance pay of 5,400 Kronen from the government. When Kun became a commissar, the representatives of the radical veterans showed up in his office expecting to collect the amount for members of their association, only to be told "to get out . . . or otherwise you get 5400 machine-gun bullets in your head." Böhm, *Két forradalom tüzében*, p. 269.

[130] "A Tanácsköztársaság ideiglenes alkotmánya" [Temporary constitution of the Soviet Republic], April 3, 1919, in *MMVTD* vi/A, 100-103.

rights the constitution made provisions for the formation of a Slovak, Ruthenian, and a German federated republic with generous provisions for local autonomy.[131]

However, the democratic pretensions of this constitution were severely compromised by the ideological commitments of the new Hungarian Soviet elite which saw itself not so much as the executor of popular will, as an instrument to carry out the mandate of history. This commitment did not necessarily vitiate the democratic principle, for majorities could presumably be persuaded to see the logic and purposes of history. But in reality, the Hungarian radical elite was deeply pessimistic about the ability of the masses to see their own enlightened self-interest and to take a "correct" position at every turn of history. Thus from the very inception of the Republic, Kun and his associates made little attempt to hide the fact that theirs was "a dictatorship of an active minority on behalf of the by and large passive proletariat,"[132] and that this minority would have to "act in a strong and merciless fashion . . . at least until such time that the revolution spread to the [other] European countries."[133]

In this spirit, the political elite loaded the dice in its own favor even while writing the constitutional document. Thus not only was the "exploiting" class—including thousands of peasant farmers using hired help—excluded from the exercise of political rights, but the electoral system was so designed as to favor heavily the urban over the rural proletariat. Moreover, the Soviet parliament, the National Congress of Councils, was to consist of delegates elected by the councils rather than by the electorate at large. And if in form the democratic principle was compromised, in practice it was well-nigh perverted by the way in which the elections for the councils were held. Thus, when on April 7, 1919 millions of Hungarians went to the polls, they did so in order to elect representatives whose names appeared on a single list. By the letter of the law, working people all over the country were free to propose alternative lists of candidates. But in the Eighth District of Budapest, the only place where such a list won the majority of the votes, the results of the elections were quickly annulled

[131] No explicit provisions were made for creating federated republics for the Rumanians and South-Slavs, perhaps because they were out of the reach of the Budapest government. Halfhearted attempts were nevertheless made to appeal to them. For an excellent discussion of these, see Keith Hitchins, "The Rumanian Socialists and the Hungarian Soviet Republic," in Andrew C. Janos and William B. Slottman, *Revolution in Perspective: Essays on the Hungarian Soviet Republic* (Berkeley and Los Angeles: University of California Press, 1971), pp. 109-144.

[132] Kun, quoted in Tőkés, *Béla Kun*, p. 178.

[133] Ladislas Rudas, Ibid., p. 180.

and new elections held.[134] After the elections the new councils were duly and festively invested, but immediately reduced to purely ceremonial functions, for the day-to-day conduct of their business was entrusted to the so-called *directoria*, or executive committees, often consisting of outsiders appointed by the government. By May 1919, it was these *directoria* rather than the councils proper that made decisions on any matters of substance on the local level.

Even so, perfect political uniformity could not be attained. This is not surprising in view of the fact that the Republic was very young and during most of its tenure in office the conduct of military operations had made communications difficult between the countryside and the urban centers. Consequently when the 378 delegates of the National Congress of Councils convened on June 14, 1919,[135] many of the provincial delegations showed a sharply critical attitude toward the revolutionary government, and turned the sessions of the congress into a massive demonstration against the "Soviet bureaucracy" and the Revolutionary Governing Council. While some delegates spoke of the need to end the "dictatorship over the proletariat," others reminded the people's commissars that they were accountable to the congress, and threatened to conduct an investigation into the abuses of power by Kun and the members of his inner circle.[136] Against such opposition, the Soviet government retaliated by pushing through drastic changes in the rules of procedure, by denouncing the "immature and counterrevolutionary prattle" of the provincials, and finally, as things were getting out of control, by adjourning the congress and entrusting its functions to a standing committee.[137] Clearly, the voice of "artificial majorities" was not to interfere with the pursuit of the higher purpose. Thus while the Hungarian Soviet Republic of 1919 did not de facto attain the monolithic qualities of later Communist regimes, de jure political power remained concentrated in the hands of its Revolutionary Governing Council and some of the affiliated workers' and soldiers' councils.

However, we ought to be reminded at this point that the Soviet

[134] *MMVTD*, vi/A, 161.

[135] It was characteristic of the prevailing confusion that 413 delegates showed up at the congress but only 348 were found to have proper accreditation. Another thirty delegates were co-opted. See *A tanácsok országos gyűlésének naplója, 1919 junius 14-23* [Proceedings of the National Congress of Councils, June 14-23, 1919] (Budapest: Athenaeum, 1919), especially proceedings for June 14, pp. 1-5. From here on *TOG*.

[136] *TOG*, June 15, pp. 4-6; June 18, pp. 1-7; June 20, p. 13.

[137] For these and other details concerning the congress, see Andrew C. Janos, "The Agrarian Opposition at the National Congress of Councils" in Janos and Slottman, *Revolution in Perspective*, pp. 85-108.

regime was, as its adherents frequently claimed, a dictatorship of a new type, a revolutionary dictatorship. It was such not only because it set out to revolutionize the world, but because in attempting to do so it felt emancipated from institutional and moral restraints. It justified itself by a grand design of delivering all mankind for all time from conflict, deprivation, and even such anxieties that the traditionalist would regard as part and parcel of the human condition. Such chiliastic salvationism, by no means restricted to Marxist orthodoxy, has a logic of its own: given the magnificence of the design, the revolutionary may cast himself into a heroic mold, may require inordinate sacrifice or total devotion from his followers, and may replace cumbersome procedure and obedience to objective law with revolutionary instinct and expediency. Whatever its outward form, revolutionary organization is not bureaucratic but charismatic in character.[138]

In the case of the Soviet Republic, this subjectivism and emancipation from legal restraints was amply evident in the conduct of affairs,[139] but nowhere more sharply manifested than in the administration of justice. If the judiciary of the old regime was sheltered from direct political influence and obsessed with legal procedure, the judiciary of the new regime was a political arm of the government that operated under extremely broad charters which left everything to the discretion of the political commissar or public prosecutor. Thus, only three days after the proclamation of the Republic, martial law was declared with the stipulation that "capital punishment be applied in every instance of armed resistance or incitement to rebellion against the councils." The decree left unspecified which courts were to have jurisdiction over such cases.[140] Four days later a system of "revolutionary justice" was established by a directive that ruled out "formal investigative procedure, written charges [Article 4] . . . appeals or recourse to clemency [Articles 5-6]."[141] In a clear case of redundancy, on April 9 the Revolutionary Governing Council issued yet another decree, ordering that "anyone who [broke] any of the decrees of the Soviet Republic should be judged by revolutionary tribunals," adding that "in exceptional cases . . . the jurisdiction of these tribunals [might] be extended to cases not specifically covered by revolutionary decrees."[142] On May 16, some attempt was made to specify crimes to be

---

[138] For a difference between these two, see Reinhard Bendix, *Work and Authority in Industry*, especially pp. xl-xli.

[139] For many references to this problem see the debate on the economy and the reports of Commissars Varga, Nyisztor, and Lengyel, *TOG*, June 16, 1919.

[140] *MMVTD*, vi/B, 3.

[141] Ibid., p. 32.   [142] Ibid., p. 167.

judged by the tribunals and to establish procedures of appeal, but excepted from these provisions were "criminal acts against the Soviet Republic committed in or near the areas of military operation."[143] By then, of course, the entire territory of the Republic could be defined as such, and indeed, it was under this statute that Tibor Szamuelly's famous flying squads staged their campaign of red terror against villagers reluctant to part with their grain or to accept the paper money printed by the revolutionary government. By the standards of a callous century that saw millions perish in civil and international conflicts, the number of the victims of this terror was very low.[144] But numbers were less significant than method. The fact is that the Republic has the dubious distinction in Hungarian history of having resorted to arbitrary violence both as a matter of principle and as a regular instrument of statecraft.

The Soviet Republic: A Balance Sheet

In any attempt to draw up a balance sheet on the record of the Soviet Republic, it is incumbent on the chronicler to point out that during its short, 133-day existence the regime had a number of significant achievements to its credit. The Republic succeeded in mobilizing a war-weary nation for the defense of its territory in the face of incredible adversity. Moreover, it was doing so while effectively dismantling the economic and political institutions of the old regime, socializing the means of production, and instituting a number of cultural and welfare measures—such as training centers and summer camps for the children of the Budapest proletariat—within its limited means. As official representatives of the ensuing counterrevolutionary regime bitterly conceded on numerous occasions, without foreign intervention the national disgrace of the Soviet Republic would have persisted for a very long time.

Yet there were a number of issues with which the Revolutionary Governing Council and its radical socialist members could not come to grips, and their failures to do so were subsequently analyzed by friend and foe alike as "mistakes." These mistakes are worth examining here because over time they resulted in tactical adjustments that reveal the nature of the learning process in the international Communist movement of those days. But from our perspective they are even more interesting because they make manifest certain fundamental contradictions between global ends and national means, and

---

[143] Ibid., pp. 496-497.

[144] The low estimate appears to be 370, the high estimate, 587. See Böhm, *Két forradalom tüzében*, p. 398.

thus provide certain points of departure for the dynamics of change in revolutionary regimes.

The first and most frequently discussed of these mistakes[145] was the alleged readiness of the Communists to enter into an alliance with the Socialists without insisting on a party of the Leninist type. Here there is some question whether the Communists, confined to jail cells right up to the moment of unification, had any real choice. But whether they did or not, the Socialist Party of Hungary (and later the Socialist-Communist Workers' party) emerged from this unification as a party typical of social democracy. And while many of the members and leading cadres of the Social Democrats were as radical as the Communists, the party organization itself, with its mass membership and close association with the trade union movement, could not function as an effective instrument of revolutionary political control and mobilization. As a result, the government had to create its own mobilization instruments. The revolutionary cadres became directly involved in the administrative and production process, where they became caught up in the conflicting pressures between political purity and economic expediency. This was quite evident during the sessions of the National Congress of Councils when the two most important commissars responsible for production, Eugene Varga and George Nyisztor, were roundly criticized by the rank and file for some of their production decisions and for their delegation of authority to bourgeois experts.[146]

A second contradiction or "mistake" of the Republic arose out of its relationship to the agrarian population. In this respect, the old central European socialist consciousness prevailed over the tactical wisdom of Leninism. In brief, this consciousness manifested itself in a contemptuous attitude toward the peasantry and an inability, or unwillingness, to deal with the rural populace. Upon the proclamation of the Republic, young socialist agitators flocked into the villages and their behavior was calculated to hurt the sensibilities of the peasants. At times they turned churches into movie houses, ridiculed the institution of the traditional family, and mocked the communal senti-

[145] For one of the most authoritative statements on this issue see G. Zinovyev and K. Radek, *Mit mond a III. Internacionále a magyarországi proletár forradalomról?* [What does the Third International say about the proletarian revolution in Hungary?] (Vienna, 1920).

[146] See *TOG*, June 17, 1919, p. 27; especially the exchange between L. Jankovics and Production Commissar George Nyisztor. For Varga's own critique, see Jenő Varga, *A magyar tanácsköztársaság gazdasági szervezete* [The economic structure of the Hungarian Soviet Republic] (Berlin: Kommunista Kiskönyvtár, 1921), especially pp. 3-28.

ments of the backward peasantry. Such insensitivity incensed not only the "rich" peasants but the majority of the agrarian proletariat as well.[147] To make things worse, the Republic did not follow the Leninist strategy of distributing land among the agrarian proletariat, but socialized all estates over 100 acres, often leaving the previous owners on the premises as commissars responsible for production. The adverse consequences of this were considerable, and the lessons were not lost on a future generation of Communists. When it re-emerged from hibernation in 1945, the party was the chief sponsor of land reform. Rural cadres were busy rebuilding churches and postponed their final assault on the "idiocy of rural life" until such a time as they had accumulated sufficient power to destroy all resistance in the way of a socialist agriculture.

The third and most significant, though probably less clearly articulated, "mistake" of the Republic stemmed from their doctrinaire attitude toward nationalism. Once again, as revolutionary purists, socialists of all persuasions remained not only true to their internationalist persuasion, but went out of their way to offend national sentiment. A few examples will suffice to illustrate the point: upon the proclamation of the Soviet Republic the statues of national kings and heroes were torn down in public ceremonies, the national anthem was banned, the display of the national colors became a punishable offense, and on one occasion such a display resulted in the shooting of the offending person. In view of this attitude it is somewhat ironic that Kun and his colleagues should subsequently be denounced as the fathers of national communism. For while Kun may have toyed with the idea of mobilizing anti-German national sentiments,[148] after his return to Hungary he steadfastly denounced all "petty bourgeois overtures . . . to social patriotism and bourgeois nationalism,"[149] and never tired of repeating that he felt "no more akin to the Hungarian proletariat than, let us say, to the American, Czech or Russian."[150] And while at one time he spoke of the need to kindle "a kind of proletarian chauvinism,"[151] this had nothing to do with the symbols or appeals of nationalism. Indeed, throughout the lifetime of the Republic he rejected suggestions that the army hoist the national flag next to the red one or permit the use of national emblems on the caps of red

[147] *TOG*, June 17, 1919, p. 26-27.

[148] Tőkés, *Béla Kun*, p. 210.

[149] Béla Kun, *Mit akarnak a kommunisták?* [What do the Communists want?] (Budapest: Kommunisták Magyarországi Pártja, 1919), pp. 66-67.

[150] Quoted in Tőkés, *Béla Kun*, p. 130.

[151] *TOG*, June 18, 1919, p. 29.

soldiers,[152] a rejection that resulted in the desertion of large numbers of officers and peasant conscripts.

Once again, the Communist movement learned a lesson, for when it returned to Hungary in 1945 the statues of national kings remained in their places, the national anthem was not banned, and the national colors were hoisted next to the red flag. In eastern Europe, and all over the world, the parties now made a great effort to identify their cause with national revolutions. Initially, this adaptation was tactical and represented a compromise between ideals and the immediate means available to attain them. But in too many instances the simulation of the nationalist role resulted in the rise of a genuine national sentiment among the cadres whose parochialism and particularism was the very antithesis of original Marxist stipulations.

[152] See Political Commissar Landler's telegram from the Rumanian front, Böhm, *Két forradalom tüzében*, p. 414.

V.

The Restoration of
Neo-Corporatism (1919-1931)

Historical Background

Counterrevolution and Reinstitutionalization

The circumstances surrounding the demise of the Soviet Republic were reminiscent of those surrounding the fall of its short-lived democratic predecessor. On July 30, 1919, the Rumanian army broke through Hungarian lines of defense on the eastern front, whereupon the units of the Red Army disintegrated in a hasty and disorderly retreat. In the ensuing panic, the Revolutionary Governing Council resigned. Kun and his fellow commissars fled the country, and the remnants of the Revolutionary Workers' and Soldiers' Council of Greater Budapest bequeathed the government of the country to a group of moderate socialists and trade union leaders who were untainted by the events of the previous weeks. A few days later, on August 3, the Rumanian army entered Budapest. Under its auspices the moderate socialist government was quickly replaced by one still farther removed from the revolutionary socialism of the Soviet regime.

When the Soviet government fell in Budapest, counterrevolutionary committees had already been active abroad and in areas outside the jurisdiction of the Republic of Councils. In the city of Szeged one such committee enjoyed the benevolent protection of the French expeditionary army to the Balkans. It was under French auspices that a new Hungarian National Army was formed, to be commanded by Admiral Nicholas Horthy, the ranking officer of the now defunct Austro-Hungarian navy. Encouraged by the French, this army joined hands with a number of semi-private officers' detachments, and their combined forces occupied western Hungary. Later, after the withdrawal of the Rumanians, the same forces occupied Budapest and the eastern provinces of the country. Wherever the army and the free corps went, its officers meted out summary justice, terrorizing not only the officials and sympathizers of the fallen red regime, but also the entire Jewish community, which the counterrevolutionaries now squarely blamed for the events of the preceding year. By any account, this terror was more savage than the random violence practiced by the Red Guard, and, unlike the latter, it quite often became an instrument for settling personal accounts, and even for achieving personal gain by means of extortion and plunder.[1]

When the National Army entered Budapest in November 1919, yet another government was formed, and preparations were made for the election of a National Assembly. Upon the prodding of the victorious Entente powers, franchise was broadened by decree: while some educational qualifications remained, the voting age was now set at twenty-four years, property qualifications were abolished, and women were included in the electorate. Even more significantly, for the first time in Hungarian history the elections were to be held under the secret ballot.

The elections of January 1920 produced an assembly that was mainly notable for the presence of new parties and faces. Neither Tisza's old neo-liberal Party of Work, nor the National Independence (1848) party, were reconstituted. Nor were individual members of these parties eager to re-enter a public life tainted by violence and marked by uncertainties. In the place of the old parties there emerged two loosely-knit parliamentary formations, one under the Christian, the other under the Agrarian Smallholder label. Both of these would have qualified as right of center in the classical political nomenclature. Yet both were also divided between old-line conservatives and radicals of the Right, whose views will be discussed at some length in the last chapter of this work. In addition to these parties, there was a smattering of republicans and liberal democrats in the House. But the socialists were absent, for just a few days before the voting they decided to boycott the elections, claiming harassment by the white detachments. Such claims were not without foundation. Nevertheless, one cannot entirely dismiss the charge raised by their opponents, that the withdrawal of their candidates was prompted by fears of a humiliating defeat in an environment where public opinion had swung

[1] Whereas the number of victims of the red terror has been estimated by different authors to lie between 342 and 578, the victims of the white terror are numbered between 626 and over 2,000. For its history, and the number of victims, see Gusztáv Gratz, A forradalmak kora. Magyarország története, 1918-1921 [The epoch of revolutions. A history of Hungary, 1918-1921] (Budapest: Franklin, 1935); Gusztáv Gratz et al., A bolsevizmus Magyarországon [Bolshevism in Hungary] (Budapest: Franklin, 1921); Dezső Sulyok, Magyar tragédia [Hungarian tragedy] (Newark: Published by the author, 1954), pp. 254-276; Joint Labor Delegation for Hungary, ed., Report on the White Terror in Hungary (London: Trade Union Council and the Labour Party, 1920).

violently from Left to Right in the wake of two unsuccessful revolutions, and in the face of the impending territorial mutilation of the country.

The newly elected assembly had to deal with a number of constitutional issues arising out of the dissolution of the Dual Monarchy. Thus, as its first order of business (Public Law I/1920) parliament abrogated the Pragmatic Sanction of 1723, declaring the country's constitutional ties to Austria null and void. This was easily done, for the act merely recognized a fait accompli. But the issue of dynastic rights and succession was not so easily tackled. While the National Army and the radicals in both major parties were "free electors" who favored the dethronement of the Habsburgs and the election of a national king, the conservatives were "legitimists" who abhorred such a "revolutionary" act and wanted to recall King Karl IV to the Hungarian throne. After considerable haggling, a compromise was worked out between these two conflicting points of view: the monarchical form of government was retained, but instead of filling the vacant throne, parliament created a regency until such time as the issue could be resolved in a calmer atmosphere. Such a solution was not entirely without precedent in Hungarian history: Louis Kossuth and John Hunyady had served as regents of the country in the nineteenth and fifteenth centuries respectively. Following these precedents, the National Assembly vested regal powers in the office, except for the power of veto over ecclesiastic matters, and the prerogative of granting titles of nobility. The remaining constitutional prerogatives, however, were still considerable: like the king, the regent could appoint prime ministers, exercise suspensive veto over legislation, dissolve or adjourn parliament, and would act as the commander in chief of the army. In time, these powers were further increased, for the Parliament Act of 1925 granted the regent the prerogative of appointing life peers to the reconstituted upper chamber of parliament.

Under prevailing circumstances, the choice of the person to occupy the position was as important as the office itself. In this respect, the assembly's freedom of action was severely curtailed, for the National Army and the white detachments let it early be known that they would brook no opposition to their own candidate, Admiral Horthy. A few brave conservative legitimists still voted against him, but the Admiral was duly elected to the office on March 1, 1920, in the intimidating presence of military officers. Thereafter he would be the sole bearer of the office, and the head of the Hungarian state until the cataclysmic events of October 1944.

While these all-too-evident signs of pressure tainted the legality of the election and gave it the appearance of a coup d'état, Horthy was really a compromise candidate of sorts, acceptable by virtue of his particular background to both the conservatives and the radicals of the Right. Indeed, Horthy was something of an exception: he was a member of the Protestant east Hungarian gentry, who had nonetheless earned his reputation not in nationalist politics, but in imperial service, first as a personal aide to Francis Joseph, then as Emperor Karl's commander in chief of the navy. Thus while his religion and family ties were apt to please the more radical "free electors," his service record was somewhat reassuring to those who wanted the traditions of the Habsburg monarchy to continue in independent Hungary. Indeed, from the point of view of Hungary's ruling classes, his election must be regarded as truly felicitous in retrospect. At many a critical historical juncture he could serve as an effective broker among the different factions of an increasingly divided establishment, thus saving the country from the upheavals of violent infighting that plagued the elites of other East European countries in the interwar period.

For the time being, however, the army and the free corps had the upper hand, and with their candidate installed in the office of the regent, their members felt free to dictate the terms for the legislative business of parliament. These terms were above all evident in the passage of three acts. The first of these was the Numerus Clausus Act (Public Law xxv/1920) in which the National Assembly set religious quotas for admission to institutions of higher learning so as to cut back on Jewish enrollments and thereby prevent the rise of another generation of left-wing intellectuals. Appropriately, this act was followed by Public Law xxvi/1920, providing for the restoration of corporal punishment for certain types of criminal offenses. The third act, Public Law xxxvi/1920, then provided for a modest scheme of land reform by transferring some 900,000 acres of land from large latifundiary estates to peasant proprietors.[2] The provisions of these acts were subsequently repealed, ignored, or sabotaged by the "consolidationist" regime of Count Bethlen (1921-1931). But the issues they addressed—the status of Jews, land reform, and a new, harsher form of social discipline free from the rationalist-humanist considerations of the nineteenth century—remained important rallying points for the new generation of right-wing radicals throughout the entire interwar period.

[2] The law envisioned the distribution of 1,129,219 acres, of which 948,682 appear to have been actually transferred to new owners. See Kerék, *A magyar földkérdés*, pp. 199-210, and Eckhart, *A magyar közgazdaság*, p. 228.

Peace Treaty

Apart from producing this package of constitutional and social legislation, the National Assembly had to face the unpopular task of ratifying the peace treaty of Trianon, imposed by the victorious powers of the Entente. The outlines of the treaty had for some time been familiar to the public. Still, when its final draft was published in the spring of 1920, its contents sent shock waves across the country. Yet another government resigned in frustration, and a caretaker ministry had to be found to affix the needed signatures to the document. This having been accomplished, the treaty was voted upon by the legislature under protest and amidst calls for national mourning.

The terms of the treaty were very harsh indeed, much harsher than those imposed on Germany at Versailles. The territory of the political unit was reduced from 111,493 square miles—or 128,879 square miles if we include Croatia-Slavonia—to 36,311 square miles; the population of the country from 18.2 million—20.8 million with Croatia-Slavonia—to 7,980,143 in 1920, or 8,603,922 in 1928.[3] The rest of the territory and population of the old kingdom of Hungary were divided among Rumania, Czechoslovakia, Yugoslavia, and Austria, with Poland and Italy eventually acquiring a few square miles each from the Czechoslovak and Yugoslav portions respectively. The detached territories included such "historical" provinces as Transylvania—long regarded as the cradle of the Hungarian national state—a circumstance that added extra fuel to the revisionist propaganda of the forthcoming years. Much of the population of these territories, of course, consisted of hitherto oppressed, non-Magyar ethnic minorities who wanted little to do with the historical Hungarian state. But the presence on the wrong side of the border of some 2.5 to 3 million Magyars was salt in Hungarian wounds and a grievance that legitimated the objective of restoring the "territorial integrity" of the old kingdom of "Greater Hungary" (see map, p. 207).

The transfer of these territories and populations changed the country's ethnic and economic profile. Ethnically, the rump country became more heterogeneous than its predecessor: 89.8 percent of its population—93.0 percent a decade later—were Magyars, 6.8 percent Germans, and the rest were divided among the minuscule Slovak, Croat, and Rumanian minorities.[4] Meanwhile economically, the country became more "advanced" and industrialized. While rump Hungary retained only about 30 percent of the territory and 40 percent

---

[3] *The Statesman's Yearbook*, 1920, p. 5; 1928, p. 5.
[4] Ibid.

of the population of the old kingdom, it retained 48.6 percent of its wheat, 64.6 percent of its rye, and 35.8 percent of its corn-producing areas.[5] Even more significantly, the rump country retained 50.9 percent of the total industrial population, 55.6 percent of all industries, 82 percent of the heavy industries, and 70 percent of the banks of the pre-Trianon political unit.[6] The agrarian population was now only 55.8 percent of the total population, and nearly one-third of the national income derived from manufacturing.[7] But for the time being, the new country was richer on paper only, for the terms of the international settlement deprived industries of their domestic supplies of fuel and raw materials, while agriculture lost the benefits of a substantial and well-protected market in the western provinces of the empire.

Consolidation

For at least another year after the signing of the peace treaty the country remained in a state of turmoil, if not of anarchy. During this year ex-King Emperor Karl made an attempt to reclaim his throne—an attempt repeated in October 1921—but was successfully repelled by his erstwhile admiral and by the radical officers of the National Army. Meanwhile, the white detachments were still running rampant, terrorizing Jews, socialists, and left-wing intellectuals. The authority of the government was at a low ebb. Prime ministers, in the words of a contemporary, commanded less respect than corporals in the detachments or than county sheriffs in the old days.[8] Refugees were streaming into the country from the occupied territories, putting an unbearable strain on the economy. The classes that had served as the pillars of the old order were utterly demoralized. The civil servants were impoverished, the entrepreneurs intimidated, the landowners apprehensive and insecure in their rights.

By mid-1921, however, the country seemed ready for a greater degree of public order and stability. The peasantry was sullen, but compliant; the workers were browbeaten; and the middle classes were tired of social experiments, and even more, of the excesses of white detachments. From abroad, too, there was constant pressure to curb domestic unrest. Above all, foreign capital would not be forthcoming until public authority and effective government were restored.

The era of consolidation began with the appointment to the pre-

[5] Buday, *A megcsonkított Magyarország*, p. 104.
[6] Ibid., p. 209.   [7] Ibid.
[8] Miklós Surányi, *Bethlen* (Budapest: Singer és Wolfner, 1927), p. 15.

206

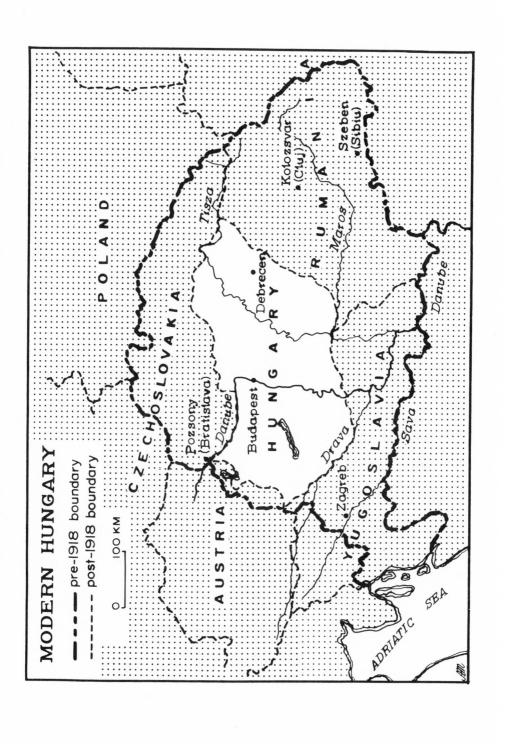

MODERN HUNGARY

—— pre-1918 boundary
------ post-1918 boundary

0   100 KM

POLAND

CZECHOSLOVAKIA

Tisza

Danube

Pozsony
(Bratislava)

AUSTRIA

Budapest

HUNGARY

Debrecen

Kolozsvar
(Cluj)

Szeben
(Sibiu)

R U M A N I A

Maros

Drava

Zagreb

Sava

Danube

YUGOSLAVIA

ADRIATIC SEA

miership of Count Stephen Bethlen. The date was April 1921, and the choice of the man once again reflected a desire to find a candidate acceptable to both radicals and conservatives. Bethlen qualified as such, for he was another Calvinist and a refugee from occupied Transylvania, two factors which seemed to guarantee that he would follow an aggressively revisionist and nationalist policy. But he was also a member of one of the great historical families, which seemed to be a sufficient assurance that he would not abridge the established privilege of the aristocracy. In this respect, he may well be compared to Horthy himself. But unlike Horthy, Bethlen was also an experienced politician, blessed with a keen intellect and sense of pragmatism that soon assured his ascendancy not only over the contending factions of the establishment, but also over the person and the office of the regent. Thus the years of his premiership may be appropriately referred to as the "era of Bethlen" in Hungarian history. During this period, it was the premier and not the regent who shaped the destiny of the nation, steering a careful middle course between extremes. Such a policy earned Bethlen's brand of politics the label of liberal-conservatism.

As soon as he became premier, Bethlen vowed to restore public order by liquidating both revolution and counterrevolution. This, of course, was easier said than done, for while the revolutionaries lay prostrate, the counterrevolutionaries—student radicals, the detachments, and the army—had to be taken "off the streets" and out of politics. This was a seemingly impossible task, but Bethlen accomplished it by a combination of persuasion and payoffs, the latter often bordering on outright bribery on the part of the state. The most rambunctious of the student leaders were given jobs in the bureaucracy, and quickly dispatched to provincial posts far from the capital. The commanders of the most dangerous detachments meanwhile were "given" seats in parliament, provided adequate positions in the ministries, or else, after a quick promotion to higher rank, they were transferred to the regular army.[9] Meanwhile, the army itself was pacified by improvements in salaries and pensions, and by assurances that, contrary to the stipulations of the peace treaty, adequate budgetary provisions would be made for military expenditures. Thus while the treaty limited the army to 35,000 officers, non-commissioned of-

---

[9] Of the leaders of the most notorious officers' detachments, I. Héjjas became councillor in one of the ministries, G. Sefcsik became a deputy, E. Kovarcz and S. Soltész were promoted from lieutenants to lieutenant colonels, Major J. Takách-Tolvay became lieutenant general and later a member of parliament, while Colonel Babarczy was made superintendent for the collection of excise. Sulyok, *Magyar tragédia*, p. 285.

ficers, and enlisted men, a somewhat larger contingent was kept under arms, with the extra appropriations carefully hidden among the expenditures of civilian ministries and administrative departments.[10]

Such a policy of payoffs, however, was subject to major fiscal constraints, for in 1921 the Hungarian state was bankrupt. With the economy in shambles, the government had no proper base for the collection of the necessary revenue. Bethlen thus had to gamble, and he did so by selling off the country's last reserves of gold and foreign currency.[11] In 1921-1922 fifty-two percent of budget expenditures came from this source; in 1922-1923 seventy-nine percent were covered by such means.[12] The risks were enormous, but the gamble paid off. At the first signs of the successful restoration of public order Bethlen negotiated a stabilization loan of $50 million (250 million Pengő in the new currency introduced in 1926). Small as this amount was, the "trickle started a real flood of money,"[13] and fiscal stability was restored. Yet the pressures to pay off both friends and potential enemies resulted in a bloated budget and a steady deficit, which in turn was financed by new loans contracted in each and every year of Bethlen's premiership: 168.7 m. P. in 1926, 294.6 m. P. in 1927, 299.8 m. P. in 1928, and 234.4 million in 1929.[14] In 1931, the last year of Bethlen's tenure in office, the total foreign debt of state and local government was 755.5 million Pengő, or seventy percent of the country's GNP, while service on outstanding debts cost 260 m. P. per annum.[15] This was a tenuous arrangement. But it could work as long as short-term loans were available on the international money market and the confidence of foreign lenders was not shaken by some untoward economic or political development.

BUREAUCRACY AND DEVELOPMENT

Etatism in Theory and Practice

While the success of such fiscal wizardry set the stage for the restoration of political civility, such civility was not to mean democracy

---

[10] For Bethlen's relations to the army, see Béla Kovrig, *Hungarian Social Policies, 1920-1945* (New York: Hungarian National Council, 1954), p. 144.

[11] Aylmer C. Macartney, *October Fifteenth: A History of Modern Hungary, 1929-1945*, 2d ed. (Edinburgh: Edinburgh University Press, 1961), I, 65.

[12] Alexander Eckstein, "Economic Development in Hungary, 1920 to 1950," Ph.D. dissertation, University of California, Berkeley, 1952, p. 133.

[13] Macartney, *October Fifteenth*, I, 65.

[14] Ibid.

[15] This was over and above some 3.5 billion P. in private debts to foreign lenders.

or popular government, only a return to the quasi-liberal principles and practices of the old regime. Not that Bethlen was philosophically or emotionally opposed to democracy. To the contrary, unlike the radical malcontents of the Right, he was ready to extoll democracy as the most civilized form of government, best exemplified by the institutions and public life of Britain, which he, like so many other Hungarian aristocrats, still greatly admired.[16] However, Bethlen also maintained that democracy would remain ineffective unless societies reached a certain degree of maturity, that is, a certain state of economic, social, and cultural development. In the absence of such development, democracy would quickly degenerate into mob rule and anarchy. To quote his own words: "Democracy is a political form suitable only to rich, well-structured and highly cultured countries, countries that are free from serious external constraints. In countries where the above conditions are absent, democracy may become seriously debilitating to national existence, especially in times of national crisis, or when the country is faced with social problems of considerable magnitude. In such instances, democracy easily degenerates into ruthless political conflict, because the complete freedom of speech and assembly are potent instruments of misguiding the masses."[17]

Quite obviously, in Bethlen's opinion Hungary had not yet attained the requisite levels of economic and cultural maturity, nor was she free from external constraints or from internal problems of great magnitude. These circumstances together seemed to rule out democracy as impracticable. But if Bethlen rejected the notion of full-fledged democracy as a "threat to national progress,"[18] he also rejected the idea of arbitrary power as a menace to civilization and common decency. What Hungary needed in her present condition was a golden mean "between unbridled freedom and unrestrained dictatorship."[19]

See Eckstein, "Economic Development," pp. 127-133; Kovrig, *Hungarian Social Policies*, p. 37.

[16] To be sure, Bethlen's definition of democracy was whiggish to boot. As he once wrote: "Democracy is a political system that secures equal rights and opportunities to every social class. Democracy, therefore, does not mean rule by the crude masses. . . . Real democracy grants a leading role to the educated and the cultured element. Any political system that tries to negate this principle does not deserve the democratic label, for it merely engenders demagoguery and mob rule." See *Bethlen István beszédei és írásai* [Speeches and writings of Stephen Bethlen] (Budapest: Genius, 1933), ii, 159.

[17] István Bethlen, "Hagyomány és forradalom a politikában" [Tradition and revolution in politics], *Magyar Szemle*, 20 (1933), 105.

[18] Bethlen, *Beszédei és írásai*, i, 159.

[19] Quoted in Sándor Kónya, *Gömbös kísérlete a totális fasiszta diktatura megteremtésére* [Gömbös' attempt to create a totalitarian fascist dictatorship] (Budapest: Akadémia, 1968), p. 33.

In quest of this golden mean, Bethlen quickly fell back on the pragmatic etatism of the two Tiszas, especially on the political legacy of Stephen Tisza, whose writings were soon to acquire the status of a quasi-official doctrine under the Bethlen regime. In this pragmatic etatism the state was to be powerful, indeed supreme. But state power was not to be free from the checks of public opinion. State supremacy was not to be an end in itself, only a means toward the achievement of a number of "higher" historical ends: material progress, national independence, and even democratic government, which Bethlen expected to arise in Hungary at some point in the future.[20]

Tactically, the restoration of the old regime required considerable maneuverings, and was accomplished in several stages. First, rather than forming a political party of his own, Bethlen and his personal entourage entered the Smallholders party, and quickly captivated its "jackbooted" (csizmás) peasant members by his seigneurial presence. Peasant politics in Hungary had yet to acquire structure, experience, and coherence of purpose. In the absence of these, Bethlen could soon engineer a fusion between the Smallholders and some of his own partisans from the Christian National camp, welding them together into a new Unitary party (Egységespárt) under his own leadership. Next he was to persuade this party and the parliament to abandon the relatively liberal franchise under which the National Assembly of 1920-1922 was elected. Here he met some resistance. While the Smallholders were softened by Bethlen's arguments concerning the dangers of agrarian socialism as well as by impending revelations about the venality of some of their erstwhile leaders, a number of old whigs balked at Bethlen's suggestion to abandon the franchise. Under the leadership of the venerable Count Apponyi, they vowed to filibuster the passage of the bill. At this point Bethlen resorted to a ruse that was reminiscent of some of Stephen Tisza's old parliamentary maneuvers: he acquired a writ of dissolution from the regent, and superseded the prevailing electoral law by an order of the Council of Ministers, rather than by an act of parliament. The constitutionality of this procedure was questionable, but it was not entirely lacking in legal foundations, for the superseded franchise had also been introduced by decree as a provisional measure. So once the mandate of the legislature expired, the government could presumably fall back on the provisions of a still earlier law, the Franchise Act of 1913. This act had never been tested in practice, but technically had not yet been repealed by any act of parliament.

The Franchise Act of 1913 that became the law of the land again

[20] Bethlen, *Beszédei és írásai*, II, 367.

by such political and legal maneuvers contained three sets of provisions that suited Bethlen's design particularly well. First, while keeping the size of the electorate well above the nineteenth-century standard of 6 percent, it reduced the number of voters from 39.5 percent
(in 1920) to 29.5 percent (in 1922) by introducing more stringent
educational and residency requirements. Contrary to the earlier franchise, the act required that voters have at least six years of education
and that they reside at least six years in one place; it set the voting
age at twenty-four for men and at thirty for women, except in the
cases of those who possessed high-school degrees, had businesses of
their own, or were mothers of at least three children. Second, the law
established a new system of "recommendations" by which candidates
were required to collect a certain number of signatures to qualify
them for the ballot, a smaller number in the case of established parties,
a larger number in the case of new parties or independent candidates.
Third, while retaining the secret ballot and list voting in forty-six
urban constituencies—including all the electoral districts of Budapest
and of seven cities with autonomous municipal government—it restored the open ballot in the 199 predominantly rural constituencies
of the country.[21]

Once the old-new Franchise Act was in force, Bethlen only needed
to restore the symbiotic relationship between the administration and
the parliament. This was accomplished by recruiting the usual bureaucratic contingent into the Unitary party (Table 26), and, conversely, by appointing a number of political stalwarts to the key posts
of local government. As before, the apparatus was "controlled by the
Minister President who appointed the *föispáns* [lord lieutenants], and
certain other political functionaries, and under him, by the Minister
of the Interior, who was the direct head of the administration and,
in particular, of the police and the gendarmerie."[22] With the help of
this machine, the two chief ministers of the cabinet were once again
able to fix the elections and ensure the return of majorities favorable
to their own persuasion.

By the testimony of observers, the above objective was pursued even
more vigorously than before the war. Electoral manipulation now
started at the pre-campaign stage, when candidates were obstructed
in their attempts to collect the necessary signatures to "recommend"
them. Also, bureaucratic pressure was applied as freely against conservative and nationalist opponents "as against any peasant tribune."[23]

[21] For this electoral law see Molnár, *Magyarország története*, II, 381.

[22] Macartney, *October Fifteenth*, I, 48.

[23] Ibid., I, 61. For the treatment of the nationalist opposition, see the letter of Julius

TABLE 26
BUREAUCRATIC MEMBERSHIP OF THE HOUSE OF REPRESENTATIVES, 1922-1931[a]
(by percentage)

Year	House	Government Party	Opposition
1922	22.0	27.2	14.3
1926	24.1	28.7	13.6
1931	26.1	32.2	16.2

SOURCE: Rudai, "Adalék a magyar képviselőház szociológiájához," pp. 215-230.

[a] Rudai apparently lists only those "bureaucrats" who entered parliament straight from the civil service. Examining the biographies of 803 deputies for the 1922-1939 period, however, I found that 56.5 percent of them had some prior experience in public service (8.0 percent of them in the military, 4.2 percent in the judiciary.)

Ironically, the expansion of the electorate—from the prewar 6.5 percent to 29.5 percent under Bethlen—made these pressures more effective than ever, for it reduced the influence of local notables. Their votes, together with the votes of their clients, were now swamped by those of the propertyless element, which in turn, was under the sway of the bureaucracy. Time and again leading members of other parties were left unopposed by the government as a matter of honor, while on some occasions the electorate of a rural district became so embittered that it braved all perils and rallied behind an opposition candidate. But on the whole, the 199 rural constituencies were effectively controlled by the administrative apparatus. In four general elections between 1922 and 1935, the Government party won 628 out of 980 available seats (64.1 percent), 578 of them in constituencies voting under the system of open franchise.[24]

While the machine routinely manipulated elections in rural Hungary, it interfered little with the process in the urban districts. This strange double standard has puzzled many observers. But the practice was quite consistent with Bethlen's and Tisza's political philosophy, with their attitudes toward the peasantry and the working class respectively, and with their desire to hold up government to public scrutiny. For one thing, while results in the rural constituencies merely measured the efficiency of the machine, the outcome of races in the "secret boroughs" provided a barometer of sorts for the measurement

Gömbös to Bethlen concerning the behavior of the gendarmerie at the by-elections in Hatvan, August 3, 1925, in Miklós Szinai and László Szücs, eds., *Bethlen István titkos iratai* [Secret papers of Stephen Bethlen] (Budapest: Kossuth, 1972), pp. 170-171.

[24] For results of elections in the interwar period, see Macartney, *October Fifteenth*, I, and Molnár, *Magyarország története*, II. Also, *Annuaire Statistique Hongrois*, XLVI (1940), 319-321.

of public opinion. For another, the prevalence of relatively clean elections in the cities guaranteed that there would always be a contingent of opposition deputies in the House of Representatives to preserve parliament as a meaningful institution. This purpose was accomplished, for while the governments of these years won 72.5 percent of the seats from the rural boroughs, their candidates captured not more than 27.2 percent of the representation of the cities.[25] Thus, just as Bethlen expected, parliament remained a forum for open and free-wheeling debate, in which the opposition could dissect policies of governments, and apply the weapons of publicity to check corruption or arbitrary behavior. Indeed, throughout the Bethlen years, and even thereafter, loud voices were raised in parliament to castigate the "pleasure trips of high officials,"[26] special railroad cars "built for the convenience of ministers,"[27] the brutality of the gendarmerie,[28] and all other forms of venality and malfeasance of which public figures, including the person of the regent,[29] were suspected. In the chagrined words of a contemporary critic:

> A revenue officer bullies a pharmacist somewhere, interpellations rattle in the House the next day. Customs agents spill the milk of a Swabian dairy woman, the speakers will castigate the machinations of the milk cartel. The district attorney has suspended a bar license, or banned a public meeting, the National Theater hires the *protégée* of a cabinet minister, and the parliament will react. It will react and react, react to everything from the forged franc scandal to the private affairs of cabinet ministers. Recently, yet another habit is gaining ground: the House is becoming the arbiter of affairs of honor. All in all, the House serves very well to diagnose, but not to cure, the illness of the body politic.[30]

The tenor of public debate was more sedate in the Upper House, but the basic rules of the political game were not much different from

---

[25] Ibid. It should be noted, however, that another 15.2 percent of all seats went to the Christian Social and Economic party, allied to the government.

[26] *Napló*, 1928, ix, 215.   [27] Ibid., 250.

[28] Ibid., 207.

[29] Conservative, legitimist deputies made the habit of referring to Horthy as the "temporary head of state," while one of their numbers, Stephen Rakovszky, spoke derisively of Nicholas Hunyady (an allusion to Horthy's more distinguished precursor in the fifteenth century). The socialists criticized the regent for meddling in politics, others raised questions concerning the costs of his special train and the expenses of his office. See *Napló*, 1922, xiv, 499; 1923, xvi; 1928, ii, 250.

[30] Jenő Papp, *A mai Magyarország erkölcsrajza* [The moral portrait of contemporary Hungary] (Budapest: Káldor, 1934), pp. 224-225.

those prevailing in the House of Representatives. The Upper House had been restored by the Parliament Act of 1925 mainly to provide representation to various economic interest groups now excluded from the Lower House by the overbearance of the political machine. It consisted of the representatives of all "recognized"—Catholic, Protestant, and Jewish—denominations, thirty-six representatives of professional and economic chambers, and thirty-eight titled aristocrats elected by their own peers to represent the "historical" classes and big landed interests. But the representatives of these classes were hamstrung by the weaker constitutional position of the second chamber,[31] and even more by the presence of other contingents that were strongly controlled or influenced by Bethlen's political machine. These included seventy-six representatives of the counties and autonomous municipalities elected for ten-year terms under the auspices of the machine, and forty (later eighty-seven) life members appointed by the regent upon the advice of the prime ministers. Most of the latter were selected from among Bethlen's personal retainers and friends. Shielded by the terms of their office, they remained loyal to their man even after his resignation from the premiership. And under his leadership, they joined hands with the arch-conservatives to fight the rising tide of Right radicalism.

The effectiveness of these institutional restraints was further enhanced by the continued presence of a press, which in the Hungarian case may truly be described as a "fifth estate." This special, practically autonomous, status of the press had evolved in the decades prior to World War I. The unique position of the press was recognized during the revolution of 1918 when the temporary ruling body, the National Council, included next to the representatives of the three major parties (and the feminists) no less than three (out of a total of twenty) representatives of the newspapers. But after 1919, because of the well-known left-wing sympathies of the press, its members were hounded by the white detachments. The institution itself became subjected to a series of repressive measures, among them Orders of Council 4680 and 5499/1919, and the subsequent Public Law vii/1922 on the Defense of the Internal Order and Security of the State that authorized the prosecutor general to ban the distribution of any

---

[31] Under the terms of the Parliament Act of 1925 the Upper House had only a suspensive veto over the bills of the House of Representatives, with no veto over money bills, which had to be sent to the regent directly for his approval. A later revision of the act called for a joint conference between the two houses, and in case of further disagreement, for a joint vote by the two houses without debate. See Macartney, *October Fifteenth*, i, 190-191; Sulyok, *Magyar tragédia*, pp. 305-307.

printed material without judicial proceedings. Under the provisions of this act, particular issues of daily newspapers were indeed banned in some fifty instances over a ten-year period. The ban was applied less frequently for incitement against the state than in order to prevent the embarrassment of the government in the conduct of foreign affairs. Irksome as they were, the restrictions still left sufficient room for public criticism, especially because the press had preserved much of its corporate autonomy and freedom from political parties, including the Unitary party of Bethlen. According to a confidential report of the superintendent of the gendarmerie in 1921, fourteen of the twenty-nine major newspapers of the country were "thoroughly inappropriate," "democratic," or "Jewish."[32] Of the remainder, five papers were described as neutral, two could not be classified, and only seven were found to be "Christian" and "national" in spirit, though not one of them was directly affiliated with the government or with Bethlen's Unitary party. Over the next decade and a half, the situation changed only very little. Thus in 1935, the country had twenty-two daily newspapers of national circulation, eleven of which were described as "Jewish-liberal," six as Christian and legitimist—i.e., sympathetic to the opposition of the Right—and only four as sympathetic to the government.[33] However, in and by themselves these figures do not tell the complete story, for the independent newspapers described as "Jewish" and "liberal" had a circulation of 713,000, the Catholic, legitimist, and conservative newspapers 165,000, while those sympathizing with the government sold only 177,000 copies daily.[34]

In the last analysis, of course, the effectiveness of this press, and of the opposition as a whole, was the function of legal and social norms that Bethlen still regarded as the keystones of a civilized state. Political rowdyism, summary justice, and an arbitrary officialdom, Bethlen explained on numerous occasions, not only besmirched the national honor, they were likely to invite economic and political sanctions on the part of the international community. Thus while the system of law enforcement became both "tighter" and more politicized than in the prewar years—above all by the abolition of jury trials—tribunals of professional judges were still independent enough to render numerous verdicts against the governments. They could annul the election of official candidates where it was obtained by obviously fraudulent or violent methods. And if under new laws for the "more effective defense of the state and the social order" political

[32] Bethlen, *Titkos iratai*, pp. 77-78.
[33] Schickert, *Die Judenfrage in Ungarn*, p. 236.
[34] Ibid.

216

cases multiplied, the courts still held their trials in public, scrutinized evidence, and invited defense attorneys to use their skills on behalf of their clients. While acquittals were less numerous than before, once the revolution was liquidated sentences meted out by the court were somewhat less than draconic. In 1927-1928, for instance, 1,029 persons were convicted for "acts against the authorities" (including many, only marginally "political" cases); of these 548 persons were fined, 372 were incarcerated for less than one month, while the longest sentence was for six months imprisonment (Table 27). In the same year, twenty-eight persons were convicted on charges of incitement; of these twenty defendants were sentenced to less than one month of confinement, eight defendants to confinement for periods of one to six months. Again, of twenty-seven convictions for *lèse-régent* and offenses against the head of state, five persons were fined, thirteen sentenced to less than one month confinement, and five to confinement up to three months.[35] Surely, there was plenty of evidence for harsh treatment by the police and gendarmerie, especially in cases where the suspects were members of the dwindling underground Communist movement. But the fact still remains that in the twenty years between 1921 and 1941, the latter could only point to two martyrs. These were persons who were sufficiently ill-advised to commit a common crime, and unlucky enough to be arrested in possession of weapons and explosives at a time when the country was in the grips of hysteria following a freak bomb attack on the Budapest-Vienna express.

TABLE 27

CONVICTIONS IN COURTS OF LAW FOR POLITICAL OFFENSES, 1910 AND 1928

Offense	1910	1928
Lèse-majesté (régent)	9	27
Crimes against the social order	14	103
Crimes against authorities	366	1,029
"Other" crimes against authorities[a]	—	91
Incitement	39	28
Sedition by means of the press	—	48
Total	428	1,326
Per 100,000 population	2.4	15.5

SOURCE: *Annuaire Statistique Hongrois*, xix (1910), 524, and xxxvi (1928), 322-323.
[a] Under Public Law vii/1922.

[35] *Annuaire Statistique Hongrois*, xxxvi (1928), 322-323.

The Politics of Development

From its forerunners in the prewar period the Bethlen regime not only inherited a political philosophy, but also a number of pressures that circumscribed its economic orientation and social policies. First of all, despite the greater differentiation and complexity of its economy, the country remained an underdeveloped backwater in relation to the core and semi-peripheral areas of the European continent. Second, just as its predecessors had been, the Bethlen government was under considerable pressure to accommodate potential malcontents. Because of its own ideological commitments, the regime labored under a set of complex restraints that prevented it from resorting to terror and large-scale repressive measures. In the absence of these, the government had to fall back on material inducements, and to provide these it had to develop the economy further. The pressing social problems of the country, Bethlen declared, would not be solved by "pursuing spectacular salvationist schemes," but by the "quiet drudgery of so many working days."[36]

While the political philosophy of Bethlen could be described as etatist, in his economic view the role of the state remained a limited and indirect one. True, the public sector was increasing its share of investments and GNP,[37] but not to the point where it would have subverted the market and the free enterprise system. Bethlen and the social classes that had gained preeminence in his machine had no appetite for running and bureaucratizing the economy. They did not want to preempt the entrepreneur but to protect him. They went about this by the old means of tariffs and subsidies, and by defending the profits of private capital, whether foreign or domestic, from the "excesses" of both Left and Right radicalism. Thus, on the one hand the government tried to keep the lid on labor unrest, while on the other it went out of its way to neutralize the adverse economic effects of right-wing demagoguery about the enslavement of the country to "mobile" capital. "If we attack mobile capital," Bethlen lectured the agrarians, "then the price of wheat will still be the same. But foreign capital will stop coming, indeed, it will escape from the country. Do you really think that if I weaken the position of capital,

[36] Bethlen, *Beszédei és írásai*, I, 5-7.

[37] The share of the public sector of investment was 18.3 percent in 1924-1925, 26.8 percent in 1925-1926, and 20.0 percent in 1929-1930. Much of the 1925-1926 figure, however, included investments in the mobile stock of Hungarian railways that had suffered considerable losses during the war, revolutions, and foreign occupation, and were replenished in that year. See Eckstein, "Economic Development," p. 111.

this will strengthen the position of agriculture? Not at all. All it would do would be to increase the number of the unemployed in the industrial sector."[38]

As in the vocabulary of Tisza, the term "economic development" for Bethlen tended to be synonymous with industrialization. In part, this priority resulted from a rational assessment of the state of the world economy, which heavily favored industrial countries over agricultural and other primary producers. In the years following the First World War, the discrepancy between the industrial and agrarian price indices continued to increase with no apparent prospect for the reversal of the trend. Even more clearly than their mercantilist predecessors in the past century, Bethlen and his economic advisers felt that the agrarian countries of Europe were at the mercy of the advanced industrial nations, and that the economic and political emancipation of the former could be attained only by attempting to replicate the economic experience of the latter. But economic and political emancipation were not the only motivations behind this policy. Under the influence of the Spencerians, and more directly of Sidney and Beatrice Webb's *Industrial Democracy*,[39] Bethlen became convinced that industrialism furnished not only greater competitive advantages on the world market, but also that it was an inherently superior form of social organization. Industrialization would provide a natural environment for the more equilibrated and pluralistic system that the premier, without using those terms, envisaged as the final stage of a process of political development. For this reason, he was quite willing to pay a social price for his policies, and industrialize the country, if need be, at the expense of the other sectors of the economy.

These priorities of the Bethlen government are well reflected in the economic legislation of the period. Having been freed from the constraints of the Austro-Hungarian customs union, the Hungarian parliament passed the Tariff Act of 1924, which extended especially heavy protection to textiles and raised the tariff on certain types of cloth as high as 75 percent. Tariff rates were set at 49.2 percent on ironware, 38.6 percent on glassware, and 33.0 percent on machines. As a sop to agrarian interests, cereals were protected from Rumanian and Bulgarian competition by a duty of 27 percent.[40] But the effect of this last provision was partly countermanded by articles in the

[38] Bethlen, *Beszédei és írásai*, ii, 328.

[39] According to the testimony of Kovrig, his personal secretary in those years. See his *Hungarian Social Policies*, p. 41.

[40] Eckstein, "Economic Development," p. 156; Hertz, *Economic Problems of the Danubian States*, pp. 69-72.

Tariff Act that permitted the duty-free entry of industrial raw materials, while levying heavy duties on finished products utilized in the farming sector. Most injurious to farming interests, a duty of 200 percent was applied to nails, hoes, and agricultural machinery, even though there were no domestic industries to be protected.[41] The proceeds from these tariffs were then used to subsidize new industries. The Industrial Act of 1907 remained in force, providing generous exemptions from taxes, tariffs, and license fees. In this manner, "the productive forces of agriculture [were] carrying the burden of industrialization in the public interest."[42] The net effect of these policies, of course, was to diminish agricultural profits and to freeze the already low real income of the agricultural labor force.[43] This provoked further bitter attacks on the government by both agrarian radicals and conservatives. Bethlen parried them personally in the annual parliamentary debates on appropriations,[44] usually urging agrarian producers to bury their selfishness, and to be enlightened enough to see their own long-range interests. As he put it in 1923:

> We either will, or will not have an industry of our own. But once we make the decision to industrialize the country, we will have to accept the fact that the interests of agriculture will temporarily suffer. Surely, we can avoid this temporary sacrifice by abandoning our policies of industrialization. But then the price of industrial products will still be high, and we will not be able to employ our surplus population. The preconditions of a healthy industrialization program are here, and we will take advantage of them, because this course of action alone will guarantee the future development of the agrarian sector.[45]

These last words may not have been much more than lip service paid to a contrary cause by a harried party politician. What was beyond doubt was the fact that the success of industrialization depended largely on the ability of agriculture to generate a substantial exportable surplus of cereals at a relatively low cost, so that the country could maintain a more or less favorable balance of trade. The key question of this neo-liberal economic policy therefore concerned the pattern of agricultural organization best suited for the production of such

[41] G. Gaál, *Napló*, 1927, ii, 330.

[42] M. Fenyő, *Napló*, 1927, ii, 331.

[43] Eckstein, "Economic Development," p. 156; J. Ferenczi, "Der neue autonome Zolltariff," *Ungarisches Wirtschaftsjahrbuch*, 10 (1925), 92.

[44] See, for instance, *Napló*, 1921, ix, 521; x, 469; 1923, xv, 186.

[45] Bethlen, *Beszédei és írásai*, ii, 306-307.

surplus. In attempting to answer this question, Bethlen was reduced to two basic alternatives: an agricultural economy of large estates, or one of peasant smallholdings to be created by some radical land redistribution scheme. In making this choice Bethlen was doubtless guided by strong and visceral feelings, for despite the fact that he no longer owned his ancestral lands, his sympathies were clearly on the side of property. But if such were his sentiments, pure emotion found support in statistics and historical experience. Thus in arguing his case, Bethlen could refer to a set of figures which showed that small farms, while capable of generating greater income per acre,[46] fell far behind the large estates when it came to cereal production for the export market (Table 28). The potential conclusions drawn from these figures were further corroborated by historical examples. On the one hand, Bethlen could point to the experience of the United States and Great Britain, the two most advanced countries in the world, both of which had attained their exalted status in the world economy without ever resorting to "harebrained" land redistribution schemes. On the other hand, Bethlen could cite the example of the Balkan countries, above all the recent experience of Rumania, where the distribution of the large estates had brought temporary relief from rural poverty, but at the same time had literally wiped out the country's cereal exports and hence its long-range prospects for modernization. In the balance hung the level of rural consumption and the peasant's standard of living. These Bethlen was quite ready to sacrifice for "progress,"

TABLE 28

CEREAL AND SUGAR BEET PRODUCTION ON DIFFERENT SIZED LANDHOLDINGS,
1926-1933
(metric quintals/acre)

Size of Holding acres	Wheat	Rye	Barley	Maize	Sugar Beets
0 — 20	7.56	6.25	7.34	8.7	103.4
20 — 100	7.63	6.21	7.77	8.99	102.61
100 — 1000	8.36	7.15	8.70	9.31	113.25
1000+	9.61	7.19	9.76	10.47	129.90

SOURCES: Eckhart, *Magyar gazdaságpolitika*, p. 230; János Adorján, *Megoldás e a földreform?* [Is land reform a solution?] (Budapest: Athenaeum, 1939), p. 18.

[46] In the 1930s, per acre income on holdings of 20 acres or less was 63.99 P.; on estates of 1,000 + acres, 31.4 P. Kerék, *A magyar földkérdés*, p. 358. It should be noted, however, that fifteen percent of the acreage of large estates was fallow land, while thirty-three percent of it consisted of forests.

partly because he saw the peasantry as the weakest of all social classes, partly because he regarded it as an anachronism, a declining social class that in time would be absorbed by the industrial economy.

NEO-CORPORATISM IN THE TWENTIES

The Division of Labor in Society

In the political system that the government of Bethlen restored, the state had a central and dominant, but by no means monopolistic, position. Unlike those of the rising totalitarian regimes of the age, Bethlen's political design did not intend to deprive other elements of society of their autonomy and identity. Nor did the system intend to preempt the operation of autonomous social forces—such as the market or the status system—by political decisions. To the contrary, the effectiveness of the economy and the social system, indeed the very exercise of power, hinged on a subtle division of labor that had emerged over the previous fifty years. In this division of labor the state, or in sociological terms, the political class, cast itself into the Platonic role of guarding the higher national purpose and arbitrating disputes among the other social classes. Next to it, the Jewish bourgeoisie was assigned the role of managing industry and finance, and of acting as intermediaries between the Hungarian economy and the world economy. Finally, the aristocracy and the landowning class were expected to provide surplus grain for exports and to act, together with the Catholic church, as the mainstays of social peace in rural Hungary. Thus, rather than possessing a single power elite, Hungary had separate elites of power, wealth, and privilege. The smooth functioning of the social mechanism rested on an effective collaboration among these three elements, a collaboration that depended on the reciprocal acceptance of each other's spheres of action and influence.

Bethlen and the Jews

Within the overall structure of neo-corporatist society no relationship was more important, or more typical of this quasi-modern system, than the one between the "native" political class and the "ethnic" enterpreneur. Yet no other relationship had been more seriously damaged by the events of 1918-1921. While the revolutionaries attacked entrepreneurs as "bourgeois exploiters," the counterrevolutionaries harassed them as Jews, leaving them demoralized and fearful not only for the safety of their assets, but also of their lives and limbs. In the wake of all this, production was sagging and relations between Hungary and the international financial community were at a low ebb.

The Jewish community that had become the target of these attacks was now smaller than in the prewar years. Of the 938,458 persons of Jewish faith, the peace treaty left only 473,310 in rump Hungary, together with an estimated 50,000-62,000 converts who did not show up in the religious census.[47] Though smaller, the community was also more homogeneous socially, and more closely identified with the bourgeoisie and the professional classes than before. According to the census of 1920, of the 204,507 gainfully employed persons of the Jewish faith, 69.5 percent were owners and salaried employees of business, 14.9 percent were teachers, professionals and the like, and 15.6 percent were wage earners in transport, industry, trade, and agriculture. According to the same census, 45.9 percent of the Jewish population now lived in Budapest, where they constituted 66.2 percent of small merchants, 90.3 percent of those active in finance, 52.6 percent of the salaried employees of industry, and 70.9 percent of those employed by commerce (the respective nationwide figures being 57.9, 88.8, 47.7, and 67.2 percents).[48] In industry, banking, and commerce alike Jews seemed to be in clear control of the commanding heights of business life. According to one, admittedly tendentious, statistical analysis, in 1935 persons who qualified as Jewish made up eighty-seven percent of the members of the Budapest stock exchange, ninety-one percent of the currency brokers' association, seventy percent of the presidium of the National Association of Manufacturers (GYOSZ), and eighty-four percent of the membership of the Textile Manufacturers' and Wholesalers' Association.[49]

As a member of the upper classes raised according to traditional norms of conduct and as one who took the economic position of the Jews for granted, Bethlen felt considerable revulsion about the Jew-baiting of the white detachments and other counterrevolutionary elements. But once again, sentiment was bolstered by rational considerations of class and national interest. For one thing, Bethlen was deeply worried about the potentially demoralizing effect of anti-Semitic excess on the lower classes. As he explained then and in the years thereafter, attacks on the person and property of Jews, if tolerated, might set a dangerous precedent. If it was right to expropriate and harass them, it might be right to expropriate and harass landowners. The ways of the rabble were unpredictable. For another thing,

---

[47] Újváry, *Magyar zsidó lexicon*, p. 554. It should be noted here that the Hungarian census, unlike the Rumanian, Polish, and Czech ones, continued to treat Jews as a religious, rather than as an ethnic or national entity.

[48] Kovács, *A zsidóság térfoglalása*, 41.

[49] Bosnyák, *Magyarország elzsidósodása*, pp. 112-113.

attacks on such a highly visible and economically important minority might give the country a bad international image with fateful consequences for its material welfare. Rightly or wrongly, but probably more strongly than any other Hungarian politician of the age, Bethlen held that the country's economic recovery depended on the goodwill and active cooperation of international high finance, and that this goodwill and cooperation could be secured only by the country's own financial community which, as it happened, was Jewish. To make this very argument, as early as August 1919 Bethlen led a delegation of notables to Horthy, beseeching him to restrain the anti-Semitism of his officers. Thereafter he continued his discreet attempts to enlist the help of the commander in chief, and later regent, to curb excesses, and when he accepted the premiership, he did so with the explicit understanding that he had a mandate for liquidating institutionalized anti-Semitism. His speeches to the "Christian" and "national" parliament were quite straightforward on this point, and were designed both to cool passions and to restore the confidence of the business community. In his introductory speech as prime minister, he stated: "This tendency [anti-Semitism] refers to itself as Christian in spirit. I take the liberty to call the attention of the House to the fact that the teachings of Christianity are not those of persecution and hate, but of equity, justice and social peace. The representatives of Christian politics here will have to find self-fulfillment in helping to restore Christian morality among the public, and in supporting honest economic endeavor in the country."[50] Or as he put it a few months later, defending the policies of his government: "The Jewish question is not, and cannot become, the cornerstone of our policy. Our policy is Christian in spirit, and hence incompatible with religious persecution. If Jews have committed crimes against the state, let us punish them because they have committed them, and not because they are Jewish. And if Christians commit the same kinds of crimes, they should not be acquitted in our courts by virtue of their Christianity."[51]

As the last sentence of this speech broadly hinted, the restoration of public order, and the liquidation of organized anti-Semitism, could not be accomplished overnight. Indeed, in both 1923 and 1925, serious bomb-throwing incidents occurred, one in a Budapest coffeehouse patronized by Jewish businessmen, another at a ball of the Jewish Ladies' Auxiliary in a provincial city. Both of these outrages were quite obviously sponsored by the anti-Semitic Association of Awakening Magyars. But the more systematic terror of the detach-

[50] *Napló*, 1921, IV, 205.   [51] Bethlen, *Beszédei és írásai*, II, 25.

ments was curbed by 1922, and thereafter, the Jewish citizens of the country could once again summon the police and expect from them protection of their persons and property. To protest this "philosemitism," seven deputies of Bethlen's Unitary party seceded in 1923, and under the leadership of T. Eckhardt and A. Zsilinszky—two gentlemen whose names will crop up time and again in this narrative—formed an opposition Party for the Protection of the Race (*Fajvédőpárt*). This, however, proved to be but a temporary irritant, for in 1926 Bethlen, much like Coloman Tisza in 1887, used the steamroller methods of the political machine to eliminate most of the professed anti-Semites from parliament. For the moment, his victory over anti-Semitism seemed complete. Thus when he looked back at the previous five years, he described this victory as one of the two most important accomplishments of his regime.[52]

If one measure of the success of Bethlen's policies was this victory over organized anti-Semitism, another was the growing prosperity of the Jewish population of the country. Thus after some years of Bethlen's premiership, the five percent Jewish element not only recovered its material losses, but was more prosperous than ever before, both in absolute terms and in relation to the gentiles. At the top of the income scale, 50 of 70 taxpayers reporting incomes over 200,000 Pengő (1930) were Jewish, as were 160 of the 291 persons whose income was between 100,000 and 200,000 P.[53] In terms of income distribution, 9.9 percent of the Jewish community fell in the "upper" and "upper middle" category, 28.3 percent in the "middle," 37.6 in the "lower middle," and 24.2 percent in the "lower" category. The comparative figures for society as a whole were 0.6, 7.7, 9.8, and 81.9 percent respectively.[54] A similar income distribution pattern has been extracted from the housing statistics of Budapest, according to which persons of the Jewish faith inhabited thirty-three percent of all dwellings with more than six rooms, thirty-seven percent of all six-room units, forty-one percent of the five-room units, and forty-three percent of the four-room apartments.[55] Altogether, the Jewish share of national wealth was varyingly estimated at from 25 to 33 percent of the total by the economists of the Right, at 19.4 percent by their counterparts on the other side.[56] None of these estimates are entirely

[52] Ibid., I, 14.

[53] Schickert, *Die Judenfrage in Ungarn*, p. 236.

[54] Bosnyák, *Magyarország elzsidósodása*, pp. 70-75.

[55] Ibid., p. 64.

[56] The 25 percent figure in Mátyás Matolcsy, *A jövedelemelosztás Magyarországon* [Income distribution in Hungary] (Budapest: Légrády, 1936), p. 19. For an estimate of

reliable. But even if some of them were inflated to exaggerate the extent of the Jewish penetration of the economy, it would be hard to dispute the validity of Macartney's observation that Hungarian Jews were still heavily identified with property and wealth, and it was precisely for this reason that they served as a "powerful prop to the ruling class"[57] during the Bethlen years.

Bethlen's policies were not only designed to protect Jewish entrepreneurship, but were also aimed at blunting the edge of some of the discriminatory measures enacted by the counterrevolutionary governments. The single most important of these was the Numerus Clausus Act of 1920, a thorn in the flesh of the upwardly mobile Jewish middle class, and of the entire Jewish community. Bethlen was aware of the depth of this resentment and gave voice to it on November 8, 1925 when he spoke in parliament about "the legitimate grievance of Hungarian Jewry," describing the act as a "purely ephemeral phenomenon," and promising to return soon to the "spirit of the Emancipation Act," which he vowed would "in no way be abridged."[58] True, even after this public declaration the act was not formally abrogated. But in the same year the High Court of Justice declared it illegal for all intents and purposes, whereupon its provisions were quietly ignored on the explicit instructions of Count Kuno Klebelsberg, Bethlen's minister of education. The results of these instructions are evident from Jewish enrollments at the universities. While the prewar proportion of 28.4 percent (and the wartime high of 33.6 percent) were never again attained, Jewish enrollments increased from a postwar low of 5.9 percent (1920-1921) to 10.5 percent in 1929-1930.[59] Meanwhile degrees acquired abroad were recognized without much ado, so that the ethnic composition of the professions underwent only slight change between 1920 and 1930. Between these two dates, the percentage of Jewish lawyers declined from 57.0 percent of the total to 55.7 percent, the percentage of Jewish physicians from 47.8 to 40.2, and of journalists from 39.5 to 36.1.[60]

28.3 percent, see, László Levatich, "Nemzeti jövedelem és jövedelemelosztás" [National income and income distribution], *Budapesti Hirlap*, January 25, 1935. The 33 percent figure in Bosnyák, *Magyarország elzsidósodása*, p. 117. The 19.4 percent, or 7 billion Pengő amount cited as "more plausible" in Jenő Lévai, *Fekete könyv a magyar zsidóság szenvedéseiről* [Black book on the sufferings of Hungarian Jewry] (Budapest: Officina, 1946), p. 75.

[57] Macartney, *October Fifteenth*, I, 20.

[58] Bethlen, *Beszédei és írásai*, II, 152.

[59] Laky, *Statistique des étudiants*, p. 29.

[60] *Magyar tájékoztató zsebkönyv* [Hungarian information handbook], 2d ed. (Budapest: Magyar Nemzeti Szövetség, 1943), p. 22.

If in most instances Bethlen followed the policies of Stephen Tisza toward the Jews, there was at least one area in which there was to be no return to the model of the immediate prewar period. While Tisza was ready to permit, and indeed to encourage, the entry of Jews into the political machine, Bethlen raised the old barriers. Whether influenced by the economic exigencies of the moment or by recent events, he made sure that no new Jewish recruits were admitted into public service. Thus while the proportion of Jews in the first postwar decade did not much change in business and in the professions, it declined substantially in the ministries (from 4.9 to 1.5 percent), in the county bureaucracies (from 4.5 to .7 percent), and in the judiciary (from 5.0 to 1.7 percent).[61] And if there were a dozen or so high officials in the governments of Stephen Tisza, there was only one Jewish minister (Baron Korányi) in all of Bethlen's cabinets, and not more than a handful of Jewish deputies in his Unitary party. In other words, Bethlen followed the model not of Stephen, but of Coloman Tisza, with its more rigid concept of the ethnic division of labor in society.

To the outsider, such exclusion from state service may have seemed a small price to pay for economic security and social mobility. But to those affected, the barriers remained prima facie evidence of discrimination which, together with the lingering memories of the white terror, continued to serve as a pointed reminder of the fact of second-class citizenship. Thus, in spite of Bethlen's best efforts, relations between Jews and gentiles remained strained. Gone were the days when the Jewish bourgeoisie conspicuously identified itself with grandiose national designs, whether they entailed independence from Austria, Magyar imperialism on the Balkans, or the cultural assimilation of recalcitrant ethnic minorities. The governments could still count on the economic support, but not on the political backing of the Jewish citizenry. Except in the villages where balloting was open, Jewish voters sought to articulate their interests through parties other than Bethlen's. The Jewish voters of Budapest split their ballots between the small Democratic bloc—the National Democratic, Citizens' Liberty, Radical, Independence, and Kossuth parties—and the Social Democrats, while the Jewish intelligentsia continued to provide the backbone of the leadership of the urban labor movement.[62]

[61] Ibid.

[62] In 1929, four of the fourteen members of the parliamentary Social Democratic party, and twenty-four of the fifty-three socialist members of the municipal council of Budapest were of Jewish parentage (Újváry, *Magyar zsidó lexicon*, pp. 858-859 and 911). As to the Democratic bloc, about half of its representatives in municipal government are said to have been Jewish, while its electoral strength was concentrated in the fifth, sixth, seventh, and eighth districts of Budapest, where most of the Jewish population

Even the great industrial and banking barons, the twenty-five or so captains of the Hungarian economy who were the keystones and chief beneficiaries of Bethlen's policies, remained somewhat ambivalent. While they provided money for the purposes of the machine, some of their secret, or not so secret, contributions went to subsidize the opposition press, the remaining radical intellectuals, and populist advocates of land reform.[63] The political class remained likewise equivocal about Bethlen's policies. While many of its members were quite ready to see the wisdom of his arguments, they continued to resent the aloofness of the bourgeoisie, and complained when the bourgeoisie would not give its undivided loyalties to the liberal-conservative camp led by Bethlen. They would do so only some time later, in the 1930s under the pressure of events that would once more briefly weld together the disparate elements of Hungarian neo-corporatism.

The Landed Aristocracy

Next to the Jews, the other element of Hungarian society that took some buffeting from the winds of revolution and counterrevolutions was the landed aristocracy, or magnates. Although quite remarkably, with the exception of Tisza, no member of this class lost his life during the events of 1918-1919, both revolutions set out to destroy the economic, social, and political privileges of the landed aristocracy. The democratic revolution of Károlyi enacted People's Law XVIII whose articles ordered the expropriation of large estates, while one of the first decrees of the Soviet Republic socialized all landholdings over 100 acres. The counterrevolution quickly annulled these decrees, but the officers of the National Army and of the various free corps remained hostile to the aristocracy. As a result of this hostility the old House of Lords was not restored, while the debates of the new National Assembly resounded with anti-aristocratic rhetoric. True, some clever maneuvering on the part of the National Association of Agrarian Proprietors (OMGE) largely emasculated the impending land reform bill. But Public Law XXXVI/1920 was still passed, and set a precedent for the expropriation and redistribution of landed estates. And while the amount of land so expropriated was far from staggering— it represented one-ninth of all the arable acres in the country—its

---

of the capital lived. See Zsuzsa L. Nagy, *A budapesti liberális ellenzék, 1919-1944* [The liberal-democratic opposition in Budapest, 1919-1944] (Budapest: Akadémia, 1972), pp. 20 and 41.

[63] Nagy, *A budapesti liberális ellenzék*, pp. 43-47.

distribution had the effect of reversing the 54-46 ratio between the acreage of farms over and under 100 acres.[64]

Bethlen put an end to anti-magnate rhetoric on the government's benches, and to further reformist schemes. "Land," as he put it with infuriating logic, "[did] not belong to the 'people' nor to those who till[ed] it, but to those under whose name it appear[ed] in the land register."[65] If one accepted the demagoguery of reformers, then, by the same logic, factories belonged to the workers, and apartment houses to their tenants. Anyway, land redistribution schemes violated the sanctity of private property, and if it was all right to expropriate his land, Bethlen argued, then one might as well expropriate his watch, coat, and pants.[66] For the time being, thus, the integrity of large estates was guaranteed. And if at first Bethlen toyed with the idea of abolishing the entailment of aristocratic estates, he soon abandoned the plan on the grounds that such protection as was afforded by the *fidei commissa* permitted members of the "historical class" to perform their economic function as grain producers, and their social functions as the country's most conspicuous elite. As before, the aristocracy was encouraged to glitter in international high society, and to use its social and family connections to further the national interest. At the same time, it was urged to show the flag in rural Hungary, and by virtue of its traditional prestige, to lend cohesiveness to the social structure.

But if Bethlen saved aristocratic property and privilege, he did not do so without imposing certain conditions, and without expecting something in return. Above all, as we have already seen, the great landowners were to acquiesce in his policies of industrialization, even though the system of tariffs and taxes cut further into the profit margins of large estates. And if he welcomed the magnates at the apex of the social structure and gave them representation in the Upper House, this was not tantamount to making them the ruling class of the country. As the roster of names indicates, Bethlen invited the aristocracy to participate in his cabinets, but they were to do so as members of the political machine, entirely on the prime minister's terms. Indeed, those who accepted positions in his cabinets—Bánffy, Klebelsberg, Korányi—were like Bethlen himself landless aristocrats, displaced persons from some other province of the old Dual Monarchy, expropriated by the successor states. The "real magnates," with

[64] The ratio between small and large holdings was not reversed until 1936. See Kerék, *A magyar földkérdés*, pp. 199-210; Eckhart, *A magyar közgazdaság*, p. 228.
[65] *Napló*, 1923, xv, 185.   [66] Ibid.

the possible exception of Julius Károlyi (Michael's conservative cousin), continued to sulk, resentful of Bethlen's autocratic ways, and of his handling of the royal succession. It would be only after his resignation from the premiership that they forgave him for his anti-legitimist stance and for his neo-liberal, mercantilist, economic policies.

As before, of course, the magnates had their own quota of eccentrics, like Counts Louis Széchenyi and Alexander Festetich, who became the country's first national socialists toward the end of the Bethlen years. But conflicts between political radicalism and latifundiary interests were not easy to manage. Neither Széchenyi nor Festetich could easily reconcile themselves to "communistic" land redistribution schemes that were an integral part of the radical program. Ironically, while his rhetoric was violently anti-Semitic, Festetich was eventually expelled from his own party for refusing to dismiss Jewish bailiffs, estate managers, and accountants from his substantial domain.[67]

The Catholic Church

In the twenties, and even more so thereafter, Bethlen was often described as a liberal, partly because of his policies toward the Jews, partly because of his rationalist-mercantilist attitude toward traditional agrarian interests. Indeed, in these respects his policies reflected significant continuities between the pre- and the postwar regimes. But Bethlen was also described, indeed, self-described, as a conservative, a label justified by some of the discontinuities between his philosophy and the old, nineteenth-century brand of liberalism.

The most important of these discontinuities concerned the relationship of the state and the Catholic church. As we may recall, in the past this relationship was often marred by antagonism. To be sure, throughout the entire era of dualism, the Church retained much of its earlier spiritual influence, and some of its political power. But its institutions and traditional prerogatives were under constant attack as the state, resentful of the supranational character and loyalties of religious Catholicism, sought to assert its authority over the Church. As part of this offensive, the liberal parliaments of the nineteenth century passed the legislative package on civil marriage, the equality of religions, and on the religion of offsprings from mixed marriages, together with a number of measures aimed at reducing the influence

[67] Nicholas M. Nagy-Talavera, *The Green-Shirts and the Others* (Stanford: Hoover Institute Press, 1970), p. 111.

of the Church in the field of education. Remarkably, in this conflict between state and Church, the most Catholic dynasty of Europe offered little solace to the embattled Church, mainly because it wanted to avoid any firm political tie between anti-clericalism and militant nationalism.

After the turn of the century, however, the anti-clerical sentiments of the Hungarian political class began to fade, and, in the face of new political challenges, even such anti-clerical stalwarts as Stephen Tisza buried their Calvinist dislike for the supranational Church. True, as late as 1908, Tisza publicly joined in the protest of Calvinist and Lutheran laity "against the renewed aggressiveness of ultramontane clericalism,"[68] urging his co-religionists to serve as the leaven of enlightenment in Hungarian society. By 1910, however, the radicalism of the Left began to loom large on the political horizon, and to combat it, Tisza was ready to seek a rapprochement with the Catholic clergy. Thus when Tisza's party reentered the political arena that year, it did so not under the old liberal banner, but under the more neutral, if somewhat awkward, label of the National Party of Work. A year later Tisza sponsored the publication of the daily *Magyar Figyelö* (Hungarian Observer) in order "to protect the religious foundations of social life against the nihilism of free-thinkers and atheists."[69] Simultaneously, he inspired the founding of a Society for Religious Equality, with the purpose of uniting Catholic and Protestant laity "against the common [Left radical] enemy."[70]

What started as ad hoc collaboration under Tisza was expanded under Bethlen, and institutionalized within the social and political framework of neo-corporatism. No charter, no formal agreement, or treaty of reconciliation was ever signed, yet the terms of future cooperation were well understood by both contracting parties. The legislative acts of 1892-1895 were neither revoked nor ignored by the government. But the state ended its earlier cultural offensive, and gave the Church virtually a free hand in matters of the primary and secondary education of the Catholic population of the country. In terms of this tacit agreement, no new state schools were to be established in Catholic villages, while those already in existence were to stop competing with their Catholic counterparts by offering significantly different, secularized curricula. The minister of education was to be a Catholic, and preferably a devout one, acceptable to the hierarchy. Apart from the filling of this particular portfolio, successive

---

[68] Quoted in Horváth, *Magyar századforduló*, p. 510.
[69] Ibid., p. 513. [70] Ibid.

governments now were to give the Church a virtual power of veto over a whole range of public appointments—judgeships, notaryships, and candidacies to the House of Representatives from overwhelmingly Catholic districts—a veto which the hierarchy made use of to weed out freemasons, atheists, and other persons whose personal life or background did not meet certain religious standards of probity.

In exchange for these concessions, the Church performed a number of useful services for the state, indeed, it became one of the pillars of the neo-corporatist order. At election time, the local clergy would support the candidates of the machine[71]; at other times it could be counted upon to exhort the faithful to be obedient to the authorities. Even more significantly, after 1920 the Hungarian Catholic church not only undertook to champion the revisionist cause of the national state, it also developed a veritable nationalist image and identity. This metamorphosis from universalism to particularism was all the more remarkable because the majority of Hungarian bishops at this time were assimilated Germans and Slovaks, rather than Magyars.[72]

Be that as it may, the Church now led the way in the nationalist indoctrination of the younger generation, and, at the same time, acted as Hungary's chief lobbyist in Rome and at various Catholic conclaves. It was mainly as a result of such lobbying that the Vatican ignored the territorial provisions of the peace treaty, and refused to make changes in the boundaries of episcopal sees. Thus, throughout the interwar period, Hungarian bishops continued to exercise their ecclesiastic authority over portions of the Czechoslovak, Rumanian, and Yugoslav states.

Neo-Corporatism and the Lower Classes

Like its economic policies, the social policies of the Bethlen regime were shaped as much by the exigencies of economic modernization as by the fashionable theories of industrial sociology that were consistent with the mercantilist, quasi-liberal orientation of the political elite. In terms of these theories, the peasantry was a historical anachronism that was doomed to be transformed in the long run into either

[71] The regularity with which this occurred may be judged from the large number of letters from Bethlen to various ecclesiastic dignitaries during the elections of 1922, 1926, and 1931. See Bethlen, *Titkos iratai.*

[72] Macartney calls our attention to the fact that in 1929 nine Hungarian archbishops and bishops—Cardinal Serédi (Sapoucek), Bishops Fetzer, Hanauer, Glattfelder, Lindenberger, Pajer, Peyer, and Rott—fell in this category. See Aylmer C. Macartney, *Hungary* (London: Ernest Benn, 1934), p. 101. So did the chaplain in chief of the army, Bishop Zadravetz, and Bishop Prohászka (died 1927), the chief political ideologue of Hungarian Catholicism.

an industrial working class or a class of wage laborers in the employ of large, mechanized agrarian production units. Given these assumptions, the regime made no serious attempt to incorporate any stratum of the peasantry into the "system." As long as they remained peasants, the lower classes of rural Hungary were to be citizens only in name. True, as a legacy of the first, turbulent, postwar years official pronouncements continued to extoll the peasantry as the principal bulwark of the nation against left-wing radicalism and internationalism. On numerous occasions Bethlen also insisted that rural smallholders were to be the class on which his whole governmental edifice would rest. But his deeds belied his words. The "jackbooted" deputies of the first National Assembly were quickly ushered out of parliament. If Bethlen's government had any meaningful peasant policy, it was to treat the rural smallholding class as a reservoir from which the membership of the national elite could be replenished. As a reflection of this attitude, the educational mobility of the children of peasant smallholders was encouraged, or at least not looked upon with disfavor. But the peasantry itself was to remain mere cannon fodder in the battle for industrialization, forbidden to make any claim on national resources or to have any meaningful representation in national politics. The agricultural proletariat was written off completely, and remained totally excluded from any of the social, health, and unemployment benefits that the Bethlen government introduced over the years.[73]

In constrast to this indifference, Bethlen took an active interest in the affairs of the industrial working class. This is not to say that Bethlen liked industrial workers. On the contrary, like most of his peers, he alternately loathed and pitied them. But like his farsighted predecessor, Tisza, Bethlen studied his industrial sociology. He came to the conclusion that the industrial working class was there to stay, not only as an incidental "precipitate" of the industrial revolution, but as a major force that would occupy a strategic position in the society of the future. How strategic this position was became amply evident in the course of the events of 1918-1919 when a single industrial city, Budapest, could temporarily impose its will upon the rest of Hungary. For Bethlen, politics was the art of the possible, and while it seemed possible to disenfranchise the peasants effectively, it did not seem possible to replicate such a policy vis-à-vis industrial workers. So, under the long shadow of the revolutions, Bethlen not only continued Tisza's policies of "oiling the social machinery" with material benefits,

[73] For some of Bethlen's thinking about the peasantry see Kovrig, *Hungarian Social Policies*, pp. 149-153.

but also proceeded to grant workers a limited political status within the neo-corporatist institutional order.

These measures designed to pacify the working class came straight out of Tisza's book, and like those of the latter, were twofold. On the one hand, the Bethlen government restored the worker's right to strike—taken away de jure during the war, and de facto during the years of the white terror—and with it the opportunity to improve industrial wages within the limits set by the profit rates of the enterprise. On the other hand, once the economy was stabilized, the government embarked on an extensive program of social legislation. This program culminated in the Social Security Act of 1927 that set up an advanced system of social and health insurance for both workers and salaried employees of industry. Simultaneously, the work week was reduced to 48 hours, child and woman labor received a degree of protection, and new standards of health and safety were introduced in the factories.[74]

The steps taken to institutionalize the political status of industrial workers preceded these economic measures. While the rights and privileges of landowners, members of the clergy, and entrepreneurs rested on convention and a complex web of tacit understandings, those of the workers became incorporated in a formal document, whose language is reminiscent of medieval charters signed by the king and his subjects. Indeed, there is perhaps no other archival relic of the period that reflects the spirit of Hungarian neo-corporatism better than this agreement, signed by the "representatives of the Social Democratic Workers" and the "Royal Hungarian government" on December 22, 1921.[75]

The Bethlen-Peyer Pact—as the document came to be known, in reference to the prime minister and the head of the reconstituted Social Democratic party—consisted of twelve clauses that addressed issues of both short- and long-term political relevance. The government pledged to return the confiscated property of trade unions, of the Social Democratic party, and of the workers' cooperatives, to release all socialists detained without trial, and to grant amnesty to those who had served part of their terms in prison. In exchange, the socialists were to adopt a more "patriotic" attitude, break their ties with the emigrés of the Soviet Republic, and use their influence abroad to improve the international image of the country. Industrial workers and the Social Democratic party were to enjoy the same freedoms of

[74] Ibid., pp. 50-52, Macartney, *October Fifteenth*, I, 68-69.

[75] For the text, see Macartney, *Hungary*, p. 266; also Molnár, *Magyarország története*, II, 379. For a book-length study on the subject, see László Réti, *A Bethlen-Peyer paktum* [The Bethlen-Peyer Pact] (Budapest: Magyar Történelmi Társaság, 1951).

speech and association as all other parties. Their press was to be free from harassment, as were all strikes, as long as they were purely economic and not political in nature. Yet, at the same time, the activities of both the party and the trade unions were to be circumscribed, for both were to refrain from organizing agricultural workers, miners, public employees, and transportation workers.

The issues of suffrage and representation were not formally included in the document. But when the electoral law was introduced the next spring, its provisions were drawn up in the spirit of the pact. For while the secret ballot in the cities permitted the free expression of working-class sentiment as well as the election of socialist deputies, the system of open franchise in the countryside effectively prevented the Social Democratic party from mobilizing the mass of agricultural workers. In the course of the next decade, both parties to the agreement accused the other of bad faith and of breaches of the letter and the spirit of the agreement. But even so, the pact continued to provide a framework for socialist and working-class politics throughout the interwar period, and indeed almost until the closing days of World War II.

Letters and Politics under Bethlen and After

If only for obvious generational reasons, the dominant element within the cultural elite of the period remained the "westernizers" (*nyugatosak*), that is those who continued to be inspired by the philosophical, artistic, and political currents of the Occident. As before the war, they congregated around the journal *Nyugat* (Occident) as proud arbiters of literary taste. They formed the nucleus of an artistic opposition to the governments of the day, including Bethlen's, which they regarded as yet another example of the perversion of the true meanings of democracy and liberalism. But if these "westernizers" or "bourgeois" artists were critical, their voices were muted. Before 1918, most Hungarian intellectuals had believed that the institutions of their country could be reshaped in their own image of democratic humanism. But the October revolution had collapsed of its own weight, and after the experiences of the Soviet Republic and the white terror, there was justified diffidence concerning the feasibility of another democratic experiment. More than ever before, after 1920 Ady's (and Széchenyi's) metaphor of the "great fallow" became a forbidding reality, which the artist could not change only escape from, either by emigration—as did some of the best composers or painters, like Bartók and Tihanyi—or by taking refuge in the world of art and fantasy, as did most of the writers.

In his escape from reality, the "westernized" artist of the period would follow one of several avenues. Some, like the writers Márai, and later Füsth, and Németh (under the all too obvious literary influence of Cocteau and André Breton), retreated into the depths of the human soul, producing a string of psychological novels that were the first of their kind in Hungarian literature. In his autobiographical *Confessions* (*Egy polgár vallomásai*), Márai, born Goldschmied, writes of a prosperous, provincial bourgeois family, depicting it with nostalgic warmth, but with touches that make it appear forlorn even in its heyday. Márai abandoned not only his ancestors' trade, but also rejected an *ars militans* that would have vindicated the social and political ideals of his class. Instead, he produced a series of elegant novels filled with an airy symbolism, novels that were incomprehensible to the average reader and found sympathetic reception only among a handful of connoisseurs in the literary salons of the capital.

Others, like the brilliant Frederick Karinthy, made their retreat from reality by travelling from the bizarre to the surreal, and ultimately, to the absurd. Similarly, many poets proceeded from substance to pure form, as did the members of the "great trio" of interwar lyricists, Babits, Kosztolányi, and Árpád Tóth. In the poetry of the latter, exquisite harmony in form combined incongruously with the utter disarray of moods to produce an effect every bit as precious as in the poems of their master, Paul Valéry. However, even more remarkable than the escape into surrealism or pure form was the route taken by a number of the less remembered writers of the urban *petite bourgeoisie*—Harsányi, Földi, Renée Erdős, and the Marxist sympathizer Déry—who spun fanciful tales of a bourgeois world that simply did not exist in Hungary. Seemingly oblivious to the idiosyncrasies of Hungarian society and its differences from the West, writers like Harsányi in his *Whiskey and Soda* (*Whiskey szódával*) populated their novels with captains of industry, financiers, corporate executives, or with figures borrowed straight from the saga of the Forsytes or from the home of the Buddenbrooks. In retrospect, the effect is at least as bizarre as in Karinthy's theater of the absurd. But in its own time, this literature catered to the very real fantasies of a bourgeoisie that was yearning for the milieu of Paris, London, and New York.

If all "westernizers" were escapists, not all literati were "westernized," and those who were not produced a body of blatantly political literature that reflects a search not just for a new Hungary, but for a new world, whose epicenter lay elsewhere than in the Occident. A few of these men of letters were urban socialists, the most notable figure among them being the deeply troubled Attila József. During his brief but remarkable literary career József moved cagily between surrealism and communism until he was expelled from the underground Communist party for the not too unreasonable suspicion of anarchistic tendencies. There were still others of his persuasion, like the proletarian writer Kassák, who had been marginally involved in the events of the Soviet Republic. But the most strident voices came from a different quarter, from two robust men claiming to represent not the city, but forgotten rural Hungary. One of them was Sigismund Móricz, whose powerful novel *Gold in the Rough* (*Sárarany*), published before World War I, was a magnificent celebration of primordial peasant strength and instinct, with a hero cast in the mold of Artsybashev's Sanin. The other writer was Desider Szabó, a Transylvanian schoolteacher. His novel *Village Adrift* (*Elsodort falu*) shocked the polite literary and social circles of the immediate postwar period with both the sensuousness of his imagery, and the vileness of his outbursts against a racially and culturally alien urban civilization with its Jewish and Swabian denizens. Both Móricz and Szabó were geniuses who burnt themselves out quickly. While Móricz remained highly productive, much of his later oeuvre consists of long-winded historical trilogies paid for, so it is said, by the line, which explains their scope and length. Szabó meanwhile retreated into Olympic haughtiness, throwing vitriolic barbs at all factions and parties without bestowing any favors. But the seed they had sown took root, and from it grew the populist literary and sociological movement of the 1930s, as young peasant writers turned away from urban and cosmopolitan modes of literary expression. Just as their models and mentors, Móricz and Szabó, these young populists tried to approach the peasant for what he was, and not what he should be. They treated him as an integral part of the social structure, and not as a mere adjunct to modern civilization, or as a potential recruit into the urban labor force. But then, again like their mentors, the "village explorers" were divided as to the best way of redeeming peasant society. The touchstone of this difference was the racial issue, specifically the issue of anti-Semitism. For while a minority of populists—led by the poets Erdélyi and Sinkai—became converts to the idea of a *völkisch* Europe consisting of purified peasant peoples, the majority of the generation—led by Julius Illyés, Francis Erdei, and Zoltán Szabó—took a view more akin to that of the Balkan populists. They envisaged, with perhaps too little political realism, the rise of a democratic, peasant Europe that would become a counterweight to both Germany and the Soviet Union.[76]

---

[76] Mikós Lackó, *Válságok—választások* [Crises—dilemmas] (Budapest: Gondolat, 1975), pp. 35-117.

VI.

The Revolution of the Right
(1932-1945)

THE CRISIS OF NEO-CORPORATISM

Economic Development—Political Decay

From a purely economic point of view Bethlen's policies of industrialization and development may be described as quite successful. Once again a right combination of political intervention and entrepreneurial skill bore fruit: within less than a decade the country's economy not only recovered from the chaos of defeat, but by most conventional yardsticks made remarkable progress. True, agricultural production continued to stagnate at prewar levels. But as the agricultural population of the country declined from 58.1 to 51.8 percent, the number of workers in factories increased from 136,808 to 236,284. The index of industrial production rose from 100 to 294 (1929), the horsepower capacity of factories from a half million in 1920, to 931,000 in 1925, and 1,297,000 in 1930, and the percentage share of industry in the gross value of the national product from 23.3 to 31.3 percent.[1] In but four years, between 1924 and 1928, the GNP of the country rose from 4,631.2 million to 5,728.3 million Pengő (U.S. $900 million to $1,150 million),[2] averaging a respectable annual growth rate of 6 percent, almost all of it in the industrial sector. In terms of these figures the Bethlen years do indeed "invite comparisons with [their] predecessor, the Compromise Era,"[3] and if the comparisons are actually made, the material achievements of the former do not much lag behind those of the latter.

By all accounts, the chief beneficiary of the boom was the urban entrepreneurial class, whose profits represented the driving force behind the development of the economy. But next to the entrepreneur the industrial working class, too, was favored by both government

---

[1] Kovrig, *Hungarian Social Policies*, pp. 36-38.

[2] Mátyás Matolcsy and Stephen Varga, *The National Income of Hungary, 1924/25-1936/37* (London: King).

[3] Macartney, *October Fifteenth*, i, 65.

238

policy and the forces of the market. Thus after the deep slump of 1919-1921, the cash wages of workers began to rise again, until in 1929 they reached the prewar level (at an average of 1,498 P. per annum),[4] though some of the increases were offset by increases in the costs of housing.[5] Altogether, 12.0 percent of the active labor force employed in the manufacturing industries in 1929 received an 11.1 percent share of the national income—9.3 percent in wages, .7 derived from rents, and 1.1 percent in the form of social services[6]—a ratio still more favorable than the one prevailing in the advanced industrial countries of the Continent.

Regretfully from the point of view of the Bethlen regime, these indices of material progress did not readily translate into a sense of well-being or active political support for the government. To be sure, the steady increase of wages throughout the twenties stilled the most acute complaints of the working class and forestalled any violent manifestations of discontent. But Bethlen and his system enjoyed little popularity, and even less legitimacy, in the cities where the industrial proletariat continued to vote for the socialists and persisted in harboring fond memories of the Soviet regime. When the urban working class at long last defected from the socialists in 1938-1939, it did so not in support of the liberal-conservatives of Bethlen's stripe, but in support of the national socialists and other right-wing radical movements.

The reasons for this failure of the government were twofold, and at least one of them was directly related to Hungary's economic backwardness and the location of the country on the European periphery. Above all, there was the age-old problem of relative deprivation caused by the international demonstration effect of the advanced countries whose standard of living continued to shape expectations in the less developed countries. The Hungarian worker may have had a larger share of the GNP of the country than his German or British counterparts, but in absolute terms his wages, and his general standard of living, remained far below the English and German levels. But then the sense of working-class frustration was further aggravated by the "feudal" spirit of the neo-corporatist order, its emphasis on heroic exploit, and, alternatively, on hereditary privilege. It was one of the

[4] Frederick Hertz, *Economic Problems*, p. 197.

[5] According to the calculations of Hertz, in 1929 the real wage of Hungarian workers was ten percent below the 1913 level, if we include the cost of housing; two percent above the prewar level if we disregard this item. Ibid., p. 196.

[6] Kovrig, *Hungarian Social Policies*, pp. 202-206; Matolcsy, *A jövedelemelosztás Magyarországon*, pp. 1-19.

great contradictions inherent in this regime and its predecessors that while they permitted considerable upward mobility from the lower classes, they continued to project an image of uncompromising rigidity. The political establishment of the twenties, as we will see subsequently, was open to plebeians. But when an outsider began to climb the social ladder, he was often forced to repudiate his origins, and to pretend that he was the scion of an ancient noble family. Instead of proudly advertising its openness to popular talent and thereby pleading for legitimacy in modern terms, the Hungarian elite attempted to derive its inner strength from a kind of pseudo-exclusiveness, frequently hiding its most attractive features under the cloak of an ostentatious contempt for achievement. As long as this was the case, the abyss between the industrial worker and the ruling political class could not be successfully bridged.

If the urban working class was influenced by an international demonstration effect, the peasantry defined its own status and expectations by comparisons with the condition of the lower classes in the city. With the exception of the immediate postwar years, the living standard of the peasantry did not conspicuously slide from the prewar level. Overall, between 1913 and 1927 the consumption of cereals remained stable at about 546 kgs. per head, the consumption of sugar increased from 8.7 to 10.6 kgs. While the consumption of meat declined from 50.6 to 41.3 kgs. per head, and the consumption of cotton from 4.12 to 3.00 kgs., the decline did not adversely affect either life expectancy or infant mortality in the country.[7] The Hungarian peasantry was a barefoot and ragged lot whose housing and nutrition was poor by modern standards, but it was not a class that was becoming hungrier every year. Peasant frustrations were nurtured not by growing misery but by the increasing discrepancy between the urban and the rural living standard. At the height of the interwar boom in 1928 the average income of the rural wage earner was as little as 325 P. (much of it received in kind), or a bare twenty-eight percent of the average earnings of the industrial population.[8] This discrepancy lent considerable substance to the rhetoric of radicals of both Left and Right about the "land of three million beggars,"[9] or about contrasts between the "European city and the Asiatic countryside,"[10] and accounted for the alienation of the peasantry not only from the regime, but from

[7] Hertz, *Economic Problems*, pp. 199-200.

[8] Matolcsy, *A jövedelemelosztás Magyarországon*, p. 8; also, *Napló*, 1937, XIII, 407.

[9] This popular phrase originated with George Oláh, a radical journalist of the Right.

[10] Ferenc Erdei, *A magyar falu* [The Hungarian Village] (Budapest: Athenaeum, 1938), p. 156.

the whole rural way of life. Thus when the "village explorers" of the thirties surveyed the attitudes of school-age children in the countryside, they found that only thirteen percent of them wanted to remain farmers, and that the rest of them were dreaming of careers as chimneysweeps, janitors, porters, garbage collectors, and conductors in the quasi-mythical city.[11] Alas, while the urban economy was expanding, it was not expanding fast enough to accommodate all these rural malcontents. So the majority of them would stay put and in the 1930s turn the Hungarian countryside into a boiling cauldron of unrest.

Adding to the level of rural tension was the fact that the peasants of the age were still better informed and more aware of the world than those of the previous generation. By 1930 literacy reached almost ninety percent; newspapers made their way to the villages, copies were passed from hand to hand, and the contents were further spread by word of mouth, even among the poorest peasants.[12] Moreover, the war itself contributed to increasing levels of information, for a good part of the adult male population had left the villages, and traveled to the cities or to foreign countries. As a result, as one rural sociologist noted, "the horizon of the village extended from Siberia to the Pyrenees. . . . Ever since the war France, the Italians, the Russian winters are standard conversational topics."[13]

But if social awareness increased, this did not mean that there was a greater "insight into the social mechanism," or a real appreciation of the complexities of modern society. As before, the Hungarian peasant retained an uncanny ability to reduce the world to simple categories derived from the narrow experience of the rural household and the simple economy. If newspaper stories now freely circulated in the village, the substance of these stories was quickly distorted beyond recognition as items were passed on from one person to another.[14] In political discussions among peasants, present and future, fact and fancy, design and reality mixed freely. Nor was the awareness of the peasant tantamount to a genuine appreciation of civic politics. Parliament was, at best, a distant place where educated people conducted their own business at the expense of the peasantry. And if a

---

[11] Zoltán Szabó, *A tardi helyzet* [Report on the village of Tard] (Budapest: Cserépfalvi, 1936), p. 200. This matches the observations in Ferenc Erdei, *Futóhomok* [Quicksand] (Budapest: Athenaeum, 1937), p. 30.

[12] In the village of Tard, 2,317 inhabitants subscribed to thirty-one dailies and fifty-three weeklies. But the contents of these became known to most of the adult population. Szabó, *A tardi helyzet*, p. 140.

[13] Ibid., p. 22.

[14] This point is well illustrated by Szabó in his Tard survey. Ibid., pp. 140-142.

deputy from the lordly estate was expected to be impervious to peasant needs, a deputy of the peasant caste was even worse, for he "would be too awkward in the company of gentlemen,"[15] either ineffectual or corruptible. "The bailiff is always worse than the master, the sergeant more trouble than the lieutenant,"[16] the peasants of Tard were quoted as saying. Clearly, the peasants had very little faith in any system that offered piecemeal solutions through legislative bargaining and bickering. Rather, they expected their salvation from a strong leader blessed with prophetic gifts and standing above the petty squabbles of parties or the tedium of administrative minutiae.

Crisis of the Global Order

However, like the fate of its predecessors, the trials and tribulations of the Bethlen regime cannot be solely explained in terms of domestic scarcities and relative deprivations. For while the latter did indeed account for the conflict between the haves and have-nots, this conflict found ideological rationale and political expression within the context of a more profound crisis of the international system.

This crisis must be approached from two separate points of departure. First there was the international division of labor and the pattern of international inequality which not only persisted but further increased throughout the postwar decade. Thus, whether we measure it in terms of income or productivity (Tables 29 and 30), we will find that the gap between core and peripheral countries further widened, in spite of the fact that a number of peripheral countries,

TABLE 29

AGRICULTURAL PRODUCTIVITY IN EUROPE NORTHWEST-SOUTHEAST AXIS, 1925-1935
(metric quintals/ha)

Country	Wheat	Potatoes	Cattle
Holland	30.0	189.3	102.5
Denmark	28.5	142.6	102.2
Switzerland	22.6	150.2	73.3
Germany	19.8	135.4	62.7
Czechoslovakia	17.1	119.4	54.3
Austria	15.1	123.0	49.6
Poland	12.3	106.4	36.9
Rumania	9.2	98.7	24.5

SOURCE: F. Hertz, Economic Problems of the Danubian States, p. 110.

[15] Ibid., p. 201.
[16] Ibid. For a similar conclusion, see Gyula Illyés, A puszták népe [The people of the puszta] (Budapest: Nyugat, 1936), pp. 10-12.

242

TABLE 30
Average Income Produced per Working Population Core - Periphery,
1913 and 1930
(International Units)

Country	1913	1930
Core:		
U.S.	1,386	1,783
Great Britain	1,017	1,230
Belgium	666	823
Sweden	664	818
Switzerland	633	889
France	627	761
Semi-Periphery and Periphery:		
Germany	881	776
Czechoslovakia (Bohemia)	577	528
Hungary	427	392
Rumania	393	318
Yugoslavia	336	312

Source: Clark, *The Conditions of Economic Progress*, 2d ed., pp. 46-47, 63, 80, 84, 87, 100, 108, 116, 136, 158.

among them Hungary, made concentrated efforts to overcome their economic backwardness. Second, while international inequality increased, the legitimacy of inequality was further undermined by the war and by the postwar treaties of peace. Whatever their true intentions may have been, these treaties appeared to reinforce privilege and lent credence to the argument that the distribution of resources across the world was a matter of naked force rather than of industry. All over the periphery there were voices heard condemning the rich countries of the Northwest: while the vanquished accused them of plunder, erstwhile allies—like Italy and Rumania—raised the issue of perfidy, and joined the chorus of critics who suggested that the injustices of a system of force could only be rectified by force.

This conflict between more and less privileged nations on the Continent was further complicated by the rise of the Soviet state as the embodiment of the revolutionary ideology of proletarian internationalism. Significantly, this ideology was not only directed against the prevailing distribution of economic resources in particular societies, but also against the political division of the world into competing nation states. Consequently, the elites of the weak nation states of the Continent found themselves under pressure from two opposite directions. On the one hand, they were threatened by the competition of powerful imperial states; on the other, they saw their very raison d'être challenged by the groundswell of proletarian internationalism. Under such pressure the political response of these elites acquired a dual character: it was revolutionary vis-à-vis the possessing nations of the core, but counterrevolutionary toward the proletarian internationalism of the periphery. It was this dualism that set apart the new Right from the old, the latter having been merely concerned with the defense of established privilege. Thus, while previously it would have been a contradiction in terms, the idea of right-wing radicalism now came to be political reality.

While in the main, this rebellion against the status quo that culminated in the events of World War II was a rebellion of nation states, in each of these states the radicalism of the Right was spearheaded by different social coalitions and political movements that envisaged different remedies. On the one hand, there were those who regarded the power and the welfare of the nation as their ultimate ends, and believed that in order to attain these objectives they were justified in casting off all the restraints of international law, convention, and morality. On the other, there were those who were not content to fight for a mere "place under the sun" in the name of *sacro egoismo*, but set out to create a new world order, based on either religious or racial principles. Thus from the 1920s onward, the political spectrum of continental countries was not only divided between the old Right and the new, but also between the competing and sometimes clashing movements of national radicalism, Christian radicalism, and national—in reality, racial—socialism.

The Depression and Its Consequences

These tensions, latent in the Hungarian as well as the global social system, were brought to the fore by the Great Depression of 1929-1934. Triggered by the crash of the New York stock exchange, the crisis soon acquired global dimensions, affecting commodity prices, production, and terms of credit, with further repercussions for the stability of both international and national political systems.

In the case of Hungary, the crisis was painfully and immediately evident in the catastrophic fall of cereal prices. Most disastrously for the rest of the economy, the price of wheat dropped from 25.84 P. per metric quintal in 1929 to as low as 7.15 P. in 1933. During the same period, the price of rye declined from 20.66 P. to 3.65 P., that of maize from 17.51 P. to 7.75 P.[17] The volume of agricultural exports

---

[17] Budapesti kereskedelmi és iparkamara [Hungarian Chamber of Commerce and Industry], *Hungarian Commerce and Industry in 1938* (Budapest: Pátria, 1939), p. 56.

fell by 49.2 percent, the gross value of exports by 70.3 percent.[18] Inevitably, profit margins followed suit: in 1932 only six percent of Hungarian farmers reported a return of five percent or more over their capital investment, while fifty-seven percent of the agrarian producers reported a net loss.[19] Not surprisingly, the production index went down from 100 (1929) to 61.6 in 1931 and 44.8 in 1932.[20] With thousands of acres left fallow, the agricultural proletariat was on the verge of famine. The smallholders dropped out of the market and produced only for their households. Nor did the great landowners, already deeply indebted, escape the consequences of the crisis, for they quickly ran out of cash and credit and were forced to lapse into a kind of self-sufficiency. The British historian of this period recalls a winter journey from the countryside to the capital in the company of "a member of one of Hungary's historical families, himself the owner of some 10,000 acres." They traveled third-class and by the slow train carrying sacks of food from the estate. Their supper, "eaten in a lovely baroque room in his palace, came out of the sacks. The room and bedrooms were unheated for lack of firewood."[21]

The collapse of the agricultural economy had serious secondary consequences, for it not only deprived the state of its revenues, but also industry of its internal market and of needed cash to pay for vital imports of raw materials. Thus as the agricultural economy weakened, industrial output and employment, too, began to decline. The gross value of industrial production slid from 2,867 m. P. in 1929 to 1,763 million in 1933,[22] urban unemployment rose to a quarter million, including twenty-seven percent of the industrial labor force of the country.[23] Those who were still employed had to take substantial cuts in pay: over a three-year period the average industrial wage fell from 1,438 P. to 1,172 P., not to rise again to the 1929 level for the rest of the interwar period.[24] To further darken this bleak economic picture, in 1931 the financial props of the system fell out almost overnight when short-term credits were cancelled, foreign capital left the country, and nearly 5 billion P. were reconverted into foreign currencies on the international money market.[25]

---

[18] Ibid.; see also, Budapesti kereskedelmi és iparkamara, ed., *Hungarian Commerce and Industry in 1935* (Budapest: Pátria, 1936), p. 16.

[19] Budapest: kereskedelmi és iparkamara, *Hungarian Commerce and Industry in 1938*, p. 56.

[20] Ibid.   [21] Macartney, *October Fifteenth*, i, 98.

[22] Hertz, *Economic Problems*, p. 191.

[23] Kovrig, *Hungarian Social Policies*, pp. 39-40.

[24] Hertz, *Economic Problems*, p. 197.   [25] Macartney, *October Fifteenth*, i, 92.

Adverse political consequences were not far to follow. In the capital unemployed workers organized demonstrations and hunger marches. One of them, on September 1, 1931, resulted in a clash with the police and considerable bloodshed. The villages likewise were in a state of uproar and under the sway of a variety of chiliastic movements, some religious, others political, and again others a successful combination of religion and political radicalism. Of the latter most notable was the Brotherhood of the Scythe Cross, led by one Zoltán Böszörményi, a journalist of minor accomplishments who called himself the "prophet of the poor" on a mission from God. He issued ten commandments of his own, and called upon the peasantry of the Tisza region to march against the "lords and communists" of Budapest.[26]

The discontent of the masses reverberated throughout the entire body politic, and by mid-1931 a rebellion was afoot among the back-benchers of Bethlen's Unitary party. Spurred on by the rapid succession of economic and political developments, the old counterrevolutionary spirit was rekindled again within the establishment. Even some of the liberal-conservative stalwarts were coming to the conclusion that the system could be saved only by sacrificing its most conspicuous representatives. Ever the grand seigneur, Bethlen obliged by resigning on August 19, 1931 in favor of Count Julius Károlyi. The latter was a personal friend of Bethlen and a relation of Regent Horthy by their children's marriage. Károlyi was a man far more conservative than Bethlen, but he was not blessed with his predecessor's skill for compromise. The change of guard only added fuel to the flames of discontent in all quarters. Soon there was open revolt in the caucus of the Unitary party, which climaxed in a vote of no confidence. Prolonged consultations followed, in the course of which the regent asked for the advice of Bethlen and of a number of senior politicians and churchmen. Finally the decision was made to call for Julius Gömbös, the most prominent figure among the erstwhile Szeged men, and the acknowledged leader of the radicals within the establishment. Thus on October 5, 1932, the man who was considered most likely to pacify

---

[26] Such a march was in fact organized in 1936, when ten thousand of Böszörményi's followers gathered at Dévaványa, expecting to move from village to village, and hoping to snowball to three million by the time they reached the capital city. The gendarmerie, however, easily foiled the march. One hundred and thirteen peasants were tried for sedition, while Böszörményi escaped to Germany. See Kálmán Szakács, *Kaszáskeresztesek* [Scythe-crossmen] (Budapest: Kossuth, 1963); Bernát Klein, "Hungarian Politics from Bethlen to Gömbös. The Decline of Liberal-Conservatism and the Rise of Right Radicalism." Dissertation, Columbia University, 1962, especially pp. 170-177; Imre Kovács, *A néma forradalom* [The silent revolution] (Budapest: Cserépfalvi, 1937), p. 248.

the masses was appointed premier. Gömbös introduced a new, more populist style into Hungarian politics and his appointment ushered in a period of Right radical ascendancy which, with a few ups and downs, was to last until the end of World War II.

RIGHT RADICALISM IN HUNGARY

Crisis of the Political Class

More so than any of its predecessors, the Bethlen regime had to contend with the problem of intellectual overproduction and the frustrated social aspirations of the educated classes. In part, this was the result of the lost war and the subsequent treaty of peace. Not only were the educated classes heavily concentrated in Budapest and on the territory of the rump country, but their numbers were further augmented by the influx of educated refugees, above all former civil servants seeking physical and economic security in the mother country. Thus if old Hungary with its almost twenty-one million inhabitants had 251,534 citizens (1910) who were in possession of certificates of maturity (from gymnasia), the new country, with its less than eight million inhabitants, inherited 209,826 of them (1920) within its truncated territory.[27] But apart from these conditions, the problem was aggravated by the government's own policies which, in response to pressures to maintain Hungary's "cultural superiority" in the Danubian Basin and to demands for new avenues of social mobility, were designed to maintain the prewar system of higher education. The University of Pozsony (Bratislava) and Kolozsvár (Cluj) were repatriated to Pécs and Szeged respectively, and, together with the old University of Budapest and the more recently organized University of Debrecen, turned out graduates at a rate even higher than before the war.[28]

The Bethlen government dealt with the problem of intellectual overpopulation by using the traditional recipe of absorbing as many

[27] Of these, an estimated 60,000 were refugees from the succession states. György Szombatfalvi, "Az értelmiség válsága" [The crisis of the intelligentsia], *Társadalomtudomány*, 4 (1924), 5-6. The above figures exclude graduates of *Realgymnasia* and other schools of a non-Latin-oriented curriculum, hence the discrepancy between them and the figures quoted above in Chapter iv.

[28] University enrollments (exclusive of enrollments in academies of law and agricultural colleges) averaged 11,893 in the years 1910-1915. Mainly because of the influx of female students, enrollments did not substantially change during the war (11,312 per annum). Then they increased to an annual average of 15,126 in the years 1920-1925, and leveled off at 12,778 in 1925-1930. Laky, *Statistique des étudiants*, p. 17.

graduates as possible into the apparatus of the state. As a result, administration, and the public sector in general, became monstrously oversized in view of the changes in the territory and population of the country. This was especially true with respect to educated personnel in the employment of the state. Thus while the number of public employees in the "worker" and "service" categories declined from 172,922 (1914) to 46,221 (1921), the number of clerks and office personnel remained more or less stationary (at 93,097 vs. 93,949), and the number of persons in the administrative and executive categories actually increased from 65,049 to 69,765.[29] Subsequently, the government carried out a much publicized, and later lamented, program of administrative rationalization that affected 21,651 employees.[30] As a result of this program the number of public servants was reduced to 169,758,[31] while the number of persons in the administrative class was consolidated at 42,861 (1930).[32] But most persons affected by the reorganization were apparently pensioned off rather than removed from the public payroll altogether, for in the interim (1921-1924) the number of pensioners of the state increased from 60,617 to 98,644.[33]

Because these salaries and pensions could only be paid by constantly raising the ceiling for the public debt and then financing the debt itself by short-term foreign loans, the budget was strained to the breaking point. To keep the large number of persons on the public payroll salary scales had to be depressed, or at least not raised anywhere near the prewar figures. The differences in pay scale are quite striking indeed. In 1920 the real income of bureaucrats, ravaged by war and inflation, was less than twenty percent of their prewar earnings (Table 31), and even after successive raises in 1923, 1925, and 1928, the average bureaucrat earned only about half of what his counterparts had made in 1913 (Table 32). Thus, unlike the earnings of the entrepreneurial and industrial working classes, those of the bureaucracy failed to recover, a circumstance that at least in part explains the ever growing resentment of the political class toward the classes associated with the urban economy. In addition, and in contrast to the prewar years, the remuneration scales of Hungarian civil ser-

[29] Ottó Szabolcs, *A köztisztviselők az ellenforradalmi rendszer társadalmi bázisában, 1920-26* [Public employees within the social structure of the counterrevolutionary regime] (Budapest: Akadémia, 1965), p. 28.

[30] Ibid., p. 32.

[31] *Annuaire Statistique Hongrois*, xxxvi (1928), 288.

[32] Macartney, *October Fifteenth*, i, 96.

[33] Szabolcs, *Köztisztviselők*, pp. 31-32.

TABLE 31
Comparison of Nominal and Real Earnings,
1913-1920
(1913 = 100)

	Unskilled Worker	Semi-skilled Worker	Skilled Worker	Private Official	State Official	Military Officer
Nominal Wage	2,919	2,703	2,253	920	921	896
Real Wage	62.6	57.5	47.9	20.6	19.6	19.1

Source: Szabolcs, *A köztisztviselők*, p. 65.

vants fell far below those prevailing in the more advanced countries of the Continent, including Austria and Germany (Table 33). Consequently, Hungarian public servants could no longer sustain a "decent," or "European," style of life. In the rueful words of one contemporary:

> Under the inexorable economic pressures of the day the living standard of the civil servants began to slip. At first, they had to drop the theater, the concert, the books, the newspapers, and the dinner parties. Then their clothes and shoes began to acquire a more threadbare look. They had to cut the number of courses at mealtime, let go the inexpensive all-around maid, and begin to sell their furniture and jewelry. While the state and the economy were being put on a more stable footing, the better part of our middle class had reached the depth of material ruin.[34]

TABLE 32
Salary of Civil Servants, 1925-1928
(Executive Class)
(1914 = 100)

Rank	1925	1928
I	29.0%	34.8%
II	32.2	36.6
III	32.6	37.9
IV	27.6	32.2
V	27.4	32.0
VI	33.9	36.8
VII	33.2	36.5
VIII	33.0	37.4
IX	36.3	40.8
X	39.6	46.2
XI	44.0	45.5

Source: Szabolcs, *A köztisztviselők*, pp. 110-113.

[34] Gaszton Gaál. *Napló*, 1927, ii, 326.

TABLE 33
A COMPARISON OF BUREAUCRATIC SALARIES, 1924-1925
(Hungary-Austria-Germany)

A. Austrian and Hungarian Salaries, 1924			
Equivalent Ranks		Salaries	
Hungarian	Austrian	Hungarian	Austrian
IV	I	57.8%	100.0%
V	II	60.8	
VI	III	62.1	
VII	IV	66.0	
VIII	V	67.8	
IX	VI	64.4	
X	VII	67.2	
XI	VIII	74.4	

B. Hungarian and German Monthly Salaries, 1925
(in gold Kronen)

Hungarian		German	
Equivalent Rank	Salary	Equivalent Rank	Salary
Minister	800	Reichsminister	2,475
State Secretary	540	Staatsekretär	1,650
Councillor	400	Ministerialrat	1,320
Section Chief	220	Ministerialdirektor	880
Secretary	170	Oberinspektor	379
Junior Secretary	100	Kanzleisekretär	171

SOURCE: Szabolcs, A köztisztviselők, pp. 106-113.

These policies of the Bethlen government not only strained the meager resources of the state, but also resulted in a growing internal conflict within the bureaucracy. While a substantial number of the new recruits now came from families of petty bureaucrats, artisans, and rural smallholders,[35] under the pressure of scarcities and increasing competition, the gentry quickly fell back on the "sacred principle of great-grandmotherhood," activating family connections in the defense of class prerogatives. Indeed, at no other time in modern Hungarian history was nepotism more rampant than during the Bethlen years. True, the gates of the bureaucracy and of the political machine had been thrown open wider than ever before to the newcomers, but at the same time the highest echelons of politics and public employment continued to be reserved for those with the proper social connections and a gilded name. Thus, if overall the proportion of members of the historical classes in the bureaucracy had declined to as

[35] The sons of petty officials, gendarmes, policemen, etc. are concealed behind such broad and vague designations as "functionaries of the state" and "pensioners." But in

250

little as 14.5 percent, in the top positions of the ministerial and county administration, it still hovered around the 55 percent mark (Table 34). The phenomenon did not go unnoticed by contemporaries. "Before the war," wrote one observer of the social scene, "most leading families were content to see one of their members in public office. Since Trianon, however, one can easily detect entire clans in high offices: fathers, sons, brothers and other relations who, not surprisingly in this small country with its limited opportunities, are trying to help each other to attain a more tolerable standard of living."[36]

In response to such widespread nepotism the newcomers attempted to create their own alternative social networks consisting of secret or semi-secret patriotic organizations whose immediate purpose was to gain access to the bureaucracy or to secure promotion to higher ranks once their members were inside the political machine. Thus while

TABLE 34
SOCIAL COMPOSITION OF BUREAUCRACY,
1927

Branch	Aristocrat	Gentry[a]	Commoner	Don't Know	Total
Office of the P.M.	1	13	8	3	25
	4%	52%	32%	12%	100%
Interior	1	7	5	3	16
	6.2	43.8	31.3	18.7	100
Finance	—	11	16	6	33
		33.3	48.5	18.2	100
Foreign Affairs (non-diplomatic)	6	33	25	9	73
	8.2	45.2	34.2	12.4	100
Counties (Deputy Lord Lieutenants)	—	13	9	2	24
		54.0	38.0	8.0	100
Civil Service (random sample)[b]	—	29	152	19	200
		14.5	76.0	9.5	100

SOURCE: *Magyarország tiszti cim- és névtára, 1927.*
[a] Includes all other members of the former common nobility.
[b] Includes the first entry of two hundred pages listing the following: municipal, state, county administrators of executive rank, postal service, railways, National Bank, National Institute for Finances (O.P.K.), Social Security Administration (O.T.I.).

1927-1928, the parents of 24 percent of the students of gymnasia, and 12.4 percent of the students of universities belonged to one of the following categories: smallholder, laborer, industrial worker, and shop assistant. *Annuaire Statistique Hongrois*, xxxvi (1928), 237-238.
[36] Szekfű, *Három nemzedék*, p. 412.

before the war such organizations were virtually nonexistent, in 1918 we can already identify six of them, in 1919 twenty-two, and in 1920 a staggering one hundred one.[37] In time, having accomplished their primary purpose of securing modest positions for their members, the majority of these patriotic societies withered away (leaving forty to be counted in 1921 and forty-nine in 1922).[38] But some of the most important—among them the Etelköz Association (EKSz or X) and the Alliance of Blood (Vérszövetség)—continued to function clandestinely. They served not only as mutual aid societies, but also as the nuclei of an opposition which saw the salvation of the nation in radical reforms that would vastly expand the functions and the powers of the state.

The leaders of neo-corporatist Hungary, Horthy and Bethlen among them, were aware of this social cleavage, and made conscious attempts to bridge the gap in order to create a well-integrated and solidary elite. Their problem was that ennoblement, the single most important integrative mechanism of the prewar period, was no longer available to them, for the granting of noble titles was a royal prerogative that could not be exercised in the absence of a crowned king. To make up for the loss of this prerogative in a highly status-conscious society, the government set up a new knighthood, the Order of the Gallants (*vitézi rend*), with Horthy as its commander in chief. Members of this order received the hereditary title of gallant (*vitéz*), sometimes accompanied by a small plot of land, granted to an individual for valor in combat, or for a commensurate act of self-sacrifice in the service of the nation. The title, the land grant, the ritual of initiation— including the touching of the shoulder of the new liegeman with a sword wielded by the regent—were all reminiscent of the medieval act of ennoblement. The principles of the order were to be those of a "true" nobility: a nobility of achievement, though not one of achievement by speculation on the commodity or stock exchange. Over the Bethlen years alone some 4,400 individuals were granted such titles of gallantry, amidst all the stipulated solemnity of the ceremony, and accompanied by a grant of 72,000 acres of land in plots of 5-25 acres,[39] but without the desired social effect of greater solidarity among the elite. The members of old families looked down upon this ersatz nobility. The title of gallantry remained something of a badge to mark the parvenu, while the Order of the Gallants became one of the pillars of national radicalism within the establishment. Within it, the

---

[37] Macartney, *October Fifteenth*, i, 30.　　[38] Ibid.

[39] Kerék, *A magyar földkérdés*, p. 177.

"Christian middle class"—as the upwardly mobile intelligentsia preferred to be called—remained deeply ambivalent about itself as well as about the gentry and the aristocracy, whose social style they tried to imitate, while denouncing the decadence of entrenched rank and privilege.

The social conflict between the gentry and plebeians was aggravated by ethnic conflict among the members of the political machine. The strained relations among the ethnic groups resulted from the fact that the small German and Slovak minorities of the country accounted for a disproportionately large share of the rural artisan and smallholder classes that provided the chief reservoir of new recruits into the establishment. The presence of these ethnic groups, of course, was not a new phenomenon. Assimilated Slovaks as well as Germans had for generations contributed more than their share to the country's political, military, and clerical elites.[40] But with political spoils declining, competing groups were ready to seize any pretext to keep others out of the political machine,[41] and plebeian Magyars were quick to plead the case for ethnic purity in order to improve their chances of advancement at the expense of the "Swabians." Their case found sympathy and the support of a number of populist writers, among them the aforementioned Desider Szabo, whose anti-Swabian literary outbursts outdid the vulgarities of the most bitter anti-Semitic philippics of the age. Confronted with this sudden outburst of hostility, the assimilated, or assimilating, members of minority groups suffered an acute crisis of identity, only faintly mitigated by institutional attempts to alleviate it.[42] Indeed, government sympathy only exacerbated the

[40] This was especially conspicuous among professional officers in the military, an occupation that traditionally attracted few recruits from among the ranks of the Magyar gentry. As a result, in 1941, twenty-one of Hungary's twenty-seven two- and three-star generals on the active list were members of the German ethnic minority. Colonel General Werth, the chief of the general staff at the time of Hungary's entry into World War II, while a Hungarian citizen, listed his nationality as German. His successor, Francis Szombathelyi, chief of staff during most of the war, was a member of the German minority, born with the name of Knaus. Nicholas Kállay, *Hungarian Premier* (New York: Columbia University Press, 1954), p. 95.

[41] Apart from the ethnic and social conflict, there was also some tension between Catholics and Protestants. The former complained about the disproportionate number of Protestant appointees to the civil service, charging discrimination. The Protestants responded that the figures were inflated, and, at any rate, whatever disproportion existed was the result of aptitude rather than favoritism (Kovrig, *Hungarian Social Policies*, pp. 46-47). Yet another division, and a source of resentment, was regional—between the Magyars of the mother country and the Transylvanians who were favored by the Bethlen government in both politics and in the civil service.

[42] For one, the earlier strict rules concerning the Magyarization of names were re-

TABLE 35
ETHNIC COMPOSITION OF BUREAUCRACY,
1927

Branch	Magyar	German	Other	Total
Office of the P.M.	18	3	4	25
	72%	12%	16%	100%
Interior	10	3	3	16
	62.0	19	19	100
Finance	20	10	3	33
	60.6	30.4	9	100
Foreign Affairs	44	20	9	73
	60.3	27.4	12.3	100
Counties (Deputy				
Lord Lieutenants)	17	5	2	24
	71.0	21.0	8.0	100
Civil Service (random sample)	112	57	31	
	56.0	28.5	15.5	100

SOURCE: As Table 34; based on the inspection of family names. "Magyar" includes all Magyarized names.

"Swabian debate" and provoked ironic suggestions from diverse quarters that the "Jews [were] being squeezed out of public life merely to make room for the Swabians."[43]

To such attacks the assimilated minorities responded in a variety of ways. Some of them, no doubt, took things in their stride. But others felt the need to compensate by carrying their Magyar nationalism to excess, or by leading campaigns against other minorities. The very leader of the ultra-nationalists, Gömbös, hailed from a Swabian family (presumably by the name of Knöpfle, or Knöpfler), a circumstance that he denied all his adult life and tried to conceal not only with chauvinistic rhetoric, but also with a fake title of nobility, which contemporary books of heraldry pointedly ignored. Likewise, in the

---

laxed: henceforth selected applicants, officers, meritorious civil servants, as well as members of the Order of Gallants, were not only encouraged to pick Magyar names, but were permitted to use hitherto protected archaic spellings—above all, the letter *y*—suggestive of noble origins. In this manner Secretary of State Löffler became Szakváry, Generals Berger and Ranzenberger, Beregffy and Ruszkay. On the other hand, when Francis Szálasi (Salosjan), leader of the opposition Arrow Cross, arbitrarily changed the spelling of his name to Szálasy, there were interpellations in the House of Representatives, public protest, and the threat of a lawsuit for the illicit use of an alias.

[43] See "A sváb vita" [The Swabian debate], *Új Magyarság*, July 2, 1939. Published in István Milotay, *Az új világ felé* [Toward a new world] (Budapest: Stádium, 1942), II, 235.

1920s, the extremist Awakening Magyars, and later the Party for the Protection of the Race, were founded by gentlemen with the names of Eckhardt, Ulain, and Zsilinszky (later to be changed to Bajcsy-Zsilinszky).[44] All three of these men made political careers out of Jew-baiting. But while Eckhardt and Ulain praised Swabians—among other things, for their "instinctive" anti-Semitism—Zsilinszky mixed his anti-Semitic tirades with denunciations of Swabian influence in order, as some would say, to divert attention from his own, less than obvious Magyar origins.

Yet there were others who took the very opposite route, and, in increasing numbers after 1933, returned to the German master race. Again others sought to elude the whole questions of origin, and hoped to establish a new, ethnically neutral, social identity. These people found refuge and moral support in the various Christian and national socialist movements, whose doctrine subordinated the nation to a higher, supranational order, within which religion (Christianity) and race (Aryanism) were more important than ethnicity in determining the status and rights of individuals. In this respect, there was a more than superficial analogy between their political behavior and the political behavior of the upwardly mobile Jewish intelligentsia, whose members found succor in the radical Marxist movements of the turn of the century.

If throughout the 1920s an open rift within the Christian middle class had been averted through the slow but steady improvement of bureaucratic salaries, in the 1930s these divisions were exposed by the economic adversities of the depression years. In the first few months of the crisis, bureaucratic salaries had to be reduced by twenty percent, a cut that more or less wiped out the gains of the previous six years. While dismissals were to be kept to a minimum, they followed inevitably, and created widespread anxiety that renewed the acrimony concerning the inequitable distribution of the spoils of the political machine. Worse still, under the new conditions of stringency, the state lost its ability to absorb new graduates from institutions of higher learning. Thus while Bethlen merely had to cope with the malcontents of an underpaid civil service, his successors would have to face up to the festering problem of chronic intellectual unemployment. In the years of the crisis, 30 percent of new medical doctors, 48 percent of law school graduates, 55.2 percent of young engineers, 70.1 percent of prospective teachers, and 90.2 percent of future agronomists found

---

[44] Bajcsy was the maiden name of Zsilinszky's mother. See Endre Bajcsy-Zsilinszky, *A nemzeti radikálizmus* [National radicalism] (Budapest: Stádium, 1930), p. 1.

no employment whatsoever.[45] Suddenly, next to the frustrated and underpaid civil servants and military officers, the country had a new political counterclass that was not only "down," but "out" of the political machine and its spoils system. A powerful and vocal pressure group in its own right, this intelligentsia demanded its own share. When it was rebuffed, it joined hands with politically articulate, but formally uneducated, members of the lower classes, and together with them formed a militant national socialist opposition. This opposition pitted itself not only against the entrenched liberal-conservative leadership, but also against the "gentleman's radicals" of the political machine.

Origins and Evolution of National Radicalism

As has already been briefly mentioned, the origins of Hungarian national radicalism go back to the autumn of 1919. It was then that, following the collapse of the Soviet regime, the officers and hangers-on of Admiral Horthy's National Army returned to the capital bringing with them their own brand of "positive nationalism" from the counterrevolutionary city of Szeged. Though rather vague and ill-articulated, this "idea of Szeged" had two cardinal elements whose seeming contradictions baffled many contemporary liberals and conservatives. One of these was a militant anti-bolshevism and an aggressive reassertion of the supremacy of the national state. The other was an openly stated distaste for the structure, institutions, and ideological underpinnings of pre-1918 Hungary, and of the world order of which it had been an integral component. The men of Szeged were counterrevolutionaries with a vengeance. But they "did not set out to restore privileged Hungary . . . Rather, they wanted to create a strong state with a sense of social justice, and a hierarchical society ruled by an elite of virtue."[46] In terms of these principles, they had as little use for the class barriers of Hungarian neo-corporatism as they had for the "dream world of Jacobin egalitarianism."[47]

The slogan of the strong state, of course, was nothing new in Hungarian politics. It had been, after all, part and parcel of the rhetoric of the two Tiszas, and of Bethlen, who likewise justified it in reference to the national interest. But still, there were significant, indeed critical, differences between the two forms of etatism. For while the Tiszas subscribed to the notion of political restraints and invoked the prin-

[45] Ferenc Olay, "Állástalan diplomások az 1934-es évben" [Unemployed graduates in the year 1934], *Társadalomtudomány*, 14 (1934), 288.

[46] Julius Gömbös. *Napló*, 1933, xv, 513.

[47] Ibid.

ciples of Roman law and of the medieval political heritage of Hungary to justify them, the radicals rejected these principles as alien to the national character. They were ready to return to the legacy of pagan Hungary,[48] to justify methods that were the trademarks of the roving bands of counterrevolutionary officers. "Violence," Julius Gömbös orated in 1922, "[was] an acceptable means of statecraft as long as it [was] used to shape the course of history, not in the interest of a narrow clique, but of an entire nation."[49] Furthermore, while the leaders of the old regime were prepared to reduce the concept of the state to the bureaucratic apparatus of the political machine, the radicals suddenly stepped forward as the champions of popular participation in politics. To be sure, this kind or participation had nothing to do with the "comedy" and "barley-mush politics"[50] of parliamentary democracy. Rather, it implied a design for mass political organization, since only by "inspiring mass faith and dedication," and "by mobilizing millions,"[51] could the radicals hope to raise the nation once again to a position of international respectability.

It was mainly through this need for mobilization that the national radicals arrived at the idea of social reform. Only by providing convenient social symbols of injustice and by eliminating the grossest inequities of the old society could the prospective elite hope to activate popular commitment to its aspirations for national greatness. The design for reform, of course, tended to reflect the narrower interests of the political class. It proposed to correct the inequities of the old order not at the expense of the "Christian middle class," the lower stratum of the state bourgeoisie, but at the expense of Jewish capitalists and aristocratic landowners, the two rather conspicuous pillars of Hungarian neo-corporatism. Of the two, one stood condemned as the embodiment of speculative gain, the other as the symbol of parasitic idleness. Both of them were regarded as "aliens," for even if some aristocratic families were Magyar by name, they were the creations and instruments of a foreign dynasty, intent on stifling the national

[48] This was, above all, evident in the rituals of patriotic societies, many of which imitated the religious ceremonies of pagan Magyars. To the consternation of the devout, some of these societies denounced King Stephen I as a "traitor" who had "sold out" to Christianity, and initiated a new cult around the figure of Koppány, one of the pagan Magyars executed upon orders from Stephen. See Szekfű, *Három nemzedék*, p. 489; also, Joseph Kessler, "Turanism and Pan-Turanism in Hungary, 1890-1945," Ph.D. dissertation, University of California, Berkeley, 1967, p. 226.

[49] *Napló*, 1922, II, 85.

[50] Barley mush (*gerstli*) was not only soft, it was also a dish popular with the Jewish lower middle class.

[51] Milotay, *Az új világ felé*, I, 90.

257

spirit. Moreover, in the radical mind the aristocracy was inseparably connected with the upper stratum of the Jewish entrepreneurial class, not only because the two groups were heavily intermarried, but also because the aristocracy was the chief protector of Jewish banking and industrial interests. On all these grounds, radical "anti-feudalism" matched radical anti-Semitism. The leader of the radicals, Gömbös, had "no use for counts unless they worked," and professed no concern as to "where a man came from, only where he was going."[52] Others were downright vituperative, and spoke of the aristocracy as "pernicious, treacherous, hateful, and deserving expropriation."[53] As a starter, they suggested the expropriation of holdings in excess of 5,000 acres, though in exchange for due compensation.[54] As to the Jews, the radical Right supported religious quotas for university enrollment, exhorted the government to facilitate the entry of gentiles into certain economic pursuits (mainly by means of preferential licensing), and advocated, as yet unsuccessfully, the reclassification of Jews as a national minority, with appropriate restrictions on their exercise of citizen's rights.

During the immediate postwar years, radical antipathy for the neo-corporatist order was closely linked to antagonism toward the old regime's economic policies. Whether influenced by their own agrarian origins, or by the ideas then floating about in neighboring East European countries, most radicals of the Right were "agrarians," hostile to industry and industrialism. Whatever its psychological mainspring, this agrarianism rested on two doctrinal pillars. One of these was the old physiocratic hypothesis, resuscitated by the populists of the Continent, according to which only agriculture produced value, hence industry was parasitic, or else a "luxury" that only rich countries could afford. "Are the countries of the Occident rich because they have industries?" one militant right-wing member of the National Assembly queried in 1920, and he hastened to provide the appropriate answer: "No, they have industries, because they are rich."[55] Such rudimentary economic theories were then complemented by the old sociological argument of political Catholicism, according to which industrialization was responsible for the rise of the proletariat, and hence for the destruction of social peace and of the whole fabric of traditional society. Inspired by these arguments, some zealots in the radical camp not only wanted to slow down but to reverse the trend toward industry,

---

[52] Quoted in Macartney, *October Fifteenth*, I, 34.
[53] Quoted in Bodrogközy, *Magyar agrármozgalmak*, p. 272.
[54] See Gömbös in *Napló*, 1923, XVII, 367.
[55] N. Grieger, *Napló*, 1920, IX, 269.

and to solve the social problems of the country by resettling the industrial population in the villages. There, in the words of one legislator of the counterrevolutionary period, they could learn the virtues of honest labor instead of a life of idleness and theft.[56] The Hungary of the future, the leaders of the Szeged men agreed, would have to be an agricultural country of small and medium-sized estates. "Our swastika, and our Heimwehr," wrote one of their numbers a few years later, "can arise only out of the soil of our small agrarian country. The profile of our nationalism must reflect the spirit of agrarian laborers, and of the homestead of the peasant smallholder."[57]

But while such ideas reigned supreme during the early years of the movement, in the course of the next decade and a half, the economic concept of the national radicals underwent significant transformation. True, a small minority of the erstwhile Szeged men—among them Andrew Zsilinszky, Tibor Eckhardt, together with such lesser figures as Francis Barcsay and Stephen Csicsery-Ronay—remained staunch adherents of the agrarian idea, whether they stayed inside or went outside the Government party. But the vast majority of radicals eventually succumbed to the inexorable logic of their militant nationalism once they realized that the exigencies of military power, and of agrarian overpopulation, made the industrialization of the country inevitable. By the end of the twenties the parliamentary spokesman of the Right was therefore "ready to accept the policy of industrialization despite the sacrifices it require[d], as long as it served the higher national purpose and not the interests of big banks and foreign capitalists."[58] Meanwhile the *völkisch* idiom of earlier years was retained together with ritualistic incantations about the virtues of the peasantry. But under this rhetorical smoke screen, the rapid industrialization of the country became once again the sine qua non for an effective nationalist policy.

This shift in economic priorities had significant consequences for radical thought and action. Industrialism has a logic of its own: by accepting it as an objective, the radicals had to reconcile themselves to the idea of a complex and interdependent society, whose functional prerequisites left little room for tribal primitivism, or the simple, heroic virtues handed down to posterity by the pagan Magyars. Gradually but inexorably, therefore, the shift in economic priorities re-

[56] N. Forgács, *Napló*, 1920, ii, 250.

[57] G. Oláh, *Magyarság*, November 23, 1930.

[58] F. Krudy in the appropriations debate of 1928. *Napló*, 1928, ix, 371. For a more elaborate statement of the Right, see *Mit akar a Wesselényi Reform Club?* [What is the program of the Wesselényi Reform Club?] (Budapest: n.p., 1930), p. 24.

sulted in what Gömbös himself referred to as the "rationalization of the national spirit," and the "abandonment of the romantic tendency, especially in the realm of production."[59] In this new socioeconomic context, leaders could still reach back to the past for political symbols, as when Gömbös gave back Hungarian officers their sabres, or when Imrédy picked an ancient totemic figure to serve as the emblem of his movement. But now the substance was unmistakably that of technocracy, with due regard for the importance of managerial skills over and above the raw heroism that the radicals had celebrated in the 1920s.

From a practical point of view, the most immediate consequence of the shift was the sudden rise to prominence of the "Sofort boys," a number of talented technocrats (Kunder, Antal, Szakváry-Löffler), who until then had been kept out of the radical limelight because of their all too obvious "Swabian" ethnic origins. Behind their rise to power in 1932-1933 was a new radical theory which held that the nation, while quintessentially an ethnic entity, could admit into its fold men who could render dedicated and useful service to the community. Indeed, for a brief period it seemed that this concept would be flexible enough to accommodate assimilated Germans, Slovaks, and even Jews. Thus in 1930 Gömbös publicly revised his position on the Jewish question,[60] and when he finally acceded to the premiership in 1932, he spoke effusively about the Jewish military heroes of World War I, described assimilated Jews as his brethren, and promised not to raise the Jewish question during his tenure in office.[61] If between 1932 and 1935 there was a "Jewish problem" at all, it seemingly could be resolved by separating the good ones from the bad ones, that is, the military heroes, technical experts, and loyal businessmen from the socialist literati, commissars, and trade union leaders. It is true that Jews (as well as magnates) were excluded from Gömbös' cabinets. But during the years of his premiership there were once again Jewish deputies on the government benches, as well as a number of high officials of Jewish parentage in the bureaucracy.[62]

[59] *Budapesti Hirlap*, June 25 and 30, 1935.

[60] *Napló*, 1930, xxxi, 417.

[61] His introductory speech as premier contained these words: "I regard as my brothers all Jews who accept the destiny of the nation. . . . I have seen them as heroes, praying for the nation as any other Magyar." *Napló*, 1932, xi, 51.

[62] In 1935 Gömbös' Party of National Unity nominated two Jewish candidates, Robert Szurday and Mór Ledermann, for parliamentary seats in Budapest, and Gömbös had no objection to the Jewish Paul Sándor serving as president-pro-tempore of the newly convened House of Representatives. See Lévai, *Fekete könyv a magyar zsidóság szenvedéseiről*, p. 18. At the same time two men of Jewish parentage, I. Ferenczi and L. Barcza, served

The shift in economic priorities, however, also raised questions concerning the economic and social costs of industrialization. This was especially true in view of the radicals' aversion to foreign credits, and to any dependence on the advanced capitalist countries, sentiments that by 1932 were fully reciprocated by international high finance. In terms of classical or "mainline" economic theory, avoidance of foreign capital left only one viable alternative, and this was the extraction of surplus from agriculture by depressing consumption and investment in that particular sector. This the radicals opposed both on the grounds of principle and of sheer expediency. For if the conventional model of the semi-servile large estate was ideologically as unattractive as was the Soviet model of the *kolkhoz*, the Balkan model of an economy of peasant smallholdings promised very little surplus capital for industrialization (a fact clearly demonstrated in Rumania and Serbia). The elimination of the agrarian route to industrialism left only a few options, one of which was to tax and expropriate the ethnic entrepreneur, whose functions could be, theoretically at least, rendered superfluous by the gradual expansion of the economic functions of the state apparatus. By following such a course of action, the radicals could accomplish two purposes with one master stroke: they would acquire financial reserves for development, and would create new jobs for the oversized and underemployed native intelligentsia. This dual prospect created an irresistible temptation to which the Right would succumb after Gömbös. They would abandon the technocratic radicalism of the latter in favor of a more rigid, racial concept of the nation, later to be embodied in the "Jewish laws" of 1938-1942. To the old generation of Whig liberals and conservatives such a course of action was anathema. It was a violation of traditional norms, if not an act of open theft that would stigmatize and demoralize all classes of society. But to the radicals of the Right, as to those of the Left, "property-ownership was not a right but a privilege, whose exercise had to be subordinated to the higher national purpose.... If private property furthered the healthy development of the nation, it [was] to be pro-

---

as state secretaries in the ministries of Commerce and Agriculture respectively, while a man of the same background, I. Hetényi, was deputy chief of the royal state police, and until 1939, chief of its political division (Schickert, *Die Judenfrage in Ungran*, p. 252). Indeed, so conspicuous was Gömbös' turnabout that one of the most prestigious members of the Jewish business community, Francis Chorin, was led to reminisce a decade later that the prime minister had "completely dropped the issue of anti-Semitism." See István Vida, "Három Chorin levél" [Three letters of Chorin], *Századok*, 111 (1977), 380.

tected. But if it hindered such a development, expropriation was the only possible remedy."[63]

These changes in the social design of national radicalism were accompanied by some important changes in the movement's concept of the national state and its orientation toward the outside world. Initially, this concept and orientation were borrowed straight from the political programs of the prewar National Independence (1848) party, heavily influenced by the particularism and parochialism of Hungarian Calvinism, hostile toward the Habsburgs, and indeed toward anything that was imperial or German. In this spirit, the national radicals of the twenties were to a man opposed to the restoration of the dynasty, and fought the two attempted royal coups with arms in hand. Their chief spokesman in the daily press, Stephen Milotay, never seemed to tire of denouncing the two Tiszas for "selling out to Vienna the most precious legacy of [the nation's] struggles for independence." Indeed, so intense were his feelings that his essays from this period were published under the title *In the Shadow of Independence.*[64]

The fact was, however, that even before 1918 Hungary was too small a country to pursue an ambitious yet independent foreign policy, to maintain or augment her influence over her eastern neighbors while also thumbing her nose at the Austrian half of the Monarchy. And if before the war, small-power imperialism coupled with an aggressive quest for independence made little practical sense, after the war the idea became nothing less than absurd. By then Hungary had been transformed into a truly minute international entity that could not pursue its revisionist objectives without a strong and sympathetic ally. Since the idea of abandoning Magyars across the borders was unacceptable to all, the question was where to find such an ally and at what expense to other policy objectives. Bethlen and the liberal-conservatives pinned their hopes on Italy, a power that could offer little else than sympathy. A handful of national radicals—most of them from the agrarian-populist wing of the movement—hoped against hope that Britain or France would "come around," or else that there would be a genuine possibility for creating a federated "Hungarian-Slav peasant state," within which Hungary's worst grievances could be redressed. This idea—later to reappear in the platform of the Independent Smallholders party in the forties—was put forward by Andrew Zsilinszky, and presumably rested on the "logic of geo-

[63] Kerék, *A magyar földkérdés*, p. 377.

[64] István Milotay, *A függetlenség árnyékában* [In the shadow of independence] (Budapest: Stádium, 1930). The quote is from an article published on May 25, 1924, ibid., p. 13.

politics."[65] But in truth this was little more than wishful thinking, for the neighboring Slavic states, Yugoslavia and Czechoslovakia, were intractable on the issue of revising the peace treaties, while the great core powers, England and France, had little sympathy for the realignment of forces in the region. So Hungarian national radicals had to look elsewhere, and when the continental balance of power began to change after 1933, most of them were ready to discard their earlier antipathies, and to throw in their lot with renascent Germany. The same men who once denounced Tisza and Andrássy now quickly expropriated their argument, to wit, that Hungarians and Germans were linked together in a community of fate under the common threat of pan-Slav imperialism on the Balkan peninsula and in the Danube Valley.[66]

But if the rationale was the same, the nature of the alliance was to be quite different from the one engineered by Andrássy and the two Tiszas. The latter, while tying the fate of the country to that of the German-speaking peoples of Europe, never regarded their country as other than a fully equal partner, and proudly, indeed arrogantly, rejected any suggestion to modify the institutions or social structure of Hungary as a price for the alliance. In this respect, Stephen Tisza's haughty dismissal of the Austrian premier and his "dilettantish views" are worth remembering. More than that, for good or ill, both Tisza and Andrássy had treated the alliance as a framework within which Hungary could acquire leverage over Austria, and through Austria, over powerful Germany. This contrasted sharply with the views of Germanophiles of the thirties and forties, who quickly resigned themselves to playing the role of a subservient junior partner. Thus the same Milotay who in the 1920s had penned intemperate articles denouncing Stephen Tisza for "selling out" the nation to Vienna now cautioned his countrymen to restrain their passion for empty nationalistic rhetoric, to "swallow their pride in alliance," and to "give themselves up in friendship to the stronger party."[67] More than that, Milotay and the Germanophile ultras also advised their countrymen that the vitality of the alliance would depend on Hungary's willingness to streamline her institutions and policies, above all her policies toward

[65] Endre Bajcsy-Zsilinszky, *Helyünk és sorsunk Európában* [Our place and fate in Europe] (Budapest: Gergely, 1941), pp. 1-4. See also, Károly Vigh, "Adalékok Bajcsy-Zsilinszky Endre francia orientációs külpolitikai koncepciójához" [The francophile orientation of Andrew Bajcsy-Zsilinszky's foreign policy], *Századok*, 105 (1971), 736-745.

[66] Milotay, *Az új világ felé*, II, 149.

[67] *Új Magyarság*, April 3, 1940.

the Jewish minority. They cautioned their countrymen pointedly that if the proper reforms were not undertaken they might well be imposed from the outside, by Germany.[68] In the given context, all this could be easily construed as a bit of *Realpolitik*, reflecting the inexorable logic of extreme weakness. But if so, the formula came perilously close to compromising nationalist principles as they had been understood since the beginning of the nineteenth century.

The Rise and Fall of Christian Radicalism

Of all the factions of the modern Right that of Christian radicalism had the longest pedigree, for its ideology and organization could claim the parentage of the prewar Catholic People's party. To be sure, like all others of old Hungary, this party became defunct in October 1918, as its demoralized leaders scattered under the impact of the successful revolution of the Left. But in August 1919, the earlier Catholic critique of liberalism, capitalism, and socialism seemed particularly well justified in the light of recent events. So under the Christian National,[69] later Christian Social and Economic, label the party was revitalized by a group of younger men just back from the trenches or from skirmishes with the two revolutionary regimes. Under their influence, the new party became far more militant than its predecessor in the prewar years. The anti-liberalism of the latter now became an outright negation of parliamentarism, its anti-socialism reemerged in the form of a retributive anti-bolshevism and anti-Octobrism, while its anti-capitalism turned into a strident attack on the Jewish entrepreneur.

---

[68] In October 1940, when the ultra-Germanophile wing of the Government party seceded to form the Party of Hungarian Renascence under the leadership of Béla Imrédy, "the view became predominant in this party that even if it were to fall victim to the government's electoral terror machine, Imrédy could lead the country by assuming the role of a Hungarian Seyss-Inquart." Péter Sipos, *Imrédy Béla és a Magyar Megújulás Pártja* [Béla Imrédy and the Party of Hungarian Renascence] (Budapest: Akadémia, 1970), p. 202.

[69] The Christian National party (KNEP) itself was an agglomeration of a number of political groups sporting the Christian label, among them the Christian Social, the Christian National Radical, the Hungarian Radical Christian Socialist, and the Christian Socialist parties. In years to come the party splintered a number of times among pro- and anti-government forces, as well as among different radical (i.e., anti-Semitic) and conservative-legitimist factions, with only a handful of individuals associated with Alexander Giesswein adhering to progressive, democratic principles. See Jenő Gergely, "A keresztényszocialisták politikai szerepe az ellenforradalom első éveiben, 1919-1923" [The role of Christian Socialists during the first years of the counterrevolution, 1919-1923], *Századok*, 110 (1976), 225-273; also, Ferenc Pölöskei, "Hatalmi viszonyok 1919 őszén Magyarországon" [Power relations in Hungary in the autumn of 1919] *Századok*, 110 (1976), 757-802.

In the short run, the avowed purposes of the party were to create a society of greater equity, and a polity strong enough to restrain the "modern cannibalism" of the market economy.[70] By adopting this new militancy, the Christian radicals easily won the sympathy of the returning Szeged men, and with their support initiated the Christian "course" (*kurzus*) of Hungarian politics in 1919-1921.[71]

But if the Christians and the national radicals tended to reach an easy agreement on their immediate objectives, the respective members of the two right-wing factions differed from one another in terms of philosophy, ultimate ends, and their images of the existing order of the world. True, the membership of both factions took a negative view of the contemporary world, regarding it as a fundamentally unjust place where the strong nations had taken advantage of the weak countries, among them Hungary. But within this common negative image, the outlook of the national radicals was essentially Nietzschean. For whether they actually read the master or not, they shared both his view that the Christian God was dead and his profound pessimism concerning human nature. In the last analysis, they would agree with Nietzsche that it was human selfishness that was responsible for the kind of dog-eat-dog international environment in which the survival of the nation required perpetual struggle and the abandonment of all sentimentalism concerning restraints.

In contrast to these stark Nietzschean views, the Christian radicals' images of the past and future were imbued with optimism and informed by a belief in the essential goodness of man, a belief that allowed for the improvement, even the perfection, of the human condition. As to the present, the imperfections of the international order were not due to man's inherent egotism, but to errors in judgment concerning institutions and organizing principles, above all the principles of liberalism and capitalism. Once the latter were smitten— whether by the sword or by rational argument—a new world order could arise. This order would not be egalitarian, but it would be just. Within it the state would once again be subject to divine law, while competition among the states would be restrained by the principles

---

[70] N. Grieger, *Napló*, 1927, I, 54.

[71] Instrumental in coordinating the work of the two groups were two secret societies, the Etelköz Association (EkSz or X) associated with the Szeged camp, and the underground United Christian League. Attempts to consolidate the two into a single, national, Christian radical organization apparently foundered on religious differences. While the former society included a large number of Protestants, the latter was a fraternity of militant Catholics. See György Borsányi, ed., *Páter Zadravetz titkos naplója* [The secret diary of the Reverend Zadravetz] (Budapest: Kossuth, 1967), especially pp. 129-145.

of Christian, i.e., Catholic, morality. As with the other Christian radical movements of the Continent, the exact nature of this new order remained unclear. To some Christian nationals, the order was to be the modern version of the universal Christian empire of the Middle Ages that would impart its values to the rest of the world. To others, it was to be a new Europe in which the Catholic southeast would reassert its predominance over the Protestant northwest. To yet others, it was to be merely a restored and perfected version of the Habsburg realm, within which Hungarians could at last come to terms with neighboring peoples and states.

However, whatever the images of past, present, and future, the principles of Christian morality were integral to them, and these principles were in sharp conflict with the professed radicalism of this new form of political Catholicism. It has been said that revolutionary power cannot be established without violating some of the Ten Commandments,[72] a circumstance that most revolutionaries deal with by referring to the higher moral qualities of their ultimate purpose. But the trouble in the case of political Catholicism was that the Ten Commandments to be broken provided the very foundation of the movement, so the clash between moral ends and immoral means created strains that other brands of radicalism did not seem to experience. Adversaries perceived this source of vulnerability, and men like Count Bethlen never ceased to query the "Christianity" of such acts as beating up Jewish university students or bombing the Jewish Ladies' Auxiliary.

It was most likely this strain between ends and means that made the Christian radical movement begin to crumble without accomplishing any of its objectives. As early as 1921, many of the Christian Nationals joined Bethlen, or, like their Austrian and Spanish counterparts some years later, drifted back toward a more traditional conservatism. Yet there were others who went in a different direction. Thus after 1932 many of the younger, more ambitious leaders of the movement joined Gömbös and the national radicals in their quest for a right-wing, but rationalized technocracy, while the more militant rank and file, the Swabian and assimilated lower middle class and intelligentsia, went over almost to a man to the rising national socialist parties.

Far more impressive than this political record was the indirect influence that the Christian radicals exercised over Hungarian politics by providing a coherent critique of liberalism and of the old order. This was largely due to the accomplishments of a few individuals,

[72] Albert Camus, *The Rebel* (New York: Vintage, 1956), p. 227.

among them the Bishop Prohászka—whose figure had loomed large in political Catholicism ever since the turn of the century, and whose works already have been quoted in these pages—and the historian Julius Szekfü who, for some time at least, found himself in the mainstream of radical Catholic movements. The latter, one of the few truly creative intellectuals of the country who lent their talent to the political purposes of the Right, started his career before the war. As a Privat-dozent, he acquired a certain notoriety for his iconoclastic volume, *The Exiled Rákóczi* (*Száműzött Rákóczi*, 1913), in which he effectively pleaded the case of the Habsburgs against the great patriotic rebel of the eighteenth century. Denounced as a Swabian and as a *schwarzgelb* traitor (after the colors of the ruling dynasty), Szekfü returned to public prominence in 1920 when he published his major work, *Three Generations*,[73] which won accolades from the entire political Right for its stinging attack on Hungarian liberalism.

Szekfü's critique of Hungarian liberalism was far-reaching and complex, but it boiled down to a single, overarching thesis that set it apart from the critique of other Catholic writers, among them from that of the Bishop Prohászka, the chief ideologue of Hungarian political Catholicism. While the latter attacked liberalism as a philosophical system and rejected it altogether as a godless creed, Szekfü's culprit was not liberalism per se, but the transplantation of culturally alien liberal ideas into the ostensibly unreceptive soil of Hungary. The results of this transplantation were not only grotesque, they were outright harmful, because the gap between form and substance could only be closed by corrupting the electoral process in politics and by perverting the market mechanism in economics. In turn, the prevailing methods of corruption—the purchase of votes by the government, and the purchase of favors by the entrepreneur—had a deeply corrosive effect on national morale. They undermined the self-respect of the elites and the legitimacy of the nation state, and in this manner they paved the way for the revolutions of 1918-1919, and for the "national tragedy" of the peace treaty.

It should be noted here that this thesis is nowhere explicitly stated in the work, but unfolds from an elegantly written text that makes *Three Generations* one of the outstanding works in Hungarian historiography despite its blatant ideological bias. The title itself refers to three liberal generations: that of Kossuth, of Coloman Tisza, and of Stephen Tisza. Of these three generations Kossuth's was well-meaning and patriotic, but it was carried away by a naive enthusiasm for the

---

[73] Szekfü, *Három nemzedék.*

seductive ideas of the French Revolution. Kossuth and his contemporaries were deceiving themselves. To paraphrase Szekfű in the language of our own days, they were "role playing," acting out the great historical drama of the French Revolution in Hungary. They failed to overthrow the dynasty, but they did succeed in sowing the seeds of liberalism, from which the institutions of the post-1867 period emerged. Once these institutions were there, even a strong and upright statesman like Coloman Tisza eventually succumbed to the spirit of the age, attempting to build a democratic polity without an enlightened public, a capitalist economy without capital or entrepreneurship, and a unitary state without a unitary nation. The third generation, to be sure, began to sense these anomalies, and made a few tentative steps in the right direction, that is, toward traditional authoritarianism. But while Stephen Tisza was a giant among his contemporaries, in Szekfű's eyes he stands condemned for his failure to perceive the need for social justice, for a reform of the system of landownership, and for a reduction of Jewish economic and cultural influence in the country. Due to this failure the masses became alienated and fell easy prey to socialist ideas, nurtured by the intelligentsia that had emerged from the culturally alien entrepreneurial class.

Throughout the volume Szekfű seems to attribute the great "historical error" of the generations not only to the *Zeitgeist,* or to the sheer accident of personalities, but to the victory of eastern, Protestant, and particularist Hungary with its mindless negation of authority, over the more sedate and Catholic western Hungary with its innate respect for gradualism and centralized government. Kossuth and the two Tiszas were representatives of the former, the products of the county system and of feudal parliamentarism, which Szekfű dismisses as irrelevant to the real interests of the nation. The greatest representative of western Hungary, meanwhile, was no other than Stephen Széchenyi, whose ideas were presented by Szekfű not only as an alternative historical model for development, but also as a valid program for the Hungary of his own time. For one thing, Szekfű celebrated Széchenyi for the agrarian emphasis of his economic program and implied that, had its prescriptions been followed, the country could have avoided the agonies of industrialism and finance capitalism. For another, Szekfű praised Széchenyi for his coolness toward political reform, for his contemptuous attitude toward the cantankerousness of parliamentarism, and for his respect for centralized government. But Szekfű reserved his greatest praise for Széchenyi's Christian universalism, for his condemnations of aggressive ethnic nationalism, and for his attempts to uphold the values of a "greater German-Christian

European civilization."[74] This kind of civilization represented for Szekfű a more perfect embodiment of the Occident than either the decadence of France or the materialism of the Anglo-Saxon countries. Had these principles of ethnic tolerance been followed, Hungary could have maintained her status as a multinational commonwealth, and preserved her integrity even in defeat.

If Szekfű's Christian supranationalism was never fully accepted by the plethora of right-wing organizations, his critique of liberalism and capitalism made him into a kind of culture hero for the radical Right. In the 1920s, *Three Generations* was perhaps more frequently quoted than any other work, and Szekfű was celebrated for his two-pronged attack on the old order and on left-wing radicalism. However, a decade later, as the strains between Christianity and radicalism began to show, Szekfű set out on a different political course and abandoned his radical constituency. Thus when Szekfű published the fifth edition of *Three Generations* in 1935, he not only wrote a highly critical codicil on the Hungarian "neo-baroque," i.e., the neo-formalist features of the Bethlen regime, but also added a ringing denunciation of Hungarian national radicalism and of the then still embryonic national socialist movement. The latter were taken to task for cultivating the heathen, the tribal, and the primitive elements of the national tradition at the expense of the country's Christian medieval heritage.[75] Elsewhere, Szekfű lamented that "for the first time in eight hundred years, the mockery of the ideals of St. Stephen and of Christianity [had] become commonplace . . . among the half-educated members of the lower middle class."[76] Even more significantly, Szekfű changed his position on the role of Germany in the prospective European commonwealth of Christian nations. Increasingly after 1933, he saw Germany not as a pillar of the Occident, but as a menace to western civilization and to the Christian ideals of an international community. By the outbreak of the war Szekfű had emerged as one of the foremost opponents of the "German orientation" of Hungary's foreign policy.

National Socialism

Though the conflict between the "ins" and "outs" of the Hungarian Right never assumed the same dimensions as in neighboring Rumania—where the Iron Guard assassinated incumbent ministers,

---

[74] Ibid., p. 57. [75] Ibid., pp. 486-489.

[76] Gyula Szekfű, "Szent István a századok tükrében" [St. Stephen in the mirror of the centuries]; in Jusztinián Serédi, ed., *Emlékkönyv Szt. István király halálának kilencszázadik évfordulójára* [Memorial for the nine-hundredth anniversary of the death of King St. Stephen] (Budapest: Akadémia, 1938), III, 28.

while the incumbents responded by the wholesale massacre of the insurgents—it was bitter enough to generate implacable reciprocal hostilities that lasted till the very end of the Horthy era, and beyond. On one side, the various national socialist factions plotted, demonstrated, distributed scurrilous leaflets, organized strikes, and spoke darkly of the coming night of the long knives. On the other, the governments, even the governments of such right-wing radicals as Imrédy, never ceased to harass them. Some of their leaders, including Szálasi, were tried and imprisoned for subversive activities. Others were forced to seek asylum in Germany, while hundreds of lesser figures in the movement were arrested, manhandled, and interned by the police authorities to ensure the security of the state. In showing such inquisitorial zeal, however, the governments may have inadvertently aided their opponents, for militant action and reaction together gave the national socialists a revolutionary credibility that neither national nor Christian radicals ever possessed among the masses. In the wake of persecutions the number of the national socialist faithful was increasing by leaps and bounds, so that in 1939 the Arrow Cross-Hungarist movement alone had over 200,000 card-carrying members.[77] At the elections of 1939, five loosely allied national socialist factions—the Arrow Cross (Szálasi), the United Hungarian National Socialist party (Baky, Pálffy, Rupprecht), the Hungarian National Socialist Labor party (Szemere, Meskó), the Christian National Socialist Front (Maróthy-Meissler), and the Party of National Will (Csóor)[78]—won fifty seats with around 900,000 votes, representing twenty-five percent of the ballots cast nationwide.[79]

Just as impressive as these aggregate figures was the fact that the national socialists drew votes from a very wide spectrum of social groups. They did well both in the Protestant regions of eastern Hungary and in the Catholic areas of the west, soaked up much of the ethnic German and the assimilated, lower middle-class vote previously cast for the Christian Social party, and outpolled the Social Democratic party in most of the major industrial centers of the country. In Budapest proper, the national socialist vote increased from 1.8 to 30.7

[77] Miklós Lackó, *Nyilasok, nemzetiszocialisták, 1935-1944* [Arrow Crossmen, national socialists, 1935-1944] (Budapest: Kossuth, 1966), p. 126.

[78] István Haeffler, ed., *Országgyűlési almanach, 1939-1944* [Parliamentary alamanch for 1939-1944] (Budapest: Magyar Távirati Iroda, 1940), pp. 99-101.

[79] Includes seven non-party, right-wing deputies. Ibid., p. 101. The 900,000 figure does not relate to the number of voters, but to the number of votes in a complex electoral system in which some persons could cast separate votes for lists and individual candidates in single-member constituencies. See below.

percent compared to the elections of 1935, while the share of the Christian Socials went down from 23.0 to 3.5 percent, and that of the Social Democrats declined from 25.5 to 14.4 percent. In Buda, the citadel of the assimilated German bourgeoisie, the national socialist vote went up from zero to 23,800, the Christian vote down from 22,800 to 2,400. Even more striking was the victory of the Arrow Cross and its allies in the so-called "red belt" of Budapest. Here the ultra-right polled 41.7 percent of the vote, as against the 27.5 percent of the Government party, the 6.9 percent of the Christians, and the 17.1 percent of the Social Democratic party. In these elections, national socialist deputies were elected in Debrecen, the heartland of Hungarian national radicalism, in the "Stormy Corner," the center of agrarian radicalism, and in the counties of Zala and Vas, the bulwarks of popular conservatism in the modern age.[80]

The ideology of these national socialist factions represented a synthesis of the ideas of the older, more established Right radical movements. Thus, from the early brands of national radicalism, national socialists borrowed tribal primitivism, authoritarianism, and the thesis that the higher ends of politics may emancipate the state from moral and institutional restraints. From the Christian Socials, in turn, they borrowed certain ideas of a "just" society and economy, together with the design for a supranational political order. Not that the national socialists denied the legitimacy of the nation state as the basic unit for the organization of mankind. But the welfare of the nation state, indeed its very existence, were not ends in themselves. Rather, they represented means toward the achievement of an ultimate end: the creation of a new global order within which harmony would be restored and remain undisturbed forever, or, at least for a thousand years.[81]

Next to such parallels, however, it will be necessary to point out some critical differences between the doctrine of national socialism and of other right-wing radical movements. For one, while national socialists shared the optimism of Christian Socials and their chiliastic

---

[80] For the election results of 1935, see the daily press, especially the issues of *Magyarság* and *Népszava*, April 3-10, 1935; for the elections of 1939, the same papers, and *Új Magyarság*, May 30-June 2, 1939. See also, Lackó, *Nyilasok*, pp. 169-170.

[81] For these elements of the doctrine see Ferenc Szálasy (*sic*), *A magyar állam felépítésének terve* [Plan for the building of the Hungarian state] (Budapest: Egyetemi Nyomda, 1933), especially pp. 39-40; József Migossy, *Mit akar a magyar nemzeti szocialista mozgalom?* [What are the aims of the Hungarian national socialist movement?] (Budapest: Nyilaskeresztes Kiskönyvtár, 1936); Hugó Borbíró, *Nemzetnevelés* [Educating the nation] (Budapest: Nyilaskeresztes Füzetek, 1937).

image of a global order of harmony, the order they envisaged was not one of a commonwealth subject to the restraints of Christian morality, but of a perfect hierarchy of raw power, sustained by the primordial solidarities of a few select peoples or races.[82] Furthermore, alone among the right-wing movements of the age, national socialists subscribed to a largely conspiratorial view of history. For while the Christian radicals blamed the abstract principles of capitalism and liberalism for the predicament of mankind, and the national radicals cursed human nature, national socialists attributed the disequilibrated state of the universe to the machinations of international Jewry. And if it is possible at all to formulate such a theory of history with any degree of subtlety, such subtlety was altogether absent from the thinking of Hungary's national socialists. None of their writings in any case showed evidence of familiarity with Nietzsche's complex theories of the "transvaluation of all values," or of the Jewish corruption of a universal "master morality." The inspiration of the movement seems to have come directly from cruder documents, such as Hitler's *Mein Kampf,* or the famous *Protocols of the Elders of Zion,* whose predictions appeared to have been proven correct by the experience of the Hungarian Soviet Republic. In this crude version, Jews acted upon their instinct for domination by manipulating such seemingly incompatible ideas as communist collectivism and liberal capitalism.[83]

This conspiratorial theory of history, in turn, engendered an apocalyptic view of politics that left little room for rational economic design

[82] One should add here, however, that Szálasi, the single most important figure in the Hungarian national socialist movement wavered between a religious and a racial concept of the new order. This is one of several reasons why his theoretical writings lack any order or coherence. Thus while in places Szálasi speaks of a "free work state resting on Christian foundations" with frequent references to God and religious morality, he speaks in others of the ideal order as one in which "all aspects of social life [would] be subordinated to the government . . . for the purposes of an active, and brutally realistic etatism" (Szálasi, *A magyar állam,* p. 39). Some of the other factions likewise wavered on this point. Thus K. Maróthy-Meissler called his party the Christian National Front, though, as it has been often pointed out, Christian in this context merely meant "non-Jewish."

[83] This is nowhere more evident than in the memorandum drafted by Szálasi's staff on May 1, 1945 to evaluate the events of the recent past, and the prospects for the immediate future. In it, the authors speak of a secret agreement between Roosevelt and Stalin, who are described as the agents of two types of Jews, the type who in Hungary used to vote for Rassay's Democratic party, and "the Béla Kun types." Their plan, the memorandum goes on, had been to eliminate all obstacles to the Jewish domination of the world, their first target having been Germany, their second target, Great Britain. See *Szálasi Ferenc naplója* [Diary of Francis Szálasi], ed. Elek Karsai (Budapest: Kossuth, 1978), p. 483.

or social engineering. Not that Hungary's national socialists were oblivious to the need for reform, or that they rejected outright the imperatives of industrialism and complex organization. To the contrary, many of them had designs for agrarian reform, and were aware of the importance of industry and industrial workers, whom Szálasi was willing to place a few notches above the "passive" peasantry in the hierarchy of his corporatist society.[84] But the building of a new order was not a matter of industrialization or modernization. It was a matter of relentless struggle against the forces of international Jewry, a task which even such a relative "moderate" on the issue as Szálasi[85] was apt to describe as the "only concrete question" facing the movement at the given historical moment.[86] In this apocalyptic vision of politics, the heroic sacrifice of the moment replaced the routine sacrifice of working days, and military valor took precedence over sustained endeavor required for gradual improvement of the standard of living. The technocrats of the establishment could worry about investment priorities and a favorable balance of trade, but the national socialists prepared for a single, epic confrontation with evil in which they would either perish or prevail.

While this chiliastic ideology provided proper inspiration to the masses tired of piecemeal reform and the prospect of long-delayed gratification, it also stimulated further questions concerning the nature of the new order that the national socialists vowed to create. One model, to be sure, was available from the official German doctrine, the inspiration of all other national socialist movements of the world. But this model was only of limited applicability, for Hungarians were neither Nordic nor Aryan in the strict sense of the word, a fact that was uncharitably pointed out in Hitler's *Mein Kampf*, the bible of national socialism. While the relevant passages[87] were discreetly omitted from the Hungarian translation, the stubborn fact remained and created an intellectual challenge to which the Hungarian national

---

[84] The workers, Szálasi would frequently state, were a "nation building," the peasantry a "nation preserving" element.

[85] Szálasi repeatedly referred to himself as being "a-Semitic," rather than anti-Semitic, and while he could see no future for the Jews in Hungary or Europe, he preferred to solve the "problem" by means of gradual immigration to overseas countries. See, for instance, *Szálasi Ferenc naplója*, pp. 260-261.

[86] Ibid., p. 229.

[87] "I was repelled," Hitler wrote, "by the conglomeration of races which the capital [Vienna] showed me, repelled by this whole mixture of Czechs, Poles, Hungarians, Ruthenians, Serbs and Croats, and everywhere, the eternal mushroom of humanity—Jews and more Jews." Adolf Hitler, *Mein Kampf*, trans. Ralph Manheim (Boston: Houghton Mifflin, 1971), p. 123.

socialists responded by offering three alternative orientations or models.

The first of these orientations had its intellectual roots in the pre-war period when a number of respectable academic scholars formed a Hungarian Turanian Society under the presidency of Count Paul Teleki, a professor of geography, and later, prime minister of the country. The initial purpose of the society was to foster linguistic, ethnographic, and historical research into the Asiatic past of the Magyar people. But this very curiosity had political and ideological overtones, for it reflected a growing ambivalence among Hungarians toward the countries and culture of the Occident. In the words of the historian of the society: "To East Europeans, and most other non-western peoples . . . the reality of the West's global dominance loomed large as the most important condition of their latter-day existence. The fact of their relative powerlessness was to generate among [them] a sense of mutual sympathy on the one hand, and a kind of collective alienation on the other. More particularly, it created feelings of sharp ambivalence—resentment and admiration, imitation and rejection, dependence and self-assertion."[88]

Defeat in World War I and the peace treaty of Trianon crystallized and politicized these sentiments by seeming to offer proof for the theory that the Magyars were an "errant people of Turan," unwanted on the European continent. Indeed, there were many who now were only too ready to believe that the victorious British and the French "conspired" with the Balkan Slavs and Rumanians to obliterate Hungary, and that their nation had no choice but to abandon an "ungrateful" Occident and to seek refuge within a larger family of Asiatic nations. In this vein, the program of a new Turanist Union proclaimed an "end to the age of servility to the West," promised defiantly not to "shed more blood in the defense of the Occident," and called for the "unification of all Turanians" against the dual evils of "Semitic corruption and Aryan decadence."[89] Other documents spoke of the need for abandoning parochial nationalism and for creating an anti-colonial, anti-imperial alliance with the nations of the "third world"—meaning Turan and East Europe—against the first world of Germanic Europe and the second world of the non-European, non-Turanian peoples.[90] From this idea of a supranational movement, it was only

[88] Kessler, "Turanism and Pan-Turanism," p. xxix.

[89] "A magyar Turáni Szövetség céljai és tevékenysége" [Aims and activities of the Hungarian Turanian Association], *Turán*, VIII (1921), 74.

[90] See, for instance, Tivadar Raith, *Keleteurópa: Ismeretlen föld* [Eastern Europe: the unknown land] (Budapest: Globus, 1927), p. 32. The "three-world" concept and the

a short step to the global order of Turanian national socialism. In some cases, Turanians were seen as competitors of Aryan Germany; in others, the German and the Turanian peoples were seen in alliance against the status quo powers of France and Britain. But in either case, Hungarian Turanists now coopted Japan into the master race, and, amidst some irreverent joking of the habitués of Budapest coffeehouses, declared it to be one of the two "swords of Turan," the other being the Magyars themselves.[91]

While Turanism was and remained little more than a fringe ideology of the Right, the second orientation of the national socialists, pan-Europeanism, had a number of adherents, and was adopted as the platform of several national socialist groups. Among them were the United Hungarian National Socialist party, associated with the names of Baky, Pálffy, and Rupprecht, and the Hubay-Vágó faction within the Arrow Cross party. Other adherents included the maverick Nazi, Andrew Mecsér, and later, after his conversion to national socialist principles, Béla Imrédy and his Party of Hungarian Renascence. For the members of these groups, national socialism was not an Asian, but a quintessentially European movement, designed for the purpose of creating unity on the Continent and of maintaining the supremacy of Europe over the rest of the world. This movement for a Euro-centered global system would have to be led by Germany, the most vigorous entity on the Continent, and the nation most representative of the values of occidental civilization. As a continental nation wronged by the major capitalist powers and threatened most directly by Jewish bolshevism, Hungary was a natural candidate for membership in this new order. But, alas, Hungary was a small nation, cursed by bad luck and perhaps also by the unfortunate Asiatic heritage of Turan that prevented her from developing fully the qualities required for leadership in the modern world. Indeed, whether measured by their self-discipline, industry, organizational efficiency, or aptitude in the martial arts, the Hungarian people were found sadly wanting. Hungarians might not be an inherently defective *Ausfallvolk*, like the Poles and the Rumanians, but they were a somewhat retrograde people (*retrogrades Volk*), and hence not one of the *Herrenvölker* called upon to rule the Continent.[92] Therefore, the members of this wing of the movement

---

term were apparently first used by the Russian writer V. I. Lamarski. See Kessler, "Turanism and Pan-Turanism," pp. 44-47.

[91] Benedek Barátossi-Balog, *Japán a felkelő nap országa* [Japan, the country of the rising sun] (Budapest: Published by the author, 1930), especially pp. 9-12.

[92] For the terminology and classification, *Szálasi Ferenc naplója*, p. 55.

not only were friendly to Germany, but clearly recognized German moral and political supremacy. The political design for their pan-European order was most explicitly formulated by Andrew Mecsér:

> The Hungarian nation is tired. It has exhausted itself and its constructive potential over centuries of ceaseless struggle. It has no capacity to lead other peoples, indeed, itself is now in need of being led. It has no elite apart from the Jews. The spirit of the age calls for new popular (*völkisch*) states. Such states (*sic*) will also arise on the territory of Hungary. The final solution will be somewhat similar to the present county system, except that it will have a folk character. Each of the folk units will be led by a German lord lieutenant, but his deputy will come from the native element. The Hungarian state will be such a state.[93]

In the conventional framework of the nation state such words could only be construed as the language of high treason. But in the larger, global context of this rising post-national age, they were also an expression of the frustration of a European elite with the backwardness of its own constituency. This elite, however, did not interpret Hungarian backwardness in socioeconomic terms, but in a racial-cultural frame of reference.

The chief competitor of these pan-European ideas, and the third ideological current in Hungarian national socialism was the doctrine of Hungarism. This doctrine was associated with Francis Szálasi, a retired major of Armenian and German origins, under whose leadership the Arrow Cross party, or Hungarist movement, emerged as the most potent radical right-wing organization in the country. Praised by true believers as prophetic revelation and reviled by opponents as a paranoid fantasy, Szálasi's doctrine took issue with the assumptions of the pan-Europeanists in that it started out from the premise that, together with the Germans and the Japanese, Hungarians were one of the three chosen peoples of the world.[94] This special status was conferred upon them by two circumstances. First, as the only Turanian people of occidental culture Magyars were in a unique position to mediate between East and West; second, by inhabiting one of the most perfect geographical units of the world, the Carpathian Basin

[93] Mecsér to Szálasi (*Szálasi Ferenc naplója*, p. 27). Szálasi angrily rejected the design, and denounced those national socialists, like Baky and Rupprecht, "who want[ed] to turn Hungary into a *Kronland* of Germany." Quoted in Éva Teleki, *Nyilas uralom Magyarországon* [Arrow Cross rule in Hungary] (Budapest: Kossuth, 1974), p. 282.

[94] Ferenc Szálasi, *Cél és követelések* [Aims and demands] (Budapest: A Nemzet Akaratának Pártja, 1935), p. 12.

of the European continent, they were in the position not only to protect their own country, but also the Balkan area and much of southern Europe as well. The new global order would consequently rest on three supranational units: an empire of the West ruled by Germany, an empire of the East run by Japan, and a third unit that Szálasi designated as the Carpatho-Danubian Great Fatherland, under the benevolent domination of Hungary. In this strange scheme, Russia, America, and England were barely mentioned, perhaps because the first would have been under German rule, the second under Japanese domination, while England, deprived of her colonial empire, would be reduced to impotence.[95]

As envisioned by Szálasi, the internal structure of the Carpatho-Danubian Great Fatherland was to be a regional federation consisting of several units inhabited by different ethnic groups. In this respect, the design was more tolerant than most which had been produced by official Hungary since the beginning of the nineteenth century. For while it was true that the Magyars would play a leading role in the federation, and occupy a territory much larger than that of Trianon Hungary, the peripheral areas were to be administered by the Slovak, German, Ruthene, and Serbo-Croat "co-nationalities." By oversight or by design the Rumanians were missing from the scheme (as they had been from Béla Kun's federated Soviet Republic of 1919). Conspicuously within the context of the times, the Germans would have no special prerogatives. They would administer the Burgenland, to be reannexed from Austria, and a few ethnic enclaves, but there was to be no question as to Magyar supremacy. The notion that Germans were inherently superior to Hungarians was squarely rejected by Szálasi. Indeed, from the point of view of continental politics, Magyars might play a more significant role than Hitler's Germany. Meanwhile, Szálasi's own charisma seemed to supersede that of Hitler's. As he put it in his collection of aphorisms:

> It is my conviction that the whole ordering of Europe can be effected only by this little people, despised by the Germans, the Magyar people following the basic principles evolved through me. He who does not identify himself with my doctrine, who does not recognize me as leader without reservations, and does not agree that I have been selected by higher divine authority to redeem Magyardom, he who does not understand me, or loses faith in me, let him go.

[95] This was in 1935. In May 1945 Szálasi speculated that the Berlin-Rome-Tokyo triangle might be replaced by a new London-Tokyo-Berlin triangle facing the U.S. and the Soviet Union. *Szálasi Ferenc naplója*, pp. 483-484.

. . . Every party member thus must accept the ideology of Hungarism . . . for the fall of Hungarism would mean the end of national socialism.[96]

But if he assigned such an exalted role to Magyardom, Szálasi was not the old-fashioned, nineteenth-century nationalist. The welfare of the nation and its survival were not the ultimate goals of his politics. The Magyar race was on a higher, historical mission to create order, and if it "had become incapable of filling this role, it should be cleared out of the Danube Basin and another put in its geographical position."[97] In 1935, this was not much more than braggadocio, another bit of political gibberish. But a decade later it was turned into a principle of policy, as Hungarian national socialists scorched the earth of their own country, and were ready to sacrifice its people for the higher purposes of history.[98] Out of such zeal then would arise the Arrow Cross myth, according to which the Hungarian people, by sacrificing themselves, had saved the rest of Europe from the total victory of bolshevism.[99]

Radical Political Elites

The fortunes of these movements over time may be followed by examining the changing composition of the Hungarian political elite in the years 1919-1945. As so often, the statistical correlations are far from perfect, if only because the samples at hand frequently refer to coalitions whose members included politicians of both the old and the new school. But still, whether we examine the composition of the cabinets, of parliaments, or of particular parliamentary parties, the samples tend to bear out the proposition that the bulk of the radicals of the Right came from a generation of educated plebeians, many of them of non-Magyar ethnic background. They came of political age around the end of World War I, but found their upward mobility frustrated by an older generation of professional politicians recruited from the members of the gentry and the aristocracy.

[96] Quoted in Macartney, *October Fifteenth*, i, 163.

[97] Ibid.

[98] The supranational principles of the movement became incorporated in the preamble of the Decree on the Corporate State, promulgated in February 1945 by the Arrow Cross regime. The drafters of this document spoke of the need to create a Social-National International (*szociálnacionálé*), and they made a distinction between "tasks to be performed in Hungary proper as opposed to the larger *Lebensraum* of the Hungarist state." The preamble ended with the slogan "Peoples of the world, unite!" (Teleki, *Nyilas uralom*, p. 251).

[99] For this otherwise well-known myth, see Sulyok, *Magyar tragédia*, p. 542.

This particular social profile first appeared during the "Christian course" of 1919-1921. In this period, legislative authority was vested in a National Assembly. The cabinets exercised this authority ineffectually in the name of the Assembly, but without the benefit of a Government party or the political machine. Both cabinet and parliament consisted overwhelmingly of men who were novices in more than one respect. For one thing, they were relatively young, at least by the standards of Hungarian politics: 38.7 percent of the parliamentarians were under 40 (compared to a mere 17.6 percent of the Liberals of 1905) with only 6.7 percent of them over 60 (in contrast to 21.4 percent of the men serving under Stephen Tisza (Table 36). For another, these men had entered politics not from the traditional triangle of bureaucracy, landownership, and law—whose representatives had made up 84.9 percent of the Government party in 1905, and 78.5 percent in 1910—but from such lesser occupations as teaching, the priesthood, pharmacy, and medicine, or from the ranks of peasant smallholders (Table 37), who in 1920 made up about two-thirds of the deputies in the "agrarian proprietor" category. As to social origin, a substantial majority of the members of the National Assembly were recruited from outside the "historical" classes. Thus while in the prewar decades nobles of one category or another made up 61.9 percent of the membership of the Lower House,[100] in 1920 this ratio had been reversed: commoners comprised 62.9 percent of the deputies, and only 29.4 percent of the total number of deputies were clearly certifiable as members of the gentry (including the petty nobility) and the aristocracy (Table 38). The contrast was even more pronounced at the cabinet level. Here 71.9 percent of the members were commoners (compared to the approximately 30 percent for the prewar period), with 55.6 percent of them bearing foreign, or Magyarized, names (Table 39).

The ensuing liberal-conservative period (1921-1931) was instrumental in restoring patterns prevailing before 1918. True to its reputation, the Bethlen regime provided little upward mobility for the younger generation: the men who came in with Bethlen were of his own age and grew older with him in power, so that the percentage of those under 40 gradually declined from 29.3 to 7.9 percent among the ranks of his Unitary party. With respect to occupation, the incursion of members in "new" professions was corrected in favor of the "traditional triangle" of landowners, lawyers, and bureaucrats, whose percentage was up again to 75.5 (1922), 74.8 (1926), and 75.7

[100] See Chapter III, p. 137.

TABLE 36

Age of Deputies in Government Machine, 1887-1939[a]

(by percentage)

Age Group	1887	1892	1896	1901	1905	1910	1920	1922	1926	1931	1935	1939	Nat. Soc.
-40	38.6	32.0	30.0	28.3	17.6	24.0	38.7	29.3	11.1	7.9	27.6	15.8	38.0
41-60	45.9	52.5	55.5	55.5	61.0	59.0	54.6	63.9	78.9	78.9	56.0	73.5	60.0
61-	15.5	15.5	14.5	16.2	21.4	17.0	6.7	6.8	10.0	13.2	16.4	16.7	2.0

Sources: For 1887-1931, Rudai, "Adalék a magyar képviselőház," pp. 215-230; for 1935-1944 figures are based on information in Haeffler, *Országgyűlési almanach* for 1935-1939, and 1939-1944.

[a] Figures for the 1906 "coalition" not included. Figure for 1920 refers to the members of the Christian National-Smallholder coalition.

TABLE 37

Occupational Structure: Government Machine, House of Representatives, 1905-1939

(by percentage)

Year	Agr. Prop.	Lawyer	Public Serv.	Clergy	Business	Journalists Teachers	Professionals[a]	Other White Collar	Wage Laborer
1905	30.2	20.1	34.6	.6	3.2	9.5	.6	1.2	—
1910	31.3	21.1	26.2	2.5	8.6	9.8	1.5	—	—
1920[b]	30.0	11.2	15.8	12.1	7.7	11.0	4.8	3.4	—
1922	33.3	15.0	27.2	4.1	8.8	6.1	4.8	.7	—
1926	29.7	16.4	28.7	3.5	9.4	4.7	6.4	1.2	—
1931	23.7	19.8	32.2	1.3	9.2	7.2	5.9	.7	—
1935	29.9	13.7	29.3	2.4	5.4	6.5	6.0	6.8	—
1939	30.8	9.6	29.8	1.8	6.7	7.4	7.4	5.9	.6
National Socialists	14.0	12.0	24.0	4.0	12.0	16.0	4.0	6.0	8.0

Sources: As above, Table 36.

[a] Includes doctors, pharmacists, self-employed architects, engineers, etc.

[b] Members of the Smallholder-Christian National coalition.

TABLE 38
Social Composition of Parliament, 1920-1944

| | Christian Period 1919-1921 | | Liberal-Conservative Period[a] 1921-1932 | | | | National Radical Period[b] 1932-1944 | | | |
	Government Party	House		Government Party		House		Government Party		House	
Total	—	245	100%	314	100%	490	100%	348	100%	510	100%
Aristocrat	—	11	4.5	28	8.9	47	9.6	31	8.9	41	8.0
Gentry	—	61	24.9	138	43.9	168	34.3	112	32.2	138	27.1
Commoner	—	154	62.9	135	43.0	257	52.4	189	54.3	297	58.2
Don't Know	—	19	7.7	13	4.2	18	3.7	16	4.6	34	6.7

SOURCE: Based on listings in the *Országgyülési Almanach* for the respective years.

[a] Elections of 1922 and 1926.

[b] Elections of 1935 and 1939.

TABLE 39

SOCIAL COMPOSITION OF CABINETS, 1919-1944[a]

	1919-1921 Christian Period	%	1921-1932 Lib-Cons Period	%	1932-1944 Nat Rad Period	%	Liberal Conservatives	%	1932-1944[d] National Radicals	%	Not Identifiable	%
Total	45	100.0	34	100.0	43	100.0	16	100.0	20	100.0	7	100.0
Aristocrat	4	8.9	7	20.6	4	9.3	2	12.5	2	10.0	—	—
Gentry[b]	7	15.6	12	35.3	15	34.9	10	62.5	3	15.0	1	14.3
Commoner	32	71.1	14	41.2	21	48.8	3	18.8	14	70.0	4	57.2
Don't Know	2	4.4	1	2.9	3	7.0	1	6.2	1	5.0	2	28.5
Magyar	20	44.4	17	50.0	23	53.5	14	87.6	6	30.0	3	42.9
German[c]	21	46.6	11	32.4	14	32.6	1	6.2	9	45.0	4	57.1
Other	4	9.0	6	17.6	6	13.9	1	6.2	5	25.0	—	—

SOURCE: Statisztikai Hivatal, Magyarország tiszti cím és névtára, and MaCartney, October Fifteenth, II.

[a] August 7, 1919—August 29, 1944.

[b] According to the standard followed throughout the tables, titles awarded throughout the lifetime of the wearer not counted. This omits Premier Imrédy; Premiers Darányi and Gömbös are likewise omitted, the former as the illegitimate issue of Ignatius Darányi, the latter because his claim to a title was ignored by books of heraldry.

[c] "German" and "other" categories include persons whose names had been Magyarized.

[d] The breakdown of ministers by faction ("ethnics" identified by *): Radicals: Antal,* Bárdossy, Bartha, Csáky, Fabinyi,* Gömbös* (Knöpfle), Hóman,* Imrédy* (Heinrich), Jaross,* Jurcsek,* Kozma, Kunder,* Lukács, Mikecz,* Rátz,* Reményi* (Schneller), Szász,* Tasnádi-Nagy, M. Teleki.

Liberal-Conservatives: Bánffy, Bornemissza, Ghyczy, Győrffy-Bengyel, Kállay, Kánya, Keresztes-Fischer,* Lázár, Losonczy, Nagybaczoni-Nagy, Puky, Széll, Szinnyei-Merse, Sztranyavszky,* P. Teleki, Varga.

Not easily identifiable politically: Darányi, Csatay, Marschall,* Radocsay, Röder,* Somkuthy, Winckler.*

(1931). Within the traditional triangle, though, the proportion of landowners declined, reflecting Bethlen's proclivity to govern with financially less independent ex-bureaucrats and lawyers. Naturally, there was also a shift back to the gentry and the aristocracy. In the parliament, their proportion rose from 29.4 to 43.9 percent—52.8 percent in Bethlen's own party—while in the cabinet the increase was from 24.5 to 55.9 percent. So presented, however, the figures understate the true extent of the change, for both the cabinet and the party sample include a number of carry-overs from the Christian course, men who for some time were kept by Bethlen as a matter of convenience. If we eliminated these carry-overs, or if we considered merely Bethlen's cabinets after 1926, the proportion of the old style politicians would be far greater.

The beginning of the second Right radical period then signalled a return to the social patterns of the Christian course, though with certain modifications. For one, the radicals were younger than the Bethlenites: they were members of the "front generation" born between 1890 and 1900. They too were growing older in office. While, in 1935, 27.6 percent of the Gömbös-led Government party (now Party of National Unity) consisted of deputies under 40, in 1939 the respective figure was only 15.8, while the proportion of middle-aged deputies increased from 56.0 to 73.5 percent. At the same time, the occupational structure of the Government party moved away slightly from the traditional triangle on account of a decline in the number of lawyers. More significantly, the composition of the "agrarian proprietor" and "public service" categories changed to include a greater number of peasant proprietors (5.5 percent) and military officers (5.2 percent) compared to the 1922-1931 period.[101]

The return of Right radicalism also resulted in a new low in the participation of the historical classes within the elite. Their proportion among the deputies of the Government party declined from 43.9 to 32.2 percent, and in the cabinets from 55.9 to 44.2 percent. However, as we will note below, more so than any of their predecessors, these cabinets were in fact coalitions of radicals and liberal-conservatives. Thus the contrast becomes truly remarkable only if we separate dyed-in-the-wool radicals from hard-line conservatives. If we do so, we will find that seventy-five percent of the radical ministers were commoners and of an assimilated ethnic background (Table 39). Among the latter we will find premiers Gömbös (Knöpfle), Imrédy (Heinrich), and

---

[101] See Péter Sipos, Miklós Stier, and István Vida, "Változások a kormánypárt parlamenti képviseletének összetételében 1931-1939," [Changes in the composition of the parliamentary Government party, 1931-1939], *Századok*, 101 (1967), 602-660.

Sztójay (Stojaković), the most outstanding representatives of Hungarian right-wing radicalism. In contrast, 75.0 percent of the liberal-conservatives were members of the historical classes, 87.5 percent of them of apparent Magyar ethnic origin.

The sample of national socialist leaders shows both similarities and differences within the general profile of Right radicalism. This sample, we should note, was extracted from diverse sources. First, there is a list culled from the daily press of the period which names ninety candidates running for parliamentary seats in the elections of 1939; second, a sample of deputies actually elected as they appear in the *Parliamentary Almanac*, published in the spring of 1940; thirdly, there is a sample of seventeen national socialist ministers and members of the Arrow Cross National Council that presided over the affairs of the country in 1944-1945 (Table 40). Of these three samples, the first one includes a high percentage (74.5) of commoners, but also a surprisingly high (62.2) ethnic Magyar component which seems to be at variance with the general profile of right-wing radicalism. A possible explanation is that at the elections, the Arrow Cross and other national socialist parties tried consciously to rid themselves of the stigma of

TABLE 40
NATIONAL SOCIALIST LEADERSHIP

	Candidates for Election, 1939		Members of Parliament, 1940		Cabinet-National Council October 1944-April 1945	
	No.	%	No.	%	No.	%
Total	90	100.0	50	100.0	17	100.0
Aristocrat	3	3.3	2	4	2	11.8
Gentry	17	18.9	12	24	1	5.9
Other	67	74.5	34	68	13	76.4
Don't Know	3	3.3	2	4	1	5.9
Magyar	56	62.2	29	58	5	29.4
German	25	27.8	17	34	8	47.1
Other	9	10.0	4	8	4	23.5

SOURCES: For candidates, *Népszava*, May 29, 1939, and Lackó, *Nyilasok, nemzetiszocialisták*, index; for members of parliament, see István Haeffler, ed., *Országgyülési Almanach*, 1940, pp. 99-101; includes seven non-party national socialist deputies, among them Rajniss, who later entered the Imrédy party; members of the national socialist cabinet and National Council ("ethnics" marked by asterisk): Beregffy, (Berger),* Budinszky,* Csia (?), Gera (?), Hellebronth,* Jurcsek,* Kassai* (Schallmeier), Kemény, Kovarcz,* Pálffy, Rajniss* (Rheinisch), Reményi* (Schneller), Szakváry* (Löffler), Szálasi* (Salosjan), Szász,* Szöllösi* (Nesluhać), Vajna. As always in these tables, in case of doubt benefit was given to the Magyar element. But the names Csia (Cea) and Gera (Gherea) almost certainly refer to Rumanian ethnic origin. If so, the ethnic distribution in the cabinet would be: Magyars, 17.6 percent; Germans, 47.1; Others, 35.3.

being a "foreign import," and to show that they were more Magyar than the prospective membership of the Government party. Among the group of 50 actually elected, however, the German assimilated element seemed to have fared well, as did the members of the historical classes, whose percentage was 22.2 percent among the candidates, but 28 percent among the elected deputies. This may suggest a number of intriguing hypotheses, but before jumping to any premature conclusions concerning these variations, we should note that the cabinet-National Council sample was overwhelmingly plebeian (76.4) and ethnic (70.6) in composition, and thus more or less replicated the profile of other elites of the radical Right.

The national socialists and the other radical elites differed in two respects, and both of these differences are indicative of the "outgroup" character of the former. First, the national socialist deputies were somewhat younger than the radicals of the establishment—thirty-eight percent of them "young," sixty "middle-aged," and only two percent "old"—that is, they included a substantial number of those born after 1900 who were not part of the original Szeged clique or who could not be absorbed by the Gömbös machine during the crisis years. Second, while the establishment radicals of the Gömbös-Imrédy stripe had entered right-wing politics from low-level positions in the machine where they had been frozen for a decade or so by conservative superiors, most of the national socialists were recruited from the "non-conventional" occupations: smallholders, small businessmen, and manual workers, as well as educated persons who had never been part of the administrative-political machine of the establishment. True, among them we will find twelve deputies under the label of "public service." But only two of these were civilians, the others being retired, or cashiered, officers of the military and the gendarmerie.

POWER AND POLITICS, 1932-1945

Radicalism in Perspective

As elsewhere on the European continent, in Hungary the main impulse for the rise of Right radicalism came from the growing insecurity of political elites, and would-be political elites. Its source was a dual threat we have already taken notice of: the prospect of political subjugation by the powerful imperial states of the core, and the parallel prospect of subversion by the global Communist movement embodied in the Comintern and the Soviet state. Due to the commonality of these perceptions and the prevalence of doctrinal borrowing, the idiom and aspirations of the Hungarian Right bore obvious resemblances to those of its counterparts in Germany, Italy, Austria, and other countries.

Within the general phenomenon of the European Right, however, we will have to identify variations not only in terms of doctrinal expressions, but also in terms of actual political outcomes. In this respect, the dividing line appears to be geopolitical, for while the movements of the radical Right were successful in establishing their institutional monopoly in the countries of south and central Europe, above all in Italy and Germany, in East Europe they failed to accomplish this short of outside intervention. Thus, in Hungary national socialism did not attain institutional monopoly until October 1944, when the Arrow Cross regime was installed by the Germans on a strip of Hungarian territory, which was still out of reach of the advancing Soviet army.

While the pattern is geographical, the reasons behind it must be sought in the relative degrees of backwardness and social differentiation. In southern, and especially central, Europe a capitalist economy had emerged around the turn of the century. There was in these societies a modernized agrarian enterprise, and, above all, an industrial bourgeoisie. Yet both of these classes, like the political classes themselves, experienced serious pressures from two directions: the pressure of competition with the most advanced core economies for the domestic and international market, and pressures from their own restless labor force for the redistribution of property and profits. Under these pressures, agrarian and industrial capitalists came to be the allies of the political classes—the bureaucrats, the military men, or else the "mobs" of armed bohemians—and to a greater or lesser extent helped to pave their way to power.[102] In these countries the new type of state had a multiple appeal. For the political classes it was to be the tool of international power and prestige, while for the entrepreneurs it was an instrument for maintaining labor discipline and for sustaining a high level of demand for locally produced commodities.

In Hungary, as in the other countries of the European periphery, economic and social configurations were different. Entrepreneurship and the insecurity of enterprise, to be sure, were not altogether absent. But here the bourgeoisie could hardly be described as national. Given the backwardness of the economy, a significant number of entrepreneurs were what Marxists call *compradores*, that is, the managers and

[102] See, for instance, Charles S. Meier, *Recasting Bourgeois Europe* (Princeton: Princeton University Press, 1975), pp. 305-308.

agents of foreign capital. Even those entrepreneurs whose interests were clearly on the side of the local economy were ethnically alien, more frightened than encouraged by manifestations of aggressive nationalism. At the same time, agrarian enterprise had yet to develop a truly modern character. Thus while large landowners abhorred the idea of a reform of rural society, the political classes had little use for an agrarian economy that required an elaborate apparatus of repression, yet was too inefficient to support the radicals' policies of industrialization by providing cheap comestibles for both export and domestic consumption.

Consequently, in Hungary, the pattern of political conflict and coalitions was to be quite different from the one we encounter in the major European countries. Instead of finding a natural ally in the bourgeoisie, and in the owners of large-scale agricultural enterprise, the political class encountered the implacable hostility of all vested interests. In the face of this hostility, the political class itself became divided between those who wanted to protect and those who wanted to liquidate the traditional landowner and the ethnic entrepreneur. For the same reason, the Hungarian Right—or at least some of its segments—was far more radical in matters of "feudalism" and "capitalism" than its counterparts in the more advanced societies of the Continent, a circumstance that should not be obscured by its long record of failure to act effectively upon this sentiment.

Two Experiments

When Gömbös and the radicals of the Right were called upon to form a government in 1932 after more than ten years in limbo, their freedom action was severely circumscribed by pledges made to the regent as conditions of their appointment. One of these was that Gömbös, as prime minister, was to refrain from tampering with the existing political institutions of the country. He was to appoint members of the "old guard" to the key portfolios of agriculture, interior, and foreign affairs, and was not to call for new elections before the expiration of the current term of the House of Representatives. Accordingly, during much of his premiership, Gömbös had to contend with a cabinet and parliamentary party whose loyalties were divided between himself and his liberal-conservative predecessors.

So constrained, the new government presented itself as one of national reconstruction, rather than one of sweeping social reforms. The resolution of the "land problem," i.e., the redistribution of large estates, was to be postponed until such time as the country's economic health was fully restored. The Jewish question was publicly laid to rest, apparently after Gömbös extracted a private pledge from the leaders of the Jewish community that business would wholeheartedly support the economic endeavors of the new government.[103] Thus while not ignoring altogether some of the right-wing shibboleths of earlier years, the ninety-five-point program of the government tended to emphasize short-term economic goals: above all, it promised to "promote the accumulation of domestic capital by all available means," and spoke profusely about the need to increase productivity and to improve the country's balance of trade.[104] To lend substance to these claims, Gömbös appointed the aforementioned Sofort boys to coordinate the technical aspects of mobilizing the economy for reconstruction and development. The three most important of these men, Petneházy, Szakváry, and Kunder, were to report to Gömbös directly, and together with him, constituted a kind of superministry in charge of the country's economic affairs.

This shift in priorities, however, did not imply that Gömbös had abandoned his radical design, only that he had postponed its execution until political conditions became more propitious. Thus while he struck a voice of moderation in the program and in his speeches to the nation and the parliament, after only two months in office Gömbös set out to create the foundations of an authoritarian regime. He reorganized Bethlen's Unitary party under the new name of Party of National Unity (NEP), and to execute his design, he appointed a right-wing stalwart, Béla Marton, secretary-general of the party. Marton was to be in charge of sections for propaganda, social work, women, popular education, and economic mobilization, with cells in each of Hungary's 4,000-odd incorporated communes. A permanent administrative staff and a cadre of 60,000 "elite fighters" (élharcosok) were to be supervised by the secretary-general. To complete this organizational network, the party was to acquire a transmission belt in the form of the newly created Alliance of Social Associations (TESZ), whose members would be available for purposes of organizing demonstrations, collecting signatures, holding mass rallies, and engaging in other forms of mass political action.[105] Thus while Bethlen's Unitary party, like the Liberal party of the Tiszas, was little more than an

[103] This pledge is said to have been formal and incorporated in a written agreement allegedly signed by Eugene Szabó and Samuel Stern on behalf of the orthodox and reform Jewish communities respectively, and by Gabriel Baross and Joseph Szörtsey on behalf of Gömbös. See Sándor Kónya, Gömbös kísérlete, p. 40.

[104] A Gömbös kormány nemzeti munkaterve [The national work plan of the Gömbös government] (Budapest: Stádium, 1932); for the quote, see p. 76.

[105] Macartney, October Fifteenth, I, 118.

extension of the administrative apparatus manufacturing parliamentary majorities, the new party was to be nothing less than an instrument for the "total control of the nation's social life."[106] In the words of Marton:

> Until now, the conventional parties have concentrated their efforts on the election campaigns. . . . In contrast, the Party of National Unity will participate in electoral politics only as part of its broader design to aid the Leader [Gömbös] in his progress toward the goal of national unity. As part of this design, the party will serve as an instrument for reshaping the whole way of life. . . . For this reason, it should be able to reach out to all of our Hungarian brethren who share the objectives of the Leader. At the same time, the party should also use its organization to preempt political ideas and action that do not emanate from its own framework.[107]

After laying down these foundations for a monopolistic political party, Gömbös stepped up his preparations for establishing an authoritarian state. In 1935, he at last persuaded Horthy to call for new elections, in the course of which he engineered a majority far more sympathetic to his ideas than its predecessor in the House he had inherited from Bethlen. Just as important as the election results, however, was Gömbös' successful maneuver to force the retirement of a number of generals left over from the old royal and imperial army, and to replace them with a number of younger officers more attuned to the ideas of social reform and straightforward political authoritarianism. Encouraged by his success, he began to make more frequent and more open statements concerning the virtues of an authoritarian state, soon pledging to Göring and to some German friends that a one-party regime would be set up in Hungary within the following two years.[108]

Whether Gömbös could ever have carried out his pledge will remain a matter for historians to debate, for before his deadline arrived he fell gravely ill, and to the barely concealed glee of his numerous opponents, passed away in October 1936. Now the regent moved to restore the changing political balance between radicalism and conservatism by appointing to the premiership the ideologically uncommitted Coloman Darányi. Under the guise of forming a "grand coalition" of all nationalist forces, Darányi quickly proceeded to dismantle Gömbös' political machine. The office of secretary-general of the NEP

---

[106] Gömbös, quoted in Kónya, *Gömbös kisérlete*, p. 176.
[107] Ibid., pp. 178-179.
[108] Macartney, *October Fifteenth*, I, 148.

was abolished, the apparatus disbanded, and the whole party was once more reduced to the status of an electoral machine based on the local bureaucracy. New talk about land reform meanwhile was laid to rest unceremoniously by no less a person than Regent Horthy, who in a broadcast speech to the nation blandly declared that since there was not enough land for all, the salvation of the nation lay not in land redistribution, but in economic development.[109]

Such overt abandonment of radical principles, however, created a considerable stir, not only among the "young Turks" of the NEP, but also among university students, the marginal intelligentsia, and others who saw their earlier hopes dashed by conservative retrenchment. Late in 1937, many of these malcontents entered national socialist groups and successfully mobilized the streets with anti-establishment and anti-Semitic slogans. Even more ominous, national socialist Germany began to loom large on the continental horizon and, after the *Anschluss* of Austria to the Reich in March 1938, became a next-door neighbor of Hungary. In the face of rising internal and foreign pressure, Darányi resorted to a dual strategy. On the one hand, his government stepped up the police harassment of extreme right-wing groups; on the other, it suddenly announced plans for drafting a "Jewish law," presumably to steal the thunder of the ultras and to preempt a political confrontation with Germany. The bill was drafted and submitted to parliament, but not without some vocal criticism by groups that included the aristocratic National Casino, one hundred leading members of the country's cultural establishment, and even twenty-four retired generals of the army who registered their protest in a formal memorandum to the regent.[110] Inside parliament, the opposition to the bill consisted of an informal coalition of assorted conservative and left-wing politicians. In the Upper House this opposition was led by Count Anton Sigray, the unofficial head of the legitimists (monarchists), in the Lower Chamber by Bethlen, who had earlier parted ways with the governments of Darányi and Gömbös. As a result of this opposition and the anticipated hostility of the Upper Chamber, the bill turned out to be a relatively moderate document. At any rate, it was a far cry from the legislation already in force in Germany. Its text used a religious, rather than a strictly racial, criterion for the definition of Jewishness. It established numerous ex-

[109] See Miklós Stier, "A kormánypárt fasiszta jellegű átszervezésének csődjéhez, 1935-1936" [The failure of the reorganization of the Government party along fascist lines, 1935-1936], *Századok*, 105 (1971), 696-709.

[110] For this memorandum, and the debate on the bill, see Schickert, *Die Judenfrage in Ungarn*, pp. 236-254. Also, Lévai, *Fekete könyv*, pp. 22-23, 50.

emptions—among them exemptions for wounded war veterans and for the holders of certain decorations—and it gave the regent broad powers to grant further exemptions to all who had performed meritoriously in the service of the nation. For the rest of the Jewish population, it established quotas of twenty percent in selected occupations, to be attained mainly by attrition.[111] Even so, the Upper House remonstrated that the bill would establish a legal precedent for discrimination. It was passed only after repeated assurances by Darányi that the act (Public Law xv/1938) would close the matter once and for all, and that no further Jewish laws would be submitted to parliament.

Such halfhearted measures, however, did not satisfy the national socialists who proclaimed 1938 to be their year, and proceeded to make good on their claim by instigating demonstrations, distributing leaflets, and causing considerable turmoil. One of the demonstrations was personally offensive to the regent, who thereafter concluded that Darányi's Janus-faced policies had failed, and that the premier would have to make room for a more resolutely conservative successor. The regent's choice was Béla Imrédy, a financial expert who travelled in Christian political circles, but who primarily had the reputation of being a hard-nosed pragmatist with excellent connections in the city of London and in the international banking community.

At first, Imrédy's reputation seemed to be well justified. In parliament he spoke of the need to defend the ancient constitutional liberties, by now a code word for defending the status quo, reiterated Darányi's pledge not to reopen the Jewish question,[112] and then initiated a number of harsh measures to repress the national socialists. By midsummer, the police arrested Szálasi, and the courts duly sentenced him to five years for conspiring to subvert the constitutional order.

But then, whether out of personal ambition, wounded pride, or conviction that the politics of the old order were beyond redemption,[113] Imrédy suddenly changed his course, and in one of the most

[111] Macartney, *October Fifteenth*, I, 218-219; Lévai, *Fekete könyv*, p. 33.

[112] See his introduction before the House of Representatives, *Napló*, 1938, xviii, 600-601.

[113] The standard explanation is that Imrédy had been impressed by German resolve and strength during a visit to Germany in August 1938. Macartney (*October Fifteenth*, I, 248) attributes his turnabout to indiscretions of British journalists and slights by the Foreign Office. However, it is more likely that, any irrational impulse aside, Imrédy may just have persuaded himself that both Britain and France were unsympathetic to the Hungarian cause; that neither were able to prop up minor allies on the Continent; and finally, that the effective solution of domestic social problems was impossible within the traditional framework of neo-corporatism.

startling turnabouts of Hungarian history, signalled to the Gömbös "orphans" that he was ready to become their leader. He did so by delivering a militant right-wing speech at a provincial political rally on September 4, 1938. In it he announced a sweeping social program, including the redistribution of large estates, and called for new, more radical anti-Jewish measures, declaring himself in favor of a pro-German foreign policy.[114] In the weeks thereafter he followed this up with more rhetoric borrowed straight from the vocabulary of fascist parties. He promised to "transform the social structure," to "realize new Hungarian life on the ancient Hungarian soil," and called for the formation of a new movement "based on firm, exactly defined, ideological foundations," adding that on such foundations would the governments of the future rest.[115] It is true that he equivocated somewhat on the issue of a one-party dictatorship, but he professed contempt for parliamentary arithmetics,[116] and in private vowed to carry out his program, if necessary, by order of council without the assent of the legislature.[117] Finally, to make good these pledges, he reenlisted the services of Béla Marton, the onetime secretary-general of Gömbös' abortive mass party, with instructions to organize a new Movement of Hungarian Life, complete with paramilitary units, uniforms, emblems, totemic symbols, and other paraphernalia of fascist-type political parties.

The new orientation seemed to have yielded its first dividends within a few weeks when, following the Munich agreement, a German-Italian committee of arbitration awarded Hungary the Magyar-inhabited areas of Czechoslovakia. These were reoccupied with due pomp and ceremony. But the domestic radicalism of the program soon put in motion powerful conservative forces whose representatives, with considerable justification, felt betrayed by Imrédy. Bethlen arranged a number of secret discussions between the leaders of the Socialist, Democratic, and Independent Smallholder parties of the opposition and some of the liberal-conservative "pick-axmen"[118] of the Government party proper. Well prepared, the conspirators struck

114 Sipos, *Imrédy*, p. 58.
115 Macartney, *October Fifteenth*, I, 307.
116 Sipos, *Imrédy*, p. 88.
117 Macartney, *October Fifteenth*, I, 110.
118 This designation—in Hungarian, *csáklyás*—originated with Gömbös, who at one time accused the conservative old guard within the establishment of attempting to spring a leak on his boat of reform. Since the metaphor was somewhat strained, and the use of the word *csáklya* something of a malapropism, the opponents accepted the label with malicious glee.

on November 23, 1938, defeating Imrédy on a motion of confidence. Sixty-two deputies of his own party voted against the prime minister.

The news of the parliamentary coup provoked widespread demonstrations in Budapest in favor of Imrédy. As so often, the regent hesitated and the dissidents retreated, permitting Imrédy to retain the premiership. But the retreat was only temporary, and their attack was soon renewed, this time by more devious means. By December 1938 the country was rife with rumors concerning Imrédy's Jewish ancestry. In February 1939 documents to this effect were indeed produced by courtesy of the chief of police, an old appointee of Bethlen, and were passed on to the regent. When Imrédy was confronted with the documents, he seemed to acknowledge their authenticity by fainting on the spot. He then tendered his resignation, leaving the radical Right leaderless and once again in a state of disarray. Imrédy's successor, Count Teleki, liquidated the incipient Movement of Hungarian Life. But as a noble gesture to the ex-premier, the Government party was rebaptized once more, to be known henceforth under the somewhat awkward designation of the Hungarian Party of Life. For another year and a half the ex-premier stayed in this party, trying to influence its policies from within. But when he failed to do so, he crossed the aisle with his political entourage to join the national socialist opposition of the wartime governments.

The Politics of Stalemate

Unlike the political institutions of so many European countries, those of Hungary underwent only relatively minor changes in the years 1932-1944. In 1937, a Regency Act was passed, designed to broaden the constitutional powers of the head of state. It granted the regent right of preliminary review of government bills, and abolished provisions for impeachment by parliament, as stipulated by the articles of the original charter under which the regent had been elected in 1920. A year later, amidst considerable bickering among equally reluctant parties, a new electoral law was passed. Under its provisions, for the first time, the secret ballot was introduced across the country, though this democratic feature was in part countered by a simultaneous raising of the voting age and of residency requirements. A more technical provision of the law introduced a system of dual balloting: 135 deputies were to be elected from single member constituencies, 125 by list voting from larger electoral districts that encompassed several individual constituencies. There were complex provisions as to eligibility requirements for franchise in the different types of electoral districts, but the net result of all of these was to reduce the size of the electorate from approximately 29 to 22.5 percent of the total population.

Far more important than these changes in form, however, were changes in the spirit and substance of politics brought about by the ever-sharpening rift between the radicals and the liberal-conservatives—for simplicity's sake, from here on, conservatives—within the very heart of the political machine. A degree of fragmentation, of course, had never been absent from the political base of Hungarian governments. But now the two major factions within the establishment differed not only on particular points of public policy, but on the very legitimacy of the institutional framework within which they were supposed to be functioning. This circumstance made mediation between them, and the formulation of effective public policy, difficult if not altogether impossible.

Apart from the constitutional issue of parliamentarism vs. the one-party state, the radicals and conservatives within the state apparatus were split on a number of critical issues. In matters of foreign policy, the radicals were pro-Axis and, with the years, increasingly favored Germany's patronage over that of weak and bungling Italy. In domestic affairs, they were committed to a more equal distribution of land and to the "solution" of the Jewish problem by setting occupational quotas, and by establishing public control over the large banking-industrial concerns. In contrast, the conservatives tended to adhere to the ground rules as they had been laid down by Bethlen in the 1920s. In foreign policy they were "Anglophiles"—a somewhat misleading designation, for most of them merely wanted to reduce Hungary's dependence on the Axis and on Germany—while in the domestic arena they seemed to lack higher principle and were merely content to "save what could be saved" from the economic and social structure of the old regime. In practice, of course, the dividing line between conservatives and radicals occasionally became blurred, for there were a number of radicals who remained doubtful about the wisdom of a pro-German orientation in foreign policy, just as there were a number of conservatives who felt that to save the quintessence of the old regime, at least some concessions would have to be made to the "mob," whether at the expense of the magnates or of the Jewish bourgeoisie.

At first, the machine was split horizontally, between younger men at the lower echelons, and older men at the higher echelons of the bureaucracy and political life. But later, these horizontal cleavages were cut across by vertical ones, as the old guard diminished by natural attrition, and as younger men of radical sentiment were appointed to positions of responsibility by the Gömbös and Imrédy cabinets. In this manner, the radicals captured some of the departments of government from top to bottom, while the conservatives managed to hold on to others. Thus for much of the time after 1935 the radical Right could call as its own the Ministries of Finance, Industry, and Defense, together with the rural gendarmerie whose officers had long been known for their anti-liberalism, anti-socialism, and anti-Semitism. The conservatives on the other hand retained control over the Interior Ministry (much of the time under the direction of the indomitable Keresztes-Fischer), of Agriculture, and of the state police, including its important political division under the direction of Hetényi, and later of J. Sombor-Schweinitzer, the scourges of underground communism as well as of overground national socialist movements. Other ministries, among them Foreign Affairs and Justice, were split more or less evenly between radicals and conservatives with the balance of power shifting back and forth depending on the minister in charge of the department.[119] The organs of local administration were likewise divided between the adherents of the two factions, some "belonging" to the radicals, others to the conservatives. Again others were split right down the middle, or else divided between the local officialdom and the lord lieutenant appointed by the prime minister of the moment. In a few counties the lord lieutenant lost control over the local machine altogether. Among them was the strategic county of Pest—excluding the city proper—where an officialdom of national socialist sympathies gained the upper hand as early as 1938.

The split within the machine was reflected in the changing balance of forces in the parliamentary Government party. Thus while in the years 1932-1935 conservative "pick-axmen" still had a significant edge over the radicals in the ruling NEP, after the elections of 1935 the ratio was reversed. A perfect count is impossible.[120] But when the

[119] For the ministries, see Kovrig, *Hungarian Social Policies*, pp. 164-182; for the counties, Ferenc Glatz and Miklós Stier, "Megyei küzdelmek a gömbösi reformtörekvések körül" [Struggles in the counties for and against Gömbös' reform endeavors], *Történelmi Szemle*, 14 (1971), 157-188; Ervin Hollós, *Rendőrség, csendőrség, VKF 2* [Police, gendarmerie, and the secret general staff] (Budapest: Kossuth, 1971), pp. 42-43, 88.

[120] It has nonetheless been attempted. Thus according to a recent study Gömbös had inherited from his predecessors sixty-three staunch Bethlenite conservatives and thirty-five "agrarians," who opposed Bethlen's economic policies, but who were not necessarily in favor of Gömbös' brand of political radicalism. Of the rest only eighteen were unqualified supporters of Gömbös. The same study writes that after 1935 there remained in the party twenty-six hard-core Bethlenites, twenty-nine agrarians, and seventy-one unqualified supporters of Gömbös, together with forty-five apparent waverers. See Sipos, Stier, and Vida, "Változások," pp. 613-614.

great confrontation of 1938 took place, 102 deputies of the Government party went for Imrédy, while 71 became "dissidents" siding with Bethlen.[121] In the course of the next year, the Government party was reconstituted under Teleki's auspices, but Imrédy remained one of its members, and exercised considerable influence in the selection of candidates for the forthcoming general elections of 1939. The net result of this was a further shift in the direction of radicalism, so much so that some observers were ready to pronounce conservatism dead in the new parliamentary contingent of the Government party. Upon closer examination, however, we will find that some 60 of the 180 deputies of the Hungarian Party of Life (MÉP) were Teleki's men, not much different in social and political cast from the old Bethlen-ites.[122] Others could not be easily identified with either faction, for they were men picked on the grounds that they were acceptable to both Teleki and Imrédy. Estimates on the numerical strength of these groups vary,[123] but none of these is probably as accurate as the one suggested by Veesenmeyer, the Germans' top expert on Hungarian politics. According to a confidential report of his, the membership of the parliamentary MÉP was more or less evenly divided among three groups of deputies: 1) reliable right-wingers and friends of Germany; 2) unreliables in the pay of the Jews and magnates, and 3) political opportunists, who were ready to bend with the prevailing political wind.[124]

It should be noted here that over the following years attempts were made both by the radicals and the conservatives to tip the parliamentary balance in their own favor. An expedient for this was provided by the co-optation of deputies from the recovered territories, on the theory that conditions there were too unsettled to hold regular elections. This game of numbers started in 1938-1939 at which time twenty-six—and later ten more—deputies were appointed to represent the reannexed territories of southern Slovakia and the Carpatho-

[121] Only sixty-two members of the NEP actually voted against Imrédy, but nine more deputies resigned from the party subsequently. Sipos, *Imrédy*, p. 91.

[122] *Népszava*, June 23, 1939.

[123] One historian offers the following breakdown for the political composition of the parliamentary MÉP in 1939-1940: ultra-Right (Imrédy's personal entourage), twenty-six; right-wing, seventy-six; agrarians, thirty-five; Teleki's confidants, fifteen; not identified, twenty-eight (Sipos, *Imrédy*, pp. 121-122). Most of the latter and at least half of the agrarians, however, were political conservatives, so this breakdown is not as much at variance with the other sources as it appears at first sight.

[124] Secret report, quoted in Elek Karsai, *A budai vártól a gyepüig, 1941-1945* [From Buda castle to the western frontier] (Budapest: Táncsics, 1965), p. 359.

Ukraine.[125] Since the administrative machinery of these territories was set up by Imrédy's men, and patronage there was controlled firmly by Andrew Jaross, one of Imrédy's closest political allies, the majority of the contingent turned out to be partisans of the radical Right. However, an opportunity to correct this imbalance arose in 1940 when, upon its reannexation to Hungary, northern Translyvania was given a representation of fifty-one (and later, seven more). This time, the local administrative machine was set up by men closely linked to Bethlen and Teleki, both of them natives of the region. Their influence was manifest in the exercise of patronage: most of the appointees came from the local landowning class and were much more conservative (and anti-German) than the majority of the MÉP deputies.[126] Another year later the "Southlands," or Bácska, were regained from Yugoslavia, and a new delegation of twenty-six was admitted to the House. While the prime minister of the day, Bárdossy, was distinctly a man of the radical Right, he was thoroughly inexperienced in matters of domestic policy, so that the new administration was set up by his conservative minister of the interior, Keresztes-Fischer, "out of hand-picked elements loyal to himself and sympathetic to his ideas."[127] Consequently, twenty-two out of the twenty-six members were members of the "Magyar landowning and official classes in the area,"[128] on the whole conservative rather than radical by political affiliation. Altogether these changes tended to favor the old Right over the new, and helped to tip the balance of power against the radicals of the MÉP caucus, already weakened by the defection of Imrédy and nineteen of his cohorts in October 1940 (see Diagram).

If one consequence of the split in the machine was the political fragmentation of the parliamentary Government party, another was a loosening in the grip of the government over the electoral process. In 1935, Gömbös could still control electoral results with almost mathematical precision: he had "consented" to twenty-five Independent Smallholder deputies, and the same number was actually elected.[129] But in 1939, despite the impressive majority of seats garnered by the Government party, the machine could not, or would not, repeat this feat. For one thing, the MÉP's majority of the popular vote (as opposed to seats) was a razor-thin 50.5 percent. And next to the "traditional" opposition—of Smallholders, Social Democrats, Democrats, and con-

[125] Haeffler, *Országgyűlési almanach, 1939*, p. 99.
[126] Macartney, *October Fifteenth*, i, 430; ii, 100; also, Sipos, *Imrédy*, pp. 218-219.
[127] Macartney, *October Fifteenth*, ii, 78.
[128] Ibid.   [129] Macartney, *October Fifteenth*, i, 129.

servative Christians (monarchists)—the government had to put up with the 50 or so national socialist deputies, elected with 25 percent of the popular vote. For another, the divided sympathies of the local administrations did not permit the same rigor as had been applied earlier toward "extremists." So, despite recurrent harassment, the national socialist Arrow Cross now dominated the "street," and became the only party capable of mobilizing the masses for political action.

The split in the party and in the administrative machine restored some of the past influence of the propertied classes, particularly of the landowning class in the villages. Where the gendarme and the village notary grew hesitant, the local landowner reemerged as a patron and as an authority figure. Even more significantly, the stalemate of the Government party brought about a certain *immobilisme* in the Lower House, which in turn restored the Upper House to a position of influence that it had not enjoyed since the 1840s. This did not mean that the aristocrats, clerics, and industrialists of the Upper House could dictate public policy. But the advice of the peers was listened to intently by conservative premiers like Teleki and Kállay, as well as by the regent.[130] And the very prospect of a legislative veto, or even the free-wheeling bluntness of a debate, made the Upper House a significant brake on the potential radicalism of bills emanating from the caucus of the Government party.

Finally, the conservative-radical split within the body politic had the consequence of elevating the regent to a key position in the system of government. Although the designation "Horthy regime" is freely used by posterity to describe the political order of the entire interwar period, the term is fully justified only when applied to the years after 1935. Beforehand, as it has been argued on these pages, the hub of the political system was the machine controlled by the prime minister who, on account of this control, had the chief responsibility for the conduct of state business. But thereafter the machinery of the state became increasingly paralyzed, and the regular conduct of public affairs required a powerful arbitrator standing over the hubbub of administrative and party politics. More by default than by design

---

[130] Premier Kállay writes in his memoirs that he could only confide in the Foreign Affairs Committee of the Upper House, presided over by former Foreign Minister Coloman Kánya, and seek the advice of its members, including Bethlen, Sigray, George Prónay, "several Jews and baptized Jews." Another author meanwhile identifies Horthy's closest advisers as Bethlen, Chorin, Goldberger, Count Maurice Eszterházy, Keresztes-Fischer, Ullein-Reviczky, and Eugene Ghyczy. The first four of these seven were members of the Upper House. See Kállay, *Hungarian Premier*, pp. 185-186; Karsai, *A budai vártól*, p. 275.

Diagram

Overview of Parliamentary Parties and Factions, 1939-1944

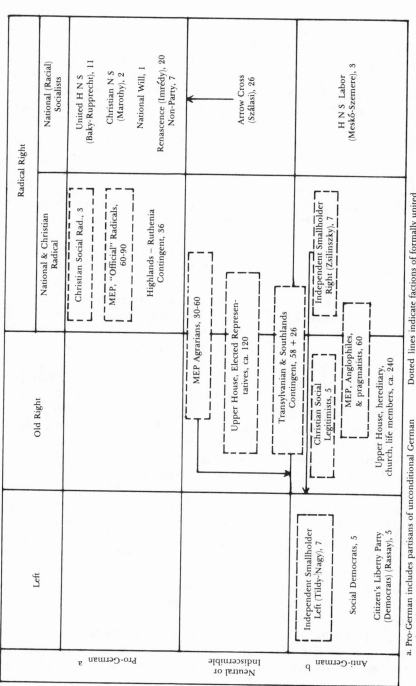

a. Pro-German includes partisans of unconditional German orientation.

b. Anti-German includes Anglophiles, "pragmatists," Turanists, and those of an "eastern," Balkan-Slav orientation.

Dotted lines indicate factions of formally united parties.

Arrows indicate shifts in position over the years 1939-1944.

Horthy assumed this role. He performed it more or less effectively by virtue of his prestige with most right-wing groups, whether radical or conservative. The Regency Act of 1937 did not so much create this situation as it acknowledged an already accomplished fact. But whether exercised de facto or de jure, Horthy's powers were still subject to many informal restraints. Precisely because his powers were the function of a delicate equilibrium, he could not eliminate one or the other major faction within the political establishment by fiat, or by means of a coup d'état. In other words, he could only tilt, but not fundamentally alter, the balance of domestic forces. He did so by appointing alternately premiers of opposite political persuasions, and then dismissing them when they went "too far" in asserting their political identity at the expense of their opponents. That in the process he made errors, especially when advancing age took a toll on his judgments, should not be too surprising.

Given the propensities and the constitutional powers of Regent Horthy, the political history of Hungary became one of alternating radical and conservative governments, interspersed with futile attempts to bring the two wings of the establishment together in some form of coalition. Thus the radical government of Gömbös (1932-1936) was followed by a government of reconciliation under the ideologically colorless Coloman Darányi, who tried to hammer out a compromise between the "old guard" (of Bethlen) and the "orphans" (of Gömbös). The attempt failed, but when the conservatives had their chance again their man, Béla Imrédy, made his dramatic turnabout to become the champion of radicalism. Imrédy's experiment (1938-1939), as we have seen, was too bold and offensive, and he was forced to resign under circumstances that were narrated above. But instead of an outright conservative government another uneasy coalition followed (1939-1941) under the premiership of Count Paul Teleki, a conservative who in earlier years had acquired some radical and anti-Semitic credentials, but who now tried to balance these by a professed Anglophile orientation in his foreign policy. Contrary to his personal inclinations, however, the drift of world events brought Hungary closer to the Axis powers, and when confronted with the choice of attacking Yugoslavia or resisting Germany, Teleki took the gentleman's way out by committing suicide. His desperate act and prior vacillations prompted the regent to appoint a pro-German and radical premier, Ladislas Bárdossy (1941-1942), under whose tenure of office the country entered the war on the Axis side, first against Yugoslavia, then against the Soviets, and finally, against the western Allies. But Bárdossy was too accommodating towards Germany and too oblivious to the sensitivities of conservatives on the domestic scene. So the opposite faction had its chance once again, as Horthy appointed Nicholas Kállay, an old-style gentry politician, to preside over Hungary's last conservative cabinet (1942-1944).

An examination of the Hungarian political process of the period would be incomplete, however, if we restricted it entirely to a survey of domestic political forces and interests. For after 1938 some of the most important stimuli for political decisions originated from the German Reich, whose leaders had a triple leverage over Hungarian developments: an economic leverage they acquired as the major trading partners of the country[131]; a diplomatic leverage as the arbitrators of Hungary's territorial disputes with her neighbors, Rumania, Czechoslovakia, and Yugoslavia; and finally, a military leverage they exercised by veiled, and later open, threats of occupying the country, which they eventually carried out. This triple leverage was used chiefly to steer the country on a pro-Axis course, and to maximize the country's contribution to the German war effort. But domestic politics were not immune from German influence either. While Germany was not interested in sweeping agricultural reforms that would have interfered with the flow of comestibles from the country, German leaders did persistently, indeed obsessively, pressure Hungarian governments to seek more radical solutions to the Jewish "problem."[132] Inevitably therefore, the German nexus furthered the social and political designs of the radical Right.

Whatever the motor forces behind them, these designs made considerable headway between 1938 and 1944 when the partisans of radicalism succeeded in enacting a number of measures that, together with the accompanying official rhetoric, gave public life a distinctly fascist color. Yet, at the same time conservative influence both inside and outside the formal structure of government remained sufficiently strong to slow down the pace of radicalization, and to blunt the edge of radical legislative acts by quiet bureaucratic or political sabotage. As a result, throughout these years there remained a considerable discrepancy between radical political form and conservative political substance.

In domestic affairs, the radicals scored their most important vic-

---

[131] In 1939 Hungary sent 52.2 percent of her exports to Germany, and exactly the same percentage of her imports originated from there. Iván Berend and György Ránki, *Magyarország a fasiszta Németország életterében* [Hungary in the economic space of fascist Germany] (Budapest: Közgazdaságtani Kiadó, 1960), p. 189.

[132] For an excellent summary of these, see Mario D. Fenyo, *Hitler, Horthy and Hungary* (New Haven: Yale University Press, 1972), pp. 66-78.

tories by enacting a number of increasingly repressive measures designed to curtail Jewish economic and civil rights. Thus the discriminatory, but relatively mild Jewish law of 1938 (Public Law xv/1938) was soon superseded by a much harsher second act (Public Law IV/1939), the articles of which introduced a new, stricter definition of Jewishness—one parent born into the Jewish faith—and reduced the number of exemptions. This act cut occupational quotas from twenty to six percent in the professions, and to twelve percent of the payroll of salaried employees in business, quotas that were to be attained not by attrition but by the hiring of gentiles or the dismissal of Jewish personnel.[133] As a result of these measures, tens of thousands lost their regular source of income.[134] But other acts were still to follow. Thus Public Law xv/1941 forbade marriage between Jews and gentiles; Public Law xII/1942 called for the expropriation of Jewish landholdings and Public Law xIV of the same year, passed as a summary of a number of earlier ministerial decrees, excluded Jews from the regular army, consigning them to auxiliary labor units.[135]

While it may well be argued that the conservative establishment could have done more than it actually did to stem the fascist tide, its prominent members did fight these laws in caucus, in the private chambers of the regent, and on the floors of both houses of parliament, where the resistance was led by Bethlen, Count Sigray, Baron Prónay, and other members of the aristocracy.[136] And if these conservative politicians failed to prevent the passage of the bills, or were unsuccessful in attaching some of their pet amendments to them—

[133] Lévai, *Fekete könyv*, pp. 36-42; Sipos, *Imrédy*, pp. 84-85.

[134] The estimated effect of the Second Jewish Law was to dislodge 50,772 employees, and to diminish Jewish wealth by 1.5 billion Pengő (representing 18.75 percent of Jewish assets, and 4.2 percent of total national wealth). See Miklós Kósa, *Hová, mivel, hogyan?* [Where to, with what, and how?] (Budapest: Published by the author, 1941).

[135] The last two of these measures were passed under the tenure of the Kállay government, a fact that has raised justified questions concerning the genuineness of its whiggish credentials, especially in view of the shrillness of one of Kállay's parliamentary speeches in March 1942. But in his memoirs (*Hungarian Premier*, p. 70) Kállay reminds us that he inherited the bills from his predecessors, that the labor service was already in effect, and that he was bending to intense German pressure when submitting them to parliament. Kállay also maintains that he had no intention to carry out the provisions of the laws meticulously, and that he so advised some of the leading members of the Jewish community. Kállay's version is supported by the subsequent statements of Messrs. Stern and Chorin (Lévai, *Fekete könyv*, p. 65; Vida, "Három Chorin levél," p. 373), by the tardiness with which the provisions of Public Law xII were executed, and by Kállay's choice of the liberal General Nagy to supervise the execution of Public Law xIX. See below.

[136] Lévai, *Fekete könyv*, p. 50.

such as exemptions for all members of the nobility—the summary result of their intervention was still to mitigate the harshness of the legislation.[137] Thus while tens of thousands suffered from economic deprivation and were reduced to the status of second-class citizens, for the time being at least, Hungarian Jews were spared the worst features of the Nuremberg laws that the radicals of the Right held up as a model for the Hungarian legislators. Accordingly, up until the German occupation of the country in March 1944, the Jewish citizenry of Hungary was not subjected to restrictions on personal freedom or domicile, the expropriation of personal property, or the wearing of discriminatory insignia.

The only somber exception to the rule were the Jews in the auxiliary labor force who, together with other "unreliables,"[138] were attached to front-line units under the supervision of right-wing radicals in the corps of officers. Members of these units were required to wear yellow arm bands—white for gentiles and converts—and, more often than not, were subject to gross abuse as well as needless jeopardy to life and limb.[139] To remedy the situation, the conservative Kállay government appointed General Nagybaczoni-Nagy, an officer of pro-Jewish sympathies, minister of defense in November 1942. His appointment brought about immediately noticeable improvements.[140] But then came the great military debacle of January 1943, and in the general confusion of the retreat, thousands of forced laborers perished, together with tens of thousands of the regular army.[141] Their ranks were soon replenished by new recruits, whose treatment deteriorated once General Nagy had been forced out of the Ministry of

---

[137] This opinion is shared by a number of writers favorable to the legislation. See Schickert, *Die Judenfrage in Ungarn*, p. 237; János Makkai, *A zsidótörvény* [The Jewish law] (Budapest: Egyetemi Nyomda, 1939), p. 41.

[138] At the end of 1941, there were 14,413 Jews and 6,319 non-Jews among those called up for auxiliary labor service. Randolph L. Braham, *The Hungarian Labor Service System, 1939-1945* (Boulder and New York: East European Quarterly and Columbia University Press, 1977), p. 26.

[139] For a detailed documentation of the travails of labor servicemen, see Elek Karsai, ed., *Fegyvertelenül álltak az aknamezőkön* [Unarmed on the minefields, documents concerning the wartime Hungarian labor service] (Budapest: Magyar Izraeliták Országos Központja, 1962), I-II.

[140] Ibid., I, lxxiv.

[141] While the regular army lost 140,000 of its 200,000 troops, official reports put the losses of the labor units at 23,308. According to various confidential estimates, however, the losses were as high as 43,000 of a total of 50,000. Not all of these losses were casualties. The official report lists 20,234 as missing in action, and the number of those captured by the Soviets was in the thousands. See Braham, *Hungarian Labor Service*, p. 37. Karsai, *Fegyvertelenül*, I, lxxv.

Defense through the successful machinations of a right-wing cabal of politicians and officers.

As so often in analogous situations, the brunt of the economic and physical burdens of discrimination had to be borne by the small men— the Jewish working class, the small merchants and shopkeepers, and to some extent, the professional class—who lacked the cushions of social connections and wealth. Contrariwise, the prosperous were shielded from adversity by the natural sympathies of the conservative establishment for wealth and status, and by its tendency to differentiate sharply between gentlemanly (*úri*) Jews and the rest. Nor was the Jewish economic elite entirely helpless on its own. Its members still had their hands on the arteries of the economy, and possessed an expertise that could only be replaced with difficulty and not without cost to production and the standard of living. This gave them a few chips in the game of covert politics. Moreover, in conservative Hungary rank and wealth had an aura that continued to shine, and it would be some time before a royal Hungarian policeman would raise so much as an eyebrow at a royal privy councillor or baron of the realm, whatever his ancestry.

All these factors naturally conspired to protect property irrespective of the letter or intent of legislation. A case in point is the fate of Jewish landholdings, which became subject to partial expropriation under Public Law iv/1939, and to total expropriation under Public Law xii/1942. While the intent of these laws seemed to be clear-cut, their execution progressed, if at all, in a hesitant and desultory fashion, partly because the laws did not provide for methods of transfer to new owners. There were some inconclusive discussions concerning the future of these properties in both the caucus of the MÉP and the Council of Ministers, as a result of which some land was transferred to the Order of the Gallants, to be distributed more or less as bounty among Right radical stalwarts. In the interim, however, some of the provisions of the law were countermanded by a ministerial decree that permitted the sale of Jewish properties by their legal owners under certain circumstances.[142] Thereafter, a few smaller holdings were registered and expropriated. But, to quote Macartney on the subject, "most of the large estates were never touched at all."[143] The same conclusion was reached by the anti-Semitic Karl Schickert, who in his work on Hungarian Jews complained that, by late 1943, only 149,000 of the 608,593 acres of Jewish owners had been expropriated

[142] Macartney, *October Fifteenth*, ii, 100, n. 3.
[143] Ibid., n. 4.

and redistributed.[144] Even less affected, it seems, were the big industrial concerns in Jewish hands. Given their large aggregate payroll, these enterprises could easily comply with the twelve-percent quota of the second Jewish law simply by adding the requisite quota of gentiles to their boards of directors and staffs of executives. Adding insult to right-wing injury, these appointees were as a rule not selected from among the ranks of militant anti-Semites, but from among the more sympathetic members of the old gentry-aristocratic establishment, whom Stephen Milotay angrily denounced as "Aladárs," a first name of distinctly upper-class flavor, though in the argot of the underworld also used in reference to pimping.[145] Through such expedients, the largest industrial plants thus remained under the effective control of their Jewish owners, and during the war continued to function as before, often making substantial contributions to the war effort of the Axis powers.

Not surprisingly perhaps, conservative resistance was even more effective in defending the economic interests of the landed classes. True, the radicals had made some progress in 1940 in that they put before parliament a land reform bill and secured its enactment as Public Law II of that year. But even before reaching the floor, the bill had "travelled a rugged road."[146] Its scope had been gradually whittled down from 2.6 to 1.2 million acres as a result of the persistent lobbying of conservative aristocrats and Catholic prelates at all levels of the government. When the bill finally reached the floor, it was presented by an agrarian deputy, who pragmatically quoted the exigencies of the times, and added caveats about the dangers inherent in expropriation.[147] And by the time the bill was passed, its last fangs were removed by the attachment of a codicil that provided for a twelve-year period of enforcement, not to begin before the end of the "current European war."[148] In sum, until the very end of the period, the system of large estates remained intact.

The most remarkable accomplishment of the old establishment, perhaps, was the preservation of a degree of political freedom and pluralism in the face of repeated attempts by the radical Right to introduce a one-party dictatorship. True, even compared to the Bethlen years, the civil and political rights of the citizenry had eroded considerably. After 1939, the minister of the interior could detain subversive elements without trial, the minister of defense could call

---

[144] Schickert, *Die Judenfrage in Ungarn*, p. 254.
[145] *Új Magyarság*, April 28, 1940.   [146] Sipos, *Imrédy*, p. 128.
[147] *Napló*, 1940, II, 247-248.   [148] Macartney, *October Fifteenth*, I, 325.

up unreliables for labor service, and the public prosecutor's office could suspend the publication of press organs with relative ease. It is also true that the principles of parliamentarism had been gravely compromised by the practice of co-optation, as a result of which 113 of the 373 members of the House of Representatives in 1942 sat by virtue of appointment rather than election. Nor was parliament as regularly convoked as before. In 1943, by his own admission, Kállay had its sessions adjourned for several months to avoid confrontations with the oppositions of the Left and the Right, both of which he subsequently labeled as nuisances and as impediments to a reasonable policy.[149] But still, for good or ill, and quite often for the benefit of the ultra-Right, the nuisances remained. Hungary persisted as one of the few countries of the Continent, and the only one in East Europe, that permitted the functioning of a multi-party system and some freedom of assembly and of the press. As late as March 1944, the Hungarian press offered a choice among conservative, liberal, socialist, monarchist, Catholic, fascist, and different national socialist points of view, some of them pointedly critical of pathologically sensitive Germany. And when parliament was in session, question-time remained a time for potential embarrassment, for members of the cabinet and the prime minister still had to answer questions concerning their foreign and domestic policies. By means of such questions, the opposition could on occasion directly influence public policy. Thus it was in parliament that Bajcsy-Zsilinszky, by then a major figure in the nationalist and anti-German Independent Smallholders party, revealed and denounced atrocities committed by Hungarian troops in Yugoslavia.[150] This revelation created unprecedented commotion in the House, but eventually led to the indictment and conviction of a number of high-ranking officers before a military tribunal.[151] Less effective, but equally dramatic, was the occasion on which a member of the opposition rose at the brief session of May 24, 1944 to protest the arrest of members of parliament by the German occupation authorities. A similar protest was lodged during the session of September

[149] Kállay, *Hungarian Premier*, pp. 188 and 222-223. It should be noted here that while the proceedings of the House of Representatives between June 1939 and December 1942 occupy sixteen volumes, those between January 1943 and September 1944 are printed in two and a half volumes.

[150] December 5, 1942. *Napló*, xvi, 1942, 490-492.

[151] Fifteen officers, including three generals, were tried; five of them were sentenced to death (Kállay, *Hungarian Premier*, p.109). The detractors of the Kállay government, however, point out that the principal defendants were allowed to escape to Germany, whence they returned in the tow of German troops in March 1944. While Kállay did not engineer this escape, he probably greeted the news of it with relief.

21, 1944, at which time one deputy raised the matter of the deportation of Jewish citizens.[152]

The delicate internal balance of power between radicals and conservatives was also reflected in the conduct of Hungary's foreign policy.[153] Indeed, from 1935 on the governments themselves were often divided on its proper course. Between 1935 and 1939, the radical prime ministers Gömbös and Imrédy favored a closer alignment with Germany, while the cautious and conservative Foreign Minister Kánya (1932-1939) preferred to maintain Hungary's neutrality in the European conflict. In the fateful years of 1939-1941 the cleavage further deepened: Prime Minister Teleki emerged as the leading representative of nonalignment, while his foreign minister, Stephen Csáky, acted as the chief spokesman of radical groups clamoring for an unequivocally pro-German foreign policy. Horthy, a key figure in decision making as the arbiter of this dispute, was of two minds. On the one hand, like most members of his class, he wanted to see the restoration of Hungary's "territorial integrity," and knew that this could not be accomplished without the help of Germany; also, like most officers, he had fond recollections of German-Hungarian comradeship-in-arms during World War I. On the other hand, he regarded Hitler as a loathsome parvenu, and feared national socialism as a revolutionary movement that would subvert the traditional social and international order. Moreover, as a former naval officer, he had considerable respect for British sea power, and doubts about the long-range military prospects of Germany. But if such were his doubts, the quick, unbroken series of German successes, together with the inducements of the boundary changes under the two Vienna Awards, still favored the radical faction in politics, and set the country on a course that anxious conservatives could not effectively change. Thus in 1940 Hungary joined the Tripartite Alliance, and in the next spring, Teleki having committed suicide, the government would support German military action in Yugoslavia. Two months later, following conspiratorial maneuvers bordering on a coup d'état, Hungary entered the war against the Soviet Union and Great Britain.[154]

[152] For these two instances, see *Napló*, 1944, xix, 247 and 254-265.

[153] The best accounts of Hungarian diplomatic maneuverings are Macartney, *October Fifteenth*, ii; Fenyo, *Hitler, Horthy and Hungary*; Gyula Juhász, *Magyarország külpolitikája, 1919-1945* [Hungarian foreign policy] (Budapest: Kossuth, 1969). For personal accounts, see Kállay, *Hungarian Premier*; Stephen D. Kertész, *Diplomacy in a Whirlpool* (South Bend: University of Notre Dame Press, 1953).

[154] German aircraft disguised under Soviet markings bombed the city of Kassa, whereupon Premier Bárdossy and the chief of staff, Henrik Werth, prevailed upon Horthy to declare a state of war between Hungary and the Soviet Union. The extent of de-

This last act was a radical triumph, a fait accompli that committed the country to the fateful war effort of the Axis. Yet as early as August of that year a change of heart and policy were evident in Budapest.[155] The coterie of "defeatist" and Anglophile advisors of the regent recovered from their shock, and apparently reminded Horthy of his old belief in the invincibility of England and its allies. Partly as a result of this, Horthy dismissed General Henrik Werth, the army chief of staff—a man whose role had been critical in bringing about the state of war—even though under prevailing circumstances this dismissal could be construed as a direct affront to Hitler.[156] Immediately afterwards, lobbying began for the withdrawal of the Hungarian contingent from Russia, internally justified by the ever present "Rumanian danger." However, neither the Bárdossy government nor its conservative successor under Kállay were successful in extricating the Hungarian units from the campaign, and the greater part of the expeditionary army eventually perished in the great battles of the Don in January-February 1943.[157] Thereafter, the Kállay ministry refused to put another army in the field, and no Hungarian military units saw front-line duty until the spring of 1944. In the interim, Kállay put out feelers to the Allies, made secret preparations for a surrender—it was hoped, to the western powers—and on September 8, 1943 concluded a secret and conditional armistice with British emmissaries in Constantinople. In later years, this agreement turned out to be an elaborate ruse, designed to mislead German—and possibly, Soviet—intelligence by making references to an Allied landing on the Balkans. But for the time being, its terms secured Hungary immunity from aerial bombardments, while Allied aircraft could roam over the country without interference from the air and ground defenses.

Pyrrhic Victory

This surreptitious, but increasingly brazen conservative-Anglophile course of public policy was abruptly reversed on March 19, 1944. On that day Horthy was detained at Klessheim on a visit to Hitler, while the country was quickly occupied by a force of eleven German divisions. In Horthy's absence, confusion reigned in the military com-

---

ception, and the knowledge of the key participants thereof, are matters of historical debate. But the fact remains that war was declared without consulting either parliament or Horthy's coterie of conservative elder statesmen.

[155] Fenyo, *Hitler, Horthy and Hungary*, p. 30.

[156] Werth was asked to resign only a few days after Hitler asked that he be made a member of the delegation to visit Germany. Ibid.

[157] See n. 141 above.

mand and except for one garrison in Transdanubia the Hungarian army offered no resistance. Together with the army, German police units entered Budapest with instructions to round up all anti-fascist elements, not only the members of the "Jewish Left" but those of the conservative old guard was well. Thus together with a number of Socialist, Democrat, and Independent Smallholder deputies—among them Bajcsy-Zsilinszky, whom the Gestapo apprehended after a gun duel—the German security police also arrested and subsequently deported to Buchenwald Count Sigray of the monarchists and Keresztes-Fischer, the longtime minister of the interior. Kállay sought asylum in the Turkish embassy, where he eventually surrendered and was transported likewise to a concentration camp. Bethlen, the chief culprit in German eyes, eluded his captors.

The regent was allowed to return nevertheless, and under duress appointed a new cabinet. Presided over by Döme Sztójay, Hungary's former ambassador to Berlin, this cabinet consisted of politicians from Imrédy's Party of Renascence and from the radical wing of the Government party, together with two national socialists, L. Endre and L. Baky, appointed under German instructions as secretaries of state in the Ministry of Interior in charge of "Jewish affairs." As part of an overall agreement—hammered out with Hitler, and his personal emissary to Hungary, Edmund Veesenmeyer—Horthy was to remain head of state, though he was to retire from the active conduct of affairs and give his cabinet free hand in the shaping and execution of policy. The Hungarian army and economy were to be fully mobilized. The Jewish question was to be solved without meddling by either the regent or the parliament, which henceforth would be convened only for three brief, and largely pro forma, sessions. The political aspects of these arrangements were to be overseen by Veesenmeyer, while the solution of the Jewish problem was placed under the supervision of Adolf Eichmann, who was dispatched to Hungary immediately after the entry of German troops. Within a few days after his arrival, a new Jewish law was promulgated by order of council, rather than by act of parliament. It decreed that all persons designated as Jewish wear a discriminating mark, be concentrated in designated areas, and subjected to various restrictions. A few weeks later, by secret order of the Ministry of Interior, the deportation of the Jewish population began from the provincial cities and the countryside.[158]

While now the radicals were at the helm, their victory had been a

[158] Some 223.3 thousand persons from the territory of Trianon Hungary, another 292.2 thousand from territories reannexed after 1938 (according to the estimates of the World Jewish Congress). See Braham, *Hungarian Labor Service*, p. 120.

309

hollow one, for it was hard to overlook the fact that they had been put in power by a foreign army. To most, the German presence in the country was a source of acute embarrassment, and the "solution" of the Jewish problem was not only too brutal, but produced no tangible economic benefits for the state. Indeed, the very opposite was the case, for in a startling move, the German SS had seized control of the country's twenty or so largest industrial companies, among them the Manfred Weiss Plant of Csepel. The Germans granted safe passage to the owners and their families in exchange for their assets in the country.[159] Meanwhile the assets of lesser Jewish companies, together with the personal property of the rest, were looted by uncontrollable mobs, or by officials put in charge of the inventories.

Such was the state of government and country when, in the early summer of 1944, the conservative phoenix reemerged from its ashes, and, for the very last time in Hungarian history, attempted to take control of the rudderless ship of state. The initiative was taken by Bethlen who, while still in hiding, wrote Horthy a long memorandum on June 25. It was to be the swan song of the man, and of the whiggish principles he represented in Hungarian politics. In it, he roundly condemned the "inhuman and stupid persecution of Jews with which the present government stain[ed] the Hungarian name . . . and threaten[ed] to corrupt once and for all large segments of gentile society," then urged the regent to "chase away the present cabinet from its place," concentrate the Hungarian troops in the country proper, appoint a new government of non-political experts, and sue for armistice.[160] Prodded further by the pleas of neutrals, and his resolve stiffened by continuing German reverses on the front, Horthy complied. On June 30, he ordered Endre and Baky dismissed from their posts as secretaries for Jewish affairs. A week later he ordered a loyal armored division to foil a planned coup by Baky, and an attempt by the German SS units to start the deportation of Jews from the capital. He was less successful on July 17 when he tried to dismiss the entire Sztójay cabinet. Veesenmeyer remonstrated, and Horthy backed down in the face of open threats. But by late August, the military situation deteriorated further. Rumania surrendered and in the ensuing confusion Horthy did appoint a new cabinet. Following Bethlen's advice, it consisted mostly of generals and statesmen of the

---

[159] The owners and their families were flown to Lisbon by aircraft provided by the SS. On the transaction itself, see Francis Chorin's memorandum to Horthy, May 17, 1944. *Horthy Miklós titkos iratai* [Secret papers of Nicholas Horthy], ed. Miklós Szinai and László Szücs (Budapest: Kossuth, 1962), pp. 440-442.

[160] Ibid., pp. 458-464.

old school, loyal to the regent. The mandate of the new premier, Géza Lakatos, was to negotiate an armistice agreement.

The agony of Hungarian conservatives at this critical juncture must be appreciated by the historian. On the one hand, they faced arrest and deportation by the Germans whose troops and security police were present in the country. On the other, they were convinced that the arrival of the Soviet troops would not only doom their social position, but their physical existence as well. Nor were their expectations entirely groundless. In the course of the next few months some of them, including Horthy himself, landed in Dachau and Buchenwald, while others, including Bethlen, were marched off in the opposite direction, never to be seen again in their own country. Standing between the devil and the deep sea, the conservatives were bound to be halfhearted, and it should not come as a surprise to anyone that their attempt to surrender on October 15 was bungled from beginning to end.

Following this unsuccessful attempt to surrender to the Soviets, a German coup d'état liquidated the last vestiges of the old regime, and replaced Horthy's regency with the Arrow Cross regime of Francis Szálasi. By then, however, the Soviet army was at the gates of Budapest, which was soon to be subjected to a devastating siege. Thus, the authority of the new Hungarist state became effective only over a few thousand square miles of Transdanubia, where the front line quickly moved as far west as Lake Balaton. Under such inauspicious conditions, Szálasi was reduced to a world of fantasy that left little room for social or institutional experiments. By decree, the state was transformed along modern corporatist lines, with rights of representation granted to fifteen autonomous functional groups, among them soldiers, workers, traders, peasants, and mothers.[161] In reality, however, the principle of functional autonomy clashed with the Arrow Cross' totalitarian repudiation of institutional and legal restraints.[162] In the absence of such restraints, statecraft deteriorated into a reign of terror against erstwhile opponents, the evaders of universal conscription, and, above all, against the remaining Jews, now largely concentrated around Budapest. Toward the latter, Szálasi personally

---

[161] Karsai, *A budai vártól*, p. 612; Macartney, *October Fifteenth*, ii, 444, n. 4; Teleki, *Nyilas uralom*, p. 251.

[162] Characteristically, when the professors of the relocated universities asked to exercise their traditional autonomy, Rajniss, member of the Arrow Cross Council of State, denounced them as "old stuffed heads," and "asses," who had not yet understood the spirit of the changing times. He then threatened to teach them "a lesson about autonomy that they [would] never forget." See Karsai, *A budai vártól*, p. 612.

may have favored a more "humane" solution of forced labor and eventual resettlement in some remote part of the world.[163] But his subalterns introduced their own final solution by indiscriminate killings and forced marches in the winter of 1944-1945.[164]

The Hungarian Arrow Cross regime lasted for a period of 170 days, a month or so longer than the revolutionary experiment of the Left in 1919. Like the latter, the former was overthrown by force of arms, and when this force prevailed the country not only changed its form of government, but also its place within the larger, global system. At the same time, the global system also passed through a significant threshold of historical development. In the place of loosely structured networks of nation states, there arose more tightly knit regional and ideological blocs, competing with each other for military and political supremacy. Within this new global system, Hungary would belong neither to the First, nor to the Third, but to what came to be known as the Second World, with its own peculiar problems and dynamics that will be better examined elsewhere.

[163] See above, n. 81; also E. L. Carsten, *The Role of Fascism* (Berkeley: University of California Press, 1969), p. 180.

[164] The number of Jews to perish between October 1944 and April 1945 is set at 85,453. See Braham, *Hungarian Labor Service*, p. 120, and Teleki, *Nyilas uralom*, p. 136.

Conclusions

THE POLITICS OF BACKWARDNESS

From this study of Hungarian history, the age of modernity emerges as one of far-reaching social and political changes stimulated by the technological revolutions of the Occident. This formulation takes us back to the works of Comte, Marx and Spencer, although the conventional concept of modernization will require substantial modifications. For upon a closer examination of the evidence we will find that we deal not with a single process, but two separate processes. One, the process of innovation in the Occident; two, the gradual diffusion of these innovations from the core area to the peripheries of the world system. The dynamics of these two processes vary considerably. These variations will permit us to identify two distinct patterns of social and political change.

The dynamics of the process of innovation may be gleaned from some of the major events of western history between the sixteenth and twentieth centuries. A convenient point of departure is provided by the epochal changes in the technologies of transport and production, which together accounted for the material progress of the Occident. In turn, material progress gave rise to new social configurations, attitudes and degrees of complexity. Political development and the rise of the modern nation state implied adaptations to these changes, above all to the new complexity of social relations, and to the rise of politically conscious mass publics, by creating new administrative organizations, by subordinating these organizations to the civic polity, and by incorporating the new social element into already existing institutions of representative government. The best example and model for this institutional evolution is provided by the political history of Britain, starting with the establishment of the cabinet system in the eighteenth, and culminating in the gradual extension of suffrage in the nineteenth century.

The dynamics and nature of the process of diffusion meanwhile appear from the Hungarian experience to which this volume has been devoted. Here, too, the rise of the modern state may be loosely linked to technological and material progress. But this progress was not the country's own. Rather, political changes were stimulated by the prog-

313

Conclusions

ress of the core countries, thus reversing the historical experiences of the Occident. This is to say that the modern state took shape before the modern economy; it came into being not as a product, but as a potential instrument of social change. This reversal of the historical "sequences" of development then had important secondary and tertiary consequences, but overall was responsible for the ascendancy of the state over all aspects of social life. For, having been established in a backward society, the state gradually preempted the public in politics, subverted the market by slowing down the commercialization of land and labor, two of the basic commodities of a capitalist economy, and became responsible for a particular pattern of social mobility by diverting talent from entrepreneurship into professional politics. Thus instead of gradual democratization we encountered a progressive narrowing of political regimes; instead of the development of a capitalist economy we could only witness a gradual increase in etatism; and in the place of a "bourgeois society" we would find a society of pariah entrepreneurs, and of political classes competing for the spoils of the state.

The reversal of the historical experiences of the West, however, did not only affect the structure of society, but public attitudes as well. In the Occident, public attitudes had been shaped directly by the industrial and commercial revolutions, leaving few groups untouched in the eighteenth and nineteenth centuries. Of these two revolutions, that of industrialism engraved in the public mind a record of success in dealing with the material and social environment, and instilled in people a deep sense of personal and collective efficacy. If not everybody had become a Robinson Crusoe, most denizens of Britain, Holland or France did come to believe that people had the power to affect their social environment. At the same time, the market economy served as a school for impersonal modes of conduct that are indispensable for the effective functioning of complex societies and large-scale polities. The result in sum was the rise of a modern *Gesellschaft* that is described in the writings of Tönnies, Weber and Mannheim.

Not so in the countries of the periphery, where, as the example of Hungary has shown, public attitudes are shaped by different forces and means. Here, too, to be sure, industrialism and commercialism lurk in the background. But the experience is vicarious. Attitudes are not changed by exposure to the factory or the marketplace, but by distorted images of modern life, disseminated through various networks of communication, above all through the modern educational system which, like the modern state, arises not in response to social exigencies, but in anticipation of them. Through this modern edu-

314

cational system, people do indeed gain a certain insight into the social mechanism, particularly into the vulnerability and manipulability of elites. But these insights are not reinforced by the kind of experience that gives individuals their sense of personal efficacy and autonomy, so important for the effective functioning of a civic polity. What emerges thus is not a western-style *Gesellschaft*, but a fusion between the patterns of a *Gemeinschaft* and a *Gesellschaft*, with elements of the former predominating.

Most significantly, however, the process of diffusion affects attitudes in a peripheral society by means of the international demonstration effect. In the western societies where the epochal innovations of the modern age first struck root, public attitudes toward material standards changed gradually, following the growth of productivity in the economies. As new techniques of production were gaining ground in agriculture and manufacturing, a surplus of goods was created, and began to trickle down from the top toward the bottom of the social pyramid. In the process, the luxuries of yesteryear—body linen, toiletries, better housing, more nutritious food—became necessities of the day, and part of what most people began to regard as the normal condition of life. On the world periphery, however, the process unfolds differently. For, as the Hungarian case suggests, images and expectations are disseminated faster than the means of material improvement, creating a deep sense of relative deprivation, indeed bitter frustration, since between aspiration and fulfillment lie not only marginal differences in degrees of leisure and comfort, but fundamental differences in the quality, and the very quantity, of life. Worse still, economic progress in and by itself will not necessarily alleviate the sense of deprivation, for as the backward country experiences a measure of economic growth, so will, often at a much faster rate, the advanced societies of the core, subverting all the potential political benefits of peripheral development. In the short run, popular discontent may be neutralized by promises of a better future, or by the skillful manipulation of sentiments by political elites. But in the long run, pent-up frustrations are likely to resurface time and again, to act as the single most important destabilizing factor in peripheral politics.

While the relative deprivations of the public at large are mainly of a material nature, stemming from a sense of fundamental injustice about being denied a "condition of life fit for humans," those of the political elites will be of a different character. Elites, by definition, are people with access to the levers of power, who, in a backward society, will rarely be able to resist the temptation of using these levers for the satisfaction of their own material needs. But even if they are

Conclusions

successful in raising their own material condition to a globally accepted standard commensurate with their status, the political elites of backward societies will continue to live with nagging frustrations that arise from invidious comparisons with the status and power of their counterparts in the great economic, cultural and political centers of the world. Whereas the latter govern rich, powerful and sophisticated nations, they themselves preside, in the famous words of one Hungarian, over "little, ugly homelands," often the objects of derision by the denizens of the core countries. Thus the ruling classes of these countries will at best be ambivalent members of the international gentry class, for even if they possess great personal wealth and power, their identity will be stamped with the poverty and backwardness of their country of origin. No less painful to bear than material deprivation, this sense of ambivalence and inadequacy is likely to become a major factor in the quest for change, not only within the narrow confines of the backward country, but also within the larger structure of the world system with its apparent inequities.

VARIATIONS ON THE THEME

If such relative deprivations are perennial facts of life in backward societies, the ideological expressions of these deprivations do undergo transformations over time, reflecting changes in the images of the pioneering core countries, as well as in the legitimacy of the larger world system. Variations on the general theme of peripheral politics should therefore be approached from this vantage point, rather than from the perspective of developmental stages in a teleological scheme of history.

To follow a chronological outline, we may begin to examine these variations by recounting some of the characteristics of the nineteenth-century world system. Its central feature, of course, was that it was dominated by the nations of the Occident, whose own ideology, liberalism, provided both a model for social behavior and a coherent justification for the prevailing global division of labor and resources. Significantly, the acceptance of the model and justification was universal, or near-universal. Traditional conservatism was on the decline, and while radicals (like the Hungarian Forty-Eighters) frequently challenged liberal incumbents, they did so by invoking their very own doctrine, castigating their opponents for being liberal only in name and not in substance.

True, in the process of transferring liberal symbols and institutions from the core to the periphery, the original meanings attached to them underwent significant transformations. But even after the "corruption" of liberalism, some elements of the original formula and intent remained intact. Thus with respect to economics, liberal elites maintained their commitment to material progress by industrialization, while in politics they never abandoned their cardinal principle that the power of the state should not be absolute, but subject to legal and institutional restraints. It was mainly on account of this commitment that revolutionaries were acquitted in the courts of St. Petersburg, Budapest and Bucharest, and that irate policemen in these cities would chase rambunctious student radicals to the gates of the universities, but not one step beyond, lest they violate the institution's territorial autonomy and integrity. Violations of legal norms did, of course, occur. But peripheral elites—prime ministers, judges, chiefs of police, and perhaps even village gendarmes—were too deeply imbued with the desire to be seen as "civilized" human beings to stray too far from certain universally accepted norms of public conduct by engaging in the wholesale massacre or degradation of their own citizens. If they still did so, their excesses were not only roundly condemned, but often rectified by direct intervention on the part of powerful and self-righteous core governments.

The fatal weakness of this system was that it had been rendered illegitimate by the perversion of its own charter and identity. Thus it was regarded as corrupt long before, and irrelevant after, the general ideological decline of liberalism. Indeed, the liberal states of the periphery were rendered impotent by their single most attractive feature, the modicum of public liberties and dignity they were willing to grant to their citizens. To put it in different words, today as much as in the past, neo-liberal, pro-western regimes suffer from a basic incongruity between their professed goals and the available means. As a result, they become repressive enough to be resented as nondemocratic, or even anti-democratic, but they are not repressive enough to be able to break through the web of traditional vested interests, and other barriers to the progress of their economies. In this respect, the dilemmas of Tisza and Bethlen earlier in this century are strikingly similar to those of Chiang Kai-shek, Diem, and Reza Pahlavi in more recent years.

These contradictions notwithstanding, the crisis of peripheral liberalism was brought forth only by the decline of the collective charisma of the Occident. The reasons for this decline have been examined above and need not be reexamined here. Suffice it to say that after 1900, and even more so after 1918, the core countries of the West were no longer regarded as knights in shining armor. Even as their

317

material conditions and technological sophistication continued to advance, the sermons about their own virtue, and about the superior qualities of their civilization, began to sound hollow. And as the charisma of the global elite of industrial democracies was fading, so was the magnetism of their institutions, and of their model for the solution of human problems.

To be sure, even after World War I, this crisis of legitimacy was not universal, and it did not result in the overnight disappearance of liberal neo-corporatism from the periphery. Rather, the peripheral political spectrum now became divided between those still committed to the old, highly imperfect institutions of peripheral liberalism, and those who, under the new national radical label, clamored for a new economic, social and political design. In Hungary, these two camps were represented by the partisans of the two Tiszas and Bethlen on the one hand, and by the followers of Gömbös, Imrédy and Sztójay on the other. This split had many parallels in prewar East Europe and Latin America. But it has even more numerous counterparts in the contemporary world. The cases of Faruk versus Nasser, Idrin versus Khadaffi, Aramburu versus Peron, the Shah versus the Ayatollah, are only some of the most obvious and best-known examples.

Whether in the past or present, the differences between these two camps arise not out of ends but out of chosen means. For while both liberals and national radicals espouse the welfare and power of the national state, the radicals eschew the liberal institutional design, and propose to attain their objectives by casting off all legal and moral restraints. In international relations this implies the rejection of the principles of comity among states, in domestic affairs the espousal of economic mobilization within the organizational context of the one-party state.

The problem with this Nietzschean design is that while the national radical can proudly eschew the "hypocrisy" and "bourgeois sentimentality" of institutional restraints, he cannot easily rid himself of the restraints imposed on him by the logic of his own design, above all by the logic of development within a nationalist frame of reference. In order to mobilize the people and the resources of a backward society effectively, great sacrifices are required from broad segments of the population. The imposition of these sacrifices, in turn, often necessitates terror and massive violence, methods that the radical nationalist will find hard to apply against the very constituency he has set out to save. A few recalcitrant members of the national community may be cast out as alien in spirit. But it will be more difficult to cast out the large and inert rural masses from the national community, or to sacrifice them on the altar of economic expediency. This being

318

the case, the ruthlessness of the national radical will eventually turn to ethnic minorities and other aliens in the midst of the nation: compradores, foreign companies, and, above all, ethnic entrepreneurs. If Nasser, Nkrumah, Amin, or other Third World dictators have not been carbon copies of Gömbös, Imrédy or Sztójay in Hungary, their capabilities and limitations have been the same. They all have failed to mobilize an inert peasantry and an exhausted agrarian sector, and ended up expropriating foreigners or liquidating pariah capitalists. The fate of Jews in Hungary and in other East European countries thus anticipated those of the Indians in East Africa, of the Chinese in Indonesia and Malaysia, and of other upwardly mobile groups of outsiders sacrificed by native politicians in the name of nation-building and economic development.

If radical nationalists reject the notions of moral and legal restraint, the revolutionaries of the modern age go one step further, in that they also reject the notion of development. This is to say that they reject the idea that the condition of a given society may be improved by the accumulation of capital, or by the gradual transfer of technologies from the core to the periphery. Thus, despite their considerable differences, the great ideologies of this century, communism, populism, and national—in reality racial—socialism, all go beyond the economic and political designs of modernization, and, instead of proposing to develop the material or spiritual potentialities of individual nations, they set out to change the structure and rules of the larger world system. If the populists envisaged a "green international" in which the agrarian societies of the world could feel secure from the corruptive influences of the industrial capitalist countries, the communists wanted to create a world of equality beyond the nation state. Christian socialists wanted to replace the market with religious morality, while national socialists nurtured the hope of a world of perfect inequality, sustained by the primordial solidarities of a few master races.

For purposes of studying these revolutionary ideologies, the Hungarian case is particularly revealing, because it allows us to study and to juxtapose a plethora of movements. True, populism had few advocates in Hungary, perhaps because by 1900 the country was too far advanced economically to return to the innocence of folk ways. But communism, national socialism (and, to a somewhat lesser extent, Christian socialism) had, at different times, substantial numbers of supporters. This fragmentation of the revolutionary movements is in and by itself an interesting phenomenon that can be only partly explained by the ethnic fragmentation of the counterelite. In part, the reason for the dichotomy must be sought in Hungary's past, and in

Conclusions

her ambivalent position within the larger international community. On the one hand, Hungary was a dispossessed proletarian country of the periphery, where the socialist call for the sharing of international wealth made as much sense as in Russia, or in the Balkan countries. On the other hand, the country had a heroic tradition and was occidental in cultural makeup, an impoverished cousin of the West, so to say, for whom the idea of saving the Occident from its own decadence had a natural appeal.

None of these ideologies and revolutionary movements, of course, has a perfect writ free from internal contradictions. True, whether compared to the liberal or the national radical, the revolutionary of the Left or Right can exact enormous tribute in resources and blood without violating either the letter or the spirit of his own political charter. His formula of millenarian salvation is the formula of total devotion and sacrifice. In its name, the revolutionary can drive thousands, if not millions, into factories, wars, gas chambers, or collective farms, and thus can break through the barriers of traditionalism and neo-corporatism. But if the revolutionary movements of the past and present have been able to break through the formalism of the liberal state, the question still remains what such revolutionary systems can accomplish in the larger scheme of human affairs? This question is especially relevant because so far in human history revolutionary elites of both Right and Left have been fighting their battles from within the boundaries of national states. There the question soon arises whether to continue their struggle relentlessly for a perfect world, or whether to conserve their energies for a more propitious future date. The trouble is that in taking the first option revolutionaries may well destroy themselves—as did the fascist states of the interwar period— while in taking the second, they may jeopardize their revolutionary identity. Accommodations to the imperatives of an orderly economy and polity may well extinguish their revolutionary fervor, and result in the ritualization of their original global objective. For this process of regression, or bureaucratization, the history of the pre-1945 period offers few insights. In order to examine the problem in any detail, we would have to turn to the post-1945 years, an epoch that lies beyond the chronological boundaries of this study.

BACKWARDNESS AND MOBILITY IN THE GLOBAL SYSTEM

Obviously, the narrow focus of inquiry into the affairs of a single country does not allow us to test or develop a grand theory on the sources and origins of international inequality in the modern world.

320

Conclusions

But it should enable us to make a few observations concerning the nature of those "confining conditions"[1] that make it difficult for backward countries to acquire international mobility, that is, to move from the periphery to the center of the global economy.

According to the now popular hypothesis, the most pervasive of these conditions are the dependence of the backward nations on the more advanced ones and the transfer of surplus from one geographical sector of the world economy to another. The problem is, in other words, exploitation of the weak by the stronger members of the international community. This proposition is attractive to many observers of the world scene, for time and again in modern history we have encountered such blatant forms of expropriation. Indeed, in the case of Hungary, too, such exploitation by classical, colonial-mercantilist methods was the order of the day in the eighteenth century, when the Austrian imperial government imposed a highly discriminatory system of tariffs on the country, with the purpose of developing the industries of Bohemia and German Austria at the expense of the consumers of Hungary. But if so, these policies were not long-lived. Thus while Hungarian nationalists never stopped complaining about the depredations of Austria—using many of the phrases of the dependency idiom of our own days—the economic relationship between the two halves of the realm was gradually reversed, until it had reached the point where it could be safely said that Hungary exploited Austria, by refusing to pay her fair share of common defense and overhead expenses, and by forcing upon the empire a system of protective tariffs, highly injurious to Austro-German and Bohemian industrial interests. In sum, contrary to accepted wisdom, the imperial nation was paying an economic price for the empire, and the weaker nation had the subtle means to transfer resources to its own economic sphere.

Likewise, looking at particular segments of economic history, one can make the case that the Hungarian economy suffered from deteriorating terms of trade and from precipitous falls in the price of primary products. Most patently this was true during three chronological periods, the years of 1815-27, 1878-96, and 1929-33. But once again, as this study has attempted to show, the secular consequences of these crises have been grossly exaggerated by historians as well as contemporaries, and a more careful examination of the evidence will show that the crises were preceded and followed by cycles during which the terms of international, and intra-imperial, trade favored the Hungarians. As the most dramatic instances of this, the years

---

[1] Bodenheimer, "Dependency and Imperialism," p. 158.

Conclusions

1790-1815 and 1850-78 may be cited. During these years, the price of primary products soared, while the price of textiles declined in the wake of technological breakthroughs in various manufacturing industries. And if, despite such favorable currents, Hungarians ended up with a negative balance of trade, and in a state of private and public indebtedness, these outcomes cannot be readily attributed to manipulative core behavior or to the labor intensive character of the local economy, but to the rapid redefinition of needs stimulated by the example of new lifestyles in the advanced industrial societies of those days. Nobody, for instance, forced Hungarians to increase their consumption of textiles as fast as they did in the early nineteenth century. But they did so anyway, and in doing so slowed down the rate of domestic saving and increases in the productivity of agriculture. In this way, the international demonstration effect itself became a "confining condition" setting limits to economic development.

Another one of these confining conditions stems from the broader historical context in which the modern state arises in the backward societies of the periphery. In part, at least, the premature rise of the state is the result of the desire of elites to create a modern economy. The problem is that the costs of maintaining a modern state apparatus are likely to become a serious drain on scarce resources, which tends to diminish the purchasing power of the public and to prevent the rise of a viable domestic market. While in some backward societies the consequences are truly stark, in Hungary the state did not prevent a measure of economic development. But the transfer of surplus from the public to the state, from the economy to the polity, may well have been far more substantial than any transfer of surplus from the country to the more developed sectors of the world economy.

If this study thus suggests that at least some reservations are in order concerning the validity of the dependency hypothesis, it also presents us with a note of caution concerning attempts to link successful economic and political development to western culture, or its functional equivalents. Clearly, in the case of Hungary, we did not deal with functional equivalents, but with the culture itself, embodied in a political tradition of legalism, and in a religious experience that included, among others, the Protestant reformation. These elements of the culture, and especially the heritage of religious Calvinism, are closely linked in our minds to modern capitalism, democracy, and to the progressive rationalization of human relations. Yet neither capitalism nor democracy flourished in Hungary, and instead of the progressive rationalization of public attitudes, we have encountered a gradual regression to the value orientations of the traditional *Gemeinschaft*.

But if so, this observation alone should not induce us to cast out culture—the injunctions of collective memories and religious heritage—from the conceptual arsenal of social science. For while the Hungarian case casts doubts on the validity of these starker versions of the cultural hypothesis, it tends to corroborate some of the more subtle and sophisticated formulations, above all, the formulation concerning the persistence of cultural patterns and their importance in shaping certain choices and outcomes. In this respect we may return once more to the example of Hungarian Protestants, whose religious commitments, as we noted, failed to give rise to successful capitalist enterprise in the country. Nevertheless, they did turn out to be entrepreneurs in the political realm, in the bureaucracy, in parliament and the cabinets, over which they presided for forty-five of the seventy-six years of constitutional government. Cultural patterns did, indeed, behave like metal.[2] If they bent under the exigencies of backwardness, they certainly did not melt, or evaporate without a trace.

At any rate, cultural configurations are more relevant as necessary, than as sufficient conditions of economic, social, and political change. Religion and tradition, we are reminded by an astute observer, become truly meaningful only within a hospitable institutional and international environment.[3] The fact that for a hundred years the relative development of European countries barely changed is ample proof that the old, pre-1945 world system did not provide such an environment. Whether the present world system will be able to provide one for today's backward societies may turn out to be its greatest test, and the very condition of survival in an age when international inequalities are keenly felt, yet no longer accepted as legitimate.

[2] For this paraphrase, see Joseph Schumpeter, *Capitalism, Socialism and Democracy*, 3rd ed. (New York: Harper and Row, 1950), p. 12.
[3] Bellah, "Reflections," p. 244.

Bibliography

BOOKS

Acsády, Ignác. *A magyar jobbágyság története* [History of Hungarian serfdom]. 2d ed. Budapest: Faust, 1942.

Ágoston, Péter. *A zsidók útja* [The Jewish way]. Nagyvárad: Társadalomtudományi Társaság, 1917.

Almond, Gabriel A. and Powell, G. Bingham. *Comparative Politics: A Developmental Approach.* Boston: Little Brown and Co., 1966.

Andics, Erzsébet. *A bethleni konszolidáció és a fehér terror* [The consolidation policy of Bethlen and the white terror]. Budapest: Szikra, 1948.

———. *A magyar nacionalizmus kialakulása és története* [Formation and history of Hungarian nationalism]. Budapest: Kossuth, 1964.

Apponyi, Albert. *Memoirs.* New York: Macmillan, 1935.

———. *Ötven év* [Fifty years]. Budapest: Pantheon, 1922.

Apter, David A. *Ghana in Transition.* New York: Athenaeum, 1963.

———. *The Politics of Modernization.* Chicago: Chicago University Press, 1965.

Asboth, János. *Magyar conservativ politika* [Hungarian conservative policy]. Budapest: Légrády, 1876.

Bajcsy-Zsilinszky, Endre. *Helyünk és sorsunk Európában* [Our place and fate in Europe]. Budapest: Gergely, 1941.

———. *A nemzeti radikálizmus* [National radicalism]. Budapest: Stádium, 1930.

Balla, Antal. *A magyar országgyűlés története* [History of the Hungarian parliament]. Budapest: Légrády, 1927.

Ballagi, Géza. *A nemzeti államalkotás kora* [The age of building the national state]. Budapest: Athenaeum, 1897.

Barabási-Kun, Béla, ed. *Tisza emlékkönyv* [Tisza memorial]. Debrecen: Egyetemi Nyomda, 1928.

Bárány, George. *Stephen Széchenyi and the Awakening of Hungarian Nationalism, 1791-1841.* Princeton: Princeton University Press, 1968.

Barátossi-Balog, Benedek. *Japán a felkelő nap országa* [Japan, the country of the rising sun]. Budapest: Published by the author, 1930.

Barta, István. *A fiatal Kossuth* [The young Kossuth]. Budapest: Akadémia, 1964.

———, ed. *Kossuth Lajos az utolsó rendi országgyűlésen* [Kossuth at the last diet of the estates]. Budapest: Akadémia, 1951.*

———, ed. *Kossuth Lajos összes munkái* [Collected works of Kossuth]. Budapest: Akadémia, 1951.*

* Cross-referenced item.

325

Bibliography

Beksics, Gusztáv. *I. Ferenc József és kora* [Francis Joseph I and his times]. Budapest: Athenaeum, 1896.

Belitzky, János. *A magyar gabonakivitel 1860-ig* [Hungarian grain exports until 1860]. Budapest: The Domanovszky Series on the History of Hungarian Agriculture, 1932.

Bendix, Reinhard. *Nation-Building and Citizenship*. New York: Wiley, 1964.

————. *Work and Authority in Industry*. 2d ed. Berkeley: University of California Press, 1974.

Benz, Ernest. *The Eastern Orthodox Church*. Chicago: Aldine, 1963.

Berend, Iván T. and Ránki, György. *A gazdasági elmaradottság* [Economic backwardness]. Budapest: Közgazdaság és Jogi Könyvkiadó, 1979.

————. *Magyarország a fasiszta Németország életterében* [Hungary in the economic space of fascist Germany]. Budapest: Közgazdaságtani Kiadó, 1960.

————. *Magyarország gyáripara, 1900-1914* [The manufacturing industries of Hungary, 1900-1914]. Budapest: Akadémia, 1955.

Bernát, Gyula. *Az abszolutizmus földtehermentesítése Magyarországon* [The land redemption policies of the absolutist government in Hungary]. Budapest: Egyetemi Nyomda, 1935.

————. *Az új Magyarország agrárpolitikája, 1867-1914* [The agrarian policy of the new Hungary, 1867-1914]. Pécs: Egyetemi Könyvkiadó, 1938.

Bernát, István [Stephen]. *Das verpfändete Ungarn*. Budapest: Pátria, 1896.

————. *Tanulmányok az agrárpolitika és a magyar agrármozgalom köréből* [Studies on agrarian policy and the Hungarian agrarian movement]. Budapest: Pátria, 1927.

Bernstein, Béla. *A magyar szabadságharc és a zsidók* [The Hungarian war of independence and the Jews]. Budapest: Franklin, 1898.

Berzeviczy, Albert. *Az abszolutizmus kora Magyarországon* [The age of absolutism in Hungary]. Budapest: Franklin, 1922.

Berzeviczy, Gregorius. *De commercio et industria Hungariae*. Lőcse: Podhoranszki, 1797.

————. *De conditione et indole rusticorum in Hungaria*. Sopron: Joseph Máriássy, 1806.

Bethlen István beszédei és irásai [Speeches and writings of Stephen Bethlen]. 2 vols. Budapest: Genius, 1933.

Bethlen, Stephen [István]. *The Treaty of Trianon and European Peace*. London: Longmans Green Co., 1934.

Bethlen Miklós önéletleírása [The autobiography of Nicholas Bethlen]. 2 vols. Budapest: Szépirodalmi Könyvkiadó, 1955.

Biró, Karl. *Die ungarische Arbeiterbewegung seit dem Sturz der Räterepublik, 1919-1925*. Hamburg: Haym, 1925.

Blum, Jerome. *Noble Landowners and Agriculture in Austria, 1815-1848*. Baltimore: Johns Hopkins University Press, 1948.

Bodrogközy, Zoltán. *A magyar agrármozgalmak története* [History of agrarian movements in Hungary]. Budapest: Egyetemi Nyomda, 1929.

Bódy, Paul. *Joseph Eötvös and the Modernization of Hungary, 1840-1870*. Philadelphia: Transactions of the American Philosophical Society, 1972.

Bibliography

Böhm, Vilmos. *Két forradalom tüzében* [In the crossfire of two revolutions]. Vienna: Bécsi Magyar Kiadó, 1923.

Bontoux, Eugen. *Ungarn und de Ernährung Europas.* Wien: Waldheim, 1861.

Borbiró, Hugó. *Nemzetnevelés* [Educating the nation]. Budapest: Nyilaskeresztes Füzetek, 1937.

Borsányi, György, ed. *Páter Zadravetz titkos naplója* [The secret diary of the Reverend Zadravetz]. Budapest: Kossuth, 1967.*

Braham, Randolph L. *The Hungarian Labor Service System, 1939-1945.* Boulder and New York: East European Quarterly and Columbia University Press, 1977.

Bright, Richard. *Travels from Vienna to Lower Hungary.* Edinburgh: Constable, 1818.

Bunzel, Julius. *Studien zur Sozial- und Wirtschaftspolitik Ungarns.* Leipzig: Duncker and Humblot, 1902.

Camus, Albert. *The Rebel.* New York: Vintage, 1956.

Cardoso, Fernando H. and Faletto, Enzo. *Dependency and Development in Latin America.* Berkeley: University of California Press, 1979.

Carsten, E. L. *The Role of Fascism.* Berkeley: University of California Press, 1969.

Clark, Colin. *The Conditions of Economic Progress.* London: Macmillan, 1940. 2d ed. London: Macmillan, 1951.

Cockroft, James P.; Gunder-Frank, André and Johnson, Dale L., eds. *Dependence and Underdevelopment.* New York: Doubleday, 1972.

Csaplovics, Johann von. *Gemälde von Ungarn.* Pest: Hartleben, 1829.

Czoernig, Karl. *Österreichs Neugestaltung, 1848-1858.* Augsburg and Stuttgart: Crotta, 1858.

Deák, Ferenc. *Beszédek,* 1829-1873 [Speeches]. Budapest: Franklin, 1898.

deSchweinitz, Karl Jr. *Industrialization and Democracy.* Glencoe: The Free Press, 1964.

Dessewffy, Aurél. *Elmélkedés a megnyíló országgyűlés felől* [Thoughts on the forthcoming diet]. Kassa: Werfer, 1839.

Dessewffy, József. *A "Hitel" című munka taglalatja* [A critique of the work "Credit"]. Kassa: Werfer, 1831.

Deutscher, Isaac. *Stalin.* New York: Random House, 1960.

Dobrogeanu-Gherea, Constantin. *Neoiobagia* [Neo-Serfdom]. Bucharest: Socec, 1910.

Domanovszky, Sándor, ed. *Magyar művelődéstörténet* [The cultural history of Hungary]. 4 vols. Budapest: Magyar Történelmi Társulat, 1939.

Eckhart, Ferenc. *A bécsi udvar gazdaságpolitikája Magyarországon, 1780-1815* [The economic policies of the Viennese court in Hungary, 1780-1815]. 2d ed. Budapest: Akadémia, 1958.

————. *Magyar alkotmány és jogtörténet* [Hungarian constitutional history]. Budapest: Politzer, 1946.

————. *A magyar közgazdaság száz éve, 1841-1941* [One hundred years of the Hungarian economy, 1841-1941]. Budapest: Posner, 1941.

Bibliography

Eckhardt, Sándor. *A francia forradalom eszméi Magyarországon* [The ideals of the French Revolution in Hungary]. Budapest: Franklin, 1924.

Eckstein, Alexander. "Economic Development in Hungary 1920-1950." Ph.D. dissertation, University of California, Berkeley, 1952.

Eisenstadt, S. N., ed. *The Protestant Ethic and Modernization*. New York: Basic Books, 1968.

Emmanuel, Arghiri. *Unequal Exchange: A Study of the Imperialism of Trade*. New York: Monthly Review Press, 1972.

Eötvös, József. *A falu jegyzője* [The notary of the village]. Pest: Hartleben, 1845.

———. *Die Garantien der Macht und Einheit Österreichs*. Leipzig: Köhler, 1859.

———. *Báró Eötvös József összes munkái* [Eötvös' collected works]. 20 vols. Budapest: Révai, 1904.

———. *Die Reform aus Ungarn*. Leipzig: Köhler, 1846.

———. *Magyarország 1514-ben* [Hungary in 1514]. Pest: Heckenast, 1847.

Erdei, Ferenc. *Futóhomok* [Quicksand]. Budapest: Athenaeum, 1937.

———. *A magyar falú* [The Hungarian village]. Budapest: Athenaeum, 1938.

Fann, K. T. and Hodges, Donald C., eds. *Readings in U.S. Imperialism*. Boston: Porter Sargent, 1971.

Fellner, Frigyes. *Magyarország nemzeti jövedelme* [The national income of Hungary]. Budapest: Akadémia, 1916.

Fenyo, Mario D. *Hitler, Horthy and Hungary*. New Haven: Yale University Press, 1972.

Ferenczi, Zoltán. *Báró Eötvös József* [Baron Joseph Eötvös]. Budapest: Tudományos Akadémia, 1903.

———. *Deák, Ferenc élete* [The life of Francis Deák]. Budapest: Tudományos Akadémia, 1904.

Finkle, Jason L. and Gable, Richard W. *Political Development and Social Change*. 2d ed. New York: Wiley, 1971.

Futó, Mihály. *A magyar gyáripar története* [History of Hungarian manufacturing industries]. Budapest: Magyar Gazdaságkutató Intézet, 1944.

Gerschenkron, Alexander. *Economic Backwardness in Historical Perspective*. Cambridge: Harvard University Press, 1962.

Gompers, Samuel. *Labor in Europe and America*. New York: Harper, 1910.

Gratz, Gusztáv et al. *A bolsevizmus Magyarországon* [Bolshevism in Hungary]. Budapest: Franklin, 1921.

———. *A dualizmus kora* [The age of dualism]. Budapest: Magyar Szemle, 1934.

———. *A forradalmak kora: Magyarszág története, 1918-1921* [The epoch of revolutions: A history of Hungary, 1918-1921]. Budapest: Franklin, 1935.

———. *The Situation in Hungary*. Budapest: Pallas, 1925.

Grosz, Joseph and Boggs, Arthur W., eds. and trans. *Hungarian Anthology*. 2d ed. Toronto: Pannonia Press, 1966.

Gruntzel, Joseph. *Handelspolitik und Ausgleich in Oesterreich-Ungarn*. Wien: Hoerder, 1912.

Bibliography

Grünwald, Béla. *A felvidék* [The highlands]. Budapest: Ráth Mór, 1878.

———. *Az új Magyarország* [The new Hungary]. Budapest: Franklin, 1890.

Gvadányi, Jozsef. *Egy falusi nótáriusnak budai utazása* [The journey of a village notary to Buda]. Pozsony-Pressburg and Komárom: Weber Simon, 1791.

Hertz, Frederick. *Economic Problems of the Danubian States.* London: Gollancz, 1947.

Hevesi, Gyula. *Egy mérnök a forradalomban* [An engineer in revolution]. Budapest: Europa, 1959.

Hitler, Adolf. *Mein Kampf.* Translated by Ralph Manheim. Boston: Houghton Mifflin, 1971.

Hoitsy, Pál. *Nagymagyarország* [Greater Hungary]. Budapest: Lampel, 1902.

Hollós, Ervin. *Rendőrség, csendőrség, VKF 2* [Police, gendarmerie, and the secret general staff]. Budapest: Kossuth, 1971.

Hóman, Bálint and Szekfű, Gyula. *Magyar történet* [Hungarian history]. 5 vols. Budapest: Egyetemi Nyomda, 1936.

Horthy, Miklós [Nicholas]. *Memoirs.* London: Hutchinson, 1956.

Horváth, Mihály. *Huszonöt év Magyarország történetéből, 1823-1848* [Twenty-five years from the history of Hungary]. 2d ed. 3 vols. Pest: Ráth Mór, 1867.

——— in German. *Fünfundzwanzig Jahre aus der Geschichte Ungarns.* 3 vols. Leipzig: Brockhaus, 1867.

Horváth, Zoltán. *Magyar századforduló* [The turn of the century in Hungary]. Budapest: Kossuth Kiadó, 1961.

Hoselitz, Bert, ed. *The Progress of Underdeveloped Areas.* Chicago: Chicago University Press, 1952.*

Huntington, Samuel P. *Political Order in Changing Societies.* New Haven: Yale University Press, 1968.

Illyés Gyula. *A puszták népe* [The people of the puszta]. Budapest: Nyugat, 1936.

Inkeles, Alex and Smith, David. *Becoming Modern.* Cambridge: Harvard University Press, 1974.

Janos, Andrew C. and Slottman, William B. *Revolution in Perspective: Essays on the Hungarian Soviet Republic.* Berkeley: University of California Press, 1971.*

Jászi, Oszkár [Oscar]. *The Dissolution of the Habsburg Monarchy.* 2d ed. Chicago: University of Chicago Press, 1958.

———. *Magyar kálvária, magyar feltámadás* [Hungarian calvary and resurrection]. 2d Hungarian ed. Munich: Aurora, 1969.

———. *Magyarország jövője és a dunai egyesült államok* [Hungary's future and the Danubian United States]. Budapest: Új Magyarország, 1918.

———. *A nemzeti állam kialakulása és a nemzeti kérdés* [The rise of the national state and the national question]. Budapest: Társadalomtudományi Társaság Könyvtára, 1912.

———. *A történelmi materializmus állambölcselete* [The theory of the state in historical materialism]. Budapest: Társadalomtudományi Társaság Könyvtára, 1908.

Bibliography

————. *A választójog reformja és Magyarország jövője* [The reform of the electoral law and the future of Hungary]. Budapest: Deutsch Zsigmond, 1908.

Juhász, Gyula. *Magyarország külpolitikája, 1919-1945* [Hungarian foreign policy]. Budapest: Kossuth, 1969.

Juhász-Nagy, Sándor. *A magyar októberi forradalom története* [The history of the Hungarian October revolution]. Budapest: Cserépfalvi, 1945.

Kállay, Nicholas. *Hungarian Premier.* New York: Columbia University Press, 1954.

Kann, Robert. *The Multi-National Empire.* New York: Columbia University Press, 1950.

Károlyi, Árpád. *Az 1848-diki törvénycikkek az udvar elött* [The legislative acts of 1848 before the royal court]. Budapest: Magyar Történelmi Társaság, 1936.

Károlyi, Mihály [Michael]. *Faith Without Illusion.* London: Jonathan Cape, 1954.

————. *Fighting the World.* New York: Albert and Charles Boni, 1925.

Karsai, Elek. *A budai vártól a gyepüig, 1941-1945* [From Buda castle to the western frontier]. Budapest: Táncsics, 1965.

————, ed. *Fegyvertelenül álltak az aknamezökön* [Unarmed on the minefields, documents concerning the wartime Hungarian labor service]. 2 vols. Budapest: Magyar Izraeliták Országos Központja, 1962.

————, ed. *Szálasi Ferenc naplója* [Diary of Francis Szálasi]. Budapest: Kossuth, 1978.*

Katona, Béla. *Die Volkswirtschaft Ungarns.* Budapest: Légrády, 1913.

Kautz, Julius. *Entwicklungsgeschichte der volkswirtschaftlichen Ideen in Ungarn.* Budapest: Grill, 1876.

Kazinczy, Ferenc. *Pályám emlékezete* [Recollections of my career]. Budapest: Franklin, 1900.

Kazusi, Okhawa. *The Growth Rate of the Japanese Economy since 1878.* Tokyo: Kinokiniya, 1957.

Kebschall, Harvey G., ed. *Politics in Transitional Societies.* New York: Meredith, 1968.

Keleti, Károly. *Hazánk és népe* [Our country and people]. Budapest: Ráth Mór, 1889.

————. *Magyarország közgazdasági és müvelödési állapotai* [Hungary's economic and cultural condition]. Budapest: Pesti Könyvnyomda, 1879.

————. *Visszapillantás közgazdaságunk egy negyed századára* [Looking back at a quarter-century of our economy]. Budapest: Akadémia, 1875.

Kemény, Gábor, ed. *Iratok a magyar nemzetiségi kérdés történetéhez Magyarországon a dualizmus korában, 1867-1918* [Documents concerning the nationality problems in Hungary during the period of dualism]. Budapest: Tankönyvkiadó, 1952.

————. *A magyar nemzetiségi kérdés története* [History of the nationalities problems in Hungary]. Budapest: Gergely, 1946.

Kerék, Mihály. *A földreform útja* [The road to land reform]. Budapest: Magyar Élet, 1942.

330

Bibliography

————. *A magyar földkérdés* [The land problem in Hungary]. Budapest: Mefhesz, 1939.

Kéri, Gyula. *A magyar szabadságharc napi krónikákban* [A day-by-day account of the Hungarian war of independence]. Budapest: Franklin, 1899.

Kertész, Stephen D. *Diplomacy in a Whirlpool.* South Bend: University of Notre Dame Press, 1953.

Kessler, Joseph. "Turanism and Pan-Turanism in Hungary, 1890-1945." Ph.D. dissertation, University of California, Berkeley, 1967.

Kiss, István. *Az utolsó nemesi felkelés* [The last feudal levy]. Budapest: Franklin, 1909.

Klein, Bernát. "Hungarian Politics from Bethlen to Gömbös: The Decline of Liberal-Conservatism and the Rise of Right Radicalism." Ph.D. dissertation, Columbia University, 1962.

Kölcsey, Ferenc. *Minden munkái* [Collected works]. 4 vols. Pest: Hackenast, 1866.

Kónya, Sándor. *Gömbös kísérlete a totális fasiszta diktatura megteremtésére* [Gömbös' attempt to create a totalitarian fascist dictatorship]. Budapest: Akadémia, 1968.

Kossuth, Lajos. *Felelet Gróf Széchenyi Istvánnak* [Response to Count Stephen Széchenyi]. Pest: Landerer és Heckenast, 1842.

————. *Összes munkái* [Collected works]. Edited by István Barta. Budapest: Akadémia, 1951.*

Kossuth Lajos az utolsó rendi országgyűlésen [Kossuth at the last diet of the estates]. Edited by István Barta. Budapest: Akadémia, 1951.*

Kovács, Imre. *A néma forradalom* [The silent revolution]. Budapest: Cserépfalvi, 1937.

Kovrig, Béla. *Magyar szociálpolitika és törvényhozás, 1920-1945* [Hungarian social policies and legislation]. New York: Hungarian National Committee, 1954.

———— in English. *Hungarian Social Policies, 1920-1945.* New York: Hungarian National Committee, 1954.

Kubinszky, Judit. *Politikai antiszemitizmus Magyarországon, 1875-1890* [Political anti-Semitism in Hungary, 1875-1890]. Budapest: Kossuth, 1976.

Kühne, Roland. "Geschichte des Getreidehandels und der Getreidepreisbildung in Ungarn." Ph.D. dissertation, Moson-Heidelberg, 1910.

Kun, Béla. *Mit akarnak a kommunisták?* [What do the Communists want?]. Budapest: Kommunisták Magyarországi Pártja, 1919.

Lackó, Miklós. *Nyilasok, nemzetiszocialisták, 1935-1944* [Arrow Crossmen, national socialists, 1935-1944]. Budapest: Kossuth, 1966.

————. *Válságok—választások* [Crises—dilemmas]. Budapest: Gondolat, 1975.

Lakatos, Ernő. *A magyar politikai vezetőréteg, 1848-1918* [The Hungarian political elite, 1848-1918]. Budapest: Élet Nyomda, 1942.

Lerner, Daniel. *The Passing of Traditional Society.* Glencoe: The Free Press, 1958.

Lévai, Jenő. *Fekete könyv a magyar zsidóság szenvedéseiről* [Black book on the sufferings of Hungarian Jewry]. Budapest: Officina, 1946.

331

Bibliography

Levy, Marion, Jr. *Modernization and the Structure of Societies*. Princeton: Princeton University Press, 1966.

Lippay, Zoltán. *A magyar birtokos középosztály és a közélet* [The Hungarian landed middle class and public life]. Budapest: Franklin, 1919.

Lipták, László. *Egy veszedelmes nép* [A dangerous people]. Budapest: Cserépfalvi, 1937.

Lishchenko, P. *History of the National Income of Russia*. Moscow: International Publishers, n.d.

Litván, György. *Magyar gondolat—Szabad gondolat* [Hungarian thinking—free thinking]. Budapest: Magvető, 1978.

Lockwood, William. *The Economic Development of Japan*. Princeton: Princeton University Press, 1954.

Macartney, Aylmer C. *A dunamedence problémái* [Problems of the Danubian basin]. Budapest: Keresztes, 1942.

————. *Hungary*. London: Ernest Benn, 1934.

————. *Hungary and Her Successors, 1919-1937*. New York: Oxford University Press, 1937.

————. *National States and National Minorities*. New York: Oxford University Press, 1934.

————. *October Fifteenth: A History of Modern Hungary, 1929-1945*. 2 vols. Edinburgh: Edinburgh University Press, 1957.

McCagg, William O. *Jewish Nobles and Geniuses in Modern Hungary*. Boulder and New York: East European Quarterly and Columbia University Press, 1972.

McLellan, David, ed. *Karl Marx: Selected Writings*. Oxford: Oxford University Press, 1977.

Maier, Charles S. *Recasting Bourgeois Europe*. Princeton: Princeton University Press, 1975.

Makkai, János. *A zsidótörvény* [The Jewish law]. Budapest: Egyetemi Nyomda, 1939.

————. *Urambátyám országa* [The country of *urambátyám*]. Budapest: Singer and Wolfner, 1942.

Mannheim, Karl. *Man and Society in an Age of Reconstruction*. New York: Harcourt, Brace and World, 1958.

Marczali, Henry. *Hungary in the Eighteenth Century*. Cambridge: The University Press, 1910.

Márki, Sándor. *Az 1848-49-ik évi szabadságharc története* [History of the war of independence of 1848-1849]. Budapest: Athenaeum, 1898.

Marx, Karl. *Capital*. Translated by S. Moore and E. Aveling. 3 vols. New York: International Publishers, 1975.

May, Arthur. *The Habsburg Monarchy, 1867-1914*. Cambridge: Harvard University Press, 1960.

Mercator [pseud.]. *Die Nationalitätenfrage und die ungarische Reichsidee*. Budapest: Ráth, 1908.

Mérei, Gyula. *Mezőgazdaság és agrártársadalom Magyarországon, 1791-1848*

Bibliography

[Agriculture and agrarian society in Hungary]. Budapest: Teleki Pál Társaság, 1948.

Metternich, Clement. *Nachgelassene Papiere.* 8 vols. Wien: Braumüller, 1881-1884.

Migossy, József. *Mit akar a magyar nemzeti szocialista mozgalom?* [What are the aims of the Hungarian national socialist movement?]. Budapest: Nyilaskeresztes Kiskönyvtár, 1936.

Milotay, István. *A függetlenség árnyékában* [In the shadow of independence]. Budapest: Stádium, 1930.

———. *Az új világ felé* [Toward a new world]. 2 vols. Budapest: Stádium, 1942.

Mitchell, B. R. *European Historical Statistics, 1750-1950.* New York: Columbia University Press, 1975.

Mitrany, David. *The Land and the Peasant in Romania.* New Haven: Yale University Press, 1930.

Mitterspacher, Lajos. *Elementa rei rusticae.* Pest: Typis Universitatis, 1794.

Mód, Aladár, ed. *Forradalom és szabadságharc 1848-49-ben* [Revolution and war of independence in 1848-1849]. Budapest: Szikra, 1948.

Molnár, Erik et al. *Magyarország története* [History of Hungary]. 2 vols. Budapest: Gondolat, 1971.

Montgomery, John F. *Hungary: The Unwilling Satellite.* New York: Devin-Aldair, 1947.

Moore, Barrington. *Social Origins of Dictatorship and Democracy.* Boston: Beacon Press, 1966.

Nagy, Zsuzsa L. *A budapesti liberális ellenzék 1919-1944* [The liberal opposition in Budapest, 1919-1944]. Budapest: Akadémia, 1972.

Nagy-Talavera, Nicholas M. *The Green-Shirts and the Others.* Stanford: Hoover Institute Press, 1970.

Pach, Pál Z. *Magyar gazdaságtörténet* [Economic history of Hungary]. 2 vols. Budapest: Tankönyvkiadó, 1963.

Paget, John. *Hungary and Transylvania.* London: John Murray, 1855.

Pap, Dezső. *A magyar szociálpolitika a világháborúban* [Hungarian social policy during the World War]. Budapest: Grill, 1934.

Papp, Jenő. *A mai Magyarország erkölcsrajza* [The moral portrait of contemporary Hungary]. Budapest: Káldor, 1934.

Pardoe, Julia. *The City of the Magyars, or Hungary and Her Institutions in 1839-1840.* London: G. Virtue, 1840.

Páter Zadravetz titkos naplója [The secret diary of the Reverend Zadravetz]. Edited by György Borsányi. Budapest: Kossuth, 1967.*

Pethe, Ferenc. *Pallérozott magyar gazdaság* [Rationalized Hungarian farming]. Sopron: Nemzeti Gazda-Hivatal, 1805.

Petrassevich, Géza. *Zsidó földbirtokosok és bérlők Magyarországon* [Jewish landowners and tenants in Hungary]. Budapest: Stephaneum, 1904.

Pikler, Gyula. *Az emberi egyesületek, különösképen az állam keletkezése és fejlődése* [The origins and development of human associations, and especially of the state]. Budapest: Társadalomtudományi Társaság Könyvtára, 1905.

Bibliography

Polányi, Karl. *The Great Transformation*. Boston: Beacon Press, 1957.

Prest, A. R. *Consumers' Expenditures in the United Kingdom, 1900-1918*. Cambridge, England: The University Press, 1954.

Prohászka, Ottokár. *Produktiv e a pénz?* [Is money productive?] Budapest: Szentistván Társulat, 1898.

Prokopovicz, Serge. *Histoire économique de l'URSS*. Paris: Flammarion, 1952.

Pukánszky, Béla. *Német polgárság magyar földön* [German bourgeoisie on Hungarian soil]. Budapest: Franklin, 1936.

Pulszky, Ferenc. *Meine Zeit, mein Leben*. 2 vols. Pressburg and Leipzig: C. Stampfel, 1883.

Pye, Lucian W. *Aspects of Political Development*. Boston: Little Brown and Co., 1966.

Raith, Tivadar. *Keleteurópa: Ismeretlen föld* [Eastern Europe: The unknown land]. Budapest: Globus, 1927.

Réti, László. *A Bethlen-Peyer paktum* [The Bethlen-Peyer pact]. Budapest: Magyar Történelmi Társaság, 1951.

Rettegi, György. *Emlékezetre méltó dolgok* [Things worth remembering]. Bucharest: Kritérion, 1970.

Rézler, Gyula István [Julius Stephen]. *A magyar nagyipari munkásság kialakulása* [Rise of the working class in great industry]. Budapest: Faust, 1945.

———. *Die soziale und wirtschaftliche Lage der ungarischen Arbeiterschaft*. Budapest, 1942.

Riggs, Fred. *Administration in Developing Countries*. Boston: Houghton and Mifflin, 1964.

———. *Thailand, the Model of a Bureaucratic Polity*. Honolulu: East-West Center, 1966.

Rostow, Walt W. *The Stages of Economic Growth*. Cambridge, England: The University Press, 1962.

Rubinek, Gyula. *Vámpolitikai kérdések* [Problems of tariff policy]. Budapest: Stephaneum, 1904.

Rumy, Károly. *Populäres Lehrbuch der Oekonomie*. Wien: Schaumburg, 1808.

Salacz, Gábor. *A magyar kulturharc története* [History of the Hungarian culture struggle]. Pécs: Egyetemi Könyvkiadó, 1938.

Sándor, József. *Az EMKE megalapitása* [The founding of the Transylvanian Hungarian Cultural League]. Kolozsvár: EMKE, 1910.

Sándor, Nicolaus. "Die Lage der ungarischen Landarbeiter." Ph.D. dissertation, Leipzig, 1911.

Sándor, Pál. *A XIX. századvégi agrárválság Magyarországon* [The agrarian crisis of the end of the 19th century]. Budapest: Akadémia, 1958.

Schickert, Klaus. *Die Judenfrage in Ungarn*. Essen: Essener Verlag, 1943.

Schmitter, Philippe. *Interest Conflict and Political Change in Brazil*. Stanford: Stanford University Press, 1971.

Schumpeter, Joseph. *Capitalism, Socialism and Democracy*. 3rd ed. New York: Harper and Row, 1950.

Schwartner, Martin. *Statistik des Königreichs Ungern*. Ofen-Buda: Gedruckt mit königlichen Universitätsschriften, 1809.

334

Bibliography

Sebess, Dénes. *Magyar agrárevolúciok* [Hungarian agrarian evolutions]. Budapest: Egyetemi Nyomda, 1933.

Serédi, Jusztinián, ed. *Emlékkönyv Szt. István király halálának kilencszázadik évfordulójára* [Memorial for the nine-hundredth anniversary of the death of King St. Stephen]. 3 vols. Budapest: Akadémia, 1938.*

Serres, Marcel de. *Voyage en Autriche.* Paris: A. Bertrand, 1814.

Seton-Watson, Robert W. *Electoral Corruption and Reform in Hungary.* London: Constable, 1911.

————. *Racial Problems in Hungary.* London: Constable, 1908.

Sieghart, Rudolf. *Zolltrennung und Zolleinheit.* Vienna: Manz, 1915.

Simonyi, Iván. *Judaismus und die parlamentarische Komödie.* Pressburg: Published by the author, 1883.

Sipos, Péter. *Imrédy Béla és a Magyar Megújulás Pártja* [Béla Imrédy and the Party of Hungarian Renascence]. Budapest: Akadémia, 1970.

Spira, György. *A magyar forradalom 1848-49-ben* [The Hungarian revolution of 1848-1849]. Budapest: Gondolat, 1959.

Spohr, Ludwig. *Die geistigen Grundlagen des ungarischen Nationalismus.* Berlin and Leipzig: Walter de Gruyter, 1936.

Springer, Rudolf [Karl Renner]. *Grundlagen und Entwicklungsziele der österreichischen Monarchie.* Vienna and Leipzig: F. Deuticke, 1906.

Stallings, Barbara. *Economic Dependency in Africa and Latin America.* Beverly Hills-London: Sage Publications, No. 01-031, 1972.

Süle, Tibor. *Sozialdemokratie in Ungarn.* Köln: Böhlen, 1967.

Sulyok, Dezső. *Magyar tragédia* [Hungarian tragedy]. Newark: Published by the author, 1954.

Surányi, Miklós. *Bethlen.* Budapest: Singer és Wolfner, 1927.

Szabó, Ervin. *A munkásmozgalom 1903-ban* [The labor movement in 1903]. Budapest: A Huszadik Század Kiskönyvtára, No. 2, 1904.

————. *Társadalmi és pártharcok az 1848-49-es magyar forradalomban* [Social and political conflicts in the Hungarian revolution of 1848-1849]. Vienna: Bécsi Magyar Kiadó, 1921.

Szabó, István. *Tanulmányok a magyar parasztság történetéből* [Studies from the history of the Hungarian peasantry]. Budapest: Athenaeum, 1948.

Szabó, Zoltán. *A tardi helyzet* [Report on the village of Tard]. Budapest: Cserépfalvi, 1937.

Szabolcs, Ottó. *A köztisztviselők az ellenforradalmi rendszer társadalmi bázisában, 1920-26* [Public employees within the social structure of the counter-revolutionary regime]. Budapest: Akadémia, 1965.

Szakács, Kálmán. *Kaszáskeresztesek* [Scythe-crossmen]. Budapest: Kossuth, 1963.

Szálasi, Ferenc. *Cél és követelések* [Aims and demands]. Budapest: A Nemzet Akaratának Pártja, 1935.

Szálasi Ferenc naplója [Diary of Francis Szálasi]. Edited by Elek Karsai. Budapest: Kossuth, 1978.*

Szálasy [Szálasi], Ferenc. *A magyar állam felépítésének terve* [Plan for the building of the Hungarian state]. Budapest: Egyetemi Nyomda, 1933.

335

Bibliography

Széchenyi, István. *Beszédei* [Speeches of Stephen Széchenyi]. Edited by Antal Zichy. Budapest: Történelmi Társaság, 1897.*

————. *Hirlapi cikkei* [The newspaper articles of Count Stephen Széchenyi]. Edited by Antal Zichy. Budapest, 1894.*

————. *Irói és hirlapi vitája Kossuth Lajossal* [Count Széchenyi's literary and journalistic polemics with Louis Kossuth]. Edited by Gyula Viszota. Budapest: Magyar Történelmi Társulat, 1927.*

————. *Hitel* [Credit]. 3rd ed. Fontes Series. Budapest: Magyar Tudományos Akadémia, 1930.

————. *Világ* [Enlightenment]. In *Széchenyi István művei* [Collected works]. Budapest: Tudományos Akadémia, 1903-1904.

Szekfű, Gyula, ed. *A mai Széchenyi* [Topical Széchenyi]. Budapest: Magyar Szemle Társaság, 1934.

————. *Három nemzedék és ami utána következik* [Three generations, and whatever has happened after them]. 3rd ed. Budapest: Egyetemi Nyomda, 1935.

Szterényi, József. *Die ungarische Industriepolitik*. Wien: Hofverlag, 1913.

Szücs, Ábrahám. *A pipás nemesek véleménye az adó, háziadó, örökváltság, hitel, ősiség, és a magyar nyelv iránt* [The opinion of pipe-smoking nobles on matters of taxation, the house tax, redemption, credit, entail, and the use of the Magyar language]. Kecskemét: Szilády, 1844.

Teleki, Eva. *Nyilas uralom Magyarországon* [Arrow Cross rule in Hungary]. Budapest: Kossuth, 1974.

Tisza, István. *Magyar agrárpolitika* [Hungarian agrarian policy]. Budapest: Athenaeum, 1897.

Tőkés, Rudolf. *Béla Kun and the Hungarian Soviet Republic*. New York: Praeger, 1967.

Tömöry, Márta. *Új vizeken járok: A Galilei kör története* [On uncharted waters: history of the Galileo Circle]. Budapest: Gondolat, 1960.

Townson, Robert. *Travels in Hungary*. London: Robinson, 1797.

Troeltsch, Ernst. *Protestantism and Progress*. Boston: Beacon, 1958.

Tucker, Robert C., ed. *The Marx-Engels Reader*. New York: Norton, 1972.

Vadnay, Andor. *A Tiszamellékről* [Report about the Tisza region]. Budapest: Budapest Hirlap, 1900.

Vámbéry, Rusztem. *Hungary: To Be or Not To Be*. New York: Ungar, 1946.

Varga, Jenő. *A magyar tanácsköztársaság gazdasági szervezete* [The economic structure of the Hungarian Soviet Republic]. Berlin: Kommunista Kiskönyvtár, 1921.

Viszota, Gyula, ed. *Gróf Széchenyi István írói és hirlapi vitája Kossuth Lajossal* [Count Széchenyi's literary and journalistic polemics with Louis Kossuth]. Budapest: Magyar Történelmi Társulat, 1927.*

Wallerstein, Immanuel. *The Modern World System*. New York: Academic Press, 1974.

Warriner, Doreen, ed. *Contrasts in Emerging Societies*. Bloomington: Indiana University Press, 1965.

Bibliography

Weber, Max. *The Protestant Ethic and the Spirit of Capitalism*. Translated by Talcott Parsons. New York: Charles Scribner and Sons, 1947.

————. *The Theory of Social and Economic Organization*. 2d ed. Glencoe: The Free Press, 1964.

Weis, István. *A mai magyar társadalom* [Hungarian society today]. Budapest: Magyar Szemle, 1930.

Wirth, Max. *Europa und die Bodenschätze Ungarns*. Leipzig, 1868.

Zichy, Antal, ed. *Gróf Széchenyi István hirlapi cikkei* [The newspaper articles of Count Stephen Széchenyi]. Budapest, 1894.*

————. *Széchenyi István beszédei* [Speeches of Stephen Széchenyi]. Budapest: Történelmi Társaság, 1897.*

Zichy, Jenő. *Emlékirat a magyar ipar fejlesztése érdekében* [Memorandum concerning the industrial development of Hungary]. Budapest: Pesti Könyvnyomda, 1880.

Zinovyev, G. and Radek, K. *Mit mond a III. Internacionale a magyarországi proletár forradalomról?* [What does the Third International say about the proletarian revolution in Hungary?]. Vienna, 1920.

Zsoldos, Jenő, ed. *1848-49 a magyar zsidóság életében* [1848-1849 in the life of Hungarian Jewry]. Budapest: Neuwald, 1948.

ARTICLES

Achim, András. "A vitás parasztpárti programmról" [About the controversial program of the Peasant party]. *Huszadik Század*, 18 (1908), 308-316.

Albrecht, Ferenc. "A magyar demokrácia válsága" [Crisis of the Hungarian democracy]. *Társadalomtudomány*, 8 (1928), 34-51.

Apter, David A. "System, Process and the Politics of Economic Development." Pages 135-159 in Hoselitz, Bert and Moore, Wilbert. *Industrialization and Society*. The Hague: Mouton, 1963.*

Arató, Endre. "A magyar nacionalizmus kettős arculata" [The two faces of Hungarian nationalism]. Pages 79-143 in *A magyar nacionalizmus kialakulása és története* [Formation and history of Hungarian nationalism]. Edited by Andics, Erzsébet. Budapest: Kossuth, 1964.

Barta, István. "A magyar polgári reformmozgalom kezdeti szakaszának problémái" [Problems of the initial phase of the Hungarian movement of bougeois reform]. *Történelmi Szemle*, 6 (1963), 307-343.

Bellah, Robert N. "Reflections on the Protestant Ethic Analogy in Asia." Pages 243-252 in Eisenstadt, S. N. *The Protestant Ethic and Modernization*. New York: Basic Books, 1968.

Berend, Iván T. and Ránki, György. "Nemzeti jövedelem és tőkefelhalmozódás Magyarországon, 1867-1914" [National income and capital accumulation in Hungary, 1867-1914]. *Történelmi Szemle*, 6 (1963), 187-203.

Bethlen, István. "Hagyomány és forradalom a politikában" [Tradition and revolution in politics]. *Magyar Szemle*, 21 (1933), 105-118.

Bibliography

Bodenheimer, Susanne. "Dependency and Imperialism: The Roots of Latin American Underdevelopment." Pages 155-181 in Fann, K. T. and Hodges, Donald C., eds. *Readings in U.S. Imperialism*. Boston: Porter and Sargent, 1971.

Brezezinski, Zbigniew. "The Politics of Underdevelopment." *World Politics*, 9 (1958), 55-76.

Cushing, G. F. "Hungary." Pages 29-116 in Warriner, Doreen, ed. *Contrasts in Emerging Societies*. Bloomington: Indiana University Press, 1965.

Deutsch, Karl. "Social Mobilization and Political Development." *American Political Science Review*, 55 (1951), 493-502.

Dos Santos, Theotonio. "The Structure of Dependence." In Fann, K. T. and Hodges, Donald C., eds. *Readings in U.S. Imperialism*. Boston: Porter and Sargent, 1971.

Eötvös, József. "Szegénység Irlandban" [Poverty in Ireland]. In Vol. 12, pages 38-181 of *Báró Eötvös József összes munkái* [Eötvös' collected works]. Budapest: Révai, 1904.*

————. "Vélemény a fogházjavitás ügyében" [An opinion on the improvement of jails]. In Vol. 12, pages 3-37 of *Báró Eötvös József összes munkái.**

————. "A zsidóság emancipátiója" [The emancipation of Jewry]. In Vol. 12, pages 109-158 of *Báró Eötvös József összes munkái.**

Geöcze, Sarolta. "Konzervativizmus és keresztény szocializmus" [Conservatism and Christian socialism]. *Huszadik Század*, 9 (1904), 272-285.

Gergely, Jenő. "A keresztényszocialisták politikai szerepe az ellenforradalom első éveiben, 1919-23" [The role of Christian socialists during the first years of the counterrevolution, 1919-1923]. *Századok*, 110 (1976), 225-273.

Gerschenkron, Alexander. "The Rate of Growth in Russia since 1885." *Tasks of Economic History*, 7 (1947), 144-174.

Glatz, Ferenc and Stier, Miklós. "Megyei küzdelmek a gömbösi reformtörekvések körül" [Struggles in the counties for and against Gömbös' reform endeavors]. *Történelmi Szemle*, 14 (1971), 157-188.

Gratz, Gusztáv. "A liberalizmus" [Liberalism]. *Huszadik Század*, 9 (1904), 165-182.

Gunder-Frank, André. "Economic Dependence, Class Structure and Underdevelopment Policy." In Cockroft, James D.; Gunder-Frank, André; and Johnson, Dale J. *Dependence and Underdevelopment*. New York: Doubleday, 1972.

Hitchins, Keith. "The Romanian Socialists and the Hungarian Soviet Republic." Pages 109-144 in Janos, Andrew C. and Slottman, William B. *Revolution in Perspective*. Berkeley and Los Angeles: University of California Press, 1971.*

Huntington, Samuel P. "Political Development and Decay." *World Politics*, 17 (1965), 386-430.

Inkeles, Alex. "Making Men Modern." *American Journal of Sociology*, 75 (1969), 138-150.

———. "The Modernization of Man," in Weiner, Myron, ed. *Modernization: The Dynamics of Growth.* New York: Basic Books, 1966.*

Iványi, B. G. "From Feudalism to Capitalism: The Economic Background of Széchenyi's Reform in Hungary." *Journal of Central European Affairs,* 20 (1960), 270-288.

Janos, Andrew C. "The Agrarian Opposition at the National Congress of Councils." Pages 85-108 in Janos, Andrew C. and Slottman, William B., eds. *Revolution in Perspective: Essays on the Hungarian Soviet Republic.* Berkeley and Los Angeles: University of California Press, 1971.*

———. "Gentry in the Modern World: Hungarian Nobles and Romanian Boyars in the Politics of the Rising National State." Paper presented at the Third Congress of the International Association of South-East European Studies, Bucharest, September 6, 1974, pp. 1-39 with 19 tables.

Jászi, Oszkár [Oscar]. "A latifundium elleni küzdelem" [Struggle against the latifundium]. *Huszadik Század,* 16 (1907), 478-480.

———. "Az új Magyarország felé" [Toward the new Hungary]. *Huszadik Század,* 15 (1907), 1-15.

Komlós, John. "The Efficiency of Serf Labor: The Case of Austria-Hungary." Paper presented at the Ninth Annual Meeting of the American Association for the Advancement of Slavic Studies, Washington, D.C., October, 1977.

Kornfeld, Móric. "Bethlen István gazdaságpolitikája" [The economic policies of Stephen Bethlen]. *Magyar Szemle,* 22 (1934), 167-173.

Mályusz, Gyula. "A reformkor nemzedéke" [The generation of the reform period]. Századok, 57-58 (1923-1924), 6-75.

Matolcsy, Mátyás. "A buzaértékesités problémája Magyarországon" [Problems of wheat marketing in Hungary]. *Magyar Szemle,* 20 (1932), 215-220.

McCagg, William O. "Hungary's Jewish Commissars and Ministers, 1905-1924." Paper presented at the Berkeley Conference on the Hungarian Soviet Republic, March 19-20, 1969. Published with substantial revisions as "Jews in Revolutions: The Hungarian Experience." *Journal of Social History,* 5 (1972), 78-105.

Miskolczy, Ágost. "Államvédelem és pártmozgalom" [The security of the state and the party system]. *Magyar Szemle,* 21 (1933), 86-89.

Mutschenbacher, Emil. "Bethlen István gazdaságpolitikája" [The economic policies of Stephen Bethlen]. *Magyar Szemle,* 22 (1934), 176-182.

Návay, Lajos. "Az alföldi munkáskérdés" [Labor problems on the Plainland]. *Budapest Szemle,* 84 (1895), 36-68.

Olay, Ferenc. "Állástalan diplomások az 1934-es évben" [Unemployed graduates in the year 1934]. *Társadalomtudomány,* 14 (1934), 282-294.

Pölöskei, Ferenc. "Hatalmi viszonyok 1919 őszén Magyarországon" [Power relations in Hungary during the autumn of 1919]. Századok, 110 (1976), 757-802.

Pye, Lucian W. "The Nature of Transitional Politics." Pages 538-550 in Finkle, Jason L. and Gable, Richard W. *Political Development and Social Change.* 2d ed. New York: Wiley, 1971.*

Bibliography

Rézler, Gyula István. "Die soziale und wirtschaftliche Lage der ungarischen Arbeiterschaft." *Ungarische Hefte*, 1 (1942).

Rudai, Rezső. "Adalék a magyar képviselőház szociologiájához, 1887-1931." [Notes on the sociology of the Hungarian House of Representatives, 1867-1918]. *Társadalomtudomány*, 13 (1933), 215-230.

Schmitter, Philippe. "Still a Century of Corporatism." *Review of Politics*, No. 85 (January 1974), 85-128.

Sipos, Péter; Stier, Miklós and Vida, István. "Változások a kormánypárt parlamenti képviseletének összetételében, 1931-1939" [Changes in the composition of the parliamentary Government party, 1931-1939]. *Századok*, 101 (1967), 602-620.

Spira, György. "Egy pillantás a Hitel irójának hitelviszonyaira" [A glimpse at the credit record of the author of "Hitel"]. *Történelmi Szemle*, 6 (1963), 344-355.

Stier, Miklós. "A kormánypárt fasiszta jellegű átszervezésének csődjéhez, 1935-36" [The failure of the reorganization of the Government party along fascist lines, 1935-1936]. *Századok*, 105 (1971), 696-709.

Szekfű, Gyula. "Szent István a századok tükrében" [St. Stephen in the mirror of the centuries]. In Serédi, Jusztinián, ed. *Emlékkönyv Szt. István király halálának kilencszázadik évfordulójára*. [Memorial to the nine-hundredth anniversary of the death of King St. Stephen]. 3 vols. Budapest: Akadémia, 1938.*

Szombatfalvi, György. "Az értelmiség válsága" [The crisis of the intelligentsia]. *Társadalomtudomány*, 4 (1924), 4-14.

Takács, Imre. "Agrárszocialista mozgalom a háború elött" [Agrarian socialism before the war]. *Társadalomtudomány*, 12 (1932), 249-272.

Temperley, Harold W. V. "Introductory Essay" to Marczali, Henry. *Hungary in the Eighteenth Century*. Cambridge, England: The University Press, 1910.

Ungár, László. "A magyar nemesi birtok eladósodása" [Indebtedness of the landholdings of the Hungarian nobility]. *Századok*, 68 (1935), 39-60.

————. "A magyar polgári osztály kialakulásáról" [Formation of the Hungarian bourgeois class]. *Századok*, 76 (1942), 306-328.

Vida, István. "Három Chorin levél" [Three letters of Chorin]. *Századok*, 111 (1977), 362-389.

Vigh, Károly. "Adalékok Bajcsy-Zsilinszky Endre francia orientációs külpolitikai koncepciójához" [The francophile orientation of Andrew Bajcsy-Zsilinszky's foreign policy]. *Századok*, 105 (1971), 736-745.

Wagner, Francis S. "Széchenyi and the Nationality Problem." *Journal of Central European Affairs*, 20 (1960), 289-311.

STATISTICAL AND DOCUMENTARY MATERIALS

Annuaire Statistique Hongrois. Nouveau Cours. Vols. 1-47 (1892-1940).

Bernátsky, Kornél. *Rural Standard of Living in Hungary Since World War I*. New York: Mid-European Study Center, 1954. Microfilm, Library of Congress.

Bibliography

Bethlen István titkos iratai [Secret papers of Stephen Bethlen]. Edited by Miklós Szinai and Laszló Szücs. Budapest: Kossuth, 1972.*

Bosnyák, Zoltán. *Magyarország elzsidósodása* [The Judaization of Hungary]. Budapest: Held, 1937.

Budapester Handels- und Gewerbekammer, ed. *Beiträge zur Geschichte der Preise ungarischer Landesprodukte im 19. Jahrhundert.* Budapest: Pesti Könyvnyomda, 1873.

Budapesti kereskedelmi és iparkamara [Hungarian Chamber of Commerce and Industry], ed. *Hungarian Commerce and Industry in 1935.* Budapest: Pátria, 1936.

————. *Hungarian Commerce and Industry in 1938.* Budapest: Pátria, 1939.

Budapesti kereskedelmi és iparkamara, évkönyve [Yearbook of the Hungarian Chamber of Industry and Commerce]. Budapest: Pesti Könyvnyomda, 1898.

Buday, László. *A megcsonkított Magyarország* [Dismembered Hungary]. Budapest: Pantheon, 1921.

———— in English. *Dismembered Hungary.* London: Grant Richards and Co., 1923.

Censor [pseud.]. *Társadalmunk és társadalmi hivatásunk* [Our society and calling]. Budapest: Published by the author, 1887.

Danyl, R. and Dávid, Z., eds. *Az első magyarországi népszámlálás, 1784-1787* [The first Hungarian official census, 1784-1787]. Budapest: Állami Nyomda, 1960.

Fényes, Elek. *Magyarország statistikája* [The statistics of Hungary]. 3 vols. Pest: Trattner, 1842-1843.

Germany, Statistisches Reichsamt. *Statistik des Deutschen Reiches No. 402. Berufaufzählung.* Berlin: Reimar Habbag, 1929.

A Gömbös kormány nemzeti munkaterve [The national work plan of the Gömbös government]. Budapest: Stádium, 1932.

Great Britain, Census Office. *Census of England and Wales, 1931.* Occupation Tables. London: H.M. Stationery Office, 1934.

Haeffler, István, ed. *Országgyülési Almanach* [Parliamentary almanac]. Budapest: Magyar Távirati Iroda, 1935 and 1940.

Horthy Miklós titkos iratai [Secret papers of Nicholas Horthy]. Edited by Miklós Szinai and László Szücs. Budapest: Kossuth, 1962.*

Hungarian Ministry of Foreign Affairs. *Hungarian Peace Negotiations.* 3 vols. Budapest: Horánszky, 1922.

International Labor Office, ed. *Wages in Germany 1800 to the Present.* Studies and Reports, Series No. 15. London, 1945.

Joint Labor Delegation for Hungary, ed. *Report on the White Terror in Hungary.* London: Trade Union Council and the Labour Party, 1920.

Kempelen, Béla. *Magyar nemesi családok* [Hungarian noble families]. 11 vols. Budapest: Grill, 1911-1931.

————. *Magyarországi zsidó és zsidóeredetü családok* [Families of Jewish origin in Hungary]. 3 vols. Budapest: Grill, 1937-1939.

341

Bibliography

Kósa, Miklós. *Hová, mivel, hogyan?* [Where to, with what, and how?]. Budapest: Published by the author, 1941.

Kossuth, Lajos. *Országgyűlési tudósitások* [Parliamentary reports]. Budapest: Magyar Történelmi Társulat, 1948.

Kovács, Alajos. *A zsidóság térfoglalása Magyarországon* [The ascendency of Jewry in Hungary]. Budapest: Kellner, 1923.

Központi Statisztikai Hivatal, ed. *A magyar birodalom gyáriparának üzemi és munkásstatisztikája* [The statistics of Hungary's manufacturing industries and laborers]. Budapest, 1910.

Kun, Andor; Lengyel, László; and Vidor, Gyula, eds. *Magyar országgyűlési almanach* [Hungarian parliamentary almanac]. Budapest: Magyar Távirati Iroda, 1927, 1931.

Laky, Dezső ed. *Statistique des étudiants des universités hongroises.* Budapest: Pátria, 1933.

League of Nations, ed. *Industrialization and Foreign Trade.* Geneva, 1945.

Lóczy, Lajos [Louis]. *A Geographical, Economic and Social Survey of Hungary.* Budapest: Kilián, 1919.

————. *A magyar szentkorona országainak leírása* [Description of the countries of the Hungarian Crown]. Budapest: Kilián Frigyes, 1918.

A magyar munkásmozgalom történetének válogatott dokumentumai [Selected documents of the Hungarian labor movement]. 6 vols. Budapest: Kossuth, 1955-1959.

Magyar tájékoztató zsebkönyv [Hungarian information handbook]. 2d ed. Budapest: Magyar Nemzeti Szövetség, 1943.

Magyarország Szabadkőműves nagypáholyának névjegyzéke [Membership list of the grand lodge of Hungarian free masons]. Budapest: Aigner, 1886.

Matlekovits, Sándor [Alexander]. *Das Königreich Ungarn volkswirtschaftlich und statistisch dargestellt.* Leipzig: Duncker and Humblot, 1900.

————. *Die Landwirtschaft Ungarns.* Leipzig: Duncker and Humblot, 1900.

————. *Wekerle Sándor emlékezete* [Eulogy of Alexander Wekerle]. Budapest: Magyar Lapkiadó, 1922.

Matolcsy, Mátyás [Mathias]. *A jövedelemelosztás Magyarországon* [Income distribution in Hungary]. Budapest: Légrády, 1936.

Matolcsy, Mátyás [Mathias] and Varga, Stephen. *The National Income of Hungary 1924/25-1936/37.* London: King, 1938.

Mérei, Gyula. *Magyar politikai pártprogrammok* [Platforms of Hungarian political parties]. Budapest: Egyetemi Nyomda, 1935.

Mit akar a Wesselényi Reform Club? [What is the program of the Wesselényi Reform Club?]. Budapest, 1930.

Napló. See Országgyűlés, Képviselőház.*

Országgyűlés [National Assembly]. Képviselőház [House of Representatives]. *Napló* [Proceedings], 1867-1944. Quoted as *Napló.* Also Országgyűlés [National Assembly]. Felsőház [Upper House]. *Napló* [Proceedings], 1926-1944.

Országgyűlési Almanach [Almanac of the National Assembly]. See Sturm, Végváry, Kun, Haeffler.*

Rege, Károly. *A magyar buza áralakulása és termelési költségei* [Price and production cost of Hungarian wheat]. Budapest: Pátria, 1931.

The Statesman's Yearbook, 1872-1938.

Sturm, Albert, ed. *Országgyűlési Almanach* [Parliamentary almanac]. Budapest: Pester Lloyd, 1887, 1892, 1897, 1901, 1905.

Szinai, Miklós and Szücs, László, eds. *Bethlen István titkos iratai* [Secret papers of Stephen Bethlen]. Budapest: Kossuth, 1972.*

——. *Horthy Miklós titkos iratai* [Secret papers of Nicholas Horthy]. Budapest: Kossuth, 1962.*

A tanácsok országos gyűlésének naplója, 1919 junius 14-23 [Proceedings of the National Congress of Councils, June 14-23, 1919]. Budapest: Athenaeum, 1919.

Újváry, Péter. *Magyar zsidó lexicon* [Hungarian Jewish encyclopedia]. Budapest: Pallas, 1929.

UNESCO. *The Progress of Literacy in Various Countries.* Paris: UNESCO, 1953.

Végváry, Ferenc and Zimmer, Ferenc, eds. *Országgyűlési Almanach* [Parliamentary almanac]. Budapest: Pester Lloyd, 1910.

NEWSPAPERS CONSULTED

Budapesti Hírlap, 1895-1935
Budapesti Szemle, 1891-1895
Egyenlőség, 1878-1883
Életképek, 1838-1848
Ellenzék, 1896-1900
Hetilap, 1846-1848
Huszadik Század, 1900-1919
Magyarság, 1930-1944
Március Tizenötödike, 1848
Nagyváradi Napló, 1900-1902
Népszava, 1906-1942
Pester Lloyd, 1922-1938
Pesti Hírlap, 1842-1849
Pesti Napló, 1882-1890
Új Magyarság, 1937-1944
Új Nemzedék, 1916-1918, 1922-1934
Világ, 1914-1919

Index

Index

Index

Budapest, capital, 1872-
  age of dualism, 95-96, 123, 152, 173;
  elections, 99, 166n; press, 102; Jews
  in, 113-14, 117, 179; industry and labor, 140, 150, 157-58; population,
  150-51; radicals in, 186, 317
  revolutions of 1918-19, xxxiv, 189,
  191-92, 194, 197
  counterrevolution of 1919-21, 201
  interwar period, 246, 275, 293; elections, 212, 227, 260n, 270-71; Jews in,
  223, 225, 227-28
  World War II, 308-309, 311
  institutions: University of, 124n, 185,
  247; Chamber of Commerce, 133;
  City Library, 189; Central Prison, 191;
  Vienna express, 217; Stock Exchange,
  223
Budapesti Hírlap, 116
Budinszky, Ladislas (László), 284n
Bulgaria: Hungarian plans for, 140;
  economy, 150n; agriculture, 219
bunkókrácia, 58
Bunzel, Julius, 158
bureaucracy
  age of reform: designs to modernize,
  66, 76-77
  age of absolutism, 89
  age of dualism: establishment of, 92-
  93; recruitment of, 94, 109-110, 134,
  141; centralization, 95-96; and political machine, 97-100, 166; economic
  base of, 105-108; composition of,
  106n, 110-12, 173, 177-78; and Jews,
  113-14, 178; salaries, 249
  interwar period: and political machine, 212, 257, 294-97; composition
  of, 227, 250-51, 254; recruitment of,
  247-48, 250-51; salaries, 248-50, 255;
  as political class, 286
  See also administration; political
  class; political machine
Burgenland, 277
burghers, *see* bourgeoisie; feudal society
Byzantium, 4, 11, 12

cabinet
  revolution of 1848-49: establishment
  of, xxxiii, 85, 92

age of dualism: social composition of,
  111; Jews in, 178-79
  counterrevolution of 1919-21: social
  composition of, 278, 279
  interwar period: social composition
  of, 229, 278, 282, 283; under Gömbös, 287
Calvin, John, 14
Calvinism, Calvinists
  feudal society: of Transylvania, 6, 20;
  influence of doctrine, 14, 322; nobility, 15, 19; in politics, 15-16
  age of reform: number of, 6; of Wes-
  selenyi, 70; and Magyar culture, 78;
  and Jews, 80
  age of dualism: voters, 99; and Jews,
  142, 181; in politics, 148, 231
  interwar period, 208, 262
  See also Protestantism
Carpatho-Danubian Great Fatherland,
  277
Carpatho-Ukraine, *see* Ruthenia
Catholic, -s: and Protestants, 5-8, 231;
  number of, 1839, 6; European, 6;
  doctrine, 12-14; social mobility, 15; in
  nobility, 19; and anti-Semitism, 142;
  in bureaucracy, 253n; political, 258,
  264-68; in secret societies, 265n; in
  Hungarian culture, 268; and national
  socialism, 270. *See also* Christianity
Catholic church, clergy
  feudal society: invited to Hungary, 5;
  and Protestant Reformation, 5-8; privileges, 12, 19-21, 23; landholdings, 20
  age of reform: Széchenyi family and,
  50; conservatism of, 60, 71; liberal
  plan to curtail, 62; landholdings, 83
  revolution of 1848-49, 75, 85
  age of dualism: liberal legislation
  against, xxxiv, 124-25; and educational system, 125; and assimilation,
  127n; and aristocracy, 146; and Stephen Tisza, 230-31
  revolutions of 1918-19, 193
  interwar period, 230-32; and Bethlen,
  234; in politics, 298
  World War II, 305-306
Catholic People's party, 101, 146; in coalition of 1906, xxxiv; program and
  philosophy, 146-48; composition of,

Index

conservatism, conservatives (*cont.*)
261, 290; popular, 271; in cabinets,
283, 300; in political machine, 292n,
294-99
World War II: influence of, 301;
against anti-Semitism, 302-304, 311;
against land reform, 305; foreign policy, 307; of Kállay government, 308;
disarray of, 311
world-wide: compared, 316
See also liberal-conservatives
Conservative party: 1846-48, 58-59;
1876-84, xxxiv, 143, 145
Constantinople: negotiations at, 308
Constitution party, xxxiv, 101, 143
core, of world economic system, xix;
consumption patterns in, 40; Occident
as, 45, 154, 169; model for Hungary,
105, 314-17; income per capita, 157,
243; productivity compared, 218, 242-
43; rebellion against, 244, 285, 286,
318-19; innovation and political
change in, 313-14. See also Occident
Corporation of the Holy Crown, xxxi,
23
corvée, 27-28, 56, 84
Corvinus, Mathias (Mátyás), king, xxxi,
5, 27, 28, 29
cottage tenancy (*zsellérség*), 30, 32, 84
cottagers (*zsellérs*), xxxii
Council of the Lieutenancy, 25
Council of Ministers, 211, 304
counter-reformation, 6
counties
feudal society: origins, 24; functions,
25-26; in Transylvania, 26
age of reform: elections, 60-61; grievances of, 62-63; radicalism in, 71; liberal views of, 76-77; in 1848, 85
age of absolutism, 88
age of dualism: administrative reform
of, 94-96
interwar period: representation of,
215; radicals and conservatives in,
294-95
Countrywide Club (*Országos Kaszinó*),
179
courts, *see* judiciary
Croatian nationality, 8; in census, 11,
63n; in 1848, xxxiii, 86-87; under ab-

solutism, 88; social mobility of, 111;
minority in Trianon Hungary, 205;
Hitler and, 273n; Szálasi and, 277
Croatia-Slavonia
historic entity: geography, 3; Hungarian Crown acquires, 4; military frontier, 22; institutions of, 25-26
age of reform: and liberals, 69
age of dualism: Compromise with, 91
Crown, institution of
feudal society: and estates, 16-17, 22-
25; landholdings of, 18; and land tenure; 26-27; tariff policies, 47
age of reform: served by Széchenyi,
50; alliance with conservatives, 57-58,
60-61, 65, 74; in conservative program, 59; liberal reform designs of,
62, 68, 70, 71; and German cities, 78;
and Jewish rights, 83
revolution of 1848-49, 86
age of dualism: Rumanians and, 105;
and aristocracy, 131
See also monarchy
Csáky, Count Stephen (István), 282n,
307
Csanád: bishopric of, 59; county of,
162
Csatay, Ladislas (László), 282n
Csepel: industrial complex, 310
Csia, Alexander (Sándor), 284n
Csicsery-Rónay, Stephen (István), 259
Csokonai-Vitéz, Michael (Mihály), 38
Csongrád, county of, 162
Cumans, 4, 8, 21, 22
Czechoslovakia: relations with, xxxiv,
192, 193, 232, 292, 301; and Trianon
treaty, 205; economy, 242; foreign
policy, 263; Hitler's view of, 273n
Cziráky, Count, 59

Dachau: concentration camp, 311
Dalmatia, 140
Dániel, Arnold, 188
Danube Steamship Company, 55
Darányi, Coloman (Kálmán): premier-
ship, xxxv, 282n, 289-91; and first
Jewish law, 291; resignation, 291; and
Grand Coalition, 300
Deák, Francis (Ferenc), 65, 70, 71,
113n, 125

Index

351

Index

Erdélyi, Joseph (József), 237
Erdős, Renée, 236
estates: in feudal society, 16-17, 22-24
Eszterházy, Count Maurice (Móric), 298n
Eszterházy, Count Nicholas (Miklós), 37
Eszterházy, Prince Paul (Pál), 146
Eszterházy family, 17, 132
etatism: age of dualism, 145; of Bethlen, 210-11, 218; on periphery, 314
Etelköz Association (EKSz, X), 252, 265n. *See also* secret societies
Evangelical, *see* Lutheran
exports, *see* trade, foreign

Fabinyi, Tihamér, 282n
Falk, Maximilian (Miksa), 113n
Farmers' Training School: at Szarvas, 36
Faruk, king of Egypt, 318
fascism: in Hungary, 169-70, 301, 302; in Europe, 320. *See also* national radicalism; national socialism
Fejérváry, Baron Géza, premier, 179
Félegyhaza, village, electoral district, 75n
Felsőbüki-Nagy, Paul (Pál), 63, 65
feminists, 215
Fenyő, Max (Miksa), 220n
Ferdinand I, king, xxxi
Ferdinand V, king, 86
Ferenczi, Alexander (Sándor), 173
Ferenczi, Izsó, 260n
Festetich, Count Alexander (Sándor), 230
Festetich, Count George (György), 36, 37
Festetich, Prince Tassilo, 146
Festetich family, 132
Feszler, historian, 78
Fetzer, bishop, 232n
feudalism: reaction in sixteenth century, 5; institutions of, xxxi, 26-30; reform of, 56, 59-60; abolition of, xxxiii, 84
fidei commissa, 132, 141, 184, 229. *See also* entail, laws of
filibuster, xxxiv, 101-102, 165, 167, 211
Finance, Ministry of: in 1848-49, xxxiii, 86, 93, 94; in age of dualism, 110,

112, 122n; in interwar period, 251, 254, 295
florin (*forint*), currency, xxv, 35n
Földi, Michael (Mihály), 236
Foreign Affairs, Ministry of, 251, 254, 287, 295, 298n
foreign capital: debt, and Széchenyi's program, 52; and economic development, 150, 287; in counterrevolution of 1919-21, 206; under Bethlen premiership, 209, 218, 245, 248; Right radical view of, 259, 261
Forgách, Count Nicholas (Miklós), 59
Forgács, N., deputy, 259n
Forty-Eighters, party of: composition of, 135-36; program of, 138-40, 144; in parliament, 140-41; anti-Semitism of, 141; critique of liberalism, 316. *See also* Independence party
France: economic development compared, 32, 157, 158, 169; liberalism in, 62, 68; political development, 62-63, 75, 314; model for liberal reforms, 76; revolution of 1789, 76, 268; Széchenyi and, 80; capital export, 150; image of, 183, 269; Entente power, 191, 274, 275; and Hungarian counterrevolution, 201; foreign policy, 262, 263, 291n
Franchet d'Espèrey, Louis Felix, 191
franchise: in 1848, 85-86; in age of dualism, 92, 97, 144, 145, 159, 160, 184, 186, 187; in revolutions of 1918-19, 191, 193, 194; in counterrevolution of 1919-21, 202; in interwar period, 211-12, 213-14, 235, 270n, 293-94
Franchise Act of 1913, 211-12
Francis (Ferenc) I, king, emperor, xxxii, 60
Francis Joseph (Ferenc József) I, king, emperor, xxxiii, xxxiv, 87, 88, 90, 204
free boroughs, *see* cities
free corps, 204, 228. *See also* white detachments
free districts, royal, 21, 22, 23-24
free electors, 203, 204
free peasantry, 19, 22
freehold, 27
freemen, 23, 63n

Index

Index

Index

landowners: in feudal society, 36-37; in age of reform, 42; in age of absolutism, 90; in age of dualism, 92, 93, 120-21, 138; in counterrevolution of 1919-21, 206; in interwar period, 234, 279-83, 287, 298; during World War II, 297, 305

Landswehr, 91

László, Eugene (Jenő), 189

Latin: as official language, 54

Latin America: compared to Hungary, 318

Lázár, Andrew (Andor), 282n

Ledermann, Maurice (Mór), 260n

Left radicalism: in age of dualism, 173-97, 231; in revolutions of 1918-19, 194; in interwar period, 218, 233, 240, 269

legitimists: in counterrevolution of 1919-21, 203, 264n; and Bethlen, 214n; during World War II, 290, 298, 306, 309

Leipzig: Széchenyi at, 50

Lengyel, Joseph (József), 192

Lenin, V. I., Leninism, xvi, 168, 188, 189, 198

Levant, 31

liberal, -ism, -s
  age of reform, xxxii; denounced, 55; at elections, 58, 61; aristocrats and, 60n; gentry and, 60-61; and nationalism, 62-63, 75, 76, 82; eastern and western compared, 64-69; at Diets, 65; radical and moderate factions, 69-74; and Jewish emancipation, 73n, 81-83; and centralization, 76-77
  age of dualism: and Jews, 115-18, 131; etatism, 122-23; and anti-clericalism, 124-25; economic policies, 127-34; protectionism, 129, 131; and industrialization, 132-34; in House of Representatives, 136; and peasantry, 160; legacy of, 230; critique of, 267
  interwar period: press, 216, 306; Bethlen's, 230, 235; and national radicals, 256, 261; critiques of, 264-69, 272, 295
  global ideology, 316-18

liberal-conservatism, liberal-conservatives, xxxv, 208, 228, 239, 292; in Unitary party, 246; in political machine, 256, 287, 294-97; foreign policy of, 262; elites, 279-83. *See also* conservatism

liberal democrats, *see* Democratic bloc

Liberal party, 1875-1905: formation of, xxxiv; in parliament, 97, 100-101, 139; and political machine, 100-101, 288-89; patronage, 116; and Jews, 117, 141; and nationalism, 122-23; and Church, 124-25; and national minorities, 125-27, 144; economic policy of, 127-34; and aristocracy, 131-32; demise of, 135; social policies of, 164-65; in elections, 166n; social composition of, 279

life peerage, 98

Lindenberger, bishop, 232n

List, Friedrich, 66

Liszt, Franz, 78

literacy, *see* education

literature: in age of reform, 38-39; in age of dualism, 181; in interwar period, 235-37

London: medieval, 30; yearning for, 236; and Imrédy, 291

Lonovich, archbishop, 59

lord lieutenant (*főispán*), office of, xxiv, 24; in age of dualism, 95, 96; in interwar period, 212, 295

lord's bench (*úriszék*), 28

Losonczy, minister, 282n

Louis (Lajos) I, king, 4

Louis (Lajos) II, king, xxxi, 5

Low Countries: economy, 169

Lower House, *see* House of Representatives

Lower Table, *see* Diet

Lukács, Béla, 282n

Lukács, George (György), 173, 190

Lukács, Leslie (László), 103, 104, 122n, 179

lumpen-nobility, 58

Lutheran, -ism, -s: in feudal society, 6, 13-15, 16; in age of reform, 6, 46, 78, 80; in age of dualism, 127n, 231

Macchiavelli, Niccolo, xx

magnates

Index

Index

Index

Index

Slovak minority (*cont.*)
Hungary, 205; national socialism and, 277. *See also* national minorities

Slovakia: as Hungarian Highlands, 3; reannexation of southern, xxxv, 296

Smallholder party: in 1920-21, 202, 211; Independent (1930-44), 262, 292, 297, 299, 309

Smith, Adam, 66

social banditry, 44

Social Democratic party
age of dualism: attitude toward, 104; Austrian origins, 158, 187; founding of, 160; Galileo Circle and, 174; Jews in, 177; anti-nationalism, 186; radicals in, 186-89
revolutions of 1918-19: in National Council, 191; alliance with Communists, 192, 198
interwar period: in elections of 1920, 202; Jews in, 227n; Bethlen and, 234-35; in elections of 1939, 270-71; alliance with old Right, 292
World War II, 299, 309
See also socialism, socialist

Social-National International (*szociálnacionálé*), 278n

Social Security Act of 1927, 234

socialism, socialist
age of dualism: press, 103; in courts, 104-105; agrarian, 104, 159, 161-62; political organization of, 160; Tisza's view of, 165; Jews and, 176-77, 181; reformist, 182; intellectuals, 183, 187-89; and nationalism, 186; radical, 189
revolutions of 1918-19, 192, 198
counterrevolution of 1919-21, 202, 206
interwar period: agrarian, 211; in parliament, 214n, 299; under Bethlen, 234-35; writers, 236; support for, 239; Right radicals and, 260, 264, 268, 295
World War II, 306
See also Social Democratic party

Socialist-Communist Workers' party, 192, 198

Socialist Party of Hungary, 192

Society for Religious Equality, 231

Sofort boys, 260, 288

Soltész, S., white officer, 208n

Sombor-Schweinitzer, Joseph (József), 295

Somkuthy, general, minister, 282n

Somogycsurgó, village, electoral district, 142n

Sorel, Georges, 187

South Slav minorities, 11. *See also* Croatian minority, Serbian minority

Southlands, *see* Bácska

Soviet Republic, 190-200; founded, xxxv; and Jews, 175n, 182; leaders of, 190; institutions of, 193, 195; constitution of, 193-94; federated republics of, 194n, 277; judiciary of, 196-97; accomplishments of, 197; red terror in, 197; and peasantry, 198-99; land reform of, 199, 228; and nationalism, 199-200; overthrow of, 201, 256; emigrés, 234; legacy of, 235, 239, 272; writers in, 237

Soviet Union: Bolsheviks, 189; Hungarian Communist party in, 193; and Hungarian Soviet Republic, 199; populist view of, 237; ideology of, 243; *kolkhozi*, 261; Right radical view of, 277n, 285; in World War II, xxxvi, 286, 300, 303n, 307, 308, 311

Spain: Christian radicalism in, 266

Spencer, Herbert, xiii, xv, xvi, 168, 183, 185, 219, 313

squirearchy, *see* gentry

Stádium, of Széchenyi, 53

Stalin, Joseph V., 272n

Stencker, Gustav, professor, 78

Stephen (István) I, saint, king, xxiv, xxxi, 4; "Admonitions," 10; national radical denunciation, 257n; in modern writing, 269

Stern, Samuel, 288n, 302n

Stormy Corner (*Viharsarok*), 162, 271

strikes: age of dualism, 160

students: in left-wing movements, 173-76, 187, 189; Right radical, 208; graduates in Bethlen machine, 247-48; social composition, 251n

suffrage, *see* franchise

Swabian minority: immigration of, 10, 49; as voters, 148; sentiment against, 237, 253-54, 267; assimilated, 253-55, 260, 266. *See also* German minority

Index